ALSO BY NICK SEABROOK

Drawing the Lines: Constraints on Partisan Gerrymandering in U.S. Politics

One Person, One Vote

One Person, One Vote

A Surprising History of Gerrymandering in America

NICK SEABROOK

PANTHEON BOOKS, NEW YORK

Library of Congress Cataloging-in-Publication Data
Name: Seabrook, Nick (Nicholas R.), author.
Title: One person, one vote: a surprising history of gerrymandering in America / Nick Seabrook.
Description: First edition. New York: Pantheon Books, 2022.
Includes bibliographical references and index.
Identifiers: LCCN 2021050744 (print) | LCCN 2021050745 (ebook) |
ISBN 9780593315866 (hardcover) | ISBN 9780593315873 (ebook)
Subjects: LCSH: Gerrymandering—United States—History. Apportionment (Election law)—
United States—History. State governments—United States.
Classification: LCC JK1341 .S393 2022 (print) | LCC JK1341 (ebook) |
DDC 328.3/3455—dc23/eng/20211123
LC record available at https://lccn.loc.gov/2021050744
LC ebook record available at https://lccn.loc.gov/2021050745

vvww.pantheonbooks.com

Jacket images: Flag illustration by Matt Curtis; (gerrymander cartoon)
Old Paper Studios/Alamy
Jacket design by Kelly Blair

Printed in the United States of America

First Edition

2 4 6 8 9 7 5 3 1

To my parents

The conception of political equality from the Declaration of Independence, to Lincoln's Gettysburg Address, to the Fifteenth, Seventeenth, and Nineteenth Amendments can mean only one thing—one person, one vote.

—WILLIAM O. DOUGLAS

Contents

INTRODUCTION A Uniquely American Problem 3

1 The First Gerrymander 13

2 James Madison's Henrymander 37

3 Revenge of the Whigs 62

4 Honest Abe Stacks the States 81

5 Frankfurter's Political Thicket 103

6 Echoes of Slavery 128

7 A Blue Tide in the Golden State 159

8 The Prisoner's Dilemma 187

9 Win One for the Whizzer 201

10 The Handshake Deal 231

11 Hollow Hope 269

CONCLUSION If You Can Keep It 301

Acknowledgments 321

Notes 323

Bibliography 333

Index 345

One Person, One Vote

A Uniquely American Problem

Redistricting is like an election in reverse! Usually the voters get to pick the politicians. In redistricting, the politicians get to pick the voters!

—THOMAS B. HOFELLER

The results of Wisconsin's 2018 election had to be seen to be believed. The state's controversial governor, Scott Walker, running for a third term in office after surviving a closely contested and high-profile recall effort in 2012, and securing a narrow reelection in 2014, faced off against the Democratic challenger Tony Evers, the state's superintendent of public instruction. The election was expected to be a close one. *The Cook Political Report* rated the race as a toss-up, both candidates were consistently polling within the margin of error, and prediction models, including Nate Silver's *FiveThirtyEight,* had the contest ranked as one of the closest in the nation. At first blush, very little appears strange about the result. The challenger, Evers, eked out a narrow victory by almost 30,000 votes over the somewhat unpopular incumbent, a margin of slightly more than 1 percent of the nearly 2.7 million ballots that were cast.

Yet peering beneath the surface reveals some disturbing abnormalities. Despite losing the popular vote overall, Walker somehow carried sixty-three of Wisconsin's ninety-nine state assembly districts, and twenty-one of the thirty-three state senate districts. How could a candidate for governor win almost two-thirds of the districts in a state and still end up on the losing side? The answer to that question lies in what may go down as one of the most egregious instances of gerrymandering in American history. The battle over Wisconsin's legislative districts would play out in both the statehouse and the media, eventually reaching all the way to Washington, D.C., and a showdown before the nine justices of the U.S. Supreme Court.

What exactly is gerrymandering? The term has a certain elasticity to it that makes pinning down a concise and consistent definition of the underlying concept somewhat tricky. Writing in the early twentieth century, Elmer Griffith, a University of Chicago PhD student whose treatise "The Rise and Development of the Gerrymander" may be among the most cited doctoral dissertations in history, defined the gerrymander thus: "Districts would not seem, therefore, to be gerrymandered unless they were established especially for election purposes and were formed intentionally in a particular manner for partisan advantage." As a working definition for the purposes of this book, Griffith's formulation is a good start, although perhaps a little more restrictive than I would like. Nevertheless, it serves as a decent jumping-off point for the discussion to come, by laying out the three quintessential elements of the practice.

Gerrymandering requires intent. One can point to all manner of examples of unfairness, inequality, and injustice in the electoral process that occurred naturally, by accident of history, or through the aggregation of individual decisions about where to live, whom to vote for, and what rules to follow. These are not gerrymanders. At its heart, gerrymandering involves a concerted effort to make the votes of certain groups of people matter more than the votes of others. It can be directed at an individual politician, at an entire political party, at voters in certain regions, or at those who hold specific political views. It is an effort to place a thumb on the scale of representative democracy, stacking the deck before an election has even taken place.

Gerrymandering may not always be partisan, as Griffith's definition stipulates, but it is always political. Those crafting the gerrymander do so with some concrete political goal in mind. And as is the case in criminal law, it's often the intent that is the most difficult element to prove. Just as criminal defendants and their attorneys may cook up seemingly innocuous or innocent explanations for their conduct, so too may perpetrators of gerrymandering cloak their actions in subterfuge, obfuscation, or deflection. Demonstrating corrupt intent in these instances can be challenging, although sometimes the circumstantial evidence of the gerrymander itself may be sufficient to carry the burden of proof. Other times, the actions of those responsible are documented in an exquisitely detailed paper trail, the conspiracy laid bare for the courts, the media, and the voting public to peruse at their leisure. And like the criminal defendant whose lawyer labors in vain to prevent him from running his mouth, those in the business of gerrymandering have a tendency to want to brag about their exploits. These are the easy cases. To give but one high-profile example: when it comes to the recent gerrymander in Wisconsin, we have the receipts.

Gerrymandering requires manipulation. It is a departure from business as usual, from the traditional district-drawing principles of compactness, of contiguity, of following existing political boundaries, and of preserving the integrity of communities. These manipulations may be subtle, as in the case of a minor modification to a district line that suddenly places an incumbent on the other side, now forced to run for reelection in hostile territory. Or they may be overt, as when an entire state is carved asunder with reckless abandon to serve the whims of the party presently holding power.

The gerrymander is an unnatural creation, a violation of the norms, procedures, and conventions of a functioning democratic system. It can take the form of a minor violation, something akin to a speeding ticket on the highway of democracy, or a full-fledged abomination, one that makes a mockery of even the imprimatur of accountability or responsiveness to the will of the people. To gerrymander is to distort, to corrupt, to turn the institutions that should be working on behalf of the people's interests into perversions that serve only the powerful, the moneyed, or the politically connected. Whenever political machinations over gerrymandering are afoot, no matter who wins, it's always the voter who loses.

Gerrymandering always involves boundaries. They may be district boundaries, county or municipal boundaries, or even the boundaries of the states themselves. But central to the concept of gerrymandering is the drawing or redrawing of lines on a map. Similar results might be achieved by instituting a poll tax, by imposing a restrictive voter identification law, or by systematically purging individuals from the electoral rolls. These are also not gerrymanders. I would further argue, in another minor quibble with Griffith's earlier definition, that gerrymandering does not require these boundaries to be districts that are established especially for election purposes, or at least not solely for such a use. But they must have predictable electoral effects that can be logically anticipated by those who are responsible for drawing them.

Just as good fences make good neighbors, gerrymandered districts make for predictable, orderly, well-behaved voters. Nothing pleases politicians more than knowing that their district is safe, that their majority is safe, that no matter which direction the winds of popular sentiment may be blowing, their shelter is well built, sturdy, and prepared to weather the storm. But as with Frost's mended wall, sometimes cracks appear in the veneer of politics as usual. Sometimes voters break through the barriers that are erected against their will and make gaps in the well-laid foundations of properly gerrymandered districts. But these examples are few and far between. While polls show that gerrymandering remains unpopular with the general public across the political spectrum, the people who do like it also tend to be the ones who make the rules.

I would also argue that gerrymandering, or at least gerrymandering as it is practiced today, is a uniquely American phenomenon. Across the world, virtually every nation that uses districts for its elections has made at least some effort to prevent those in power from manipulating them for partisan gain. To be sure, even the best redistricting practices do not manage to eliminate all traces of electoral unfairness. Nor should they be expected to, because such unfairness is endemic to all district-based electoral systems. But at the very least, these safeguards eliminate the most egregious instances of gerrymandering, of the type that has become a widespread epidemic in contemporary American politics. In the vast majority of U.S. states, however, the political branches of government retain the responsibility for drawing the lines, giving rise to the means, the motive, and the opportunity for electoral shenanigans. Which brings us back to Wisconsin.

The effort to gerrymander Wisconsin in 2011 was merely one prong of a broader multistate strategy to maximize Republican representation in state legislatures and the U.S. Congress. Armed with the significant gains made in statehouses across the country during the wave election of 2010, the GOP undertook an unprecedented effort to use control of the redistricting process to entrench those majorities. The scheme was known as REDMAP (short for the Redistricting Majority Project) and was the brainchild of Chris Jankowski, a veteran Republican political strategist and consultant at the Republican State Leadership Committee. Their effort specifically targeted those states, like Wisconsin, that provided fertile ground for gerrymandering, bombarding them with outside money during the 2010 campaign. This was supplemented by millions of additional dollars in so-called dark money, contributed anonymously and in unlimited amounts to social welfare nonprofit groups organized under section 501(c)(4) of the Internal Revenue Code.

The second stage of REDMAP was to utilize sophisticated computer software, such as Maptitude and autoBound, combined with extensive and highly granular data on the voting population, to manipulate district boundaries with a level of precision and microtargeting never before seen in American history. What resulted in Wisconsin was a gerrymander so severe that despite winning the popular vote in both 2012 and 2018, Democrats have not controlled more than thirty-nine of the ninety-nine assembly seats (39 percent), or fifteen of the thirty-three senate seats (45 percent), in any of the elections held since. Wisconsin was the centerpiece of the successes that the REDMAP project was able to achieve, and Scott Walker himself went on to become the finance chair and chief fundraiser for the National Republican Redistricting Trust, the organization leading the effort to repeat these successes in the wake of the 2020 census.

Though the slogan of *The Washington Post,* "Democracy dies in darkness," refers to the importance of a free press in holding elected representatives accountable, the same can be said for the secretive manner in which REDMAP went about implementing its redistricting agenda. The details of the plan would not become fully known until documented in court records years later. On August 26, 2018, Thomas Hofeller, a veteran Republican political strategist and, it turned out, one of the key figures in the REDMAP project, passed away in his Raleigh, North Carolina, home at the age of seventy-five, after a long battle with cancer. Hofeller had been a major player in Republican redistricting efforts going back to the early 1970s, when he worked as a consultant for the California State Assembly, developing one of the very first computerized mapping systems for use in the redrawing of district boundaries.

While the Democrats in Sacramento had been able to successfully stymie his early computer-drawn maps, the tools Hofeller developed later proved crucial to Republican efforts in the 1980s and 1990s to crack the decades-long Democratic stranglehold over the "solid South." They would eventually propel Newt Gingrich and his band of "Contract with America" crusaders to national power in the 1994 midterm election.

And though these earlier political activities had kept Hofeller mostly behind the scenes, developing an almost cultlike following among the somewhat insulated community of hard-core redistricting operatives, it was the Republican successes in the 2010 redistricting cycle that finally catapulted him to national infamy. Hofeller masterminded the successful effort to turn the seven-to-six Democratic edge in U.S. House of Representatives seats in his home state of North Carolina into a ten-to-three landslide in favor of the Republicans, earning him plaudits from his fellow partisans and boogeyman-like infamy among his opponents. But it was not until after his death that the full scope of Hofeller's role in the Republican gerrymandering effort following the 2010 census became apparent.

While going through her father's effects, Hofeller's estranged daughter, Stephanie, with whom he had not spoken since 2014, discovered four external hard drives and eighteen thumb drives containing more than seventy-five thousand files, many of them related to his REDMAP consulting activities. These files eventually made their way to attorneys representing Common Cause, a progressive watchdog group that at the time was embroiled in a lawsuit with the State of North Carolina over the gerrymandering of their state legislative districts. The files revealed that Hofeller had been the architect of the second phase of REDMAP and had led the team that was tasked with drawing the maps that would be used in the GOP's efforts to implement partisan gerrymanders in North Carolina, Pennsylvania, Wisconsin, Michigan, and Ohio. It was a spectacular success. A decade later, the Republican majorities in the legislatures of these REDMAP-focused states have yet to be seriously threatened, let alone reversed.

And it's not only in state elections where the effects of REDMAP are still being felt. The same Republican state legislatures who redrew their own district boundaries to cement their majorities have, in most cases, also been responsible for drawing the districts for electing members of the U.S. House of Representatives, providing them with a significant advantage in the battle for control of Congress. In 2012, despite receiving in excess of 1.4 million fewer votes than their opponents, Republicans controlled 234 of the 435 House seats, 33 more than the Democrats. The journalist David Daley, in his 2016 book, *Ratf**ked: Why Your Vote Doesn't Count,* wrote the following: "The outcome of the 2016 and 2018 elections for Congress are no longer in doubt. On the Sunday morning talk shows and cable news panels from now through these elections, we will endure dozens of conversations about 'who will control the House' and 'can Democrats take the House.' They are all wasting your time. Let's answer those questions. One: the Republicans. Two: no, it's settled. There is no need to hold the vote."

With hindsight, Daley was of course completely wrong about 2018. The Democrats' Blue Wave, inspired by the insipid approval ratings of the incumbent president, was sufficiently large to crest the Republican Fortress of Gerrymandering, to the tune of a 235–199 majority. Although their popular vote margin of 8.6 percent would certainly have yielded even greater dividends in the absence of REDMAP. But replace "the House" with "the Wisconsin state legislature," and this argument, though hyperbolic, is not wrong. Ditto Michigan. Ditto Ohio. Ditto Pennsylvania. Ditto North Carolina. This was the effect of what *The New York Times* labeled "The Great Gerrymander of 2012."

Gerrymandering may not be new, but the success of REDMAP represents a new phase in the evolution of the phenomenon. No longer shackled by incomplete data, outdated technology, or uncertainty about how districts could perform in the future, line drawers can use today's software to simulate election results under a wide variety of hypothetical conditions, fine-tuning the gerrymander to remain robust in the face of incumbent retirements, adverse electoral swings, and all manner of other potential hiccups. Historical examples of the practice, and even those from only a decade or two ago, pale in comparison to the effectiveness, and the efficiency, of the modern gerrymander.

How do you solve a problem like gerrymandering? Unfortunately, the usual mechanisms by which the citizens in a democracy push for changes in government policy are short-circuited when, as is the case with redistricting reform, the underlying problem has the effect of rendering those mechanisms inoperative. Ordinarily, voters who are dissatisfied with the activities of their government could vote in new politicians who promise to chart a different course, lobby their current representatives to take action by organizing into interest groups, or at the very least hold out hope that elected officials will keep their fingers on the pulse of public opinion and adjust their behavior accordingly.

But the rise of gerrymandering creates powerful incentives for politicians to resist these political pressures. Their own reelection prospects may depend in no small part upon what happens when those district lines are redrawn. And when the underlying problem is nothing less than subversion of electoral fairness through the manipulation of the very rules of the game themselves, how can we rely on elections to fix the problem? We've created a system where the foxes are in charge of guarding the henhouse, and our only solution is to either replace them with a different set of foxes or ask them very nicely to please not eat the chickens. "*Quis custodiet ipsos custodes?*" wrote the Roman poet Juvenal in the early second century: "Who watches the watchmen?"

The answer, at least in theory, is the judges. Those who desire to put an end to the scourge of gerrymandering have always looked to courts for their salvation. Judges, at least at the federal level, are not elected. They also enjoy life tenure, which in theory should immunize them from the political pressures that stymie a legislative fix. And furthermore, our Constitution has enshrined into law the very principles of equality, democracy, and fair representation that would seem to protect us against those who would seek to sabotage the ability of citizens to hold their elected representatives accountable.

Article I stipulates that "the House of Representatives shall be composed of Members chosen every second Year by the People of the several States," but makes no reference to allowing representatives to upend this process by using gerrymandering to choose their voters. The Fourteenth Amendment provides that "no State shall make or enforce any law which shall . . . deny to any person within its jurisdiction the equal protection of the laws," and contains no exception for laws that discriminate against certain voters solely on the basis of their political beliefs. Article IV mandates that "the United States shall guarantee to every State in this Union a Republican Form of Government," but as Ben Franklin famously quipped as he left the Constitutional Convention in Philadelphia in 1787, it's only a republic if you can keep it. So why, after more than seventy years of court challenges to unfairness in districting, are things worse today than they've ever been before?

Unfortunately, persuading the judicial branch to intervene in the types of overtly political disputes that have constantly surrounded the issue of gerrymandering has always been an uphill battle. Courts like to project an image of themselves as being above the petty squabbles of their counterparts in the elected branches, of being neutral arbiters who apply the law as written and never take sides in the hot-button political disputes of the day. "Judges are like umpires," John Roberts told the senators on the Judiciary Committee when he was nominated to the bench in 2005. "Umpires don't make the rules, they apply them. . . . It's my job to call balls and strikes, and not to pitch or bat."

This portrayal has always been a fiction. From *Marbury v. Madison* to *Bush v. Gore,* the courts have repeatedly injected themselves into political disputes between Congress and the president, between the federal government and the states. Between Democrats and Republicans. But gerrymandering remains the third rail of American jurisprudence.

The Supreme Court justice Potter Stewart, when struggling to define the term "hard-core pornography" in a 1964 obscenity law case, famously threw up his hands in frustration and declared, "I know it when I see it." So too it is with gerrymandering, which has heretofore eluded the best attempts of political scientists, statisticians, and legal scholars to distill its essence into a simple enough standard to easily differentiate unconstitutional discrimination from politics as usual. But we know it when we see it. It's been around for a long time. And while the Republicans may be the ones reaping the lion's share of the benefits from gerrymandering right now, that has certainly not always been the case. Nor will it likely stay that way forever. Democrats, given the opportunity, have been no less eager to use it to gain an edge.

This book tells the story of gerrymandering in America, from the North Carolina colony of the early eighteenth century to the courthouses of the twenty-first century and beyond. From James Madison to Madison, Wisconsin, it follows through the political thicket of electoral manipulation; of cracking, packing, pairing, and dislocating; of the political question doctrine, the totality of circumstances test, the elections clause, and the adequate and independent state ground standard; of Henrymanders, Bullwinkles, water-whelps, and salamanders; of logrolling, pork barreling, vote diluting, and ratfucking; from the 111 registered voters of Loving County, Texas, to the 5.8 million of Los Angeles County, California. And in the not too distant future, perhaps we will emerge from the other side. It's going to be a challenge, for sure, but through diligent grassroots activism, coordinated legal strategizing, and just a little bit of luck, we might yet have a republic that we can keep.

1

The First Gerrymander

Legend tells us that the gerrymander originated in early nineteenth-century Massachusetts. There, the eponymous governor Elbridge Gerry, desperate to maintain his own power, crafted a somewhat bizarrely shaped state senate district that snaked around the western borders of Essex County, site of the Salem witch trials many generations before. Amid these sleepy Boston suburbs, a political coup d'état was silently brewing. Gerry, frustrated by the obstructionism of his Federalist foes, or so the story goes, hatched a plan to rig the results of the commonwealth's upcoming 1812 elections. Catching wind of the plot, an enterprising New England newspaper editor decided to blow the whistle, lampooning Gerry in the pages of his tabloid. His cartoon depicting Essex County's meandering, misshapen seat as a somewhat sad-looking salamander went viral and was republished across the nation, in one of the very earliest examples of the political meme.

If Google Ngrams had existed at the time, they would have revealed the portmanteau of "Gerry" and "salamander" taking on a life of its own. The #gerrymander was the trending topic of 1812, appearing in more than eighty newspaper articles nationwide in the nine months following the original reporting by the Boston media. By October, Maryland even had its own version, because Baltimore Democrats sought to replicate Gerry's playbook in their own state. "So adroitly have the districts been carved in the true Gerrymander style," wrote the *Federal Republican*, a Washington, D.C., paper, "that the number of democratic members is in an inverse ratio to the relative number of democrats in the state." And so, it came to be that this most pernicious of election-meddling tactics was birthed, amid the partisan bickering and postrevolutionary rancor of the early republic. And the rest, or so we've been led to believe, is history.

This is the story of the first gerrymander, or at least the one that we've always been told about. But what the history books leave out, and what only a deep dive into the colonial records of the early eighteenth century reveals, is that gerrymandering was occurring long before Elbridge Gerry signed his salamander into law. It was happening before the Constitution Gerry had helped to write was ratified, or even conceived of, before the winds of independence had first begun to blow.

Though the term "gerrymander" would be Elbridge Gerry's cross to bear, at least in posterity, the 1812 Massachusetts redistricting was by no means the first time in history that political boundaries had been manipulated for political gain. In fact, the true origins of the practice predate Columbus sailing the ocean blue in 1492. These historical antecedents to the American gerrymander may be found in the centuries-long British tradition of the rotten borough.

Rotten boroughs originated in the thirteenth century, when the Parliament of England was created to replace the royal council, or king's court, that had existed prior to the drafting of the Magna Carta in 1215. Under this new system, each historical borough sent two burgesses, or representatives, to Parliament. But as time went by and populations shifted, the boundaries of these ancient boroughs often no longer corresponded very much to the settlements they purported to represent.

In many areas, borough populations became so small that they contained only a handful of eligible voters, and so a small group of landowners were able to exert a dramatically outsized influence on the workings of Parliament. By corruptly controlling both the voters and the MPs through bribery or patronage, these medieval aristocrats, the one-percenters of their time, maintained their stranglehold on the levers of power. Hence the name, "rotten borough." One famous example was the populous city of Manchester, one of the powerhouses of the Industrial Revolution. Despite the dramatic expansion of its population, Manchester did not elect its own MPs until the nineteenth century, instead being subsumed by the larger constituency of Lancashire, itself a rotten borough. On the flip side, the historical constituency of Old Sarum, once a bustling cathedral city and site of the famous Old Sarum Cathedral, of which only the foundations survive today, retained the right to elect two members of Parliament, even as the construction of nearby Salisbury Cathedral decimated the town's population.

By 1831, of the 408 elected members of the House of Commons, 152 were chosen by fewer than 100 voters, and 88 by fewer than 50. After centuries of crippling inequality, the practice finally came to an end with the passage of the Representation of the People Act of 1832, also known as the Reform Act, which pledged to "take effectual Measures for correcting divers Abuses that have long prevailed in the Choice of Members to serve in the Commons House of Parliament."

But these historical English boroughs, no matter how rotten, do not a gerrymander make. Our working definition of the term requires not only the effect of valuing the votes of some constituents more highly than those of others but also the intentional redrawing of district boundaries themselves. The proper term for electoral inequality that arises from a failure to redraw the electoral lines, rather than a deliberate attempt to manipulate them, is "malapportionment." Malapportionment was not merely a unique and antiquated feature of the pseudo-gerrymanders of yore. It would also be central to the "creeping gerrymanders" that arose in the United States during the first half of the twentieth century, where numerical inequality came about not through the overt redrawing of boundaries for political advantage but from the unwillingness to redraw those lines in response to changes in district populations. Such creeping gerrymanders formed the basis of the very first legal challenges to redistricting that played out before the Supreme Court during the reapportionment revolution of the 1960s, and so they will be discussed in greater detail in later chapters. And while the quest to discover the first uniquely American gerrymander will now take us across the pond, it turns out that we're not quite done with the British just yet.

"I'll slit his nose, crop his ears, and lay him in irons!" exclaimed the Governor, as he hammered away at the ornate front doorway of the Chief Justice's Edenton home. "I want satisfaction of you, come out and give it to me!" But the Chief Justice, himself a veteran explorer who had survived more than his fair share of standoffs during his many expeditions into hostile Indian territory, would not be intimidated. The door remained firmly closed.

The year was 1724, and His Excellency George Burrington, only recently arrived in the colonies from England—the recipient of a royal commission from the lords proprietors that appointed him the third governor of the Province of North Carolina—was on the warpath. Burrington's short tenure as governor had been extremely eventful. He had a reputation, according to a colorful 1896 biography by Marshall De Lancey Haywood, for being thin-skinned and intemperate: "He could tolerate no opinion that was not in accord with his own, and deemed every one a personal enemy, if not a villain, who differed with him." This translated into an unfortunate habit, as documented in the colonial records of the time, of having his detractors criminally indicted for criticizing him. These included one man, Joseph Castleton, who opined that His Excellency was "a damn Rogue & villain, and that there was not a worse Rogue & villain in the world." For his trouble, Castleton "was sentenced to stand in the pillory, on the public parade of Edenton, for two hours, and to beg pardon, on his knees for the offense." He left, according to one historical account, "a less talkative, if not wiser, man."

When the Chief Justice failed to answer his calls for satisfaction, the Governor only became further enraged. "I'll lay him by the heels, I'll have him by the throat, and burn his house or blow it up with gun-powder!" he opined, stepping back for a moment, his anger boiling. The Governor raised his foot and attempted repeatedly to kick his way through the front doorway. His face, already bright red amid the rising crescendo of his rage, began turning an even deeper shade of crimson with the exertion. The door, however, sturdy and well-built from the finest Carolina oak, refused to yield.

Burrington had arrived in the New World with the best of intentions. An educated man whose royal appointment as governor had been made in repayment for an unspecified favor that his father had performed for King George I, he harbored dreams of developing the province for the betterment of all its subjects. And his well-documented truculence aside, Burrington did achieve several notable things during his stint in the colonies. These included opening up the Cape Fear peninsula to new settlement and overseeing the construction of new highways to connect the lower reaches to the more populous northern areas. He also traveled tirelessly around North Carolina on foot, conducting surveys of rivers and harbors, checking in frequently with even the most isolated settlements, and doing whatever he could to ensure the smooth operation of his colony. And, displaying a generosity of spirit that belied his frequent violent outbursts, he was also observed during his many travels distributing money from his own pockets to colonists who were struggling, for which he developed a reputation as something of a man of the people. None of these qualities, however, were on display that day in Edenton.

> After swearing a great many oaths, none of which had any effect on the steadfastly unyielding oak door, the Governor turned his attention to the window. Raising his club, he brought it crashing down through the large glass pane, the early evening sunlight glinting off the shards as they shattered to the ground at his feet. The Chief Justice, somehow maintaining his composure in the face of this onslaught, retreated to a back room. Taking out a quill and parchment, he began, in typical lawyerly fashion, to calmly document the Governor's many threats and epithets.

Later that same year, on a visit to London, Christopher Gale—a British attorney from Lancashire who had immigrated to Carolina in his early twenties and had been appointed chief justice of the province by Burrington's predecessor in 1703—would describe this encounter with the governor in exquisite detail in a deposition that was submitted to the High Court. His account was corroborated by the testimony of seven members of the Provincial Council, and his character was considered above reproach. Less than a year into the job, His Excellency George Burrington was unceremoniously dismissed from his position by the lords proprietors.

He lingered in the colony for more than a year after his firing, stirring up enmity against Gale, who was, in Burrington's words, "an ungrateful, perfidious scoundrel and an egregious sot," as well as his successor

The George Burrington historical marker in Pender County, North Carolina.

as governor, Sir Richard Everard, whom he termed "a Noodle and an ape" and a "numbskull head." He even attempted to challenge Everard to a duel in late 1725 and, once again failing to receive satisfaction, "physically attacked at least two other houses in the neighborhood," threatening to run the occupants through with his sword. Under criminal indictment for his rampage, Burrington finally returned to England in 1726.

For most politicians, threatening to murder a sitting judge would probably have been a swift career ender. But whatever services his father had rendered for the king were apparently extremely well received, for less than six years later Burrington was back, royal commission in hand, reappointed to the office that he had previously held. And this time he had his sights set on destroying the political power and influence of those who had previously defied him. He would utilize every weapon in his arsenal to exact his revenge, including the as-yet-unnamed gerrymander.

George Burrington was born in Devonshire, England, sometime in the early 1680s. That idyllic south-coast county was also the home of Sir Walter Raleigh, for whom the state capital of Raleigh, North Carolina, would later be named. The son of Gilbert Burrington, George grew up on the family estate at Ideford, in the parish of Chudleigh. In a preview of the turbulent relationships to come, he quickly became estranged from his father, having "disobliged" him at an early age. One of his relatives, Charles Burrington, is credited by historians as being among

Portrait of Thomas Pelham-Holles, 1st Duke of Newcastle,
painted by William Hoare, circa 1750.

the earliest supporters of William of Orange, who invaded England
and seized the British crown during the Glorious Revolution of 1688.
Another relative, John Burrington, was a member of Parliament from
Okehampton and an influential figure within the British navy.

Already politically well connected, George saw his station in life rise
even further in 1711 when his close friend, Thomas Pelham, inherited
the title of Duke of Newcastle from his uncle. It was Pelham's patronage that proved influential in earning Burrington an army commission
in 1715, where he eventually rose to the rank of captain. And Pelham's
connections with the lords proprietors, particularly John Carteret, later
Earl Granville, who was a close political associate of the duke's, might
also have played a role in securing his first appointment as a provincial
governor in the New World.

Things did not get off to a good start. When he attempted to throw
his weight around by directing an official order to William Reed, the
council president who had served as temporary governor prior to Burrington's appointment, the order was returned to him "with comments
not altogether refined." Indignant at being deprived of his office, Reed
began spreading rumors, based on hearsay, that Burrington had "been

in prison, before leaving England, for beating an old woman." And thus Reed became the first in a long line of political opponents to be indicted for criticizing His Excellency. The depositions recounting these events would join that of Christopher Gale on the desks of the lords proprietors and contribute in no small part to his first dismissal (yes, first—more on that later).

Ever willing to call in favors, Burrington secured his second commission as governor directly from the king, much to the chagrin of Gale, who had campaigned strenuously against the appointment. He returned to Edenton in February 1731, and his temper had certainly not cooled in the intervening years. His second term was marred by a violent attack against the attorney general of the colony, John Montgomery, "a man of innumerable villainies," according to Burrington, who he believed was involved in a conspiracy to undermine his authority. "After attacking him with a chair," writes Haywood, "the Governor had thrown him to the floor and punched him in such a manner, with his knee, that he would probably have been killed, or seriously injured, had not bystanders interposed." Predictably, having been pulled off his erstwhile adversary in the throes of battle, Burrington challenged Montgomery to "meet and fight him in Virginia." Once again, though, satisfaction would elude him. Seeking a license to return to England, quite wisely fearful for his life, Montgomery was denied by His Excellency Burrington, who informed him that he would instead "give him a license to go to the Devil, if he desired it."

"The next episode in which we see our hero recorded," recounts Haywood, "is a controversy between [his successor] Governor Everard and the Rev. Thomas Bailey, a missionary to whom Sir Richard had denied the use of the public house of worship." Sensing an opportunity to embarrass the man who had replaced him, Burrington organized a posse to march on the Edenton Court House. Breaking down the door, the congregation entered and the Right Honorable Reverend proceeded to hold services, delivering his Sunday sermon from the bench. Burrington, for his part, is described as being "a Churchman in theory, though not in practice," so the stunt appears to have been driven less by genuine ecclesiastical concerns and more by the long-running feud with his successor.

It was not only his political rivals who felt the wrath of the governor's temper. Returning one day to his sprawling five-thousand-acre Cape

Fear estate, Stag Park, and finding that an impoverished family had erected a log cabin on the edge of his property, Burrington instructed his servant to burn it to the ground. "It is a very common Practice for the People in this Province to burn their Houses," he wrote in his defense, apparently in all seriousness, "as being a cheaper way than pulling them down." Other alleged crimes included "throwing [a] colonial official's written defense of his judgeship into the fire, horse theft, and stealing the council's secretary's commissioning seals." I think you're beginning to get the picture at this point.

Burrington's retribution against his many perceived enemies was political as well as personal. He realized, amid the turmoil of the colony's fractured politics, that he could use his power as governor to secure a colonial legislature that was, shall we say, more amenable to his requests. At the time, the legislature consisted of a council, staffed with representatives of the crown who were appointed by the governor himself, and an assembly, elected by the people to represent the interests of the colonists. Chief among Burrington's targets were Nathaniel Rice, John Baptista Ashe, and Edmund Porter, three members of the legislature who he believed were plotting a coup against him. Their presence in Edenton came by virtue of Martin Bladen, a political rival of Burrington's benefactor, the Duke of Newcastle, who had personally intervened in their appointment, further stoking the governor's paranoia.

Nevertheless, things had been all smiles when Burrington had first returned to Edenton in 1731, because both the members of the assembly and the governor took pains to express the "esteem and regard" with which they held each other. "But this love feast," writes Haywood, "was of short duration." It was the issue of taxes, rather than the governor's many personal indiscretions, that first forged division between the legislature and the executive, and things very quickly went south after the assembly passed a resolution condemning the "charging [of] exorbitant fees by public officials." You can probably guess which public official they had in mind.

Burrington, in typical tone-deaf fashion, responded that "whoever the person might be who wrote this resolution, he was doubtless guilty of such abuses himself." He then further opined that the assembly's conduct "brought to mind the stratagem of a thief, who would hide himself in a house, for the purpose of robbery, and then set it on fire to escape in the smoke." He also pointed out, not entirely helpfully, that the colonial officials in Virginia levied even more extortionate fees against their constituents. But the assembly members, for their part, "did not seem to think the usages of a sister colony germane to the difficulty." The fragile peace in the province had lasted a matter of months. In May 1731, frustrated with the "divisions, heats, and indecencies" of the assembly, Burrington issued an order of prorogation, canceling the remainder of the legislative session in a fit of pique. Left open, however, was the question of who would fill the chamber's ranks when it reconvened the following year.

Having already been "constrained to put an end to their deliberations" in 1731, the governor set as his goal for the 1732 session, as is colorfully described in the colonial records of the time, "to prepossess people in a future election according to his desires, his desires herein being (as we verily believe), to endeavor by his means to get a majority of his creatures in the lower house." In other words, merely sidelining the legislature by prorogation was not enough; Burrington wanted to control it. And never one for half measures, he quickly set about flexing the muscles of his gubernatorial power.

He achieved this goal by artificially creating new districts for the lower house of the colonial legislature out of whole cloth, while also arbitrarily altering the boundaries of the existing ones, remaking the electoral map into one that would ensure the election of those who supported his agenda. This gerrymander would have the effect of bringing the chamber more in line with the upper house, which was already packed with said creatures. By manipulating the districts, some of which ended up containing "not more than thirty families," he was decisively able to bring the colony under his personal political control.

The historical record is somewhat unclear as to from where exactly Burrington derived the authority to do this. In a letter dated November 17, 1732, Rice, Ashe, and Montgomery lay out the details of the gerrymander, concluding that Burrington "proceeded with the advice & consent of such of the Council as are of his own Appointment, & never oppose his schemes be they ever so absurd, to divide old Precincts established by Law, & to enact new Ones in Places." It seems likely, then, that Burrington used the influence he had gained over the upper house through his own appointments to force through a resolution that gerrymandered the districts of the lower house.

Support for this may be found in the minutes of the council's November 1 meeting, which reference the addition of territory to the Edge-combe precinct: "His Excelly the Governour by and with the advice and consent of His Majestys Council doth Establich and Confirm the Limits before recited to be within Edgecombe precinct." The minutes also describe the creation of a new precinct, Bladen, in the Cape Fear region, stating that Burrington and the council "doth Erect and make the before mentioned bounds into a precinct to be hereafter Distin-guished & called Bladen precinct with all such rights and Privilidges as other precincts within this province have and Enjoy."

The paucity of details in the council's minutes may be explained by Burrington's heavy-handed approach to running the business of that chamber. But there is evidence in the record that the governor's actions were not without opposition. "These Considerations moved Mr Rice & Mr Ashe to offer in Council Objections and Reasons against this Method," contends the aforementioned November 17 letter, "which (as we have much reason to suspect,) he will not suffer to be entered in the Council Journal." The surviving minutes certainly suggest that he indeed did not suffer such. The letter also references opposition from the assembly itself, describing "the Governor & Council appointing Precincts, where no Precincts before were (the legality of which, more especially of late years, has been by the Assemblys deny'd)."

In another undated memorandum from Ashe and Rice, they further allege that Burrington's gerrymander was accomplished "by the Govr & Council alone without the Concurrence and Assent of the Assembly," in a manner that flagrantly circumvented the ordinary legislative proce-dures in the colony. These required bills to be passed by both chambers before being enacted into law. "We are of opinion that this method of erecting Precincts," the memorandum concludes, in an obvious appeal to Burrington's superiors to put a stop to his abuses of power, "is not only illegal and may be attended with many evil consequences; but is also not warranted by his Majesty's Royal Instructions which forbids erecting new Judicatures without His Majestys Licence." For the time being, though, the governor had achieved his goal, which, according to Griffith, was "to secure a majority in the lower house strong enough radically to oppose the people."

But this triumph would prove to be short-lived, a Pyrrhic victory that only hastened the end of his career, for the many enemies he had made along the way were about to come home to roost. And this time,

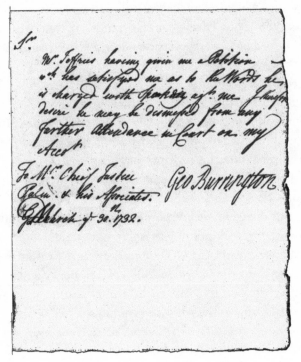

George Burrington's signature on a 1732 colonial record.
No likeness of the man himself survives to the present day.

he would not be able to rely on his friend the Duke of Newcastle to bail him out. With Burrington temporarily absent from the colony in 1734 on a visit to inspect his holdings in South Carolina, his opponents sensed an opportunity to turn the tide of opinion in London against him, at a time when he would be unable to respond in his defense. Numerous petitions flowed into the offices of the Board of Trade, alleging that Burrington's actions with respect to the legislature were in violation of his royal charter, which of course they were.

And so in April 1734, with the accusations mounting, the board decided to replace him with Gabriel Johnston, a Scottish physician, political writer, and professor of oriental languages at the University of Saint Andrews. Burrington, true to form, did not take the decision to remove him a second time particularly well. In a petition to the king appealing his dismissal, he railed against his opponents, and "their endeavors to defame him, by inventing and spreading scandalous stories." He also lamented his "deplorable misfortune to be so misrepresented to Your Majesty as to be removed, without ever knowing the causes that brought upon him an undeserved disgrace & dismal ruin." But by this time, he had burned too many bridges in London, and his desperate appeals to Newcastle to intervene went unanswered.

Not content to merely castigate the underhanded actions of his opponents with respect to his ouster, Burrington also went on to allege the existence of a conspiracy to assassinate him, orchestrated, he claimed, "by directions from some person in England." This was a clear reference to Bladen, who he had long believed was also behind the efforts to obstruct his agenda in the colony. Bladen's agents, including Rice and Montgomery, "with some others their confederates, did contrive and attempt to assassinate your petitioner, then actual Governor there by shooting him with pistols, from which danger he was rescued by the sudden and unexpected interposition of some courageous men who came to his assistance." This alleged murder plot is not documented in any historical sources outside Burrington's own writings, and so seems more likely to be a product of his mounting paranoia and invention than a genuine attempted coup against the crown's representative in North Carolina. Although, as one 1886 historical account notes, "if a tithe of what his enemies said about Burrington be true, the wonder is that he got away from the colony alive, and not that an attempt was made to kill him."

In his later years, after once again returning to London in disgrace, Burrington mellowed at least somewhat, trading in his sword for that proverbial mightier of weapons, the pen. He wrote extensively for Henry Fielding's satirical political journal *The Champion* under the pseudonym Janus the Elder, publishing frequent diatribes against the first prime minister of Great Britain, Sir Robert Walpole. But after a career marred by violent rhetoric, not to mention actual violence, Burrington himself would meet a violent and tragic end. On February 22, 1759, some twenty-five years after his return to England, his bruised and battered body was discovered in a canal in St. James's Park, London, the apparent victim of a robbery gone wrong. The crime was never solved.

"Yesterday was taken out of the Canal in St. James's Park, the Body of an elderly Man well dressed," wrote *The Public Advertiser* the next day. "His Pockets were turn'd inside out, and his Stick in his Hand, which was clinched and bruised." Ever feisty, the seventy-seven-year-old Burrington had apparently put up a spirited fight against his assailants,

The Burrington coat of arms.

but not enough to escape with his life. He was buried at St. John the Evangelist Church in the City of Westminster, following an extravagant and expensive funeral. "Far from the land of his labors and turmoils the old Governor is now laid at rest," concludes one historical epitaph. "Never will that slumber be broken by political animosity or the fiercer discords of private life that marred his earthly career."

Would that it had been so. Maintaining his long list of enemies even in death, Burrington suffered further indignity when it was falsely reported, in a story that made its way into numerous historical sources, that "rioting in his usual manner, he fell a sacrifice to his own folly, [and] was found murdered, in the morning, in the Bird Cage Walk." In his will, Burrington left his estate, flush with cash from the sale of his holdings in the New World, to his nephew, his children apparently having "disobliged" him in much the same way as he had his own father many decades before. "He died, and left the world behind; His once wild heart is cold," concludes an eighteenth-century English poem excerpted by Haywood in his biography of Burrington. "His once keen eye is quelled and blind; What more?—His tale is told."

The French film director Jean-Luc Godard once said that "a story should have a beginning, a middle and an end, but not necessarily in that order." And so it is with the story of the first gerrymander. By accident of history, the naming of the gerrymander would derive not from the practice's actual origins in colonial North Carolina but from an off-the-cuff discussion that took place in a Boston newsroom in the early nineteenth century.

Elbridge Gerry had a problem. The year was 1812, and the politician whose name would go on to become synonymous with the practice of manipulating legislative districts for partisan gain was being thwarted by the Federalist majority in Massachusetts at every turn. Seemingly always a bridesmaid in the commonwealth's politics during the founding era, Gerry spent most of his career in the shadow of titans like John Adams and Samuel Adams. He bounced around between various different political offices, flirting with periods of semiretirement, never quite able to follow through on the promise of greatness that his talent seemed to warrant. Gerry's career had been tainted by scandal, both political and personal, most seriously in the XYZ Affair, which brought the nation to the brink of all-out war with France.

Occurring early in the presidency of John Adams, the XYZ Affair presented the first major diplomatic crisis of the newly established United States. The letters represent the code names given to several French diplomats in documents circulated within the administration: Jean-Conrad Hottinguer (X), Pierre Bellamy (Y), and Lucien Hauteval (Z). Hostilities between the two nations had begun to ramp up in the wake of the French Revolution in 1789, with the United States maintaining its neutrality in the subsequent war between France and several other European powers. Things devolved further after the Washington administration negotiated the Jay Treaty with Great Britain in 1795.

With war seemingly on the horizon, Adams sent a diplomatic envoy to Paris consisting of Gerry, Charles Cotesworth Pinckney, and John Marshall. Their mission ended in failure. The nations would go on to fight several naval skirmishes in the Caribbean in what historians call the Quasi-War, before hostilities ultimately came to an end with the signing of the Convention of 1800. That Gerry took the PR hit for the breakdown in diplomatic relations is particularly ironic, not to mention spectacularly on-brand, because he remained in France for several months after the other two commissioners had left, and his informal negotiations with the French foreign minister, Charles-Maurice de

Talleyrand-Périgord, ended up laying much of the groundwork for the later accord. The XYZ Affair also led to allegations of pro-French sympathies that would dog him for the remainder of his career.

But perhaps even more embarrassingly, the disastrous decision to guarantee a loan for his brother, a chronic bungler of monetary affairs, also ruined Gerry financially. He and his two brothers had inherited from their father a successful shipping business that exported dried codfish to Barbados and Spain. But years of neglect and mismanagement by his brother, during which time Gerry was often preoccupied with his political career, left the firm heavily in debt and Gerry himself on the proverbial hook, so to speak. The man who had represented Massachusetts at the Constitutional Convention in Philadelphia now found himself in a state of relative poverty that he considered unbefitting a statesman of his caliber.

As a member of the Democratic-Republican Party, Gerry had aligned himself with the presidencies of Thomas Jefferson and his successor, James Madison, who advocated for the cutting back of federal power with respect to the states. This placed him on opposite sides from the commonwealth's most famous politician, John Adams, who along with other Federalists like Alexander Hamilton and John Marshall desired to strengthen the authority of the national government. Gerry now had the opportunity to stick it to those critics by presiding over the passage of a strong Democratic-Republican legislative agenda in a state that had to that point been dominated by his political opponents. The only thing standing in his way was the lingering Federalist majority in the state senate. The Massachusetts state constitution, however, required new state legislative boundaries be drawn that year, and it would be from the debates over the redrawing of those district boundaries that Gerry's infamy would spring.

It had been a long and arduous road to the governor's mansion for the man whose lasting political legacy was one he had never courted or desired. Born in 1744 in Marblehead, Massachusetts, Gerry was the son of a wealthy merchant seaman who had immigrated to the United States from England fourteen years prior. A precocious young man who benefited from the finest private tutors money could buy, he was admitted to Harvard College at age thirteen and earned both undergraduate and graduate degrees before his twentieth birthday. His initial foray into national politics came when he successfully sought election to the

First Continental Congress in 1774, the colonial legislature that had assembled in Philadelphia in the wake of the Boston Tea Party. But, still grieving the death of his father earlier that year, Gerry declined to take up the post.

Instead, he would come to play a key role in the colonial resistance to British rule in Massachusetts, stockpiling weapons and ammunition at Concord, which he funneled in through his hometown of Marblehead after Parliament closed the port of Boston. These activities earned him significant plaudits from his fellow Founding Fathers, including John Adams, who wrote in 1776, "If every Man here was a Gerry, the Liberties of America would be safe against the Gates of Earth and Hell." On the night of Paul Revere's famous ride, Gerry was staying at the Menotomy Tavern in Arlington, along with two patriot colonels. As a patrol of redcoats entered and searched the tavern en route to Lexington, Gerry and his pals, still clad in their nightshirts, only escaped capture by hiding out in a nearby cornfield.

Gerry first ran for the office of governor in 1788, almost a full year before the Constitution that he had helped to draft would go into effect. The campaign did not go well for him. To his misfortune, he found himself facing off against John Hancock, the wealthy merchant and patriot whose signature famously, and eponymously, graced the Declaration of Independence. Hancock had already been overwhelmingly elected as the very first governor of the newly established commonwealth back in 1780 and enjoyed the unbridled support of the Boston political establishment. Gerry had represented Massachusetts at the Philadelphia convention, and his input proved vital to the drafting. Of particular influence were his views on federalism, where he advocated a strict delineation between federal and state powers, and elections, where he championed the indirect selection of federal officers. Nevertheless, he remained concerned about the lack of protection of civil liberties in the Constitution and was ultimately one of only three delegates to vote against it, predicting that it would create "as complete an aristocracy as ever was framed."

Though Gerry was clearly mismatched against the gregarious Hancock, the scope of his loss was still spectacular to behold. His landslide defeat, which saw him garner only 19 percent of the vote to Hancock's 81 percent, would also not be his last. While the ratification in 1791 of the Bill of Rights, which added in those civil liberties protections

Portrait of Elbridge Gerry, painted by James Bogle in 1861.

whose absence had so sorely concerned him, produced a change of heart for Gerry about the wisdom of the founding document, it did not produce a corresponding improvement in his electoral fortunes. Four more unsuccessful bids for the governorship followed between 1800 and 1803, and each time Gerry was defeated by his latest political nemesis, the popular Federalist senator and fellow Philadelphia delegate Caleb Strong. Adding further embarrassment, he received a smaller share of the vote with each successive defeat to Strong, and once again in the political wilderness Gerry feared that his long career of public service might be drawing to a close.

For Elbridge Gerry, though, the sixth time proved to be the charm. Running again for governor in 1810, he defeated the incumbent, Christopher Gore, by the narrowest of margins, winning 51 percent of the vote in a bitterly contested campaign. Gerry was able to counter Gore's characterization of him as a "French-partizan" with accusations of disloyalty against his opponent, bringing up the fact that Gore's parents had remained loyal to the British crown during the revolution, negative campaigning apparently being as much a feature of elections in the early nineteenth century as it is in the twenty-first. Finally ensconced in the office that had for so long eluded him, Gerry found himself frustrated by divided government during his first term. But he also proved to be an unexpectedly savvy politician, charting a course of moderation in his political dealings and biding his time for a more fertile climate in which to push his policy priorities. This strategy served him well and allowed him to win reelection, this time with 52 percent of the vote, in an equally acrimonious rematch with Gore in 1811.

Gerry's second, and what would prove to be final, term as governor was as contentious as his first had been uneventful. Losing patience with the obstruction of his agenda, Gerry undertook a systematic purge of Federalist appointees in the executive branch and created numerous state judgeships that he was able to successfully pack with Democratic-Republican cronies. But it was his activities with respect to the legislative branch that drew the ire not only of his political opponents but the media as well and, far more than his later service as vice president of the United States, came to define Gerry's career and legacy.

The fundamental irony of what followed was that Gerry, who would be forevermore attached in history to the unseemly practice of partisan redistricting, was not even the architect of the infamous "salamander" district that bears his name. It was, in fact, the invention of his fellow partisans in the General Court, who, charged with the actual redrawing of state legislative boundaries, and frustrated with the continued obstructionism of the Federalists, viewed a continuing Democratic-Republican majority in the state senate as essential. By this time, the notion that the drawing of districts could be manipulated for partisan gain was nothing new. The practice that Burrington had pioneered in colonial North Carolina had been replicated on several occasions in the early republic, most notably in New York following the 1800 census and, as the next chapter discusses, in post-independence Virginia. The members of the General Court even attempted to frame their 1812 plan as a correction for earlier Federalist meddling in the drawing of district lines, although this justification was not especially convincing even at the time.

What is clear is that the line drawers in the General Court would stop at nothing to prevent the Federalists from undoing everything that they had been able to achieve following Gerry's reelection. There were few electoral shenanigans to which they were unprepared to stoop in order to achieve that goal, and the resulting plan was quite rightly lampooned as a fairly naked and transparent power grab. At the time, Massachusetts's eighteen state senate districts, from which forty members would be elected, were based not on population, as is the case in all state legislatures today, but on the amount of taxes that were paid in different localities. In theory, each senator represented at least $5 million worth of taxable property, or at least that was the way things had always been done. And while earlier districting plans had sometimes split counties between two or more senate districts to fit the communities of Massachusetts and the modern-day state of Maine (then part of Massachusetts) into eighteen districts, legislators had endeavored to keep these to a minimum.

The 1812 redistricting plan, however, utilized every tool in the book to manipulate the electoral playing field. Counties were split between two and even three districts with reckless abandon, Maine's seat apportionment was arbitrarily increased from seven to ten to capitalize on the Democratic-Republican strength in that region, and the principles of compactness and regularity in district boundaries were jettisoned in favor of distorted irregular lines and bizarre shapes. But it must be noted that this infamous "original" gerrymander, while certainly an egregious manipulation of the levers of democracy, bears little resemblance to the gerrymanders of today, including the REDMAP-inspired plans discussed in the introduction.

Modern gerrymandering, by virtue of the constitutional mandate of "one person, one vote," requires line drawers to distort the partisan composition of individual districts while preserving equality of population between districts across the entire electoral landscape. If unseating a Democratic incumbent necessitates moving a bloc of Republican voters into their district from neighboring localities, then a corresponding population of Democratic voters must be shifted the other way to preserve population equality. The creators of the historical gerrymanders discussed in this chapter were under no such constraints. By engaging in the kind of creative tax valuation described above, the Democratic-Republicans in the Massachusetts legislature were actually practicing a form of deliberate malapportionment, an American version of the rotten boroughs of English antiquity. While the effect was undoubtedly the same, it's hard not to conclude that the redistricting plan that gave us the term "gerrymander" was not in fact a gerrymander at all, at least not as the term is commonly understood today.

That being said, even Gerry himself was uncomfortable with the obviously partisan nature of the proposed plan, with one biographer, quoting Gerry's son-in-law, describing him as finding it "highly disagreeable" upon its unveiling. Despite his distaste, and likely harboring ambitions for higher office, Gerry nevertheless signed the legislation into law, and outrage swiftly ensued. Perhaps the biggest victims of the plan, aside from the unfortunate Federalists in the state senate, were the people of Maine. The expansion of their representation in the senate left them on the hook for $61,000 in taxes over the subsequent decade, far in excess of what would have been levied under a fair and equal apportionment of seats. These extra taxes were assessed on a town-by-town basis in a process known, quite appropriately given the circumstances, as dooming. This was a sharp departure from previous apportionment plans, which had been based on taxes actually paid, rather than those to be assessed in the future. Seven years later, the people of Maine voted to break away from Massachusetts and form their own state.

At the urging of the Federalists, a state house of representatives committee was empaneled to investigate the source of these inequalities but in a manner befitting the political argle-bargle of the entire process was then disbanded one hour before it was scheduled to deliver its report. "In this manner," wrote one understated early twentieth-century historical account, "a very arbitrary scheme of assessment and apportionment was resorted to by the Democrats."

Though Gerry himself had no direct involvement in the drawing up of the plan, and had signed it, if his son-in-law is to be believed, only grudgingly, the media went on to make him the poster child of its excesses. The most obviously distorted seat in the new senate map was that which split the Federalist stronghold of Essex County, producing a district that meandered around the western and northern county line in order to pack in as many majority Federalist towns as possible. The result was that in a county where the Federalists would have been expected to pick up all five seats under a fair plan, in the next election the Democratic-Republicans managed to win three of the five, not to mention twenty-nine of the forty seats in the senate overall, despite winning less than 50 percent of the popular vote.

The original "gerrymander" cartoon from *The Boston Gazette,*
printed in March 1812.

In a now famous, and possibly apocryphal, exchange, a reporter for
The Boston Gazette, alternatively Gilbert Stuart or Elkanah Tisdale,
depending on whose version of events you believe, drew a head, wings,
tail, and claws on a map of the Essex County district that was displayed on the wall of his editor's office. "That will do for a salamander!"
exclaimed the reporter as he stood back and admired his handiwork.
"Better say a gerrymander" deadpanned the editor, and thus political history was made. The newspaper caption that accompanied the
cartoon upon its publication proudly announces the discovery of "a

new species of Monster, which appeared in Essex South District in Jan. 1812." Its creator: none other than "his Excellency," Governor Gerry.

In one final indignity that added injury to insult for Gerry, while the redistricting plan he had signed proved effective enough to preserve the Democratic-Republican majority in the state senate, they nevertheless lost control of the state house of representatives in the 1812 election. And, matching up for a fifth time with his old foe Caleb Strong, whom the Federalists had brought out of retirement for one last rodeo, Gerry himself lost an agonizingly close race for governor in the same election, by fewer than 1,400 votes out of more than 100,000 that were cast. Though he would die two years later at the age of seventy, while serving as vice president of the United States under James Madison, Gerry was at least able to earn enough from his federal salary to finally pay off the debts he had incurred from his brother's financial folly. In the end, the map that defined his tenure as governor survived even less time than Gerry himself; it was repealed in 1813.

There's one final linguistic postscript to the story of Gerry's salamander. It turns out that the word "gerrymander" has been pronounced incorrectly for decades. Elbridge Gerry's last name, and indeed the eponymous practice to which it became attached, was pronounced with a hard *G,* rather than the now ubiquitous soft one. *The Wall Street Journal* traces the origins of the confusion to at least 1850, when the topic was discussed by the delegates to the Indiana state constitutional convention. In a debate over a proposed clause that would have prohibited lawmakers in the state from participating in the drawing of their own districts, the delegate John Pettit opined, "You are constantly gerrymandering the State, or jerrymandering, as I maintain the word should be pronounced, the g being soft." This more orthographically natural pronunciation would be the one that stuck, a fact the *Journal* credits to the print-only media of the era: "Prior to radio, you kind of winged it."

There is a concept in science known as Stigler's law of eponymy. Popularized by the University of Chicago statistics professor Stephen Stigler in the early 1980s, it posits that very rarely is a scientific discovery actually named after its original discoverer. Some famous examples include Hubble's law in physical cosmology, which was first derived by

Georges Lemaître two years before Edwin Hubble received the credit; Pythagoras's theorem in geometry, which was already well known to the Babylonian mathematicians of ancient Mesopotamia; and Halley's Comet, which had been observed by astronomers as far back as 240 BC, centuries before Edmund Halley shocked the scientific world by accurately predicting its return to the skies. To that list can now be added the gerrymander, which, while ultimately named after the unfortunate Elbridge Gerry, originated long before the drawing of the infamous salamander district in Essex County. Interestingly, and clearly by design, Stigler's law is itself an example of Stigler's law, having been first chronicled by the sociologist Robert K. Merton, to whom Stigler himself awards the credit.

Burrington's North Carolina gerrymander stands out as the only clearly documented example of the practice in colonial America, and some significant portion of the credit (or blame) for its development must surely reside with him. Nevertheless, Burrington's scheme also relied on the creative use of malapportionment, and so at the very least an asterisk must be placed after any title that we might be inclined to award him. But in the quest to find the first gerrymander, one thing becomes clear: its creator was not Elbridge Gerry, nor was he even an American. And while it may be too late at this point to introduce the term "Burrimander" into the American political lexicon, the story of the bombastic, judge-threatening, attorney-assaulting colonial governor is one that deserves far more attention in the history books.

2

James Madison's Henrymander

The fellow Founding Fathers James Madison and Patrick Henry did not get along. The two Virginians had very different philosophies on the proper role of government and its relationship with liberty, divisions that came to a head during their famous debate in June 1788 over the ratification of the U.S. Constitution. But perhaps more significantly, the two men were also from different generations and very different family backgrounds. Henry, the son of a Scottish immigrant, came of political age during the colonial era. He made a name for himself in Virginia politics with a fiery speech to the House of Burgesses in 1765, where he sharply denounced the Stamp Act and the British monarchy. Taking the floor to address men many decades his senior, the twenty-nine-year-old Henry, "in a voice of thunder, and with the look of a god," declared that "Caesar had his Brutus—Charles the First, his Cromwell—and George the Third . . . may profit by their example." As cries of "treason!" erupted from the assembled burgesses, Henry, displaying the penchant for pithy declarations that later produced his signature one-liner, "give me liberty, or give me death!" calmly responded, "If this be treason, make the most of it."

In the audience that day was a twenty-two-year-old law student named Thomas Jefferson, and it would not be the last time that the two men's paths would cross. The feud that developed between these titans of the founding era, Jefferson and Madison on one side, Patrick Henry on the other, culminated in a gerrymander that would threaten not only the careers and political reputations of those involved but the very existence of the United States itself. In 1788, with the ink on the Constitution not yet dry, Henry used his political clout in the Virginia general assembly to gerrymander Madison's home district. His goal was to deny his nemesis a seat in the First Congress, the very legislative body that gave us the Bill of Rights. If he had succeeded, the fragile compromise that shepherded the fledgling union through its turbulent early years might have been shattered. This chapter is the story of how gerrymandering almost blew up the American system of government on the launchpad.

Madison's upbringing could not have been more different from that of the man who later became his bitter enemy. While Henry's father was a first-generation immigrant and minor planter, Madison's family had settled in Virginia in the early seventeenth century and owned one of the largest tobacco plantations in the colony. Fifteen years Henry's junior, Madison cut his political teeth during the revolutionary era as a member of the Virginia House of Delegates, and later as a representative in the Second Continental Congress. Henry had also been a member of that body, although their tenures did not overlap. Henry served alongside Jefferson in 1775, leaving less than a year before the Congress adopted his Declaration of Independence, while Madison served later, observing firsthand the dysfunction of the newly established American republic under the Articles of Confederation.

Though Jefferson had been impressed, as everyone would come to be, with Henry's powerful oratory, he nevertheless viewed him as all style and no substance. "His imagination was copious, poetical, sublime," he later wrote in his memoirs, "but vague also. He said the strongest things in the finest language, but without logic, without arrangement, desultorily." In a letter to George Rogers Clark in 1782, Jefferson pulled even fewer punches: "Who he is you will probably have heard, or may know him by this description as being all tongue without either head or heart. In the variety of his crooked schemes however, his interests may probably veer about so as to put it in your power to be useful to him; in which case he certainly will be your friend again if you want him."

Henry and Madison shared a passion for constitutional law, with each man, in his own way, playing a pivotal role in the establishment of constitutional governance in the United States. For Henry, this would

Portrait of James Madison by John Vanderlyn, circa 1816.

play out at the state level in his beloved Virginia, while Madison had far loftier goals in mind. Henry, working closely with his friend George Mason, was an influential member of the Fifth Virginia Convention, which not only declared the colony to be a free and independent state but also authored the first Constitution of Virginia and drafted the Virginia Declaration of Rights. Henry's reward for his role in the push for independence, which he had supported far earlier than many of his contemporaries, was to be chosen as the very first governor of the newly established Commonwealth of Virginia. His successor in that office, much to his chagrin, was none other than Thomas Jefferson. It was here that Jefferson's alliance and lifelong friendship with Madison, who was serving as a member of the governor's Council of State, was forged. The battle lines between the three men had now been drawn.

The first shots were fired in 1783. Jefferson, along with Madison, had grown dissatisfied with the state constitution that Henry's Fifth Virginia Convention had produced. The two men now spearheaded a movement to revise its text. Virginia's 1776 constitution, as was typical at the time, limited suffrage to wealthy male landowners. This had the effect of concentrating political power among the southeastern aristocracy. Jefferson and Madison, despite being wealthy male landowners themselves, desired to extend the franchise, albeit only to a somewhat larger group

Portrait of Patrick Henry by Thomas Sully, circa 1851.

of male taxpayers in good standing. But Henry was jealously protective of his commonwealth's founding document. He proved more powerful and managed to outmaneuver his opponents to devastating effect, blocking their attempts at revision. Jefferson summed up his frustration in a letter to Madison: "While Mr. Henry lives, another bad constitution would be formed, and saddled forever on us. What we have to do I think is devoutly to pray for his death."

As Henry began focusing his attention inward, consolidating the stranglehold over Virginia politics that would prove crucial to his later gerrymander, Madison was looking outward. Not content with mere independence from Great Britain, which had left the newly established nation decentralized and fragmented, Madison instead turned his efforts, as well as his not inconsiderable talents, toward the cause of greater union. He had also found himself further embroiled in the growing rivalry between Jefferson and Henry, whose most recent disagreement concerned the relationship between government and faith. Henry, although suspicious of state-sponsored religion, nevertheless desired to impose a religious tax in Virginia, the revenues of which individuals could direct toward the support of their church of choice. Jefferson, as he would later famously state in an 1802 letter to the Danbury Baptist Association, preferred "a wall of separation between church and state."

The dispute came to a head in 1785. Henry attempted to take advantage of Jefferson's absence while serving as minister to France to force his proposed tax through the state legislature. This time, however, his attempt ended up backfiring. As Jefferson pulled the political strings by letter from Paris, Madison managed to persuade the Virginia General Assembly to reject Henry's church-financing tax. Jefferson's church-state separation bill, which he had first proposed without success during his time as governor, was instead approved in its place. The degree of bad blood between the longtime political foes grew deeper still as the date of the Philadelphia convention approached in 1787.

The first attempt at establishing constitutional governance for the newly independent states had not gone well. The Articles of Confederation, drafted between July 1776 and November 1777, and ratified by all thirteen states by March 1781, were based chiefly on the guiding principle of preserving state sovereignty and independence. As such, they created an extremely weak central government that proved itself staggeringly ineffective at dealing with the problems of a large and diverse nation. The Continental Congress had been given no independent authority to lay and collect taxes, forcing the fledgling national government to rely on the generosity of the states, loans from foreign governments, and the sale of western real estate to raise the revenues necessary to function. The new government also had no independent executive branch, instead conferring upon the leader of the legislature the title of president and creating a "committee of the states" to exercise national authority whenever they were not in session.

This arrangement suited Patrick Henry. His long-standing acrimony for the divine right to absolute power that had been lavished upon the British monarchy had fanned the flames of his revolutionary fervor. Indeed, Henry's suspicion of the centralization of executive authority in the office of the president, which he saw as not only a step backward toward despotism but also a betrayal of those who fought and died in the Revolutionary War, would go on to form the cornerstone of his case in opposition to the ratification of the Constitution.

But for others, including Jefferson and Madison, the failure of the federal government to respond effectively to Shays's Rebellion in 1787, which had to be put down by the Massachusetts state militia after Congress was unable to finance an armed response, was the final straw in this failed first experiment in governing the United States. As a delegate to the Annapolis Convention in 1786, Madison joined with Alexander Hamilton in calling for a constitutional convention to consider amendments to the Articles of Confederation. Having failed to make his case in that forum, he sought election to the Continental Congress the following year, and this time was successful in persuading his fellow legislators to authorize the Philadelphia convention.

The question of who would represent the Commonwealth of Virginia as delegates to the convention, whose original mandate was limited only to the consideration of amendments to the existing constitution, was a thorny one. Madison, who had led the call for reform, was an obvious choice. And he was joined by a retired Revolutionary War general by the name of George Washington. Washington, despite supporting Madison's case for a stronger union, had initially declined the assignment, citing concerns over the legality of the proceedings. But after an intervention by Madison and Virginia's governor, Edmund Randolph, who would also serve as a delegate, Washington reluctantly agreed, although he made it clear that he was attending under duress.

Notably absent from the delegate list were the names of Thomas Jefferson and Patrick Henry. Jefferson was still in Paris, where he was joined in 1787, five years after the untimely death of his wife, Martha, by a fourteen-year-old slave from Monticello named Sally Hemings, who worked as a domestic servant and maid in the Jefferson household. Rumors of Jefferson's ongoing sexual relationship with Hemings, which resulted in his fathering at least six of her children, first surfaced during his presidency in 1802.

The journalist James T. Callender, a former Jefferson ally who had become disaffected with his administration after failing to secure an appointment as postmaster, wrote in the *Richmond Recorder*, "It is well known that the man, whom it delighteth the people to honor, keeps, and for many years past has kept, as his concubine, one of his own slaves." The story was picked up by numerous other papers, particularly those affiliated with his Federalist opponents. Jefferson never responded publicly to the rumors, although some interpret an 1805 letter to Secretary of the Navy Robert Smith as alluding to at least a tacit denial of the allegations. DNA evidence released in 1998 would prove definitively the link between the male-line Jefferson and Hemings descendants, and most historians now accept their relationship as established fact.

While Jefferson was not physically present in Philadelphia that summer, he continued to influence events from afar through another of his signature letter-writing campaigns. Henry, however, while offered a spot as delegate by Governor Randolph, declined the appointment. In another pithy declaration that may or may not be apocryphal, he opined that he "smelt a rat in Philadelphia, tending towards monarchy." As Madison was carving out the leadership role at the convention that would see him forever immortalized as the "Father of the Constitution," Henry watched anxiously, convinced that the delegates would use their mandate to debate proposed amendments to the Articles of Confederation as a pretext for ditching them entirely, to be replaced with a system that gave greater power to the central government. His fears did not prove to be unfounded.

But it was not until after the convention ended, during the debates over the ratification of the document that Madison had played a key role, perhaps more so than any other delegate, in drafting, that the long-running feud between him and Henry reached its apex, culminating in the infamous gerrymander of 1788. Henry, always the skeptic of concentrated federal power and defender of state sovereignty and individual rights, opposed the Constitution from the very beginning. "I have to lament that I cannot bring my mind to accord with the proposed constitution," he wrote to George Washington shortly after the convention. "The concern I feel on this account is really greater than I am able to express." Both Henry and his ally George Mason, with whom he had collaborated on the drafting of the Constitution of Virginia, emerged as key Anti-Federalist voices as the ratification debates heated up.

Madison meanwhile, along with two other leading Federalists, John Jay and Alexander Hamilton, took their case to the American people. They launched in the form of the Federalist Papers a passionate defense of the document they had produced at Philadelphia. It was a product of compromise to be certain, and bearing with it all of the imperfections, concessions, and trade-offs that had been necessary to forge agreement. But it was also a product of urgency. "We have seen the necessity of the Union," wrote Madison in Federalist 14, "as the only substitute for those military establishments which have subverted the liberties of the Old World, and as the proper antidote for the diseases of faction, which have proved fatal to other popular governments, and of which alarming symptoms have been betrayed by our own."

By the end of May 1788, South Carolina became the eighth state to ratify the Constitution, one short of the nine that were required for it to go into effect. All eyes turned to Virginia, which was scheduled to hold its ratification convention in Richmond that June. It was the last stand for Patrick Henry's rapidly crumbling Anti-Federalist cause.

"Even more than the Lincoln-Douglas debate over slavery, or the Darrow-Bryan debate over evolution," wrote the influential historian Joseph Ellis in his book *American Creation,* "the Henry-Madison debate in June of 1788 can lay plausible claim to being the most consequential debate in American history." For almost four weeks the 168 delegates to the Virginia Ratifying Convention gathered in the sweltering heat of the Richmond Theatre to decide upon the future of the nation. There was no doubt who the stars of the show were going to be. According to contemporaneous transcripts, Henry spoke for almost a quarter of the entire proceeding. He was described by one delegate as "rising on the wings of the tempest, to seize upon the artillery of heaven, and direct its fiercest thunders against the heads of his adversaries." Madison, ill throughout most of the convention, by contrast spoke so softly that the stenographer often had difficulty making out what he was saying. "He held his hat in one hand," writes Ellis, "which contained notes he consulted like a professor delivering an academic lecture. But as a result his arguments arrived without flourish or affectation, in a sense the more impressive because of their austerity."

What Madison lacked in oratorical brio, he made up for in keen, calculated political strategizing. Realizing that the vast majority of those in attendance had already made up their minds, he set to work persuading the undecided delegates behind the scenes. His number one target was Edmund Randolph, the seventh governor of Virginia. Randolph had been one of only three delegates to the earlier Constitutional Convention in Philadelphia, along with Elbridge Gerry and George Mason, who had voted against that initial ratification. Figuring Henry and his allies to be a lost cause, Madison gambled that if Randolph could be brought into the fold, the remaining undecided delegates would swiftly follow.

Over the course of a long series of correspondence, he finally wore Randolph down. He persuaded the governor to abandon his sticking point of conditioning ratification upon the passage of amendments to protect individual liberty, and instead vote to approve the Constitution as written. Madison's commitment to introducing a bill of rights during the First Congress after ratification, amendments to the Constitution that would protect citizens' individual liberties against the power of the federal government, ultimately proved decisive in his appeal. Randolph and the other wavering attendees were on board.

In a last desperate gambit, Henry seized upon Randolph's now abandoned position, attempting to muddy the waters in what Madison derided as "a tactical ploy designed to confuse the undecided delegates." In his final address to the convention, in which he proposed no fewer than forty separate amendments as binding conditions upon ratification, Henry extended his appeal to the heavens. "I see beings of a higher order, anxious concerning our decision," he warned the assembled delegates as a thunderstorm appropriately began to rage outside the auditorium. "When I see beyond the horizon that binds human eyes, and look at the final consummation of all human things, . . . I am led to believe that much of the account on one side or the other will depend on what we now decide." But it was all ultimately in vain. The next day, June 25, 1788, the convention voted 89–79 in favor of ratification. "Mr. Henry had without doubt the greatest power to persuade," wrote John Marshall, the influential Federalist who would later become chief justice of the United States, but "Mr. Madison had the greatest power to convince."

As it turned out, the support of the nation's largest and most powerful state, although a major PR victory for the Federalist cause, proved largely irrelevant to the fate of the founding document under consideration that summer in Richmond. Four days earlier, New Hampshire had become the ninth state to complete the ratification process, ensuring once and for all that the Constitution of the United States would go fully into effect the following year. Nevertheless, for Patrick Henry, the defeat still stung. For those keeping score at home, the Henry-Madison rivalry was becoming a rather lopsided one. Despite successfully defending the Virginia Constitution against Jefferson's designs on amendment to expand voting rights, Henry had lost the battle over church and state; failed to defend the Articles of Confederation—of which by 1787 he might have been the only remaining supporter—against what he believed was the hijacking of the Philadelphia convention by a faction bent on sowing the seeds of its destruction; and had now lost a similar constitutional holding action to Madison at the convention in Richmond.

But Henry was not quite ready to give up just yet. While he had failed to prevent the Constitution from being ratified, he still commanded a great deal of authority in his native Virginia. In particular, the general assembly, which under the quasi-parliamentary system in place at the time also had the power to select the governor, was still dominated by his Anti-Federalist allies. George Washington was acutely aware of the influence that Henry still retained over the commonwealth's politics. In a letter to Madison from Mount Vernon, he wrote, "The Edicts of Mr. H[enry] are enregistered with less opposition by the Majority of that body, than those of the Grand Monarch are in the Parliaments of France. He has only to say Let this be Law—and it is Law." And, when the members convened later in 1787 to determine who would represent the state in the newly created U.S. Senate, as well as how their U.S. representatives and federal electors would be chosen, Henry sensed an opportunity to even the score with his old political adversary.

First, he unveiled his plan for a second constitutional convention, persuading the assembly to pass a resolution calling for other states to support him in that effort. The U.S. Constitution, he argued, was a good starting point for creating a government that followed through on the revolution's promise of liberty and state sovereignty, but it was still in need of a drastic overhaul. The forty amendments that he had proposed at the Richmond convention were no longer sufficient for fixing the broken document; what was required was a return to the drawing board, a fresh start to follow through on what had been promised at Lexington and Concord.

Under Article V of the Constitution, a new convention may be called upon the petition of two-thirds of the states. With New York heeding Henry's call and passing its own resolution endorsing a second convention, there appeared to be some initial momentum behind his proposal. But preventing Madison from quashing that momentum by following through on his promise to introduce a bill of rights before the First Congress was crucial to the plan. While Henry certainly desired to protect civil liberties, he was more concerned with blunting the power of the federal government vis-à-vis the states. Persuading enough state leg-islatures to support an Article V convention would only be possible if he could bring the civil libertarians into the fold, and Madison's proposal threatened to short-circuit that appeal.

At the request of George Washington, Madison threw his hat into the ring as a candidate to be one of Virginia's two U.S. senators, although his correspondence reveals that the House of Representatives was his preferred appointment. But Henry would stop at nothing to prevent him from making it to Congress. Taking to the floor of the assembly during the debate over the Senate nominations, ostensibly to express his support for the two Anti-Federalist candidates, Richard Henry Lee and William Grayson, Henry went on to impugn Madison in a vicious personal attack. As one delegate recalled it in a letter to Madison, "Mr. Henry on the floor exclaimed against your political character & pro-nounced you unworthy of the confidence of the people in the station of Senator, that your election would terminate in producing rivulets of blood throughout the land."

And thus it was law: the final vote was Lee 98, Grayson 86, and Madison 77—an ignominious defeat for one of the state's most famous politicians. So far, at least, everything was going according to plan for Patrick Henry. Reflecting on the loss, Madison, unaccustomed to the sting of defeat at the hands of his rival, wrote to Jefferson that he had been "defeated by Mr. Henry who is omnipotent in the present legis-lature and who added to the expedients common on such occasions, a public philippic against my federal principles." Having failed to secure election to the Senate, Madison turned to the only other avenue avail-able to him if he were to realize his promise of a bill of rights: the upcoming elections to the U.S. House of Representatives. Before a year had passed, for the only time in U.S. history, two future presidents would face off for a single seat in Congress.

The long-running enmity between Henry and the Jefferson-Madison alliance had by this point gone beyond a case of mere political dis-agreement: it was also personal. Jefferson, for his part, held Henry in extremely low professional regard, believing him to be arrogant, lazy, "insatiable in money," and unqualified for most of the positions that he had occupied during his career. On Henry's refusal to accept the position of secretary of state in George Washington's cabinet, Jefferson remarked that "his self-esteem had never suffered him to act as second to any man on earth." Madison took particular umbrage at what he saw as Henry's duplicitous rhetoric during the Virginia Ratifying Convention, characterizing his remarks as "ill-founded" and "distorting the natural construction of language." Henry's motives are a little harder to read, given his preference for oratory over the written word. In fact, the entire archive of his papers from the Revolutionary War until his death in 1799 amounts to a meager 104 pages and sheds little light on the source of his very public vendetta. In any case, it was Henry's actions that spoke louder than any words.

After leaving the governor's mansion in 1786, Henry had returned to his seat in the Virginia House of Delegates, a position that gave him significant influence over the workings of the General Assembly. His plan to use gerrymandering to deny Madison a seat in the First Congress had four components. First, he would draw a district that packed in as many Anti-Federalist majority counties as possible along with Madison's home county of Orange. Second, he would pass a law requiring all congressional candidates to be a resident of the district in which they were running. Third, he would persuade the legislature to appoint Madison as a delegate to the lame-duck Confederation Congress, forcing him to travel back and forth to New York when he should have been campaigning. And fourth, he would recruit the biggest political name he could find to run against Madison in the newly gerrymandered district. It was a testament to Madison's ability, reputation, and overall star power that despite all four stages of Henry's plan apparently coming off without a hitch, Madison still managed to win the election in a near landslide.

After dispensing with the selection of the state's two U.S. senators in October 1788, the general assembly turned its attention the next month to the question of the House. Having decided to divide the state into ten districts, the delegates assigned the responsibility of drawing up a new electoral map for the 1789 elections to a subcommittee consisting of seven Federalists and eight Anti-Federalists.

According to a letter by George Mason, a bipartisan compromise emerged to divide the state "into ten districts, as nearly equal as Circumstances will admit; the Rule of Computation being the Number of Militia in each County." And while the initial bill reported out of the committee was described in contemporaneous accounts as being somewhat beneficial to the Federalists, it was amended at least three times before final passage, twice in the House and once in the Senate. According to Madison's sources in Richmond, as proceedings unfolded, "men of both factions . . . reported that Henry and his followers were amending the bill to help the electoral prospects of the Anti-Federalists." One of the strongest pieces of evidence for the existence of a plan to gerrymander the districts comes from the papers of George Washington. He wrote to Benjamin Lincoln on November 14, "It is now much dreaded . . . that the State (which is to be divided into districts for the appointment of Representatives to Congress) will be so arranged as to place a large proportion of those who are called Antifederalists in that Station."

Madison himself also appeared to be aware of the plan. Henry Lee wrote to him on November 19 stating, "Mr. H[enry] is absolute, & every measure succeeds, which menaces the existence of the govt.—the districts will be laid off, to conform to the antifederal interest." Lest there be any confusion as to what exactly Lee was referring to, he clarifies later in the same correspondence: "I profess myself pleased with your exclusion from the senate & I wish it may so happen in the lower house—then you will be left qualified to take part in the administration, which is the place proper for you." Even George Mason, perhaps Henry's closest ally in the state, makes an oblique reference to the scheme in his correspondence, quoting an unnamed Anti-Federalist member of the assembly who states, after discussing the details of the House districting bill, that "the Feds have swallowed [it] like Wormwood."

While no records survive of the details of the original districting plan drafted by the committee, or of the amendments offered by Henry and his allies, the final electoral map enacted into law by the general assembly on November 20 certainly bore the imprimatur of partisan manipulation. Or at the very least, of a personal crusade against one man. What drew particular ire from the observers at Mount Vernon was District 5. At first look, it bears little resemblance to either the famous salamander in Massachusetts or the contorted straits, rivulets, and appendages of the districts that form the poster children for the excesses of modern gerrymandering.

It was both compact and not significantly malapportioned, at least to the extent possible at the time, because the assembly endeavored to

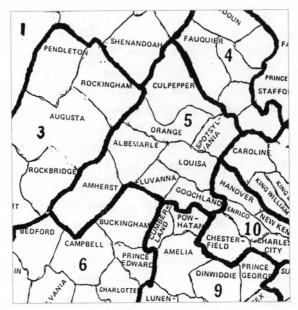

Map of Virginia's Fifth Congressional District, 1788.

roughly equalize the number of militiamen between districts, figuring this to be a rough proxy for the number of eligible voters who resided there. But beneath the surface of District 5 lurks a far more sinister intent. In the district's center sits Orange County, home to James Madison's sprawling Montpelier plantation. Joining Orange in the district are seven additional Virginia counties: Amherst, Albemarle, Culpeper, and Louisa, as well as the quirkily named Fluvanna, Goochland, and Spotsylvania.

Spotsylvania County also happened to be home to James Monroe, with whom Madison maintained a friendship despite their finding themselves on opposite sides of most of the contentious political issues of the day. Monroe had been a fellow delegate to the Richmond convention, where, much to Madison's annoyance, he had joined Patrick Henry in voting against ratification. The inclusion of Spotsylvania in Madison's district was not an accident. The remaining counties in the district were chosen for one very specific reason: five of the seven had sent a slate of delegates to the Virginia Ratifying Convention that voted unanimously against the Constitution. As an analysis by the political scientist Thomas Rogers Hunter points out, "Of the sixteen delegates from what would become the Fifth District, eleven had opposed the new Constitution." That the political leanings of an entire county could be inferred from the identities of the men who represented it seems an almost comically weak basis by today's standards for crafting a gerrymander. But Henry did not enjoy the benefits of big data that allowed the creators of REDMAP to be so successful. Working with the limited tools at their disposal, the Anti-Federalists in the Virginia General Assembly drew Madison's home county into a district that contained as many of the surrounding areas as possible that, based on their best guess, he might find electorally challenging.

Evidence for the intent behind Henry's gerrymander can be found in the correspondence between Madison and his allies at the time. The first word of a possible plot being afoot comes from Edmund Randolph, who wrote to Madison on November 9, "The faction is, I am told, endeavoring to arrange the districts for representatives, so as to place Orange, to be counterpoised." That same day, George Lee Turberville makes mention in his correspondence of an attempt "to obtain by finesse—what they could not accomplish—by fair & argumentative discussion." Three days later, he elaborates further: "The prevalence of local prejudices are not uncommon in our house—but for a majority to bend its utmost efforts against an individual is rather uncommon— The object of the majority of today has been to prevent your Election in the house of Representatives as demonstratively as if they had affirmed it . . . by forming a district (as they supposed) of Counties most tainted with antifederalism in which Orange is included."

On November 23, Edward Pendleton, after discussing Madison's exclusion from the Senate on a party-line vote, goes on to note that the Anti-Federalists "are so modeling the Districts for choice of Representatives to the other House, as to have those Elections turn on the same basis." Madison himself had not been present in Richmond for any of these events. He was now in exile in New York, appointed by the general assembly, at Henry's insistence, to serve in a lame-duck legislature that would cease to exist when the U.S. Congress met for the first time in March 1789. With the elections for the House of Representatives scheduled for February 2, it's hard not to see this move as a calculated attempt to remove Madison from Virginia, not only to prevent him from interfering with Henry's legislative skulduggery, but also to keep him off the campaign trail in the run-up to the vote. Turberville surmised as much, writing to Madison, "I do verily believe that Mr. Henry

Voted for you to [the Confederation] Congress this time with no other view but to keep you from [our] country until some more favored man, some minion of his or his party shall have the opportunity to supplant your Interest."

For Henry's plan to succeed, however, Madison had to seek election to Congress in the Fifth District, rather than somewhere else in the state where he might face an electorate more sympathetic to his Federalist principles. There was certainly no shortage of options. Of the ten districts that were ultimately drawn, six returned Federalist candidates to Congress who ran unopposed in the 1789 election. To prevent this possibility, Henry used his political clout in the general assembly to pass another law, one that required all candidates for federal office to have resided in the district in which they were running for at least twelve months prior to the election. "I am inclined to think that the Antis inserted this with a view to you," reported one Federalist in a letter to Madison shortly after the bill passed, "and that the feds have assented to it from feeling their inferiority."

Those familiar with constitutional law will immediately recognize that this restriction almost certainly violated the Constitution. In a 1995 case called *U.S. Term Limits v. Thornton,* the U.S. Supreme Court ruled that states may not impose any additional qualifications on prospective members of Congress beyond those which are found in the qualifications clause of Article I. To do so, wrote Justice John Paul Stevens for the majority, would "violate a[n] . . . idea central to this basic principle: that the right to choose representatives belongs not to the States, but to the people." While this case, decided some 207 years after the fact, obviously did not bind as precedent the members of the Virginia General Assembly, those present at the time raised similar constitutional objections to the bill.

Edward Carrington, a close friend of George Washington's who had served under the general during the Revolutionary War, was one of those who lobbied Madison to defy Henry's residency restriction and seek office in another district. "This will be against the Act concerning the Elections," he wrote to Madison on December 2, "but these gentlemen and many others are of the opinion that such a restriction was not within the power of the Legislature, and that it will avail nothing in Congress, where the qualifications of Members are to be judged." But Madison would not be cowed. Unsavory as he found the notion of campaigning in his home county, the thought of being painted as a carpetbagger running scared from Henry was even worse. And he was now beginning to face pressure from his Federalist allies to throw himself into the fray.

Madison found himself in no-man's-land, physically as well as mentally. He had left New York during a break in the Confederation Congress, traveling to Philadelphia to mull over the decision. "I came to this City with a view either to return to New York or proceed to Virginia as circumstances might require," he lamented in a December 2 letter to George Washington. "I am pressed much on several quarters to try the effect of presence on the district into which I fall, for electing a Representative," he continued, "and am apprehensive that an omission of that expedient, may eventually expose me to blame. At the same time, I have an extreme distaste to steps having an electioneering appearance, although they should lead to an appointment in which I am disposed to serve the public." Torn between returning to New York to fulfill his duties to the Confederation Congress and the prospect of a potentially humiliating campaign in Virginia that might easily end in his defeat, Madison chose Virginia, lame-duck Congress be damned. Henry, however, had one last surprise waiting for him there.

James Monroe was an obvious choice when evaluating candidates to recruit to run against James Madison in the Fifth District. As a resident of Spotsylvania, adjacent to Madison's home county of Orange, he could be drawn into the district without any great difficulty. His preexisting friendship with Madison also made him immune to accusations of being a Henry crony. Monroe was the son of a modestly successful planter and sometime carpenter, and his family had immigrated to the United States in the mid-seventeenth century from Scotland, where they had been members of the ancient and respected Clan Munro. He grew up with politics in his blood. When his father passed away in 1774, his maternal uncle, a member of the Virginia House of Burgesses and later a fellow delegate of Patrick Henry's at the Fifth Virginia Convention, took him to Williamsburg and enrolled him at the College of William and Mary.

Monroe was also a war hero, having dropped out a year and a half into his studies to enlist in the Third Virginia Regiment of the Conti-

Portrait of James Monroe by James Herring, circa 1834.

nental army. Cited for bravery personally by George Washington, after he suffered a severed artery and almost died during the crossing of the Delaware River, he rose swiftly to the rank of colonel, although financial difficulties would prevent him from being able to raise his own regiment.

Eventually returning to Williamsburg to study law, he became a protégé of the then governor, Thomas Jefferson, served as a member of the Virginia House of Delegates and the Confederation Congress, and, as already mentioned, became one of the seventy-nine delegates to vote against the Constitution at the Virginia Ratifying Convention. Even before Monroe had been drafted into his scheme, Henry had already been laying the groundwork for the campaign against Madison. His strategy, which dovetailed neatly with his broader goal of forcing a second constitutional convention to undermine the Union, was to paint Madison as an ideologue, a fanatical supporter of the Constitution as written whose myopia made him oblivious to the many flaws in the document that Henry and the Anti-Federalists believed might be addressed by a second convention. Upon returning to Virginia, Madison was shocked to discover that "it has been very industriously inculcated that I am dogmatically attached to the Constitution in every clause, syllable & letter, and therefore not a single amendment will be promoted by my vote, either from conviction or a spirit of accommodation. This is the report most likely to affect the election, and most difficult to be combated with success, within the limited period."

But combat it he did. While his pride might have made him queasy about the prospect of grubbing for votes on the streets of Orange, Madison proved himself a natural on the campaign trail. There's little doubt that he was aware of Henry's designs on a second constitutional convention, because those arguments had been aired extensively during their 1788 debates in Richmond. He must also have known that if he were able to follow through on the promise he had made privately to Randolph and others to introduce a bill of rights before the First Congress, this would surely take the wind out of Henry's sails once and for all. From this perspective then, Madison's strategy for defeating Monroe was a stroke of genius. Having denied the necessity of a bill of rights during the Philadelphia convention, and only grudgingly promising it to Randolph during their backroom dealings in Richmond, Madison now embraced it publicly. Channeling the spirit of his mentor Jefferson, he embarked on a prolific letter-writing campaign, including several that were published in local newspapers. He weaponized Henry's own arguments against him, making the case for amending the Constitution to protect individual liberties.

"The offer of my services to the district, rests on the following ground," Madison wrote to a resident of Spotsylvania County a week before Election Day. "That although I always conceived the constitution might be improved . . . I held it my duty, whilst the constitution remained unratified, and it was necessary to unite the various opinions, interests and prejudices of the different states, in some one plan, to oppose every previous amendment." So far, this was all in keeping with his prior public statements. "The change of circumstances produced by the secure establishment of the plan proposed," he continued, "leaves me free to espouse such amendments as will, in the most satisfactory manner, guard essential rights, and will render certain vexatious abuses of power impossible." And, in what appeared to be a not-so-subtle dig at Henry himself, he concluded, "With regard to the mode of obtaining amendments, I have not withheld my opinion that they ought to be recommended by the first Congress, rather than be pursued by way of a General Convention."

A more cynical opponent might have used this opportunity to go on the offensive, painting Madison as a disingenuous opportunist who changed his positions whenever it was politically advantageous to do so. After all, how could he be trusted to vote for the Bill of Rights when he had already voted against it? But James Monroe was not such an opponent. Both men ran extremely positive campaigns, often traveling together and making joint appearances around the district. Their friendship and mutual respect would allow them to attack each other's principles and policy positions but never their characters.

The biographer William Cabell Rives describes one particular debate that Madison remembered for the rest of his life. On a frigid January morning in Culpeper County, the two men faced off on the portico of a Lutheran meetinghouse. Keenly aware that his election would depend on the ability to court the votes of religious minorities in the district, which contained not only Lutherans but also a significant Baptist population, Madison took the opportunity to espouse his views on religious freedom. He also made sure to remind his constituents of the church tax Henry had proposed years earlier, and his own role in defeating it in the legislature. "Such was the extremity of the cold," writes Rives, "that Mr. Madison's ear was slightly frost-bitten while speaking. Some traces of the injury always remained; and he would playfully point to them as the honorable scars he had borne from the battle-field."

As Election Day approached, all the momentum seemed to be with Madison. Even the weather would not be able to stand in his way. As temperatures dropped to ten degrees below zero, and almost a foot of snow blanketed the ground, the voters of Virginia's Fifth Congressional District made their way to the polls. When the returns were in, Madison was victorious, and the election was not even a particularly close one. He won 1,308 votes to Monroe's 972, good for a 57–43 percent majority. While the candidates split the eight counties in the district four to four, the key to Madison's victory was to bolster the lopsided margin in his home county of Orange, where he captured 96 percent of the vote, with surprisingly strong performances in the surrounding Anti-Federalist areas. This included 38 percent of the vote in Monroe's home county of Spotsylvania, and losses by a single vote in Goochland and 21 votes in Fluvanna, both considered Anti-Federalist strongholds. Finally, in Culpeper, the county that had been considered pivotal to the outcome and in which the candidates had campaigned extensively,

Madison ran riot, winning 71 percent of the vote. Henry's plan had failed.

There's one small problem with this tale of Patrick Henry's underhanded scheme to thwart his archrival's effort to rally the country in support of the fledgling Constitution that he so despised: it might never have happened. Historians are divided as to whether Henry, though clearly not acting in Madison's best interests, actually intended to manipulate the district boundaries in an effort to keep him out of Congress. And even if the gerrymander was intentional, there is also significant disagreement as to whether it was part of some master plan to undermine the Constitution and precipitate a second convention, or merely the petty settling of a political score.

Skeptics of the gerrymander point out that the only contemporaneous sources for the allegation come in the form of accusations from persons at Mount Vernon, including George Washington, insinuations by Madison himself, a few statements made by Anti-Federalist allies of Henry before the fact, and partisan newspaper coverage afterward. None of Henry's own writings, sparse as they are, make any reference to a plan to use gerrymandering against Madison, nor do the statements of any of the legislators who were directly involved in drawing up the districting plan. Of course, none of this means that it didn't happen, and Madison himself clearly believed that he had been the victim of something untoward.

Critics of the Henrymander narrative also argue that the nature of the districting plan itself cautions against its depiction as an intentional gerrymander. Elmer Griffith, in his famous 1907 dissertation on the history of the gerrymander, maintains that "the charge that the state was gerrymandered is unwarranted, and as concerns Madison's district in shape and population it was normal." And, in the most comprehensive recent analysis of the events, the political scientist Thomas Rogers Hunter reaches a similar conclusion. He contends that "Virginia's entire 1788 districting scheme shows no marks of partisan purpose, for it was both politically fair and one of the most geographically logical plans in all of American history." He credits the origins of the Henrymander narrative to the aforementioned Madison biographer William Cabell

Rives. An associate of both Madison and Jefferson, Rives had written in the 1850s that "in laying off the State into districts for the election of representatives, ingenious and artificial combinations were resorted to for the purpose of insuring [Madison's] defeat."

But as both Griffith and Hunter correctly point out, Henry's plan did nothing of the sort. Madison's district was geographically compact, followed existing geographic and municipal boundaries, and was roughly equal in population to those in other parts of the state. Rives's source appears to be the writings of an anonymous columnist in *The Virginia Independent Chronicle,* who published twenty-three letters between January and July 1789 under the pseudonym Decius. "I call it an attempt to deprive the people of their choice of a Representative," Decius wrote in a February 23 column, "because the very idea of its being necessary to form a district in any particular way, to affect the election of any one, is sufficient evidence that the decision intended is contrary to the inclinations of the natural majority to be affected; and an attempt to form it so, is only in other words, to deny them the right of choosing for themselves." But pushed to defend his accusations by an Anti-Federalist reader, Decius appeared to backtrack on his earlier accusations. He subsequently clarifies that he was merely objecting to the "eccentric angles" of an earlier proposed version of the district that also included parts of Cumberland County, rather than its eventual form.

It's certainly true that Cumberland, which gave 81 percent of its votes to the Anti-Federalist candidate in the 1789 election, could easily have been substituted for Culpeper. This, along with the inclusion of adjacent Buckingham County, would have produced a district much more likely to bring about Madison's defeat. But none of this information was known to Henry and his allies in 1788. The most straightforward explanation of the available evidence is that Henry, constrained by a dearth of data and a desire to avoid losing his eroding majority in the general assembly—which Carrington describes as being "reduced to about ten at the completion of his projects"—cobbled together the best attempt he could muster under the circumstances to make things as difficult as he possibly could for Madison. The fact that the gerrymander was unsuccessful does not, in and of itself, mean that it wasn't a gerrymander. It certainly seems plausible that Henry originally envisioned a district that would have been more hostile to Madison, but was forced to compromise somewhat as the bill was amended before final passage.

Barring the discovery of firsthand accounts of the legislative proceedings, we may ultimately never know for sure.

What cannot be disputed is that the circumstantial evidence does support the notion of a deliberate scheme on Henry's part. Why pass a law requiring candidates to reside in the districts in which they were running if not to force Madison to contest an election on hostile turf? Why draw Madison's and Monroe's home counties into the same district if not to force the two men to compete against each other? Why appoint Madison to the Continental Congress when he clearly had no desire for the job? It's hard to put these pieces of the puzzle together and not, as Henry himself had done only a year earlier, smell a rat in Richmond, tending toward chicanery. The Republicans in Wisconsin would have behooved themselves to take a page from Patrick Henry's book, and not leave such a detailed paper trail laying out the particulars of their conspiracy.

The postscript to this story is, of course, well known. Henry's plan to force a second constitutional convention, part of his broader effort to undermine the newly established American system of government, went down in flames. When the First Congress met at Federal Hall in New York on March 4, 1789, Madison had done his homework. He arrived armed with a slate of proposed amendments that would safeguard individual liberty. These, he hoped, as outlined in a letter to Jefferson, would "give to the Government its due popularity and stability." Faced with the prospect of the undoing of the fragile compromise of 1787, and the possible dissolution of the federal government, the representatives of the First Congress got to work. After many months of debate, revision, and compromise, what emerged were ten proposed constitutional amendments that today form the cornerstone of American liberty: the Bill of Rights. Freedom of speech, freedom of religion, the right to bear arms, the right to assembly, and all the other protections that we take for granted were only made possible because Patrick Henry's plan failed.

In his twilight years, Henry became somewhat more sanguine when reflecting on his earlier jeremiad against the Constitution. Gone were the soaring rhetorical declarations of his rabble-rousing days as a revolutionary, replaced with grudging acceptance of his defeat, if not outright contrition. "Although the form of government into which my countrymen determined to place themselves had my enmity," he wrote to Monroe in 1791, "yet as we are one and all embarked, it is natural to care for the crazy machine, at least so long as we are out of sight of a port to refit." So complete was his about-face that Washington even offered him the position of secretary of state in 1795, but Henry declined, citing failing health and the financial burden of providing for his children, of which he had seventeen by two different wives. Or perhaps it was the prospect of succeeding two of the men who had played a pivotal role in thwarting his life's ambitions, Thomas Jefferson and Edmund Randolph, America's first and second secretaries of state.

Returning to the practice of law, Henry died of stomach cancer in 1799 at his home in Red Hill, Virginia. Even death could not spare him one final parting shot from his old adversary. "A man who, through a long & active life, had been the idol of his country, beyond any one that ever lived," Jefferson wrote in 1812, "descended to the grave with less than its indifference, and verified the saying of the philosopher, that no man must be called happy till he is dead." Madison, by contrast, went on to succeed his mentor as the fourth president of the United States and to become one of its most famous and lauded citizens. So go the breaks.

One thing that stands out about these early forerunners of the modern gerrymander is that they appear somewhat underwhelming when placed under the microscope of hindsight.

George Burrington marshaled every ounce of authority he possessed as the king's representative in North Carolina to lash out against his detractors in the legislature, but the districts he created to secure a majority of his creatures in the lower house were more akin to the rotten boroughs of yore than anything that might be found in a modern legislature.

Henry certainly appears, based on the preponderance of historical evidence, to have at least attempted to use the redistricting process to settle a political score with his old foe James Madison, but he lacked the tools, and the political capital, to follow through with it effectively.

And poor Elbridge Gerry, who neither authored nor particularly supported the redistricting plan that created his infamy, suffered the ignominy of having his own name repeatedly mispronounced in the portmanteau that was his most lasting contribution to the world. If there's one lesson to be drawn from this whistle-stop tour of colonial- and founding-era redistricting, it's that the milquetoast gerrymanders of yesteryear, while certainly not lacking for intent, bear little or no resemblance in terms of their effects to the REDMAP-inspired atrocities that blight the landscape of contemporary America. Moving into the mid- to late nineteenth century, however, the gerrymander would become more sophisticated, efficient, and in some cases devastatingly effective.

3

Revenge of the Whigs

The 150 years between Elbridge Gerry's famous salamander district in early nineteenth-century Massachusetts and the Warren Court's reapportionment revolution of the 1960s, which swiftly ushered in the era of the modern gerrymander, were marked with isolated instances of the practice. In 1816, for example, Maryland's Electoral College districts were successfully gerrymandered by the Democratic-Republican Party. Their efforts were sufficient to turn a 6–5 Federalist majority from the previous presidential election into an 8–0 romp in favor of their candidate, who happened to be none other than James Monroe. Why only eight electoral votes when in 1812 the state had returned eleven? The three Federalist electors, no doubt disheartened by the gerrymander, not to mention the landslide defeat of their candidate, Rufus King, failed to show up in Annapolis for the vote. The Federalist Party itself would cease to exist soon thereafter, and the void left in its place ushered in a period of relative calm known as the Era of Good Feelings. In the absence of partisan rivalries, gerrymandering too entered into a decade-long slumber, broken only when the presidency of Andrew Jackson brought about a split in the Democratic-Republican hegemony, and the Second Party System began.

Many of these early elections had made use of a twin set of practices known as at-large or multimember districting, particularly for the U.S. House of Representatives. In contrast to single-member districts, where, as the name suggests, each individual district elects only one member of the legislature, multimember systems involve districts that elect two or more representatives. At-large systems abolish the use of districts entirely, allowing the majority party in the state to control the entire congressional delegation. This itself was a form of gerrymandering, albeit a variation stemming from the complete or partial absence of district lines, rather than political shenanigans in their drawing.

The elections clause of the Constitution gives the states control over "the Times, Places and Manner of holding Elections for Senators and Representatives" while allowing Congress to "at any time by Law make or alter such Regulations." This permitted the states to take the lead in administering federal elections while also providing a congressional backstop if they were perceived to be abusing or mismanaging their power. Congress had been hesitant to avail itself of these checks in the Republic's early years, leaving state governments free to rig the results of their congressional elections in favor of their preferred party. According to a study by the University of Florida political economist Stephen Calabrese, more than half of the individual congressional elections administered by the states between 1788 and 1831 made use of some combination of at-large or multimember districting. In those elections, the majority party in the state won every single seat on offer more than 84 percent of the time. In the states that used single-member districts to choose their members of Congress, the number was only 27 percent. All of this, however, was about to change.

In response to the practice of at-large and multimember district gerrymandering, Congress passed the 1842 Apportionment Act, which attempted to impose a mandate on the states that their representatives be chosen from single-member districts. But the move was met with immediate resistance from advocates of states' rights. When President John Tyler signed the law, he attached a memorandum in which he openly expressed doubts about whether the legislation was constitutional. Many historians believe this to be the very first example of the use of presidential signing statements that have become so popular with recent chief executives. "That Congress itself has power by law to alter State regulations respecting the manner of holding elections for Representatives is clear," Tyler wrote in his memo to the House of Representatives, "but its power to command the States to make new regulations or alter their existing regulations is the question upon which I have felt deep and strong doubts."

In the debates over the proposed bill, Representative William Payne of Alabama summed up the sentiments of many of his colleagues. "Can it be reasonably expected that Georgia, under such circumstances, will quietly submit to your assumption of power, and obey your mandamus?" he asked the assembled congressmen. "No, sir, never; nor will New Hampshire, Mississippi, or any other State which has heretofore elected her Representatives under the general ticket system. They will rebuke your assumption of power, by treating your mandamus with contempt; and, as heretofore, will elect and send Representatives to Congress. Well, sir, what will you do next?" The former president John Quincy Adams, now also serving in the House of Representatives, denounced the bill too, declaring it "pernicious in its immediate operations, and imminently dangerous in its tendencies."

Payne's warning turned out to be a prescient one. In the 1842 election, New Hampshire, Georgia, Mississippi, and Missouri all chose to defy the law without consequence, and this early gerrymandering mechanism would be allowed to endure for another 125 years. While subsequent reapportionment acts did make mention of members of Congress being elected from "districts composed of contiguous territory, and containing as nearly as practicable an equal number of inhabitants," the single-member district mandate was not explicitly, or permanently, reinstated until Congress passed the Uniform Congressional District Act of 1967. At that time, only Hawaii and New Mexico still elected their representatives at large. One of the states that decided not to defy the 1842 Apportionment Act was Ohio, and later that same year it became the site of one of the most obscure yet fascinating gerrymandering attempts of the nineteenth century.

The panic of 1837 began in London. In fact, to be even more precise, it began with the 1835 eruption of the Cosigüina volcano in western Nicaragua, which spewed a massive cloud of volcanic ash into the Central American skies. Traces of the blast have since been discovered in samples taken halfway around the globe. According to an analysis by the Berkeley Earth Surface Temperature project, the ash cloud that blanketed the earth in the wake of the Cosigüina eruption was responsible for a 0.75 degree Celsius decrease in average surface temperatures over the subsequent year.

While this global cooling event was no more than a temporary blip in the long-term average, it was sufficient to cause a devastating failure of the 1836 European wheat crop. With the British forced to borrow significant amounts of money to fund the import of a large percentage of their food that year, the Bank of England suddenly noticed that its monetary reserves were running low. Following the conventional economic wisdom of the time—which held that declining reserves should be met with increased interest rates, to disincentivize borrowing and allow the replenishment of the money supply—the bank announced a gradual rate increase from 3 to 5 percent. Across the pond, the U.S. banking system happened to be uniquely vulnerable to a sudden hike in interest rates.

Five years earlier, President Andrew Jackson had vetoed a bill to recharter the Second Bank of the United States. The bank had been created in the aftermath of the War of 1812 to regulate the printing of currency and the issuing of government bonds. This meant that the central bank, whose twenty-year charter had originally been issued in 1816, would cease to exist when it expired in 1836, and so began to wind down its activities. But Jackson, ever the firebrand, was not content merely to sit on his hands and wait for the bank to destroy itself. He announced that the federal government would be withdrawing every penny of its $10 million in deposits, distributing them instead across numerous smaller institutions, known as pet banks. Many of these were located in the western regions of the country, including nine in Ohio.

Then several events occurred in short order that precipitated a full-blown panic. Real estate and commodity prices collapsed, caused in part by Jackson's "Specie Circular" executive order mandating that western lands be purchased only with gold and silver coin, which most could not afford. The price of cotton, the mainstay of the southern economy, fell by 25 percent. Rampant inflation led to currency devaluation as banks lent out more and more money to satisfy the demand, stretching reserves in the major financial centers of the East Coast to their limits.

Just when foreign investors began calling in their loans before the value of the dollar plummeted further, and Americans themselves flocked to the banks to withdraw the necessary funds to pay off their own obligations, the Bank of England decided to raise interest rates, and major New York financial institutions quickly followed suit. Suddenly unable to fulfill demand, more than eight hundred banks were forced to close their doors. Economic growth was stifled, businesses failed, unemployment soared to as much as 25 percent in some localities, and the nation entered a deep recession from which it would not emerge for another seven years.

Nowhere were the effects of the crisis felt more acutely than in Ohio. Thousands of people lost their life savings as the pet banks collapsed. Stores stopped accepting currency that wasn't backed by silver or gold, and with unsecured notes representing a large percentage of those printed by the smaller Ohio banks before the panic, thousands of people discovered that the cash they carried in their pockets was suddenly worthless. Some Ohioans resorted to printing their own money, hoping against hope that they could find a business somewhere that would accept it, so that they could buy food. The crisis also divided the major political parties in the state, the Whigs and the Democrats, and one of the key issues in the lead-up to the 1842 election was the question of banking reform.

The Whigs were still railing against Andrew Jackson, blaming his shortsightedness for the numerous bank failures that had occurred in Ohio during the panic. They favored establishing a central bank in the state, one that had enough power to be able to weather subsequent economic downturns. The Democrats, eager to shift the blame away from Jackson and his Democratic successor, Martin Van Buren, instead argued that elitist bankers in New York and other big cities had been responsible for the crisis. They pushed a populist agenda that called for Ohio to instead establish smaller local banks, but to limit their authority, keeping them on a short leash so that they could not again overextend themselves. As summer approached, political tensions threatened to reach a boiling point. Then Congress passed the Reapportionment Act on June 25, forcing the state legislature to convene a special session to come up with a new district map that could be used for the November elections.

Eighteen forty had been a very good year for the Whigs. Fueled by voter backlash against the Van Buren administration for its mishandling of the economy, the Whig challenger, William Henry Harrison, had upset the incumbent president in his bid for reelection, earning the party what would be their first of only two terms in the White House. Harrison's victory was extremely hard earned. His Democratic opponents immediately went on the attack, portraying him as elderly (he was sixty-seven), infirm, provincial, out of touch, and more at home sipping cider in his log cabin than attending to matters of state. Harrison and his running mate, fellow Virginian John Tyler, flipped the script and turned the Democratic attacks into a badge of honor. They adopted the log cabin and hard cider as their campaign symbols, even going so far as to produce banners and posters depicting log-cabin-shaped bottles of cider that they distributed to supporters. After an Ohio jeweler named Alexander Coffman Ross performed a song he had written, "Tippecanoe and Tyler Too," at a Whig rally in New York, it would go on to become the slogan of the entire campaign, effectively reminding voters of Harrison's role as the hero of the Battle of Tippecanoe in 1811.

Though the Harrison-Tyler ticket earned a narrow victory in the popular vote, they dominated the Electoral College 234–60, winning a large number of states, including Ohio, by relatively small margins. The Whig Party also swept into power in Congress, picking up thirty-three seats in the House, four of which came from Ohio, good for a twelve-to-seven majority in the state's delegation, and also taking control of the Senate. So it was that, as the summer of 1842 rolled around in Columbus, significantly more than just Ohio's banking system was on the minds of the Whig delegation in the state capital. With the Democrats in control of the state legislature and the November 1842 midterms rapidly approaching, the future control of Ohio's twenty-one congressional seats, and the jobs of the Whig representatives who currently held them, not to mention the continuing viability of the overall Whig majority in the House, were all at stake.

Things did not get off to a good start. It became immediately clear that the Democratic leadership, whom the Whigs derisively referred to as the Locofocos, were hell-bent on gerrymandering the state to within an inch of its life. Armed with far better-quality election data than had been available to Patrick Henry in 1788, namely the county-level returns from the 1840 election for governor, they set about crafting a gerrymander that enraged even many of their own backbenchers. This heavy-handedness can be seen most clearly in their attempts to browbeat their own members into submission. Unable to secure a broad consensus on redistricting within their own caucus, the leadership convened a select committee to take on the task of crafting the gerrymander. They also pressured their members into pledging to vote for the plan before any of them were even allowed to see it. Many Democrats were left feeling that their previously safe districts were being sacrificed to promote the interests of the national party, rather than what was best for Ohio.

The specifics of the legislation were laid out in some detail in contemporaneous news accounts appearing in the *Ohio State Journal*, a Whig-affiliated publication. One Democratic representative is quoted as describing the proposed plan as "perfectly ridiculous, indefensible and atrocious," but concedes that he was nevertheless forced to vote for it "under instructions." "Members were dragooned," wrote the paper on August 12, "a gross disrespect to a co-ordinate House, the like of which cannot be found in the history of legislation." And while the surrounding commentary is certainly partisan, bordering on hyperbolic, as the above quotation aptly illustrates, their coverage also included meticulous data on the political makeup of the proposed districts.

Under the Democratic plan, which underwent several revisions as it moved through committee, the state's twenty-one congressional districts were so arranged that twelve contained comfortable Democratic majorities. Whig voters were packed into seven gerrymandered supermajority districts, where their candidates were expected to triumph by large margins, while the remaining two were sufficiently balanced so as to leave the result at least somewhat in doubt. "Were the Whigs to carry the State by ten thousand," wrote the *Journal*, "they could elect only seven members of Congress, while the minority would elect fourteen. This at first-blush demonstrates that the bill proposes to disenfranchise one-half of the Whigs in the State." One Whig house member minced even fewer words when expressing his sentiments regarding the Democratic leadership: "Mr. Taylor denounced the venerable Senator from Fairfield as an old bald-headed traitor to the democracy."

The newspaper also published a series of cartoons designed to illustrate the "monstrous character" of the proposed scheme. In an homage to *The Boston Gazette*'s famous salamander drawing, various beasts, from the mundane to the grotesquely imaginary, are depicted as stand-ins for the most contorted districts.

Perhaps the least inspiring of these is District 17, whose appending of Summit County onto the shoulders of Wayne and Holmes is animalized as the "Quail," although a fairly substantial leap of imagination is required in order to see the resemblance. The adjacent caption goes to the trouble of explaining that "the above is a representation of a 'BIRD,'

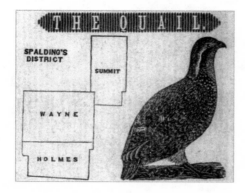

which a man named Spalding accidentally got 'in his hand' a short time ago." I'm glad we cleared that one up. But despite enduring the "pressure of Mr. Spalding's fingers upon its throat," the wily bird "darted out of his hand and flew away."

The cartoon for District 7 depicts the "Richland Roarer," an abomination of "Half Hoss, half Alligator" that would make Dr. Moreau take a step back and wonder if perhaps this time he'd gone too far. "The Roarer is an animal, which was formerly well known in the Western country," elaborates the caption, "but which has been growing more and more scarce, until it is doubtful whether it will not become entirely extinct."

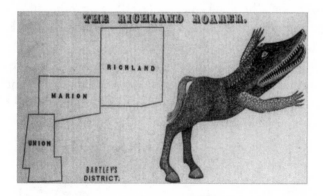

Bad news on that particular front: "The specimen figured above was caught by the Ohio Menagerie Association, . . . but with their usual ill fortune, they were not able to keep it alive a whole day." And with that, the Nobel Prize in cryptozoology remained agonizingly out of reach.

District 11 also puts in an appearance as the "Scioto Sea-Horse,"

which, somewhat confusingly, appears to be a walrus. Conveniently arranged to isolate several Whig-majority counties from the neighboring district of Mr. Latham and Mr. Byington, this particular specimen of the species *Megalatham byingtonius* is native to the frozen Northern Ocean, but made its way inexplicably to the valleys of south-central Ohio "by some subterraneous salt-water channel." "How the creature should be found on dry land," the caption muses, "at a great distance from any ocean, and in a comparatively southern clime, and that too at the hottest season of the year, is nobody's business." The Scioto Sea-Horse regrettably met the same fate as the hapless Richland Roarer: "Some bystanders . . . on looking at the animal, perceived that the hot weather was too much for him, and declared that he was 'a gone hoss; his eyes were sot.' Their judgement was verified by the event. The unfortunate creature stretched out its hind flipper and breathed its last in the early part of the next day." Tough stuff.

The body count rises still further in the form of the most mystifying of all the beasts in the Midwest Menagerie: the Gerrymander of District 16. In a somewhat baffling departure from the established theme, it bears by far the closest resemblance to the district it purports to rep-

resent. Snaking along the Ohio River and hugging the West Virginia border in a manner eerily reminiscent of Governor Gerry's salamander, the Gerrymander, "an uncommon animal, . . . was discovered in that part of the state . . . commonly called the Coal Region." Expecting "to make very large profits" by capturing the brute alive, Mr. Byington and his friends give chase but are thwarted by Mr. Schenck, who, the caption takes pains to point out, "did not belong to the menagerie association." Wounded by Mr. Schenck, who apparently "dislik[ed] the savage look and dangerous character of the varmint," and clearly also hindered by the evolutionary train wreck of its ridiculous wing appendages, the Gerrymander falls victim to a shocking display of unlicensed poaching. "As soon as they got sight of it," Mr. Schenck and his "select committee of bold sportsmen" brutally slaughter the now possibly extinct wild Gerrymander: "They fired a general volley and the ugly varmint dropped dead in its tracks." Even death would not spare the poor beast from further indignity; "its skin was immediately taken off and stuffed, and it will be exhibited through the state for the gratification of the curious."

Finally, there's the "Licking Water-whelp," which sees the head of District 9's Licking County precariously attached to the body of

Perry and Morgan. A fish or not a fish? Zero clarity may be derived from the cartoon depiction, whose half-leg half-flipper protuberances appear uniquely unsuited to both walking and swimming. Mr. Taylor, whose district the whelp steadfastly protects from its neighboring Whig strongholds, only adds to the confusion. "You call that a fish do you?" he exclaims upon first sighting the creature. "Why, it is an infernal WATER-WHELP!" "It resembles you around the head," Mr. Byington helpfully informs Mr. Taylor, "and has a most awful red mouth." Readers seeking closure regarding the whelp's fate are left on a nail-biting cliff-hanger. "Next morning the Tin Pan was seen knocked into a cocked hat," the tale cryptically concludes, "and the Water-whelp was gone."

The Whigs, despite lacking the votes to obstruct the Democrats' designs, were nevertheless determined to not go gentle into that good night of electoral oblivion. And in a move reminiscent of the futile attempts of the Democratic members of the Wisconsin state senate to obstruct Scott Walker's union busting, albeit a considerably more successful one, the Whig representatives in the Ohio legislature resigned en masse in order to deprive the majority of a quorum to pass the gerrymander. "It was designed to remain in force for ten years, and for that length of time to perpetuate the political power of this reckless faction," wrote the Whigs, in a lengthy letter explaining their actions that was published in the *Journal.* "Under these circumstances, we thought that our duty as representatives required of us to return to the people again that power, which we could no longer exercise for their benefit, but which was used by others to their lasting injury."

Lamenting that the "iron despotism" of the leadership had prevented the special session from even considering the pressing issue of banking reform, the Whigs drew a line in the sand. "Their business is destruction," bemoans the letter, "other men must re-build the ruins of their legislation." Fuming at what they saw as the Whigs' dereliction of duty, the Democrats took to the press and accused their opponents of "absquatulation," an absurd made-up pseudo-Latin term popular in the 1830s meaning to abscond, decamp, or swiftly get the hell out of Dodge. And so it was that the Licking Water-whelp, the Richland Roarer, the Scioto Sea-Horse, the Gerrymander, and even the elusive Quail never saw the light of day. The special session came to an end without a redistricting plan being passed, and the congressional elections would be delayed until 1843 to allow a new legislature to take up the mantle.

There was still time for one last parting shot in the great Ohio almost gerrymander of 1842, with both sides attempting to use the dispute to their advantage in the campaign for the November state elections. "They [the voters] will place their iron heel upon the men who resort to such partisan machinery," warned the Whigs in the conclusion to their resignation letter, "and once more fill the halls of legislation with those who will alone regard the highest interests of the state, the prosperity of the people, instead of offering up both at the altar of this Moloch of a party." But their appeal fell on deaf ears. The voters returned another Democratic majority to Columbus, the Whig governor Thomas Corwin lost his reelection bid by the narrow margin of eighteen hundred votes, and a new congressional district map was subsequently passed without incident. In the elections the next fall, the Democrats won twelve of the state's twenty-one U.S. House seats, enough to win back their overall control of the chamber, in a landslide rebuke of the unpopular Tyler administration.

The Ohio near gerrymander of 1842 stands out not because it failed but because of the unusually sophisticated nature of the attempt. Gone were Patrick Henry's ham-fisted efforts to graft the partisanship of the state's ratification delegates onto the counties they represented, a key reason why his bid to gerrymander Madison out of the First Congress was doomed to failure. Had the proposed redistricting plan been allowed to go into effect, and it was only the mass exodus of the Whigs from Columbus that prevented this from happening, they surely would have been consigned to minority status for the remainder of the decade. The Ohio plan bears by far the closest resemblance of all the gerrymanders so far considered to the REDMAP plans of the twenty-first century, making use as it did of the now ubiquitous twin gerrymandering strategies of "cracking" and "packing."

The logic proceeds thus: a gerrymander is most successful at disadvantaging the minority party when it distributes their support in the least efficient way possible across geographic space. On the flip side, the majority party's support must be arranged in an optimally efficient configuration for them to maximally benefit. The best way to achieve this is to "pack" some of the supporters of the minority party into as few supermajority districts as possible, where they run up huge majorities with large numbers of wasted votes. Then those crafting the gerrymander must also "crack" their adversary's remaining supporters into districts where they will lose by smaller margins, allowing the gerrymandering party to capture the bulk of the contested seats. At its core, gerrymandering is an exercise in maximizing the wasted votes of your opponents, while minimizing the wasted votes of your own supporters. Any votes cast in a losing effort are considered wasted, as are any surplus votes that are unnecessary for securing victory.

The Democrats created seven packed Whig districts, alongside twelve cracked districts that they would be able to secure by smaller margins.

Even if the Whigs were to win the popular vote comfortably, they would be able to pick up only the two swing districts, and still find themselves on the end of a twelve-to-nine seat deficit. While not yet anywhere close to the level of sophistication exhibited by REDMAP, the 1842 Ohio plan at least contains the seed of what would eventually germinate into the modern gerrymander. And a decade later, the Whigs, this time in the state of Tennessee, exacted their revenge. As was the case with James Madison's Henrymander, the intended victim would go on to be president of the United States.

Nobody liked Andrew Johnson. Branded by the National Constitution Center as "the most-maligned president in U.S. history," and jointly considered in a 2019 Siena College poll of presidential experts the worst man ever to occupy the Oval Office, he remains one of only three chief executives to be impeached by the House of Representatives. In his home state of Tennessee, he displayed a remarkable aptitude throughout his political career for alienating his supporters almost as effectively as he did his opponents. If Johnson, an unapologetic racist, white supremacist, and slave owner who was allegedly drunk at his own inauguration, had one redeeming feature, it might have been that he was the only Democratic senator from the South to remain loyal to the Union during the Civil War. This was almost certainly the reason why Abraham Lincoln, a Republican, selected Johnson, a Democrat, to be his running mate in the 1864 presidential election: a bipartisan gesture and call for unity amid the bloodiest conflict in the nation's history.

What began as the first, and to date only, cross-party presidential ticket would less than a year later famously become something much more, when Johnson ascended to the presidency not on his own merit but by virtue of an assassin's bullet at Ford's Theatre. "*Sic semper tyrannus!*" exclaimed John Wilkes Booth as he entered the presidential box that April evening brandishing a .44-caliber derringer pistol, "thus always unto tyrants." But what he could not have known is that the man he was elevating to the Oval Office would himself soon be branded a tyrant by the Radical Republicans in Congress during his impeachment hearings. The story of how Andrew Johnson became president of the United States began with a gerrymander.

Johnson was born in Raleigh, North Carolina, in 1808. His father a town constable and his mother a laundress, the family struggled to make ends meet, and neither Johnson nor his two siblings were able to attend school during their childhoods. When Andrew was three, his father died suddenly, the victim of an apparent heart attack shortly after rescuing three other men from drowning. His death only worsened the family's financial travails. At age ten, Johnson began serving as an apprentice to a local tailor, eventually learning to read and devouring the books that customers would bring to the shop. A lifelong love of reading would go on to serve as a substitute for his lack of formal education. He eventually settled in Tennessee after running away from his apprenticeship, establishing his own successful tailoring business in Greeneville before he had turned eighteen. After dabbling in local politics for several years, he sold his tailoring business upon winning election to the Tennessee state senate in 1841, with the financial windfall allowing him to focus on his political career full time. It also facilitated the purchase of several slaves, who worked his 350-acre farm outside Greeneville.

In an early preview of the later bipartisan presidential ticket, Johnson did not consistently vote with either the Democratic Party, of which he was a member, although not always in good standing, or the newly formed Whigs. He clashed frequently with other Democrats, including James K. Polk, whose 1844 presidential campaign he nominally supported but who later shunned his requests for patronage. By this time Johnson had been elected to the U.S. House of Representatives, defeating his Whig opponent, John A. Aiken, by fewer than five hundred votes in their 1842 contest. The political maneuvers he engaged in during that campaign to consolidate Democratic support in his district, including the displacement of a Whig postmaster, drew particular ire from the Whig establishment in Nashville.

In a manner reminiscent of George Burrington more than a century before, Johnson built his political career as a populist advocate for the poor and downtrodden. This notably did not extend to his positions on slavery, where he remained an ardent anti-abolitionist. He won three more congressional elections between 1845 and 1849 and campaigned tirelessly, albeit unsuccessfully, for the passage of his pet project, the Homestead Bill, which would have opened up the government lands on the western frontier to new settlers. His fifth campaign for Congress in 1851 had also further divided him from his fellow Democrats, who rallied around an alternative candidate, Landon Carter Haynes, in a bid to unseat him. Though he won that election by sixteen hundred votes, with the Whigs, delighting at the interparty squabbling, not even putting up a candidate, Johnson could now no longer rely on the support of his own party.

Sensing an opportunity to capitalize on the Democrats' internal divisions, the somewhat grandiosely named Gustavus Adolphus Henry, newly elected as the Whig leader of the Tennessee House of Representatives, sought to capitalize on the upcoming redistricting of the state's congressional seats. On the chopping block were the last remaining vestiges of the Democratic political establishment, which had been largely swept out of office in the 1850–51 Whig landslide. Those elections had also seen the party take control of both houses of the state legislature and the governorship.

Henry first sought to gerrymander the boundaries of the state legislature, in a bid to cement Whig control for the remainder of the decade. He then set his sights on Johnson's congressional district, bringing in numerous Whig enclaves that made his reelection close to impossible. The Henrymander, dormant for more than half a century since Patrick Henry's machinations of 1788, had risen again. "The members of the legislature have, by virtue of the authority in them vested, amended the ancient word 'Gerry-mander,' so as to make the name harmonize with modern facts," wrote the *Nashville Union* on February 28, 1852. "Henceforth it is to be set down in the political vocabulary as 'Henry-mander.' Whig papers will please note this alteration."

Johnson was stunned and disheartened by the development. "I have no political future," he lamented, "my political garments have been divided and upon my vesture do they intend to cast lots." Facing, as the *Union* somewhat hyperbolically described it, "a majority fraudulently obtained, by an act of dishonest, unjust, unconstitutional, and tyrannical legislation," Johnson opted not to run for reelection. He was not the only one. His fellow Democratic congressman Isham G. Harris, whose district had also been carved up by Henry, also declined to seek another term, and those two seats were enough to flip the six-to-four Democratic majority in the state delegation. The Whigs also captured sixteen of the twenty-three state senate seats, and scraped their way to a narrow thirty-nine-to-thirty-six edge in the state house. But Johnson's political future, not to mention his garments, were about to become a whole

Photograph of Andrew Johnson by Mathew Brady, circa 1875.

lot brighter. Having been denied his House seat, he decided instead to run for governor. And in a plot twist that a Hollywood screenwriter might reject as too implausible to be believed, he found himself facing off against none other than his old nemesis: Gustavus Adolphus Henry.

But first, he still needed to win the Democratic nomination. Even that small triumph, given the bridges he had burned within his own party, was an uphill battle. When the Democratic State Convention convened in Nashville in April 1853, the attorney Andrew Ewing was the preferred candidate of the majority of delegates. But believing that Johnson's record made him better equipped to appeal to the Whig voters whose support would be necessary to win the general election, Ewing withdrew, and Johnson found himself unopposed for the nomination. He was also perfectly positioned to turn the Henrymander narrative against his opponent in the debates and the pages of the popular press. And, in a move to further bolster his bipartisan credentials, Johnson even endorsed a Whig, Nathaniel Taylor, for his former House seat. "After an exciting canvass," writes the biographer Frank Moore, "Mr. Johnson was chosen Governor," defeating his opponent in a close race, which saw him win 51 percent of the vote. Henry, stinging from his defeat at the hands of the man whose political career he thought he had just ended, retired from politics entirely.

Despite the apparent success of the Whig gerrymander, it was John-son who would have the last laugh. In the wake of the landslide defeat of their candidate Winfield Scott in the 1852 presidential election, the Whig Party itself swiftly dissolved, and the Democrats once again returned to power in Nashville. Johnson, still harboring designs on a return to Congress, then seized the opportunity created by an 1857 vacancy in one of Tennessee's two U.S. Senate seats. At the time, sena-tors were chosen not by a popular vote of the people but by the state legislature, a practice that Johnson had ironically attempted to end. Now, in the wake of the Whigs' collapse, he was well poised to take advantage of the sizable Democratic majority in that body. And while the dwindling Whig minority denounced him as "the vilest radical and most unscrupulous demagogue in the Union," his stature as the most prominent Democratic politician in the state made his election a near inevitability.

Less than four years into his Senate term, the Confederacy secession crisis kicked off. For Johnson, there was never any question of where he stood. "I will not give up this government. . . . No; I intend to stand by it," he proclaimed in a passionate 1861 speech on the Senate floor, "and I invite every man who is a patriot to . . . swear by our God, and all that is sacred and holy, that the Constitution shall be saved, and the Union preserved."

Returning to Tennessee, which was to hold a popular referendum on the question of secession that June, Johnson risked life and limb to campaign in favor of remaining in the Union. He endured numerous threats on his life, sometimes even positioning a gun on the lectern before him during speeches, but his efforts were in vain. After the peo-ple of Tennessee voted overwhelmingly in favor of secession, Johnson fled the state through the Cumberland Gap into Kentucky, coming under fire from secessionists along the way and leaving his wife and children behind in Greeneville. But his very public displays of loyalty to the Union had earned him a new admirer in the form of Abraham Lin-coln, who appointed him the military governor of Tennessee in 1862. The man who had long harbored dreams of the presidency, while never really holding out much hope that they would ever be realized, had now positioned himself at the top of the list to be Lincoln's running mate in 1864. The unlikely chain of events that would lead to his ascension to the Oval Office had been set in motion, much to the chagrin of the enemies who had sought to destroy him, by a gerrymander.

It is evident that prior to the 1970s, gerrymandering was very much the exception rather than the norm. The few isolated examples that stand out in the historical record are in stark contrast to the ubiquity of the practice in twenty-first-century America. Lacking the constitutional mandate to redistrict every ten years, politicians did so only when it was necessary or expedient. They lacked the incentives to fully embrace the gerrymander as an everyday, or at least every-decade, component of the political battleground. And, as was emphasized at the conclusion of the previous chapter, historical gerrymandering in the United States was not particularly effective. Not only was the political will often lacking within the gerrymandering party itself, as Patrick Henry and the Locofocos discovered to their detriment, but political norms cautioned against everything but the relatively mild forms of electoral distortion that have been highlighted so far.

Line drawers expressed far less willingness to depart from county, municipal, or community boundaries when crafting districts, and even the salamanders and water-whelps that were pilloried in the pages of the popular press were far more compact and regularly shaped than most of the districts in use today. But perhaps more significantly, the tools to implement an effective gerrymander were simply not available to the politicians of the nineteenth century. Effective gerrymandering requires not only detailed and granular data on prior electoral behavior to manipulate the district populations but also the ability to forecast how those districts will behave under a variety of hypothetical future electoral conditions. Otherwise, a gerrymander that works effectively for one or two elections might collapse under the weight of even relatively minor popular vote swings or turnout variations in subsequent contests. This was what occurred with the Whig gerrymander in Tennessee.

Gerrymandering originated as a macro rather than micro phenomenon, one that placed a thumb on the large-scale levers of democracy, rather than tinkering with its individual cogs and gears. It would not be until the middle of the twentieth century that the availability of detailed election data down to the individual city-block level allowed us to remove the cover from our democratic machine and expose its inner workings. And it was not until the twenty-first that computer technology became sufficiently advanced to permit us to hack into the system itself and alter the individual lines of code. All of these developments will be addressed in good time. But before leaving history in our wake and setting sail once and for all upon the seas of modernity, there's one final example of nineteenth-century gerrymandering that demands attention. It stands out mostly because it concerns a type of gerrymandering that has not so far been considered, and will not be returned to again in this book: the gerrymandering of state boundaries themselves. It also stands out because of its devastating effectiveness.

4

Honest Abe Stacks the States

For twenty-eight years there was only one Dakota. When the territory was formed in 1861—the final vestige of the land obtained under Thomas Jefferson's Louisiana Purchase to be formally organized—no one could have foreseen its eventual admission into the Union as two separate and distinct states. Named for the Dakota branch of the Native American Sioux tribe, and including much of the modern-day states of Montana and Wyoming, Dakota was the most remote and sparsely populated of the U.S. territories of the mid-nineteenth century. Indeed, at the time of the 1860 census, only 1 percent of the American population lived in the territories in their entirety, including a mere 2,405 in Dakota. But all of that was about to change.

Within a year of the Dakota Territory's formation, Congress finally passed Andrew Johnson's Homestead Act to promote territorial resettlement. This was no doubt to his great satisfaction, although having been tapped as military governor of Tennessee earlier that year, he was by this time no longer in the Senate to see his longtime dream realized. Now, in return for a small filing fee, any free American could lay claim to a 160-acre plot of public lands on the western frontier. Signed into law by Abraham Lincoln as the Civil War raged, the legislation sought "to elevate the condition of men, to lift artificial burdens from all shoulders and to give everyone an unfettered start and a fair chance in the race of life."

Westward expansion, Lincoln argued, was essential to the nation's health and vitality. "The wild lands of the country should be distributed," he proclaimed in an 1861 speech in Ohio, "so that every man should have the means and opportunity of benefiting his condition." What followed was a massive population exodus from east to west. More than 4 million homestead claims were filed, and the deeds to 1.6 million lots were eventually distributed under the program.

Most of those who flocked to Dakota over the subsequent two decades would settle in the south, particularly in the areas around Sioux City. Southern Dakota, connected by the railroads to the major urban centers of the Midwest—particularly Chicago, which boasted a population of more than 112,000 at the time—proved more popular with homesteaders and farmers. The north, whose transit links from Fargo and Bismarck intersected with the much smaller and more isolated city of Minneapolis, grew more slowly and relied heavily on cattle ranching and fur trading, leading to frequent clashes with the indigenous Sioux population. Even with the lucrative incentives of the Homestead Act, population growth in the Dakota Territory was slow.

At the time of the 1870 census, South Dakota had reached 11,800 inhabitants, while North Dakota still lagged behind at 2,400. This left the territory far short of the numbers that would be necessary to even entertain the possibility of statehood. Resentment between the regions also began to fester. As the University of North Dakota history professor Kimberly Porter puts it, "The south half did not like the north half." By the 1880 census, however, population growth had begun to take off. Close to 100,000 people now lived in the south, a more than 700 percent increase in only a decade, compared with 37,000 in the north, representing a staggering 1,400 percent growth.

With these increased numbers, the demand for statehood also began to grow. At stake in Washington were the seats in the U.S. Senate that would follow Dakota's admission to the Union, with powerful incentives thereby existing for the Republican Party, which dominated the territory's politics. As it happened, the party already had a road map for how to gerrymander the boundaries of newly admitted states to artificially increase their Senate representation. It came from one of the unlikeliest of sources: Honest Abe himself.

America's greatest president was certainly not unfamiliar with or naive about the use of creative line drawing as a tool of political manipulation.

In fact, he himself had been a victim of gerrymandering earlier in his political career. In 1850, the Democrats in the Illinois state legislature, facing an electoral climate that was rapidly becoming inhospitable to their cause, had redrawn their districts in a desperate effort to preserve their dwindling majority. Lincoln, having served in the state legislature himself from 1834 to 1842, and then in the U.S. House of Representatives from 1847 to 1849, was an ambitious and upwardly mobile politician. He had by now set his sights on a higher office: the U.S. Senate. But the Democratic majority in the state legislature, which at the time was responsible for choosing senators, proved to be a thorn in his side. After an unsuccessful Senate bid in 1854, in which Lincoln had thrown his support behind the antislavery Democrat, Lyman Trumbull, to prevent a pro-slavery candidate from winning election, he ran again in 1858.

"A house divided against itself cannot stand," Lincoln declared in his speech accepting the Republican nomination, and it was clear that the issue of slavery would dominate the campaign. This time, his opponent was the Democratic incumbent, Stephen A. Douglas, and the election is remembered primarily for their famous series of debates on the values of republicanism, popular sovereignty, and liberty. But when the votes were in, despite Republican candidates' winning a clear majority statewide, the gerrymander was sufficient to preserve Democratic control in Springfield. The legislature dutifully reelected Douglas to his Senate seat. Stung by the loss, Lincoln decided to skip the Senate entirely and instead run for president in 1860. The Democratic attempt to sideline this rising star in the Republican Party was thwarted.

Would he still have mounted a presidential campaign if he had been less than two years into a six-year term in the Senate? It's impossible to know, but once again a gerrymander had fundamentally altered the career trajectory of a man who later became president of the United States. On such seemingly insignificant details, the fates of empires turn. And while Lincoln, despite this earlier run-in with the subversion of democracy, would go on to endorse the Republican state-stacking gerrymander of the Civil War era, its architect had been someone else: an obscure Ohio senator by the name of Benjamin Wade.

The history of the American presidency is marked with examples of almost presidents. Men (and occasionally women) who came agonizingly close to ascending to the nation's highest office, but due to bizarre or unlikely circumstances, last-minute changes of heart, or cruel twists of fate never quite made it. Al Gore's loss in the 2000 presidential election to the Texas governor, George W. Bush, came down to a disputed 537-vote margin out of almost 6 million ballots cast in the state of Florida, amid numerous election irregularities stemming from voter purges, butterfly ballots, and hanging, dimpled, and even pregnant chads. Eventually, a 5–4 decision by the U.S. Supreme Court in the case of *Bush v. Gore* finally put the controversy to rest, although the question of who really "won" the 2000 election, however one may choose to define that, is unlikely to ever be definitively resolved.

Two centuries earlier, Aaron Burr faced a similar protracted wait to discover if he would be elected as the nation's third president. Burr had technically been Thomas Jefferson's running mate in the 1800 contest against the incumbent John Adams. But under a quirk of the original Electoral College system—which until corrected by the Twelfth Amendment allowed each elector to cast two votes for president—he ended up tied 73–73 with Jefferson, with each ahead of Adams, who received 65 electoral votes. The plan had been for one of the Democratic-Republican electors to abstain, putting Jefferson one vote ahead of his running mate, who would then be elected vice president. But due to a breakdown in communication that has never been satisfactorily explained, the plan failed. No one abstained.

This triggered a contingent election, under which the House of Representatives would decide the next president. After thirty-five consecutive ballots resulted in no majority for either Jefferson or Burr, Alexander Hamilton stepped in. The arch-Federalist, who had been George Washington's Treasury secretary, finally persuaded enough members of his own party to either abstain or vote for Jefferson—whom he viewed as "by far not so dangerous a man" as Burr—to carry him to victory on the thirty-sixth ballot. Hamilton's warning about Burr's temperament turned out to be prescient. Less than four years later, Burr shot and killed him in a duel in New Jersey, while still serving as Jefferson's vice president.

And beneath these infamous and high-profile examples, there lurk a number of almost presidents whom most people have never heard of. Names that are largely absent from the history books, whose major claim to fame is that they almost, but not quite, made it to the Oval Office. Prior to the ratification of the Twenty-Fifth Amendment in

1967 (which codified the tradition that the vice president assumes the full powers and office of the presidency in the event of a presidential vacancy, rather than merely serving as acting president until a new election could be held) and the Presidential Succession Act of 1947 (which fleshed out the remainder of the line of succession: vice president → Speaker of the House → president pro tempore of the Senate → secretary of state → secretary of the Treasury, and so on), the specifics of what actually happened when a president died, resigned, was removed from office through impeachment, or was otherwise incapacitated were somewhat murky.

When President William Henry Harrison passed away from pneumonia in 1841, only thirty-one days into his term, his vice president, John Tyler, boldly declared that he was now assuming the full powers and title of president, although nothing in the Constitution clearly provided for this. Even more unclear was the question of what would happen if the office of vice president was also unoccupied. The terms of the Presidential Succession Act of 1792 suggested that the president pro tempore of the Senate, the second-highest-ranking official in the chamber behind the vice president, would become acting president in that eventuality, but this was far from settled law. The question was of no mere academic concern. Between 1800 and 1900, there were ten separate occasions on which the office of vice president became vacant for one reason or another.

Less than three years after John Tyler assumed the presidency following the death of William Henry Harrison, and with no mechanism in place at the time to appoint a replacement for him as VP, Tyler himself was very nearly killed in an explosion aboard the USS *Princeton*. Had things gone slightly differently that day, Willie Person Mangum—the North Carolina senator whose main claim to fame was having won eleven electoral votes as one of four Whig candidates for president in 1836—would have assumed the office. President Tyler (acting president according to his opponents) had been attending a demonstration cruise down the Potomac River in Washington, D.C., to celebrate the launch of the powerful new warship. Joining him on the cruise were some four hundred other dignitaries and guests that included several members of his own cabinet, as well as James Madison's widow, Dolley. Eager to show off the vessel's twelve-inch, twenty-seven-thousand-pound Peacemaker cannon, the largest in the world at the time, Captain Robert

Stockton fired off several volleys from the enormous gun along the way, to the delight of those on board.

As the ship turned for home, Secretary of the Navy Thomas Walker Gilmer—brushing off safety concerns and overruling the gun's designer, John Ericsson—ordered one final volley from the cannon in the direction of Mount Vernon as a salute to George Washington. When Captain Stockton pulled the firing lanyard, the Peacemaker exploded, spraying hot metal shrapnel into the assembled crowd. Tyler himself was halfway up the ladder to the upper deck when the explosion occurred. He had paused there for a moment to raise his champagne glass for one last toast, and so escaped unharmed. Eight people were killed in the explosion, including Secretary Gilmer and Secretary of State Abel P. Upshur. Dozens of others were wounded.

Though the explosion aboard the *Princeton* had been an accident, two other relatively obscure individuals would join the ranks of the almost presidents by virtue of failed assassination attempts. In February 1933, only twenty-three days after the Twentieth Amendment went into effect—which provided that the vice president elect would assume the office if the president-elect were killed—an Italian immigrant and anarchist named Giuseppe Zangara decided to put it to the test. Armed with a .32-caliber revolver, he approached a car containing President-elect Franklin Roosevelt and Chicago's mayor, Anton Cermak, during a rally in Miami, Florida. Zangara fired five shots into the vehicle, reportedly shouting "I hate all presidents!" and "too many people are starving!" before being restrained by onlookers.

Roosevelt, the intended target of the assassination, was unharmed. Cermak was not so fortunate. Gravely wounded in the attack, he died less than a month later, exactly two weeks before Giuseppe Zangara's date with the electric chair. Had the bullets found their mark that day, Vice President elect John Nance Garner would have assumed the office of president. "I'm glad it was me, not you," Cermak apparently told Roosevelt from his hospital bed after the shooting. The line was later engraved on his tomb.

Almost seventy years earlier, Senate president pro tempore Lafayette S. Foster had also missed being catapulted to the presidency only because of an assassination that went wrong. But on that occasion, it was very much overshadowed by an assassination that went right. The plot to murder Abraham Lincoln in 1865 involved conspirators besides

John Wilkes Booth. One of these was George Atzerodt, whose role in the plot was to assassinate Vice President Andrew Johnson, while Booth took care of Lincoln. Atzerodt even went so far as to rent a hotel room at the Kirkwood House in Washington, directly above the one being occupied by Johnson. But after a last-minute attack of nerves he decided to go drinking at the hotel bar instead of following through with the plan. Atzerodt, along with three other members of the conspiracy, was hanged in Washington, D.C., three months later. It is into this same category of almost presidents, along with the names of Burr, Foster, Garner, and Mangum, that Benjamin Wade may also be placed. Three years after Lincoln's assassination, Wade would come within a single vote in the Senate of replacing Andrew Johnson as president.

A native of Springfield, Massachusetts, Wade had worked as a laborer on the Erie Canal before trying his hand at politics. Like Lincoln he had been a member of the Whig Party before joining the Republican ranks upon its demise. After moving to Ohio initially to practice law, he was elected to the state senate in 1837. He served in that capacity until early 1842, leaving only months before the attempted Democratic gerrymander later that year, narrowly missing out on his former Whig colleagues' adventures with the Licking Water-whelp and friends. A strong advocate for women's suffrage, trade unions, and both the abolition of

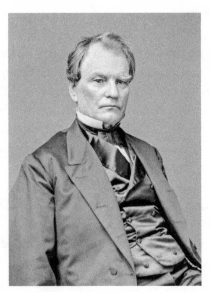

Photograph of Benjamin Wade by Mathew Brady, circa 1865.

slavery and the extension of civil rights to African Americans, Wade quickly developed a reputation as one of the most radical American politicians of the era.

He was elected to the U.S. Senate in 1851, where he opposed both the Fugitive Slave Act and the Kansas-Nebraska Act. And along with colleagues such as Thaddeus Stevens and Charles Sumner, he emerged as one of the leaders of the Radical Republican faction in Congress. When the Civil War broke out, Wade was almost captured by Confederate forces on the way back to Washington, D.C., having witnessed the Union defeat at the First Battle of Bull Run. As the war progressed, he became a vocal critic of Lincoln's pragmatic approach to the slavery question, opining somewhat uncouthly that the president's views "could only come of one born of poor white trash and educated in a slave State."

But one thing on which he and Lincoln saw eye to eye was the question of territorial expansion. Both men recognized the opportunity it created for bolstering the Republicans' control in Washington. Aside from the destruction of the institution of slavery, it was probably the number one item on the Radical Republican agenda. And Wade had a plan.

The Constitution places relatively few restrictions on the admission of new states. Article IV merely stipulates, "New States may be admitted by the Congress into this Union; but no new State shall be formed or erected within the Jurisdiction of any other State; nor any State be formed by the Junction of two or more States, or Parts of States, without the Consent of the Legislatures of the States concerned as well as of the Congress." When it comes to the granting of statehood to existing territories, therefore, Congress has almost unilateral discretion to dictate the terms, provided of course that the president is prepared to sign the legislation into law.

The rule of thumb that was used prior to the Civil War was a simple one. When and if a territory's population grew to the point that would warrant the granting of a seat in the U.S. House of Representatives, Congress would consider its petition for statehood. In 1860, that number stood at around 127,000 residents. But while conflict over slavery had dominated the congressional debates over admission during the antebellum period, the growing prospect of war saw partisan considerations rise to the forefront. Nowhere was this calculus more evident than in the Nevada Territory, which did not even exist as an independent entity when Abraham Lincoln defeated his two Democratic opponents in the 1860 presidential election. One of those opponents was none other than Stephen A. Douglas, the same man who had denied him a Senate seat two years prior.

In the four months between the election and Lincoln's inauguration, amid the chaos of the Confederacy secession crisis, Wade and the Republican majority in the House of Representatives sensed an opportunity. Though they had lost control of the Senate to the Democrats in 1858, the departure of the Democratic senators from the seven states that had seceded from the Union as of February 1, 1861, suddenly turned their thirty-eight-to-twenty-five deficit in that chamber into a twenty-six-to-twenty-five majority. In the two weeks before Lincoln took the oath of office on March 4, the Republican Congress passed, and in a decision he would surely have regretted if he'd lived to see its effects, the outgoing Democratic president, James Buchanan, signed into law, two seemingly innocuous pieces of legislation, known as Organic Acts.

Organic Acts are used by Congress to convert an existing tract of federal land into a formal U.S. territory, while Enabling Acts provide the vehicle for those territories to later obtain statehood. The first Organic Act, signed on February 28, carved off the western part of the Kansas Territory, the southwestern corner of the Nebraska Territory, and a small northern strip of the New Mexico Territory to form the brand-new Colorado Territory, population 34,277. The second, on March 2, the same day that the bill creating the Dakota Territory became law, divided the remainder of the Utah Territory in half along the thirty-ninth degree of longitude west from Washington, and designated the western portion as the Nevada Territory, population 6,857.

Around the same time, the remaining eastern portion of the Kansas Territory was admitted to the Union, in another bill signed by President Buchanan. On April 4, the new state of Kansas sent two additional Republican senators to Washington for the beginning of the Thirty-Seventh Congress. Once Lincoln took office, he and Wade wasted little time following through with the rest of the plan. What followed over

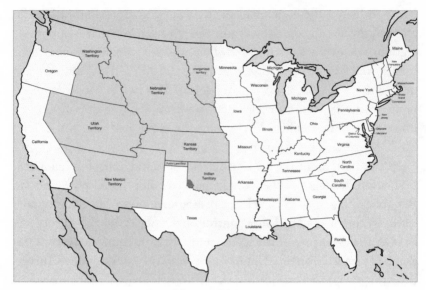

Map of the United States, 1860.

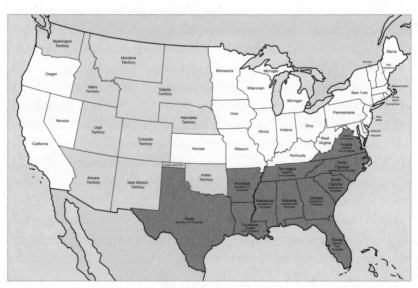

Map of the United States, 1865.

the next three years was an unprecedented flurry of territorial reorganization and statehood admission that created the geographic blueprint of the western United States as it exists today. Additional Organic Acts were passed that created the territories of Arizona (February 1863; population 9,658), Idaho (March 1863; population 14,999), and Montana

(May 1864; population 20,595). Each was passed through Congress during the Civil War, with the absence of the Democratic representatives who had left Washington to join the Confederacy, giving Lincoln and Wade unfettered control over the nation's legislative agenda. The dramatic effects of these changes to the geography of the United States can be seen in the accompanying maps, which depict the nation in 1860 and 1865.

These reorganizations were merely the opening gambit in a longer game of territorial chess, one that the political scientists Charles Stewart and Barry Weingast refer to as "America's rotten boroughs." By dividing the western territories into smaller and smaller geographic units, the Republicans would be able to later admit them as states. This process contributed in no small part to their dominance of national elections throughout the late nineteenth century. But the initial plan had more immediate goals. For Lincoln, in the midst of a brutal conflict that was already turning against the Union forces—as Robert E. Lee's Army of Northern Virginia drove first into Maryland, with shots being fired only miles from Washington, D.C., and then later into Pennsylvania—there were more pressing concerns than his party's future electoral fortunes.

The election of 1864 was fast approaching. The possibility of his losing either his majority in Congress or the presidency itself, further crippling the war effort, was a very real concern. Even after the Union victory at the Battle of Gettysburg, and Lee's subsequent retreat to Virginia, began to turn the tide of the war in his favor, Lincoln remained restless. In his mind, securing his power in Washington, and indeed his own reelection, became synonymous with winning the war and saving the Union. It was the only way he could justify to himself what followed. To fully bolster the Republican electoral prospects, additional new states would have to be admitted. Two of the most attractive prospects were West Virginia and Nevada.

In a referendum held on October 24, 1861, the people of the prounionist western counties of Virginia had voted overwhelmingly in favor of breaking away from the Confederacy and forming their own state. They began sending representatives to Washington who purported to speak for the people of Virginia as a whole. Momentum for admission also began to build among congressional Republicans, with Benjamin Wade leading the charge. There was a major obstacle in the way of this plan, however: the Constitution explicitly forbids new states to be created from within the boundaries of existing ones without their consent. Such consent from Virginia, it goes without saying, was unlikely to be forthcoming.

The validity of the secession vote itself was also significantly in doubt. West Virginia was under Union occupation at the time, and rumors that troops had been stationed at polling places to prevent Confederate sympathizers from voting were swirling. Many Republicans privately conceded that the ordinance of secession was likely illegal. But they nevertheless moved forward with a bill to admit the territory that had seceded from Virginia, which had in turn seceded from the Union, secession apparently being quite in vogue during the early 1860s. On December 21, 1862, despite his own reservations, Lincoln signed the Enabling Act that was sent to him by Congress. In June of the next year, West Virginia was formally admitted as the thirty-fifth state.

"The division of a state is dreaded as a precedent but a measure expedient by a war is no precedent for times of peace," Lincoln wrote, in an apparent acknowledgment of the tenuous legality of the admission. "It is said that the admission of West Virginia is secession," he continued, "and tolerated only because it is our secession. Well, if we call it by that name, there is still difference enough between secession against the constitution and secession in favor of the constitution. I believe the admission of West Virginia into the union is expedient." Quite. It was not the only time that Lincoln's quest to save the Union would be predicated on, to put it mildly, a somewhat tortured reading of the founding document. Representative Thaddeus Stevens of Pennsylvania, while voting in favor of admission, stated it even more bluntly: "I will not stultify myself by supposing that we have any warrant in the Constitution for this proceeding."

When West Virginia's two senators arrived in Washington that August, Senator Garrett Davis of Kentucky objected strenuously to their seating. "I hold that there is, legally and constitutionally no such state in existence as the state of West Virginia," he opined on the Senate floor, "and consequently no senators from such a state." But his Republican colleagues overruled him. The question of West Virginia's legitimacy eventually precipitated a protracted legal battle that would not ultimately be settled until 1870, long after the war, Lincoln's presidency, and, courtesy of John Wilkes Booth's bullet, also his life had come to an end. In the aptly named case of *Virginia v. West Virginia*, the U.S.

Supreme Court gave at least an implicit endorsement to the secession, ruling 6–3 that the breakaway counties had indeed received the necessary consent to be lawfully admitted as a state.

If the admission of West Virginia was constitutionally unusual, the process by which Nevada became a state broke even more dramatically with the norms and traditions of statehood politics. The Union push into Louisiana in the Red River Campaign began to stall in the spring of 1864, followed soon after in June by what would ultimately prove to be the last major Confederate victory of the war at the Battle of Cold Harbor. And with Sherman's famous March to the Sea and the fall of Atlanta still many months in the future, the need to admit Nevada became all the more pressing. Its carving off from the Utah Territory in 1861 had been driven both by the silver rush of 1859, which saw prospectors flock to the Comstock Lode in search of a cheap buck, and by a desire on the part of Republicans in Washington to blunt the influence of the heavily Democratic Mormon areas around Salt Lake City. The push for statehood, however, which was again spearheaded by Benjamin Wade and endorsed by Lincoln, was explicable only in terms of partisan politics.

Under any reasonable metric, the population of the Nevada Territory fell far short of what would be necessary to even consider an application for statehood. Fewer than seven thousand people lived in Nevada, then part of the Utah Territory, at the time of the 1860 census. Even by 1870, six years into statehood, its population had increased only to slightly more than forty-two thousand. "It was the most egregious effort in the nation's history to disregard population and economic criteria in order to admit a state for political reasons," write Stewart and Weingast. "Had Nevada waited until the standard population criterion had been met, . . . it would not have entered the Union until 1970." "Members of Congress were being asked to admit a state . . . with virtually no population," they conclude, "a violent and corrupt history, an unstable economy based on mining, and little prospect for the development of a strong agricultural base."

But admit it they did. With little debate and no recorded roll-call vote, the Nevada Enabling Act was passed by Congress and signed into law by President Lincoln on March 21, 1864, four days before the Confederate victory at the Battle of Paducah. Nevada officially became the thirty-sixth state on October 31, narrowly in time for the November elections. Two Republican senators and three electoral votes for Abraham Lincoln would swiftly follow.

What drove Lincoln, a passionate defender of both the Union and the Constitution itself, to resort to these extraconstitutional shenanigans? In one of the most definitive studies of U.S. territorial expansion, the political scientists Nolan McCarty, Keith Poole, and Howard Rosenthal make a compelling case in defense of Lincoln's actions. They argue that cynical political opportunism was not the sole motivation behind the apparent Republican power grab. After all, the very nation itself was in the process of coming apart at the seams. When the votes creating the state of Kansas and the Nevada and Colorado Territories were held, war seemed imminent. And by the time West Virginia and Nevada were admitted to the Union in the run-up to the 1864 election, it was in its full throes.

"Winning the war," they write, "involved not only preservation of the Union but also the faithful implementation of Republican policies in its aftermath." This course of events was far from guaranteed as the election approached. "Even after the secession of eleven states who had cast very few Republican votes in 1860," they continue, "Lincoln gathered only 55% of the 1864 vote in spite of a dramatic pro-Union turn in the tide of the war. As a concession to its uncertain electoral situation, the party went so far as to give the second position on its national ticket to Andrew Johnson, a slaveholding Democrat from a border state."

But was it actually necessary? Lincoln would still have won reelection by a landslide, and with a comfortable Republican Senate majority to boot, even without the votes of the newly admitted states. And the statehood gerrymander left a stain on his administration that would embolden his Republican successors to undertake far less justifiable power grabs. The actions taken during Lincoln's first term to shore up the Republican strength in the House, Senate, and Electoral College were at the very least, as in the case of Nevada, a radical departure from established procedures. And when it came to West Virginia, they arguably represented a flagrant violation of the Constitution. But what might seem inconceivable in peace can come to be regarded as unavoidable in war. Even when hostilities ceased, admission could still be justified by the necessity of protecting the integrity of Reconstruction once the states of the former Confederacy began the process of rejoining the Union. What followed over the subsequent decades, however, is far less defensible as a matter of expediency, particularly with regard to the splitting of Dakota.

The two decades between the Civil War and the omnibus statehood debates of the late 1880s were relatively quiet on the state-stacking front. But statehood gerrymandering still had a decisive effect on at least one presidential election during this period. By now, Wade had set his sights on two new territories that he hoped to add to the Republican column: Colorado and Nebraska. His designs on Colorado were thwarted on two separate occasions, first by the people of Colorado itself and then by the veto pen of Lincoln's successor, Andrew Johnson.

Congress had passed the first Colorado Enabling Act in 1864, hoping to move forward with admission before the election that November. But when a referendum was held in the territory on the question of statehood, a majority of voters rejected the idea. Three years later, another Enabling Act was passed but was vetoed by Johnson, and the Republicans fell three votes short of forcing an override. A similar effort was undertaken to admit Nebraska that was pocket vetoed by Johnson in 1865. Two years later, the Nebraska Enabling Act was back before Congress, and after Johnson vetoed it again, this time his veto was overridden. This made it the first and to date only state to join the Union through that particular legislative procedure, and the fourth new state during the 1860s. The campaign to admit Colorado, however, quickly found itself eclipsed by more urgent matters. Matters that would soon catapult Benjamin Wade into the ranks of the almost presidents.

Johnson's political capital was already rapidly dwindling. Wade and the Radical Republicans in Congress were growing increasingly frustrated with his obstructionist stance toward both their statehood gerrymandering and the cause of Reconstruction. Johnson himself did little to assuage the growing anger on Capitol Hill. In one of his first actions after assuming the presidency, he granted amnesty to many former Confederates. Then he drew further ire by labeling the Radical Republican leaders as traitors and vetoing several bills attempting to impose more stringent readmission requirements on the southern states. Things came to a head in early 1868, when Johnson attempted to dismiss Secretary of War Edwin Stanton. This was a violation of the 1867 Tenure of Office Act, which the Republicans had passed over Johnson's veto. That legislation, almost certainly itself unconstitutional, was a blatant attack on the president's authority over the executive branch, requiring as it did the Senate to consent to any removal of a cabinet-level official. Three days later, the House voted 126–47 to approve articles of impeachment.

While the Republican majority in the Senate was sufficiently large to convict Johnson and remove him from office on a party-line vote, the major obstacle to the impeachment effort turned out to be the identity of the man who would replace him. In 1867, by virtue of his status as an elder statesman and a leader of the Radical Republican faction, Wade had been elected by his colleagues as president pro tempore of the Senate. This largely ceremonial position came with the added perk of placing him next in line for the presidency, since the office of vice president had been vacant since Lincoln's assassination. For the more moderate Republicans in the Senate, the prospect of a Wade presidency was a bridge too far.

"It was believed by many at the time," wrote John Roy Lynch, the first African American to be elected to the House of Representatives from the state of Mississippi, "that some of the Republican Senators that voted for acquittal did so chiefly on account of their antipathy to the man who would succeed to the presidency in the event of the conviction of the president." While they certainly despised Johnson, Wade was, again in the words of Lynch, "the sort of active and aggressive man that would be likely to make for himself enemies of men in his own organization who were afraid of his great power and influence, and jealous of him as a political rival." When the trial was held, ten Republican senators sided with Johnson, enough for his impeachment to fail by a single vote. An editorial in *The Detroit Post* probably summed it up best: "Andrew Johnson is innocent because Ben Wade is guilty of being his successor." And when Wade himself retired from the Senate the following year, his Republican brethren were more than willing to take up the state-stacking mantle that he had previously worn.

A renewed push for Colorado statehood was instigated in the mid-1870s by the Republican territorial representative Jerome Chaffee, whose lobbying campaign to Congress was prefaced on the audacious claim that the territory now had a population of 150,000. Given that there were fewer than 40,000 inhabitants at the time of the 1870 census, this notion can at best be filed under "wildly implausible." An enterprising land speculator who had been a teacher and small business owner in Michigan before heading west to make his fortune in the mining industry, Chaffee was nothing if not an opportunist, as his later political career would soon demonstrate. Wade had attempted a similar gambit with Nevada in 1864, citing the "unexampled rapidity" with which the territory's population was growing. "I venture to predict," he boldly continued, "that in one year from this time there will be more than one hundred fifty thousand inhabitants in the Territory." His prediction was off by roughly eight decades; Nevada would not hit 150,000 residents until the 1950 census.

Notwithstanding the wildly inflated population estimates—that particular precedent having after all been unceremoniously jettisoned with the admission of Nevada—the push for Colorado statehood found a surprisingly receptive bipartisan audience in Washington. While Republicans controlled both the Senate and the presidency, the Democratic majority in the House remained a potential stumbling block. But Colorado's Democratic territorial representative to Congress, Thomas Patterson, managed to win them over with the somewhat optimistic assertion that his party would be able to successfully compete for the Centennial State's votes. A parallel effort to admit New Mexico fell one vote short of successfully passing the House, an outcome that many historians attribute to prejudice toward the territory's Hispanic majority. President Ulysses S. Grant signed another Colorado Enabling Act on March 3, 1875, eleven years after Lincoln had initially done the same. The people of the territory voted overwhelmingly in favor of statehood the next summer, and it was admitted as the thirty-eighth state on August 1.

Just in time, too. Ohio's Republican governor, Rutherford B. Hayes, was in the midst of a closely contested battle for the presidency with the Democrat Samuel Tilden. The election appeared to be going down to the wire. As politicians of both parties eagerly waited on the returns— including Jerome Chaffee, who had returned to Washington as one of Colorado's two new Republican senators—Tilden appeared to be heading for victory. When it emerged that he had won the popular vote with 52 percent to Hayes's 48 percent, Tilden's supporters began celebrating their triumph. But like other Democratic hopefuls who would come after him, the Electoral College proved to be his downfall. Having determined that there was insufficient time to organize a statewide election, the Republican majority in the Colorado legislature simply voted to appoint their own slate of electors, who dutifully cast their ballots for

Hayes. Those three electoral votes proved to be decisive. Hayes went on to capture the presidency with a 185–184 Electoral College majority, the smallest margin in U.S. history.

That result had itself been intensely controversial. The initial count of Electoral College votes gave Tilden 184 to Hayes's 165, with the votes of four states, totaling 20, still unresolved. Amid widespread reports of fraud and violent threats against Republican voters, Florida, Louisiana, and South Carolina sent competing Republican and Democratic slates of delegates to their respective capitals, each claiming that their candidate had won the state. The situation quickly reached an impasse, and as the weeks dragged on, Inauguration Day was now rapidly approaching.

The crisis was resolved when the parties entered into the Compromise of 1877, hashed out in the smoke-filled rooms of the Washington political establishment. Under the terms of the deal, the Democrats agreed to award the disputed electoral votes to Hayes, and in return the Republicans agreed to withdraw the remaining federal troops from the South. This brought Reconstruction to an end and ushered in the era of Jim Crow racial discrimination and the widespread disenfranchisement of African American voters. Not the nation's finest hour. Had Colorado not been admitted prior to the election, Tilden's 184 electoral votes would have constituted a majority even without the disputed states, and he would have become president. Add another name to the almost-presidents roster.

By the 1880s, the effects of the Republican statehood gerrymander were also being acutely felt in the Senate. From 1876 to 1888, the four states admitted in the preceding two decades—Kansas, Nevada, Nebraska, and Colorado—selected an almost-unbroken slate of Republican senators. The lone exception was the Democrat James G. Fair of Nevada, who served from 1881 to 1887. Their votes would prove crucial to maintaining Republican control of the chamber, which they held from 1877 to 1879 and again from 1881 to 1889, despite Democratic majorities in the House throughout most of these years.

With a strong demand for statehood now emerging in many of the new territories that had been created in the lead-up to the Civil War, divided government proved a stumbling block to any further admissions. But as the 1888 presidential election approached, a bipartisan push reignited the statehood debate in Washington. As it turned out, the Democrats and Republicans had very different ideas in mind as to exactly which states they thought should be admitted.

Utah, New Mexico, and Montana appeared to be the most fertile candidates for the Democrats, while Dakota and Washington were targeted by the GOP. Partisan differences stalled any real progress until Election Day, when the Republican Benjamin Harrison narrowly defeated the Democratic incumbent, Grover Cleveland. More significantly, the Republicans also captured narrow majorities in both the House and, thanks to the votes of Colorado, Kansas, Nebraska, and Nevada, the Senate. When the new administration took office the next year, the Republican Party would enjoy unified control of both the executive and the legislative branches for the first time since Reconstruction.

This put the Democrats in an extremely tough position. If they ran out the clock on the Fiftieth Congress, the incoming Republican majority would surely move to admit only those states whose Senate seats and Electoral College votes they could be reasonably sure of controlling. But on the flip side, any deal that they might be able to strike during the lame-duck session would surely come at a steep price. The Republicans had little incentive to compromise, particularly in the case of Utah, whose continuing embrace of plural marriage in contravention of federal law was a major impediment to statehood. The Democrats' sole remaining bargaining chip was Dakota, and it was from these last-minute negotiations that the two Dakotas were born.

The possibility of admitting Dakota as two separate states had already been floated prior to the election. For obvious reasons, the Democratic majority in the House had consistently opposed the idea. While the political leanings of Washington and Montana were at least somewhat up in the air, Dakota represented a home run for the Republicans. The territory was virtually certain to elect four Republican senators if admitted on their terms, and the south's burgeoning population would also provide a bonus boost for their prospects in the House of Representatives and Electoral College. The Democrats' opening salvo in the negotiations was to propose an omnibus bill admitting Dakota and Washington in the Republican column, balanced out by Montana and New Mexico on the Democratic side. Utah, seen as a lost cause, would have to wait.

All four of these candidates met the population threshold for admission, and they gambled that an omnibus approach would appeal to their opponents' desire to paint themselves as the party of inclusive statehood. Even these concessions were considered unpalatable by many within the Democratic caucus. The Florida representative Charles Dougherty was one of the most vocal opponents. "If I were in charge of this measure the plan I would pursue would be to exclude the Republican Territories . . . and admit all the Democratic Territories," he complained to his colleagues on the House floor. "Let in Arizona, and Utah; they will both be Democratic states. New Mexico will also be Democratic."

His frustration is certainly understandable. Had the senators from Nevada and Colorado, both admitted prematurely considering their populations, not been present in Washington, the Democrats would have had the votes to do precisely what Dougherty urged. But even this compromise omnibus bill was dead on arrival. The Republican counter-proposal dropped New Mexico from consideration, gave the Democrats Montana as a concession, and called for North and South Dakota to be admitted separately. Sensing defeat, the Democrats capitulated. With forty-six Democratic representatives, almost a third of their caucus, failing to show up for the vote, the House passed this revised omnibus statehood bill by a 148–103 margin. Twenty Democrats crossed party lines to vote in favor of the bill, while one Republican voted against it. North Dakota, South Dakota, Washington, and Montana were all admitted to the Union in November 1889.

Nor were the Republicans finished with the process when they ate the Democrats' lunch during the lame-duck session. Once Benjamin Harrison took office, Congress moved forward with enabling bills for Wyoming and Idaho, each of which passed along strict party lines. Their populations at the time of admission, sixty-two thousand in the case of Wyoming and eighty-eight thousand in the case of Idaho, were smaller than every state to join the Union after 1860 other than Nevada.

The Republican statehood gerrymander saw eleven new states admitted between 1860 and 1890, representing twenty-two seats in the Senate (25 percent) and forty-eight votes in the Electoral College (11 percent). It was an unprecedented flurry of territorial reorganization and state creation that defined the outline of the United States as it exists today. What began with Lincoln's noble attempt to safeguard the Union and win the Civil War devolved into a cynical scheme to preserve Republican hegemony in Washington. That the residents of the states in question had themselves supplied some of the impetus for admission provided cover for the Republicans' actions, but not justification. Residents of territories that leaned Democratic, like Utah and New Mexico, though equally deserving of representation and no less eager to see that dream realized, were left out in the cold. Abe might still have been able to lay a legitimate claim to his honesty, but those who came after him certainly could not.

Some might argue that the admission of new states, even in the service of partisan purposes, does not strictly meet the criteria for gerrymandering as I've defined it in this book. And they would have a point. But what is clear is that the artificial manipulation of territorial boundaries, most notably with the creation of Nevada and Colorado in the 1860s and the splitting of Dakota in the 1880s, does meet the standard of the intentional manipulation of political boundaries with the view toward influencing subsequent election outcomes that was established in the introduction. And in contrast to the largely ineffectual earlier gerrymanders that have so far been discussed, the electoral effects of the Republican statehood gerrymander of the second half of the nineteenth century were both significant and long lasting. The New York Democratic representative Francis Spinola surmised as much when he lamented that in accepting the 1889 compromise, his party was "[putting] the Senate of the United States where the Democratic Party can not regain control of it for the next quarter of a century."

The Republican state-stacking gerrymander was only made possible by the significant malapportionment of the U.S. Senate, a malapportionment that was enshrined in the Constitution itself. With every newly admitted state bringing with it two senators regardless of its population, Senate malapportionment created powerful political incentives for both parties to selectively admit states based on their perceived partisanship. By virtue of circumstance and the opportunities that it created, the Republicans were dramatically more successful at doing this, but not through any lack of trying on the part of the Democrats. Equal representation in the Senate had been a vital point of compromise at the Constitutional Convention in Philadelphia, not only to appease the states' rights contingent, but also to balance out the proportional representation of the House, threading the needle between large-state and small-state interests in order to make ratification possible.

So strongly did the Framers feel about this particular provision that they made it the only one to be permanently entrenched against future amendment. "No state, without its consent," concludes Article V, after outlining the various amendment procedures, "shall be deprived of its equal suffrage in the Senate." Left unresolved is the interesting question of whether this provision itself could be subject to amendment. Some legal scholars have argued that a "two step" or "double amendment" process could be employed to reapportion the Senate. The first of these would explicitly repeal the shielding clause in Article V, while the second, ratified either contemporaneously or at a later date, could amend Article I to allocate Senate seats on the basis of each state's population. Others have argued that the equal suffrage provision could only be constitutionally amended after obtaining the unanimous consent of the states.

While these arguments may seem academic, the malapportionment of the Senate continues to be a point of partisan contention to this day. As the urban-rural divide between Democrats and Republicans in national elections becomes even more pronounced, winning an overall Senate majority may become as taxing for the Democratic Party of the twenty-first century as it was for their late nineteenth-century forebears. In the wake of the reapportionment revolution of the 1960s, which is discussed in the next chapter, the U.S. Senate remains the only significantly malapportioned legislative chamber in the United States.

5

Frankfurter's Political Thicket

For most of U.S. history, the basic organizational unit of the legislative district was the county. This was the case with the 1788 Henrymander, which assembled a district out of James Madison's Orange County, James Monroe's Spotsylvania, and their surrounding Anti-Federalist enclaves. It was also true of the Licking Water-whelp and friends, whose heads, bodies, and various and sundry appendages were all assembled out of combinations of counties. When line drawers failed to respect existing county or municipal boundaries, as was the case with the mutilation of Essex County in service of Elbridge Gerry's salamander district, it was a pretty reliable sign that something untoward was occurring.

Counties represented convenient building blocks for districts because they could be easily amalgamated into geographic units that preserved communities and grouped together similarly situated constituents. Counties often had an existing political or cultural identity, allowing them to serve as a starting point for redrawing the district maps for multiple legislative chambers at a time. Frequently, states used counties as the boundaries for their senate districts, maintaining a variant of the equal suffrage blueprint that had been used for the U.S. Senate. Then they nested their state house of representatives districts within them, splitting each county into two or three slices as required. County boundaries could also be used to build a state's U.S. House districts, by combining them together so that each district was roughly equal in population. Counties were, first and foremost, an easy shorthand for politicians who wanted to redistrict in a simple and straightforward

way, without needing to resort to the kinds of "ingenious and artificial combinations" that were the hallmark of early gerrymandering.
But there was also a major downside to the use of county boundaries
for the drawing of legislative districts, and that was the problem of
malapportionment.

By the time of the 1910 census, two years before Arizona and New
Mexico finally joined the Union to complete the "contiguous 48," the
effects of urbanization, the Industrial Revolution, and the growth of the
American city were already being acutely felt in the nation's political
institutions. Fully 31 million Americans, approximately one-third of the
overall population, now lived in counties with populations of more than
100,000 people. This trend would only accelerate further over the next
half century. Both immigrants and rural Americans flocked to metropolises like New York City, whose population hit 5 million around 1913;
Chicago and its more than 2 million inhabitants; and Philadelphia,
which had recently topped 1.5 million residents. And with their interests
often being very different from the concerns of rural voters elsewhere
in their respective states, urban Americans began clamoring for fair and
equal representation in their state governments.

The early twentieth century was the apex of the Progressive movement in American government, as pro-democracy sentiments ran rampant in the political debates of the age. The Progressive Era witnessed
the birth of the direct primary election, which for the first time allowed
regular voters a voice in the selection of nominees for political office.
This process had previously been dominated by party bosses and the
Rube Goldberg black boxes of machine politics. The Seventeenth
Amendment to the U.S. Constitution was ratified in 1913, granting voters a voice in the selection of U.S. senators, who had to that point been
chosen exclusively by state legislatures. And direct democracy, in the
form of the citizens' ballot initiative, gave the average American a seat at
the policy-making table, allowing for proposed laws and constitutional
amendments to be put to a popular vote. Originating in Oregon in
1902, the initiative process permitted sponsors to place policy proposals
directly on the ballot through the collection of signatures, bypassing
the elected branches of government entirely. Direct democracy quickly
spread to numerous other states, particularly those that had once made
up the western frontier.

But as the winds of democracy were beginning to steadily pick up force, the problem of malapportionment seemed stubbornly immune to the momentum of progressive reform. While the Progressive Era did see a renewed, albeit limited, focus on redistricting reform—a handful of states redrew their legislative and congressional boundaries in the early twentieth century to more equitably distribute political power between urban and rural areas—what followed was an almost fifty-year period of inertia. Between 1910 and 1960, numerous states consistently failed to update their district boundaries in the face of rapidly accelerating population redistribution. Of the forty-eight now in the Union, only seven redistricted even one chamber of their state legislatures following the 1930 and 1940 censuses. Oregon did not redraw its district boundaries once between 1907 and 1960, while Illinois failed to do so between 1910 and 1955. Alabama and Tennessee had not redistricted since 1901. The apportionment of legislative districts in Connecticut, Vermont, Mississippi, and Delaware was fixed according to their respective state constitutions, most of which had been drafted in the late nineteenth or early twentieth century.

When redistricting did occur, it was as likely to exacerbate the problem of malapportionment as to ameliorate it. Once again, the perverse incentives created by allowing politicians to control the drawing of their own districts hindered the ability of the political process to effectively address the problem. Representatives in rural areas, which by design had been given increased representation in many state senates to counterbalance the more proportional allocation of seats in their lower chambers, feared that urban representatives would vote for confiscatory wealth redistribution if their political power was allowed to increase. These rural politicians consistently blocked any attempt to redistrict, maintaining their stranglehold on the levers of democracy. Meanwhile, urban voters, left powerless in their state capitols, were growing increasingly restless.

By the time of the 1960 census, things were reaching a crisis point. A hundred and fourteen million people, fully 64 percent of the nation's population, now lived in counties with a population of more than 100,000, an almost threefold increase over 1910. Writing in 1964, the U.S. representative Morris K. Udall of Arizona documented the full scope of the inequality that had been created by the "creeping gerrymanders" of the twentieth century. "No one can deny," he began his report to the Eighty-Eighth Congress, "that some of the States have allowed thinly-populated areas to exercise extra, and often strikingly disproportionate, power in making State laws." "This is a result," he argues, "of 1) the immense growth of cities and the decline of rural populations, and 2) a failure of these States to adjust the allocation of legislative seats as the population distribution has changed." He then went on to document some of the most egregious instances of malapportionment in the nation. His findings are so compelling that they are worth reproducing in full. Udall begins with "some of the most striking disparities in lower house apportionment":

- In Connecticut one House district has 191 people; another, 81,000.
- In New Hampshire one township with 3 (three!) people has a state assemblyman; this is the same representation given another district with 3,244. The vote of a resident of the first town is 108,000 percent more powerful at the Capitol.
- In Utah the smallest district has 164 people, the largest 32,280 (28 times the population of the other). But each has one vote in the House.
- In Vermont the smallest district has 36 people, the largest 35,000; a ratio of almost 1,000 to 1.

Turning to state senates, and noting that "many of them [were] patterned on the Federal Congress (with lower house based on population and upper house on area)," he finds that "the extreme examples are equally startling":

- In California the 14,000 people of one small county have one State senator to speak for them; so do the 6 million people of Los Angeles County. It takes 430 Los Angelenos to muster the same influence on a State senator that one person wields in the smaller district.
- In Idaho the smallest Senate district has 951 people; the largest, 93,400.
- Nevada's 17 State senators represent as many as 127,000 or as few as 568 people—a ratio of 224 to 1.
- In Arizona, Mohave County's 7,700 people have two State senators; so do the 663,000 people of Maricopa. The ratio is 86 to 1.

It must be noted, of course, that there is a difference between delib-erate action on the part of politicians in a state to create grossly unfair districts through gerrymandering and deliberate inaction to allow exist-ing inequalities to perpetuate and grow ever more dramatic over time. These creeping gerrymanders that would ignite the reapportionment revolution of the 1960s were not strictly gerrymanders at all, as the term has been defined throughout this book. But their significance to the broader history of gerrymandering in America cannot be underesti-mated. In fixing the problem of malapportionment, the courts created a new one in its place: the Frankenstein's monster of the modern gerry-mander. No one could say that they hadn't been warned.

Felix Frankfurter had been worn down. For decades, the New Dealer and titan of judicial restraint had fought a one-man holding action against his increasingly activist brethren on the U.S. Supreme Court, going toe-to-toe with legal giants like Earl Warren, Hugo Black, and William O. Douglas. In Frankfurter's mind, the involvement of the Court in cases implicating fundamental questions of fairness and equal-ity in American elections was a disaster waiting to happen. In the 1940s case of *Colegrove v. Green,* he had authored an opinion in which he spe-cifically cautioned against embroiling the judiciary in disputes over the drawing of legislative districts. Such involvement, he believed, would politicize the courts, undermine judicial independence and integrity, and set the nation on an untenable path from which there would be no coming back. Writing for a three-justice plurality, Frankfurter argued,

> Courts ought not to enter this political thicket. The remedy for unfairness in districting is to secure State legislatures that will apportion properly, or to invoke the ample powers of Congress. The Constitution has many commands that are not enforceable by courts, because they clearly fall outside the conditions and pur-poses that circumscribe judicial action.

But his warning would fall on deaf ears. In the early 1960s, in a case called *Baker v. Carr,* the Court set aside Frankfurter's earlier ruling and plunged ahead, opening the courthouse doors to precisely these kinds of challenges. Then, in a pair of decisions released only months apart

Felix Frankfurter at age twelve.
Photograph taken by W. M. Spiess of New York City, circa 1895.

in 1964, the justices created the principle of "one person, one vote," a constitutional mandate that every American's voice should count equally when it came to the election of their representatives in government. Since that time the Supreme Court has handed down numerous decisions concerning election law, delving deeper and deeper into the thicket that Frankfurter had been so unwilling to enter. The story of how the modern gerrymander rose, like a dark phoenix from the ashes of the creeping gerrymanders of the early twentieth century, is also the story of Felix Frankfurter and how he fought, and lost, the battle of the political thicket.

Frankfurter was a man of many contradictions: between his progressive and civil libertarian principles and his more conservative beliefs about the proper role of government and the courts; between the elitist East Coast legal circles in which he ran for most of his adult life and his upbringing in a poor Jewish immigrant family on the Lower East Side of Manhattan; between his cultural Zionism and lifelong support of Jewish causes and his own personal lack of religious faith; between his fundamental belief in fairness and meritocracy and the political connections and alliances he forged that ultimately catapulted him to a seat on the highest court in the land.

Frankfurter was born in Vienna in 1882, in what was then part of the Austro-Hungarian Empire, and was the descendant of multiple generations of rabbis. His uncle, Solomon Frankfurter, worked as the head librarian at the Vienna University Library, while his father, Leopold Frankfurter, was a merchant and fur trader and a former Orthodox rabbinical student. The third of six children, Felix immigrated with his family to the United States in 1894, when he was twelve years old, after Leopold had attended the Chicago World's Fair the previous year and elected to follow the American dream. Fleeing anti-Semitism in Vienna, Frankfurter arrived on Ellis Island speaking only Yiddish and Hebrew, but quickly assimilated himself into the New York cultural milieu. Young Felix, now fluent in English, excelled at his studies, first at P.S. 25 in the East Village, and then at Townsend Harris High School in Queens, reading books on Jewish history and political theory at the Cooper Union library, and attending lectures on left-wing topics such as socialism, communism, and trade unionism.

Frankfurter had come to America at the height of the Gilded Age, the era of trusts, robber barons, and unbelievable wealth and income inequality. The contrasts between the haves and the have-nots were a daily feature in the life of 1890s New York, with the sweatshops and tenements of the Lower East Side mere blocks away from the stately mansions of the Vanderbilts, Carnegies, and Astors on Fifth Avenue. His upbringing instilled in Frankfurter a strong sense of social justice, progressivism, and a desire to aid the helpless, the downtrodden, the huddled masses yearning to breathe free. It also ignited a love affair with the law that would come to define the remainder of his life.

The first step along the road to realizing his dream of becoming an attorney came when Frankfurter enrolled in the Free Academy of the City of New York, now part of the CUNY system, and the first free public institution of higher learning in the United States. He graduated third in his class of 775 and then spent time working for the Tenement House Department to raise money for law school. It was while a student at Harvard Law, to which he would later return as a professor, that Frankfurter's jurisprudential philosophy began to develop. He became a committed believer in the principle of judicial restraint, that

A young Felix Frankfurter in his boardinghouse room, circa 1905.

courts should defer whenever possible to the wisdom of Congress and state legislatures, whose status as the directly elected representatives of the people made them better suited to solving controversial social and political problems. He was described by some as the best-performing student to pass through the school since the wealthy and highly influential fellow Jewish attorney Louis Brandeis, with whom he developed a close friendship. Frankfurter graduated first in his class in 1906, also serving as an editor of the *Harvard Law Review.*

He initially eschewed partisan politics despite his strong progressive principles, spending time in private practice at the New York firm of Hornblower, Byrne, Miller & Potter, before taking a job as an assistant to the then U.S. Attorney for the Southern District of New York Henry Stimson, a close ally of Teddy Roosevelt's. This marked the beginning of a close association with the Roosevelt family. Frankfurter was an outspoken supporter of Teddy's unsuccessful Bull Moose campaign against Woodrow Wilson in 1912 and would later serve in the administration of his cousin Franklin. When Stimson was tapped by the Republican president William Howard Taft to be his secretary of war, Frankfurter followed him to Washington and was hired as an attorney in the Bureau of Insular Affairs. But frustration that his position in a Republican administration was limiting his ability to express his progressive political and social views began to mount, and he became increasingly disillusioned with the D.C. establishment. At one point he described himself as "politically homeless."

Frankfurter began seeking opportunities outside the government sphere and was eventually persuaded to return to Harvard as a professor at the behest of Brandeis, who had lobbied the financier and philanthropist Jacob Schiff to endow a position for him at the law school. Teaching mainly in the area of administrative law, he continued to refine his philosophy of judicial restraint, joining fellow professor and future SEC chairman James M. Landis in advocating for greater freedom from judicial oversight for executive branch agencies. This period also marked the beginning of a decades-long secret correspondence between Frankfurter and Brandeis, the famous "people's attorney" who two years later would be appointed by President Wilson as the first Jewish justice on the Supreme Court. More troublingly, Frankfurter's papers, which had been donated to the Library of Congress after his death in 1965, revealed that Brandeis, twenty-six years his senior, had paid Frankfurter a retainer throughout his legal and political career to act as his covert lobbyist and political lieutenant.

The outbreak of World War I brought about a return to politics for Frankfurter, who took leave from his teaching responsibilities at Harvard to become a special assistant to the secretary of war, Newton D. Baker. He occupied various roles in the War Department during the conflict, including as judge advocate general, where he supervised the courts-martial of thirty-six U.S. servicemen who were executed for desertion. He also served as counsel to the President's Mediation Commission, where he defended the socialist activist Thomas Mooney against accusations that he had participated in the 1916 Preparedness Day Bombing in San Francisco. He finished out the war as chairman of the War Labor Policies Board, where he made the acquaintance of a young assistant secretary of the navy by the name of Franklin Delano Roosevelt. Their friendship would go on to define the remainder of Frankfurter's career.

After the war, Frankfurter played a key role in the founding of the American Civil Liberties Union in 1920, contributing further to his growing reputation as a political radical. At one point, the FBI director, J. Edgar Hoover, went so far as to label him "the most dangerous man

Felix Frankfurter at Harvard Law School, 1917.

in the United States." Frankfurter himself did little to discourage the moniker. He expressed support for American recognition of the newly created Soviet Union and mounted a vocal campaign in defense of Nicola Sacco and Bartolomeo Vanzetti, the Italian American anarchists who were convicted and executed for the murders of a Massachusetts paymaster and security guard during an armed robbery in 1920.

Decades later, it also came to light that he had penned his widely read *Atlantic Monthly* article in support of Sacco and Vanzetti at the behest of his benefactor, Louis Brandeis. Frankfurter's very public advocacy on behalf of communists, radicals, and oppressed religious minorities made him many enemies among the more conservative Harvard faculty and Boston political elite during the First Red Scare. But he had also made powerful friends, including the newly elected governor of New York. And when, in the wake of the most devastating economic catastrophe in the history of the United States—the blame for which Frankfurter placed squarely in the hands of the dramatic wealth inequalities he'd observed firsthand as a boy on the streets of Manhattan—that same governor mounted a bid for the presidency, Frankfurter was among his most enthusiastic supporters.

In many ways, the events of FDR's tenure as president would go on to define the next forty years of Supreme Court history. The Court of the early 1930s was a deeply conservative institution, still steeped in the laissez-faire economic philosophy that had characterized the earlier *Lochner* era of jurisprudence. Stacked with Republican appointees—a consequence of the eight consecutive vacancies filled by the Republican presidents Harding, Coolidge, and Hoover between 1921 and 1932—the justices handed down ruling after ruling in which they undermined the ability of state and federal governments to institute progressive reforms. They struck down laws curtailing the use of child labor, establishing minimum wages and maximum working hours, and promoting collective bargaining.

Four justices in particular—Pierce Butler, James Clark McReynolds, George Sutherland, and Willis Van Devanter—stood out as marching in lockstep in their opposition to the New Deal. Alleged to have even carpooled together during their commutes to the Supreme Court building on Capitol Hill, the better to coordinate their legal arguments and case strategies, this cabal of conservative jurists was nicknamed the Four Horsemen of the Supreme Court by the D.C. press corps. Facing off against them were the Three Musketeers on the Court's liberal wing, consisting of Brandeis, Benjamin Cardozo, and Chief Justice Harlan Fiske Stone. For the first five years of the Roosevelt administration, the fate of the New Deal rested on the votes of the two swing justices. They were Charles Evans Hughes, who was more inclined to side with the Musketeers, and Owen Roberts, who at times appeared to be auditioning for the role of the fifth horseman.

Frankfurter had at this point been brought in as an informal adviser to the Roosevelt White House, a role he had also occupied during FDR's governorship in New York. The position suited him, and he turned down an offer to become FDR's solicitor general, as well as a seat on the Supreme Judicial Court of Massachusetts, in favor of the opportunity to advocate behind the scenes for a strong progressive response to the economic travails of the Great Depression. In addition to helping to craft the New Deal, Frankfurter relished the opportunity to recruit young, progressive attorneys for roles in the new administration, many of whom had been students of his at Harvard Law. Felix's Happy Hot Dogs, as the group became known, included among their ranks the future secretary of state Dean Acheson and, more regrettably, the Soviet spy Alger Hiss, who only escaped execution for espionage when he was discovered in the 1940s because the statute of limitations had expired.

The early New Deal legislation represented the most dramatic expansion of the federal government's power in the nation's history. Congress assumed unprecedented authority to regulate economic affairs, much of which was then delegated wholesale to the executive branch, giving FDR carte blanche to craft a response to the ongoing crisis. Most radical of all was the National Industrial Recovery Act, which empowered the administration to create "codes of fair competition" for the more than five hundred industries that were regulated under the law. Congress, in effect, was turning over the keys to the entire economy to the White House. The president described it as "the most important and far-reaching legislation ever enacted by the American Congress." The Four Horsemen were having none of it. In case after case, joined sometimes by only the swing vote of Roberts, and on other occasions even by one or more of the Musketeers, New Deal program after New Deal program found itself on the Court's chopping block. "This is the end of this business of centralization," Brandeis told Roosevelt's aide Thomas Corcoran, another one of Felix's Happy Hot Dogs, after the Court struck down the NIRA in 1935. "I want you to go back and tell the president that we're not going to let this government centralize everything."

The stage had now been set for the most dramatic showdown between the White House and the high court in the history of the Republic. In the meantime, however, the American people voiced their opinion on the matter. In November 1936, FDR won the largest popular and electoral vote landslide since the uncontested 1820 victory by James Monroe during the Era of Good Feelings. He picked up 523 electoral votes to the 8 of his Republican opponent, Alf Landon, who won only two states, Maine and Vermont. In an early setback for the reputation of political pollsters, *The Literary Digest,* based on a highly unscientific self-selected straw poll of its own readers, confidently predicted that Landon would win overwhelmingly. "Is Our Face Red!" blazed the giant headline on the cover of the next issue. The magazine folded in 1938.

They could be forgiven for their confidence in a Landon victory given the political climate of the time. "As goes Maine, so goes the nation" was a popular political aphorism among pundits, referencing the state's reputation as a bellwether of presidential electoral politics. And with the Republican victory in Maine's September race for governor, many had expected a repeat showing. "As goes Maine, so goes Vermont!" gleefully joked Roosevelt's campaign manager James Farley to reporters after the election, barely managing to stifle a chuckle. George Gallup's fledgling polling operation, the American Institute of Public Opinion, fared somewhat better, although even he underestimated the full magnitude of the Democratic landslide. In addition to a second term for FDR, voters returned large Democratic majorities to both houses of Congress. The only thing now standing in the way of their agenda was the Supreme Court, and Roosevelt had a plan for that.

On March 9, 1937, the president delivered his ninth Fireside Chat, broadcast on the radio to millions of Americans. In it, he laid out the case for taking decisive action to deal with the Court's obstructionism. "The Court has been acting not as a judicial body, but as a policy-making body," he charged. "We have, therefore, reached the point as a nation where we must take action to save the Constitution from the Court and the Court from itself." He then outlined what became known as his "court-packing plan," introduced before Congress as the somewhat less sinister-sounding Judicial Procedures Reform Bill of 1937. It would have granted the president the power to appoint new justices to the Court, up to a maximum of fifteen, for each incumbent member who reached the age of seventy and did not, in FDR's words, "avail himself of the opportunity to retire."

There were six septuagenarian jurists on the bench at the time, including all four of the horsemen. This fact did not exactly aid Roosevelt's somewhat transparent attempts to frame his proposal as a much-needed boost to the retirement packages of federal judges. Though the legislation would have applied to all federal courts, not just the Supremes, it was hard not to see it as a desperate power grab by the administration. FDR would lose the battle over his court-packing plan, and in spectacular style, with the Senate voting 70–20 against its most controversial provisions. But serendipity would allow him to win the broader war against the Court. And ironically, those events had already been set in motion before he had even unveiled the legislation.

Less than three weeks after Roosevelt's Fireside Chat, the Supreme Court dropped a bombshell. In the case of *West Coast Hotel v. Parrish*, Owen Roberts surprisingly defected from the conservative majority, voting with the liberals to uphold Washington State's minimum wage law. The significance of this ruling, which after all did not directly involve the New Deal whatsoever, was that less than a year earlier he had voted precisely the opposite way in a case striking down an almost identical law in New York. A month later, the Court upheld the collective bargaining protections of the National Labor Relations Act, also known as the Wagner Act, by the same 5–4 margin. This was followed in May by a trio of decisions upholding the pension and unemployment insurance provisions of the Social Security Act. After years of frustrating losses, suddenly the White House couldn't stop winning before the Supreme Court. Had the justices been intimidated by the court-packing plan into reversing course? That was certainly the popular narrative at the time. Roberts's sudden change of heart became known as "the switch in time that saved nine," a strategic retreat from the battlefield to protect the independence and institutional integrity of the Court. Nothing could have been further from the truth.

In fact, Roberts's thinking had begun to evolve long before the court-packing plan had been made public. At the *Parrish* oral arguments in December, the attorney representing the state had specifically advocated for the Court to reconsider its earlier precedent. And according to internal documents that have only recently been made public, both Roberts and Hughes appeared receptive to this argument when the justices discussed the case at their conference the same week. While the decision in *Parrish* was ultimately released shortly after Roosevelt's radio address, the outcome had been determined months earlier. Roberts provided his own version of events in a memorandum written shortly before his retirement in 1945, which he gave to his most trusted colleague on the bench, none other than Felix Frankfurter. "No action taken by the President in the interim," he wrote, "had any causal relation to my action in the Parrish case." Hughes also disputed the switch in time narrative in his autobiography, writing that the court-packing plan "had not the slightest effect on our decision."

In any event, the true story behind Roberts's evolving jurisprudence soon became a moot point, and FDR would no longer need to rely on his vote to sustain the New Deal. At the conclusion of the Court's 1937 term, Justice Van Devanter, at seventy-eight the oldest of the four horse-men, announced his retirement. The Alabama senator Hugo Black, an outspoken supporter of the New Deal, was swiftly confirmed as his replacement. Then, in January 1938, Justice Sutherland, sensing that the balance of power on the Court was shifting in a way that undermined his ability to influence it, also retired, to be replaced by Roosevelt's own solicitor general, Stanley Forman Reed. The four horsemen had now become two. Plagued by health problems, including a heart attack in late 1937 and a stroke in early 1938, Justice Cardozo finally succumbed to his illness and died that same month. And in searching for a suit-able candidate to replace only the second Jewish justice to serve on the highest court in the land, FDR would turn to his old friend Felix Frankfurter.

Originally tapped by the White House to put together a short list of possible nominees, Frankfurter was offered the job after the president found none of the proposed candidates to his satisfaction. The nomi-nation was not without controversy. Some of Roosevelt's own advisers counseled against the decision, concerned with the optics of nominat-ing another Jewish justice, so closely associated with the president, and born outside the United States. Also of concern were his earlier asso-ciations with communists and other political radicals. Possibly seek-ing to defuse these criticisms, Frankfurter agreed to testify personally before the Senate Judiciary Committee during their public hearings and answer the senators' questions, becoming the first Supreme Court nominee in U.S. history to do so. But in the end, Frankfurter's stellar credentials and impeccable legal record spoke for themselves. He was confirmed by a voice vote, becoming the seventy-eighth justice to sit on the U.S. Supreme Court. By the time Roosevelt died in 1945, less than three months into his fourth term as president, he had appointed eight new justices to the Court, remaking in his own image the institu-tion that had so frequently defied him. The lone justice who weathered the entirety of his administration was Owen Roberts, and he himself departed the bench later that same year. The legacy of the Roosevelt Court, however, would endure for decades to come.

The notion that Supreme Court justices often disappoint the presi-dents who nominate them has become a cliché at this point. But while Frankfurter certainly fulfilled the needs of the moment—providing a reliable vote for an expansive interpretation of the federal government's

Photograph of Justice Felix Frankfurter by Harris & Ewing, circa 1939.

regulatory authority—his later tenure on the bench proved far less sat-isfying to the heirs of FDR's progressive legacy. Frankfurter the advocate had been a firebrand, a passionate defender of civil liberties, meritoc-racy, and the rights of the downtrodden. But Frankfurter the justice was cautious and conservative, unwilling to use the power of the Court to champion those same causes.

He had come of age as an attorney during the *Lochner* era of the early twentieth century, observing firsthand how judicial activism could corrupt even the most well-meaning of jurists. Keenly aware that the allure of life tenure and virtually unrestricted judicial power could seduce justices into viewing themselves almost as gods—reaching down from their ivory tower to dispense justice and remake society in their own image—he took great pains never to be tempted down that path himself. It was a testament to the strength of these convictions that he found as much fault with the progressive activism of the Warren Court as he had with the laissez-faire economic paternalism of the conservative Courts of his youth. As the justices increasingly turned their attention to the causes of civil rights, religious freedom, criminal procedure, and eventually electoral fairness, Frankfurter found his influence waning. He was eclipsed by his fellow Roosevelt nominees Hugo Black and William O. Douglas, who, while cut from similar ideological cloth, lacked his aversion to flexing their judicial muscles.

For a man who had aspired to nothing more than a seat on the highest court in the land, Frankfurter's years on the bench were among the unhappiest of his life. His diaries from the 1940s portray a troubling descent into darkness, expressing bitterness toward his peers and frustration with his inability to shape the direction of the Court's rulings. He had become, in the words of his biographer Joseph Lash, "uncoupled from the locomotive of history," an anachronism amid an institution that was steaming ahead toward a new frontier in American legal thought. But history has a habit of repeating itself, and when a case involving a challenge to the drawing of congressional districts reached the Court in 1946, the opinion he authored might as easily have carried a majority of the justices in 2019.

Illinois had a malapportionment problem. The state had not redrawn its congressional districts since 1901, and in the intervening years significant population disparities had developed between the most and the least populous seats. In 1901, the House map had still been malapportioned, although to a far lesser extent. The largest district, which had 184,000 residents, was around 16 percent larger than the smallest one, which had 159,000. By 1946, this population discrepancy had ballooned to more than 700 percent, with the largest district, including significant parts of the city of Chicago and its suburbs, now containing 914,000 residents, and the smallest, a rural district in the southern part of the state, only 112,000. The state legislature's unwillingness to conduct redistricting during the intervening years was itself a product of malapportionment. Representatives from rural areas did not wish to cede political power to the city of Chicago, whose population had doubled between the 1900 and the 1940 censuses. Stop me when this sounds familiar.

Kenneth W. Colegrove was a political science professor at Northwestern University and resident of Evanston, Illinois, part of the Seventh Congressional District, that of the 914,000 inhabitants. He filed a lawsuit, along with two other voters, against the Republican governor, Dwight Green, who as the U.S. Attorney for the Northern District of Illinois had been a member of the government team that had prosecuted Al Capone for tax evasion in 1931. The suit alleged that the failure to fairly redraw the seats based on population violated the equal protection clause of the Fourteenth Amendment to the Constitution, essentially diluting the effectiveness of their votes compared with those of citizens from less populous districts.

There was little precedent at the time for such a challenge. The district court immediately dismissed the lawsuit, finding nothing in federal law that mandated either compactness or population equality in congressional districting. When the dispute reached the Supreme Court, it was decided by only seven justices. Chief Justice Harlan Fiske Stone had died between oral argument and the issuing of opinions, and Justice Robert Jackson was absent from the bench on leave to serve as the chief prosecutor at the Nuremberg Trials. Six of the seven justices who ruled on the challenge had been appointed by FDR, and they split 3–3 on the question of whether it was appropriate for a federal court to entertain it.

The decisive vote against Colegrove was cast by Harold Hitz Burton, a Truman appointee, in a 4–3 ruling that the case presented a nonjusticiable political question. Assignment of the writing of opinions on the Supreme Court is dictated by seniority, and while Stanley Forman Reed was the senior justice in the majority coalition, the opinion went to Frankfurter. It was probably the most famous piece of writing he produced during his tenure on the Court. But in a testament to his continuing inability to forge coalitions among his peers, only two other justices, Burton and Reed, would sign their names to it. Wiley Blount Rutledge wrote his own separate concurring opinion, and despite concluding that the Court should "decline to exercise its jurisdiction" in the case at hand, he was not prepared to join Frankfurter in closing the courthouse door entirely. Frankfurter's opinion is best remembered for his invocation of the metaphor of the political thicket, the notion that entertaining disputes over legislative districting would entangle the Court in a morass of partisan bickering over what was fair and unfair in the context of electoral rules and regulations.

If the more than seven-to-one population discrepancy in Illinois's congressional districts—the most severe in the nation at the federal level as of 1946—wasn't bad enough, things were looking far worse at the state legislative level. Tennessee, like Illinois, had not conducted redistricting since 1901. This despite a provision in the state constitution that mandated a reapportionment of its general assembly districts every ten years. One might wonder how the legislature could get away with flagrantly violating the state constitution over a period of almost half a century. The answer is that the Tennessee Supreme Court was apparently also asleep at the switch. An earlier state court challenge seeking to compel the assembly to act had been denied by that court in 1952. And, finding adequate and independent legal grounds in state law for the decision, the Supreme Court had declined to intervene on appeal.

Enter Charles Baker, a Republican voter in Shelby County, Tennessee, and former mayor of the city of Millington, a suburb of Memphis. Bluff City's population had grown fourfold since the last redistricting in 1901, and its politicians, including Baker, had grown frustrated with their lack of adequate representation in Nashville. The population disparities in the assembly districts should be a familiar theme at this point. The largest house district had more than five times as many residents as the smallest, while in the senate things were even more out of whack, with an eighteen-to-one population ratio between the most and the least populous. In the early 1960s, Baker filed a lawsuit against Secretary of State Joe C. Carr, seeking to force the state to redraw its district boundaries. After the lower court dismissed the case based on the *Colegrove* precedent, it would be heard before a very different slate of Supreme Court justices from the one that had been present for that earlier ruling.

Of the four justices who had voted with the majority in the Illinois lawsuit, only Frankfurter remained. And if his dissent in *Baker* is anything to judge by, he had not grown more mellow with age. Black and Douglas rounded out the trio of Roosevelt appointees still warming the bench, and they had been joined by a plethora of Eisenhower nominees, including the potent liberal coalition-building duo of Earl Warren and William Brennan. Also new to the Court were the pragmatic centrist Potter Stewart, the vacillating centrist Charles Evans Whittaker, the evolving centrist Tom Clark, and the Frankfurter-clone John Marshall Harlan.

If anyone in U.S. history had ever been born and raised to one day sit on the Supreme Court, it is undoubtedly John Marshall Harlan II. His grandfather John Marshall Harlan I had also been a Supreme Court justice—earning the nickname the Great Dissenter for his frequent jeremiads against the Court's restrictive civil liberties rulings of the late nineteenth century. Both justices Harlan had in turn been named for the great chief justice John Marshall, the Federalist champion who outmaneuvered Jefferson and Madison in the famous *Marbury v. Madison* ruling. It really was Marshalls all the way down.

All of which is to say that the outcome of the *Baker* decision was still very much up in the air when the Court heard oral arguments in April 1961. Few cases have divided the justices as significantly as the challenge to Tennessee's legislative districts. With no clear majority emerging either way following the initial conference discussion, the case was held over for reargument in October. After agonizing for months over the dispute, Justice Whittaker suffered a nervous breakdown and had to take a leave of absence from the Court, dealing a further blow to Frankfurter's attempts to cobble together a majority for his position. In the end, it would be Brennan who emerged as the consensus builder, herding the proverbial cats in the direction of a 6–2 majority that, while opening the door to subsequent equal protection challenges to the malapportionment of legislative districts, still failed to provide the Volunteer State's voters with the relief they so craved.

With only four votes on the side of striking down the Tennessee districts as unconstitutional, Brennan brilliantly outmaneuvered Frankfurter by crafting a ruling that he sold to Stewart and Clark as a narrow, fact-specific determination. In reality, though, it would end up carrying enormous weight as precedent. Sensing that a baby step in the direction of equality would be sufficient to open the floodgates, Brennan assembled six votes for his majority opinion. "The District Court misinterpreted *Colegrove v. Green* and other decisions of this Court on which it relied," he concluded, before proceeding to reformulate the Court's confusing political question doctrine. He identified six different categories of disputes that are unsuitable for judicial resolution. One of these, "a lack of judicially discoverable and manageable standards for resolving it," would go on to be hugely relevant to the Court's later partisan gerrymandering cases. More on that in later chapters. None of the six, he argued, preclude the Court from intervening to address issues of legislative malapportionment. But rather than reaching the merits of Baker's claims, he remanded the case back to the lower court for a new trial.

Frankfurter was apoplectic. He wrote a blistering dissent, joined only by Harlan, in which he railed against the majority's "massive repudiation of the experience of our whole past in asserting destructively novel judicial power." "It is as devoid of reality as 'a brooding omnipresence in the sky,'" he continued, "a disheartening preview of the mathematical quagmire . . . into which this Court today catapults the lower courts of the country without so much as adumbrating the basis for a legal calculus as a means of extrication." Waxing poetic about the majority's abrogation of what he grandiosely refers to as the "*Colegrove* doctrine," he accuses his opponents of rewriting the Constitution with their "circular talk." And at the conclusion of a pages-long discussion of the history of common-law theories of political representation, he even laments that "their reasoning does not bear analysis."

A large section of Frankfurter's opinion is devoted to the curious argument that because the problem of malapportionment in state legislatures is so pervasive and severe, far worse even than Tennessee in numerous other parts of the country, this should further caution the courts against offering relief. His lack of foresight in *Baker* regarding the direction of the nation, and the Court's jurisprudence, is breathtaking to behold. "Surely a Federal District Court could not itself remap the State," he exclaims incredulously, yet his brethren had come within a single vote of doing precisely that in the case at hand. Had Tom Clark, who switched sides at the last minute to join Brennan's majority, seen the light earlier in the deliberations, it almost surely would have happened.

Clark's concurrence sums up the degree to which Frankfurter's intransigence, which ironically might have been a welcome voice of reason on the pre–New Deal courts that he so despised, now served to alienate his brethren. "One dissenting opinion," Clark writes, in a not-so-subtle dig at his senior colleague reminiscent of Jefferson's descriptions of Patrick Henry, is "bursting with words that go through so much and conclude with so little." He then succinctly sums up the gravamen of the issue before the Court: "Tennessee's apportionment is a crazy quilt without rational basis."

Baker was the nadir of Frankfurter's twenty-three years of service on the nation's highest court. Embittered, cantankerous, and resentful of a world that had long since passed him by, he began to experience failing health soon thereafter. Less than a month after the decision was handed down, Frankfurter suffered a mild stroke while sitting at his desk on

Capitol Hill. A few days later, a second more severe stroke left him partially paralyzed on his left side. His mind still sharp, he hoped to return to the bench when the justices reconvened that October, but on the advice of his doctors he retired from the Court in late August. "I need hardly tell you, Mr. President," he lamented to John F. Kennedy in his retirement letter, "of the reluctance with which I leave the institution whose concerns have been the absorbing interest of my life."

With his departure, the locomotive of history, now firmly set on the track of redressing unfairness in districting, began to significantly pick up steam. The incoming justice, Arthur Goldberg, fell squarely into the Brennan/Warren jurisprudential camp, tipping the balance still further in the direction of political equality. And less than a year later, in an 8–1 ruling from which only Harlan dissented, the contours of the reapportionment revolution began to take shape. The case was *Gray v. Sanders,* and at issue was the county unit system used by the State of Georgia to determine the winners of its statewide primary elections. Fulton County, home to Atlanta, received only 1 percent of the unit vote, despite containing more than 14 percent of the state's population, a ten-to-one vote-power discrepancy compared with more rural counties. "The conception of political equality from the Declaration of Independence, to Lincoln's Gettysburg Address, to the Fifteenth, Seventeenth, and Nineteenth Amendments can mean only one thing," wrote William O. Douglas for the majority, before entering for the first time into the Supreme Court lexicon an immortal phrase: "one person, one vote."

Nineteen sixty-four proved to be a banner year for the Court. Freed from the confines of Frankfurter's philosophy of judicial restraint, the justices intervened to order a new trial for a state criminal defendant who had been denied access to an attorney during his police interrogation. This was merely the beginning of a dramatic expansion of the rights of the accused that would fundamentally transform the criminal justice system in the United States. In another case, the justices ruled for *The New York Times* in overturning a libel judgment from a state court in Alabama, expanding the rights of the fourth estate to criticize public officials without fear of legal reprisal. But nowhere were the effects of the Court's emerging liberal jurisprudence more acutely felt than in redistricting. Buoyed by their success in *Baker,* advocates of "one person, one vote" brought a parade of new appeals before the justices, challenging the malapportionment of U.S. House of Representatives districts in Georgia and state legislative districts in Alabama, Colorado, Delaware, Maryland, New York, and Virginia.

The Georgia case, *Wesberry v. Sanders,* presented an almost identical question to *Colegrove.* The state's Fifth Congressional District in the metro-Atlanta area had more than 820,000 inhabitants, while the Ninth District had fewer than 275,000. Their boundaries had not been redrawn since 1931. In February 1964, the Court finally delivered the hammer blow. Writing for a 6–3 majority, Hugo Black grounded his arguments striking down the Georgia districts in the constitutional mandate that members of the House be elected "by the people." Neatly sidestepping *Colegrove* without explicitly overruling it, he took pains to acknowledge Frankfurter's argument that Article I of the Constitution gives Congress sole authority to remedy issues in congressional districting. Nevertheless, he emphasized that "we made it clear in *Baker* that nothing in the language of that article gives support to a construction that would immunize state congressional apportionment laws which debase a citizen's right to vote from the power of courts."

Black's holding, an early forerunner of the originalist arguments that have come to dominate conservative legal thought in the twenty-first century, boils down to the claim that "construed in its historical context, the command of Art. I, § 2 that Representatives be chosen 'by the People of the several States' means that, as nearly as is practicable, one man's vote in a congressional election is to be worth as much as another's." This fairly torturous piece of revisionist history, which Harlan demolishes in his surprisingly well-reasoned dissent—after all, as we've seen, the Framers were no strangers to staggering electoral inequality—was made necessary by the fact that the equal protection clause, which would seem to be the more natural vehicle for imposing such a mandate, by its own terms applies only to the states. The Court eventually found a way around this problem through a doctrine known as reverse incorporation, but that jurisprudential loophole was not well established at this juncture. Black does not even address the equal protection argument in his opinion, relegating it to a dismissive footnote. He does, however, conclude with one of the most eloquent defenses of equal access to the franchise in the history of the judicial branch: "No right is more precious in a free country than that of having a voice in the election of those who make the laws under which, as good citizens, we must live. Other rights, even the most basic, are illusory if the right to vote is undermined."

All that remained after *Wesberry* was to extend the Court's holding to cover state legislative districts. These, after all, were the source of the most severe malapportionment problems that had plagued the nation for decades. That opportunity came four months later. In June, the justices handed down their rulings in a series of consolidated appeals, headlined by *Reynolds v. Sims,* a challenge to Alabama's apportionment of its state senate districts. This time the equal protection arguments were front and center, and writing for an 8–1 majority, Chief Justice Earl Warren left no doubt about what the Constitution required.

Alabama law mandated that its state senate districts be apportioned in a manner similar to that of the U.S. Senate, with each of the state's sixty-seven counties receiving one seat. This had created a situation whereby Jefferson County, home to Birmingham and the most populous in the state, had forty-one times as many eligible voters as the least populous. On the house side, the districts had not been redrawn since 1903, despite a state constitutional provision stipulating that redistricting occur every ten years. This eventually produced a sixteen-to-one discrepancy between the largest and the smallest districts. "The Equal Protection Clause demands no less than substantially equal state legislative representation for all citizens," Warren wrote, concluding that "the seats in both houses of a bicameral state legislature must be apportioned on a population basis." And with the stroke of a pen, the constitutional mandate of "one person, one vote" was applied to every state legislative chamber in the United States.

The *Reynolds* decision sparked an immediate backlash from advocates of states' rights. "While many persons were aroused and angry with the First and Second rulings," wrote Congressman Udall in his report, referencing *Baker* and *Wesberry,* "it was the Third group of cases which really touched off the storm." But while it took the remainder of the decade for the more intransigent state legislatures to be brought kicking and screaming into the Court's new reality, its legacy remains the most enduring of all of the transformations to the legal and political system that the Warren Court perpetuated. While later conservative Courts backtracked significantly on the other cornerstone of the Warren era, the expanded protections given to those caught within the crosshairs of the criminal justice system, the requirement of "one person, one vote" has only been strengthened in the decades since *Reynolds*.

In the 1968 case of *Avery v. Midland County*, the Court extended it to cover city council districts. And today there is nary a legislative body in the country, except of course the U.S. Senate, whose districts are not required to be apportioned on the basis of population. Within a few short years, and over the vigorous protestations of both Frankfurter and Harlan, the reapportionment revolution had been completed.

The Court had now solved the most pernicious and pervasive evil in the nation's electoral system: the widespread malapportionment of its legislative districts. But in fixing one problem, the justices had also opened the door to a different one. By requiring every state to redraw its electoral map every decade after each census, the temptation for politicians to allow partisan considerations to dictate the redistricting process would prove too alluring to resist. Frankfurter had been right about one thing: the reapportionment revolution did indeed lead the Court inexorably into the political thicket, and once within its tangled clutches, there could be no escaping.

After Earl Warren's retirement as chief justice in 1969, the justices continued to build on the foundations of the "one person, one vote" rulings. The more conservative Burger Court showed no less willingness toward involvement in this area than the liberal Warren Court, effectively establishing the federal judiciary as a super-legislative review body for the electoral practices of federal, state, and local government. It was during the final years of the Burger Court—a period during which, in spite of Frankfurter's warning decades earlier, the justices proved themselves, in the words of the legal scholar Lee Epstein, "willing to weigh in on virtually any aspect of election law, with often dramatic consequences"—that the Court began to lay the groundwork for its partisan gerrymandering jurisprudence. Then, as later, the issue was one that caused deep divisions among its membership. But before we consider those cases, there's another chapter in the sordid history of the gerrymander that demands attention. It concerns that most divisive issue in American government and society, the question of race.

6

Echoes of Slavery

The 1960s produced not only the reapportionment revolution in American elections but another revolution as well, one that would fundamentally transform its governing institutions and society at large: the civil rights movement. Nine years after Rosa Parks refused to give up her seat in the "colored section" of a Montgomery city bus to a white patron, and after a long campaign of protests, lawsuits, and political

"Echoes of Slavery," part of a photography series by Curtis Graves.

advocacy, often met with violent resistance, President Lyndon Johnson signed into law the Civil Rights Act of 1964. The Jim Crow institutions of disenfranchisement and racial segregation that had sprung into existence after the Compromise of 1877 were finally dismantled. This period in U.S. history, from the end of World War II through the late 1960s, has been termed "America's Second Reconstruction" by the Pulitzer Prize–winning historian C. Vann Woodward. The implication could not have been clearer. After failing for a century to follow through on the promise of delivering civil rights and liberties to all its citizens, the nation was now getting a do-over.

But there was a new menace looming on the horizon. Now under a constitutional mandate to conduct redistricting every decade, racist state legislators began to realize that the gerrymander presented them with a unique opportunity to reestablish barriers to African American voter participation. Fearful that an influx of black politicians would precipitate a takeover of their state governments, upsetting the delicate political order that had kept those communities on the sidelines and preserved their own privilege, these legislators set to work crafting districts that made it next to impossible for African American candidates to successfully compete.

Many of the tools they utilized were virtually identical to the gerrymandering strategies discussed in chapter 3. The logic of racial vote dilution, as the practice of using gerrymandering to deny minority groups a voice in government is often termed, proceeds from the same initial starting point as partisan gerrymandering. Exactly as the votes of a disfavored political party may be minimized, or canceled out, by cracking their supporters into districts where they are outnumbered, so too may a sufficiently large and geographically concentrated racial minority group be denied an opportunity to elect representatives of their choice by dividing their members among a series of districts where they are outnumbered by the white majority. A second method, known as submerging, utilizes at-large or multimember districting systems to, as the name suggests, drown out the votes of a minority group by immersing them in a sea of surrounding white communities, who vote in sufficient numbers to control all of the seats within the jurisdiction. Two related phenomena combine to make these strategies particularly effective in the arena of racial gerrymandering: residential segregation and racially polarized voting.

Residential segregation refers to the physical separation of individuals of different races into separate and distinct neighborhoods. It can occur because of deliberate government policy, through exclusionary zoning restrictions, redlining, and segregated public housing. It can also stem from private action, such as realtors engaging in racial steering, or by the aggregation of individual discriminatory decisions by landlords, homeowners, and lenders about whom to rent, sell, or lend money to. These factors combine and magnify one another over time, creating a situation where racial minority groups tend to be concentrated in certain neighborhoods, while white Americans tend to be concentrated in others. Take a drive around any major city in the nation, and it's hard not to observe this phenomenon firsthand. Residential segregation makes minority communities an easy target for gerrymandering, because they can be more efficiently identified, isolated, and then carved up to dilute their votes.

Racially polarized voting is the tendency of voters from different racial or ethnic groups to support different candidates for elective office. An article in *The University of Chicago Law Review* specifies two conditions that must be met for racially polarized voting to exist: "(1) the political preferences of majority-race and minority-race voters diverge substantially; and (2) the racial majority votes with enough cohesion to usually defeat the minority's candidates of choice." It must be noted that the existence of racially polarized voting does not necessarily require or even imply that there is widespread racism. When minority voters are outnumbered, and tend to vote for different candidates from the white majority, it has the effect of making it almost impossible for those candidates to win. But where racial animus on the part of the white population is present, the effects become even more severe.

The essence of vote dilution, in the words of the Supreme Court justice William Brennan, "is that a certain electoral law, practice, or structure interacts with social and historical conditions to cause an inequality in the opportunities enjoyed by black and white voters to elect their preferred representatives." And crucially, as the sociologist Chandler Davidson notes, it "can operate even where there are no barriers to casting a ballot, and when the group's candidates can run for office without hindrance." This made it particularly attractive to those state legislatures whose Jim Crow–era discrimination practices had now been outlawed. And while numerous, generally southern states would embrace this new tool of minority disenfranchisement, nowhere was racial gerrymandering more pervasive than in Texas.

The Lone Star State had not elected an African American to its legislature since the nineteenth century, but that did not discourage Curtis Graves. The twenty-seven-year-old Texas Southern University graduate—whose great-grandparents on his mother's side had both been the children of black slaves and white slave masters on the Evergreen Plantation in St. John the Baptist Parish, Louisiana—was ready to make his mark on the city that had become his adopted home. The Houston of the late 1950s, when Graves had arrived on the TSU campus in his blue 1951 Mercury, was one of transition. A booming oil and natural gas industry had seen the city's population grow by almost 60 percent over the previous decade, but the economic windfall was felt almost exclusively by its white residents. Houston's lunch counters, hotels, public transportation, department stores, and drinking fountains were all still segregated along racial lines. *Brown v. Board of Education,* the Supreme Court case that ordered the desegregation of the nation's public schools, had been decided only five years prior.

The university where Graves enrolled in the fall of 1959 was itself a product of civil rights litigation. In 1946, Heman Marion Sweatt, an African American school principal from Beaumont, had applied to the University of Texas Law School in Austin but was denied admission on account of his race. With the assistance of Thurgood Marshall and the NAACP, Sweatt filed a lawsuit against the school's president, Theophilus Painter, in Texas state court. In an effort to moot the litigation, which they feared might lead to a court order requiring the state to desegregate all of its institutions of higher learning, the legislature passed a bill establishing the Texas State University for Negroes in Houston, which was renamed Texas Southern University in 1951. Unsatisfied with the prospect of studying law at what was, at the time, an obviously inferior institution, Sweatt took his case all the way to the Supreme Court. In 1950, the justices ruled unanimously that the equal protection clause required his admission to the University of Texas. Curtis Graves wanted nothing more than to follow in Sweatt's footsteps as a civil rights pioneer, and like Sweatt he would lend his name to a lawsuit that eventually found its way before the nation's highest court.

Graves was born in New Orleans in 1938, the son of Fagellio "Buddy" Graves, who along with his uncle Butsy was the first African American to own an Esso gas station in the state of Louisiana. His upbringing was a study in contrasts. His father was actively involved in the NAACP and the cause of civil rights ("Thurgood Marshall slept in my bed while I slept on the couch—that's a fact!" he told *Texas Monthly* in 2015), but the family also took pains to shield young Curtis from the harsh realities of segregation and racism in the Jim Crow South. The same article recounts stories from his childhood of his mother, Mabel, engaging in subterfuge to conceal the ugly underbelly of prejudice in the Big Easy. "She told her son that they sat in the back of the bus because it was cooler, or sat upstairs at the theater to see better, or avoided meals at department stores because the glasses weren't clean."

Initially majoring in math at Xavier University in New Orleans, he dropped out and enrolled at TSU after the dean of students, observing his C average during his first two years of study, suggested that he give manual labor a try instead. It was there that he became involved in the budding civil rights movement, making the acquaintance of Eldrewey Stearns, a law student and accomplished debater, and Earl Allen, a fellow undergraduate. The three began to organize sit-ins on campus and at local grocery stores, garnering the attention of the local news media. Houston's mayor, Lewis Cutrer, a segregationist who had run on a platform of stoking racial fears about a black takeover of the city government, attempted to pressure TSU's president, Sam Nabrit, into quashing the protests. But Nabrit, whose brother was an NAACP attorney who had been involved in a successful legal challenge to the state's white primary laws—which the Supreme Court struck down in the case of *Smith v. Allwright* in 1944—was unmoved. "Primarily, you're citizens of the United States," Graves recounts Nabrit telling a student assembly at the time. "Secondarily, you're students. So you have to do what you have to do."

Graves did what he had to do. He and his fellow students hatched a plan to disrupt a parade that had been planned in the city for the astronaut and Houston native Gordon Cooper. They hoped that their protest would provoke a reaction from the city government that would ignite a broader movement for desegregation and bring national attention to their cause. The plan worked, although not in the way that they anticipated. On the eve of the parade, which 300,000 Houstonians were expected to attend, community leaders brokered a deal with local business owners to desegregate the city. But there was one condition: it had to be kept on the down low. "What was finally decided was that they would desegregate restaurants and department stores and all the Houston transit authority in one day," recalled William Lawson, a local pastor who advised the protesters, "and none of the major media—the *Post*, the *Chronicle*, the television stations—would mention it." In contrast to the fire hoses and attack dogs that had greeted student demonstrators in Birmingham, Graves and his friends had desegregated Houston without violence or fanfare. The protest they had planned for the homecoming parade never happened. "Our signs were ready," he later lamented to a reporter. "I was at the coffee shop at the Y when Eldrewey came in and said a deal had been struck."

After graduating from TSU, Graves went to work as the manager of a local savings and loan association, and at that point a career in politics could not have been further from his mind. But after attending a party at Lyndon Johnson's ranch at the invitation of his boss, the community organizer Mack Hannah—among the guests were various political heavyweights, including Chief Justice Earl Warren—he decided to get involved in a friend's campaign for school board. Discovering that his friend shared a last name with an incumbent white board member, Joe Kelly Butler, Graves devised a strategy to capitalize on the at-large system that was in use for the election. "If we can craft our campaign so we never show up at a white rally," he advised his friend, "we never allow a picture of you to be in the papers, we never do anything in white Houston, and we only campaign in black churches, the white folks will think that you are Joe Kelly Butler, . . . and you'll win." And indeed he did, becoming only the second African American to sit on the Houston school board, after Hattie Mae White in 1958.

Buoyed by his success as a campaign manager, and inspired by a visit to the state capitol in Austin, Graves decided to run for the state legislature in 1966. His timing could not have been better. Earlier that year, based on the precedent set by the Supreme Court's decision in *Reynolds,* a federal court had ruled in the case of *Kilgarlin v. Martin* that the Texas House of Representatives and Senate districts must be redrawn on the basis of population. A second parallel lawsuit, filed by the west Texas oil millionaire and future president of the United States, George Herbert Walker Bush, resulted in a ruling that struck down the state's U.S. House of Representatives districts on the same grounds.

The new redistricting plan passed by the legislature increased the number of house seats allocated to Harris County, home of Houston, from twelve to nineteen, and the number of senate seats from one to four. Meanwhile, the previous at-large system was replaced with single-member districts for the senate, and three multimember districts for the house, which followed the same boundaries as the county's redrawn congressional seats. Commenting on the new plan, the court observed that "Negroes residing in the four metropolitan districts, like all other citizens of every other color, creed and nationality, have the opportunity to vote for more Representatives and Senators than before."

Graves was not the only minority candidate to seek to take advantage of this more fertile electoral environment. He was joined by Lauro Cruz, a thirty-three-year-old Mexican American precinct judge who also sought a house seat in a county that had not elected a Latino candidate since 1836. Also running was Barbara Jordan, a thirty-year-old attorney and fellow TSU graduate who had mounted two unsuccessful house campaigns in 1962 and 1964 and was now seeking a seat in the senate. All three ran as Democrats, at first blush a curious choice given the party's continuing support for Jim Crow in many parts of the South, but a necessity in their heavily Democratic districts. The Republican Party would not even bother fielding a candidate.

Of the three, Jordan had the name recognition and political connections and was expected to win comfortably. Graves and Cruz were unknown commodities and had to work for their respective nominations. Often campaigning together, driving around Houston in a black Volkswagen Beetle, they blanketed the district with signs and visited African American and Latino churches to encourage voter turnout. In his *Texas Monthly* interview, Graves recalls one incident where a white police officer observed him hopping a fence to attach a campaign sign to the underside of a billboard and began to admonish him. "Certainly, officer," he informed the cop, "I was just taking this down."

I interviewed Curtis Graves in April 2020 by telephone from his home in suburban Atlanta, where he retired in 2003 after a long career in the federal bureaucracy. He continues to work on his memoirs while moonlighting as a critically acclaimed fine art photographer. But these days the most famous member of the Graves family is his daughter, Gizelle Bryant, the reality TV star of Bravo's *Real Housewives of Potomac*. Now eighty-one years old, Graves speaks in a slow, assured bass tone, his memory still remarkably sharp as he reminisces on events from almost fifty years prior with uncanny clarity, regaling me with numerous stories from his days as a civil rights pioneer.

The 1966 election was the first to be contested since the passage of the Voting Rights Act a year earlier, and minority voters were energized. In the end, Graves, Cruz, and Jordan all won their contests handily, while in Massachusetts the Republican Edward Brooke became the first African American to be elected to the U.S. Senate since Reconstruction. Also victorious were two Houston-area candidates for the U.S. House of Representatives with whom Graves had struck up friendships during their time on the campaign trail, one a Democrat and the other a Republican. The Democrat, Bob Eckhardt, who would go on to serve for fourteen years in Congress, had been a crucial ally to Graves and Cruz when it came to courting the votes of liberal white Houstonians. "If we went to a Latino church, Lauro was the lead person," Graves explained to me. "If we went to a white church, it was Eckhardt, and if we were in the black church, it was my responsibility."

The Republican candidate whose acquaintance they made during the campaign was none other than the man whose lawsuit had resulted in the creation of the district he was now running in: George H. W. Bush. "George Herbert Walker and I became really good friends as a result of that first campaign," Graves recalled, "when he was running for Congress and I was running for the state house. We stayed in touch, even throughout his presidency." Graves also fielded a congratulatory phone call from another president, Lyndon Johnson, at the election night victory party after the Democratic primary. He later posed with Jordan in a photo for a *Time* magazine article headlined "Texas: A Quiet Change," in which they stood together beneath a sign that simply said "Victory." "Neither Democratic candidate campaigned exclusively on race," the article noted, "but concentrated instead on bread-and-butter issues that concern whites as much as Negroes in their working-class district. The result attested to a quiet change in the minds of many white Americans." The relationship between Graves and Jordan, however, soon found itself on the rocks.

Graves received slightly more than 50 percent of the vote in his pri-

mary, narrowly avoiding a runoff election against the second-place fin-
isher. This included a strong showing of between 25 and 40 percent in
his district's white precincts. Jordan won her race with 65 percent of
the vote and performed even better with white Houstonians, capturing
between 30 and 50 percent in those precincts. Cruz was forced into a
runoff after garnering only 47 percent of the vote in his contest, short of
the 50 percent threshold to be nominated outright. Despite the *Houston
Chronicle*'s endorsing his white opponent, he won it comfortably. With
all three running unopposed in the general election later that year, victory was assured. But it did not come without substantial cost.

Graves found himself the victim of a vicious campaign of racism,
threats, and harassment, during both his state legislative race and his
later bid for mayor. "People would call and say they would castrate my
children," he told me. "I'd get death threats through the mail. Some-
body called one night and said, 'Is this Curtis Graves, the nigger?' and
I said, 'Yes, it is,' and he said, 'Nigger, you're gonna die in ten minutes.'
And what do you do then? Do you pick up your children and your wife
and run in the backyard because you think that there's a bomb somewhere? It was a tough time." Unable to count on the protection of the
Houston Police Department, whose chief he describes as "to the right of
Attila the Hun," Graves had to take his own measures to guarantee his
security during the campaign. "There were two or three guys who had
volunteered to protect me, 24/7," he remembered. "They did not allow
me to drive myself anywhere, and they were all armed. If it weren't for
them, I don't know if I'd have made it through that."

The political careers of Graves and Jordan, who entered the Texas
statehouse at the same time in January 1967, could not have been more
different. Jordan was a conciliator and consensus builder, steering clear
of controversy while diligently building relationships with colleagues
and cultivating political influence. But Graves's brazenness and confron-
tational style that had served him so well as an activist were ill-suited to
the day-to-day grind of policy making in Austin, and he quickly alienated the powers that be. "If I said I was in favor of a bill, it wouldn't
pass," he later reflected, and he largely failed to move the needle on any
of the grandiose proposals that had fueled his primary campaign.

On one memorable occasion, decked out in the spotless white suit he
often wore around the statehouse, Graves pulled a pistol on the floor of
the house during a debate on gun control and fired off a few blanks to

Curtis Graves addressing the Texas House of Representatives, 1971.

better emphasize his point. On another, he climbed on top of the press table to gain a better vantage point from which to shout questions at the Speaker. Perhaps his most notable achievement was a continuation of his earlier student activism. He led a successful campaign to desegregate the Austin Club, a popular dining hangout for members of the legislature. Though both Jordan and Graves were comfortably reelected in 1968 and 1970, and Jordan even endorsed Graves in his unsuccessful 1969 bid for mayor against the Republican incumbent, Louie Welch, their clash of personalities presaged the later deterioration of their relationship, with both harboring desires for higher political office. The same office, as it turned out.

The 1970 census marked the first time that Texas's legislative districts would be drawn afresh to comply with "one person, one vote," rather than under the aegis of litigation, as had happened in 1965. Jordan, who by this point was eyeing a bid for Congress, had been appointed by Lieutenant Governor Ben Barnes as vice-chair of the senate's redistricting committee, giving her significant influence in the drawing of the new boundaries. Graves, meanwhile, was on the outside looking in. Well aware that Houston would be gaining an additional seat in Congress, and that Jordan could use her clout to craft a district that would represent the city's African American community, one that she herself

Barbara Jordan presiding over the Texas Senate, 1972.

would be uniquely positioned to run in, Graves set his sights on her soon-to-be-vacated senate seat. But he had made many enemies during his tenure in Austin, and those chickens were about to come home to roost. "Curtis Graves wanted that seat," wrote the Houston-area representative Craig Washington. "Yet the power dynamics in the Senate would not allow that to happen; Lieutenant Governor Ben Barnes, the more conservative Senators, and the business lobby reportedly determined that they would never draw a district that Curtis could win."

The Legislative Redistricting Board redrew Jordan's Eleventh District so that it no longer contained a majority of African American voters. Graves, discouraged, resigned himself to the fact that he could never hope to compete for the seat. Jordan's exact role in this process is somewhat unclear, although Graves himself certainly believed that she had been part of the conspiracy. "She has sold us out," he told the press at the time, and even decades later he still appeared to harbor a grudge. "She put my house in the district that included River Oaks," he told *Texas Monthly.* "I called it 'the fickle finger district' because it had a little finger that went down and got my house. I was so pissed I didn't know what to do."

Other members of the legislature at the time defended Jordan, including Bob Eckhardt, who is quoted in her biography as saying, "It was not

Barbara's trade-off. Graves was rather flamboyant and they didn't want him." Shut out of the possibility of a senate bid, Graves decided to seek revenge by challenging Jordan in the Democratic primary for the newly created U.S. House of Representatives seat. "If there is a collision course between Mr. Graves and me, I shall not defer," she told the *Houston Chronicle.* "I shall not defer to him or anyone else if I think I can win."

In truth, Graves never really had a shot at this seat either. Jordan's connections to the Austin political establishment allowed her to raise five times as much money as he did during the campaign, and she earned the endorsements of the *Chronicle* and prominent local Democratic Party leaders. She appeared with Lyndon Johnson at a fundraiser, and a photograph of the two embracing ran across the pages of the local newspapers as Election Day approached. Desperate, Graves attempted to tie Jordan to the Sharpstown scandal, an insider-trading scheme that eventually ensnared the governor, Preston Smith, along with several members of the legislature. He vilified her in the press as the "Aunt Jemima of politics," but to no avail.

Jordan won the primary with 80 percent of the vote to Graves's 20 percent and went on to become the first African American woman to represent a southern state in Congress. Her career would hit even greater heights when she delivered the opening statement in the House Judiciary Committee hearings during the impeachment of President Richard Nixon, and she later became both the first African American and the first woman to deliver a keynote address at the Democratic National Convention. Graves, meanwhile, left both the house of representatives and the state of Texas in 1973, eventually settling in Washington, D.C., and embarking on a thirty-year career in the academic affairs division at NASA.

The job at NASA came with a little help from his old friend George H. W. Bush, now the director of the CIA. "When I was recruited by NASA, I had to fill out this big application form, and they asked for references," he told me. "And I thought to myself, well, George would be a good reference for me, so I called him and asked if he'd write a letter of recommendation for me. He said, 'No, I'll tell you what I'll do that's even better than that. I know [the NASA administrator] Dr. Fletcher. As soon as we're off the phone, I'll call him and tell him to hire you.'" But Graves still had one last major contribution to make in Texas before departing politics entirely. It came in the form of a federal racial gerrymandering lawsuit that he had filed in October 1971. In it, he mounted a constitutional challenge to the very redistricting plan that had denied him a seat in the state senate and a voice in that chamber for Houston's African American community.

The legal fight against racial gerrymandering had begun even before the Supreme Court's "one person, one vote" rulings made redistricting a fixture in the American political landscape, before the civil rights movement had broken down the Jim Crow–era restrictions on minority political participation. In 1957, the Alabama state legislature, at the behest of the white supremacist senator Sam Engelhardt, who was also the executive secretary of the White Citizens' Council, voted to redraw the boundaries of the city of Tuskegee. While whites were outnumbered four to one by blacks among the city's population, they had long maintained their stranglehold on political power through systemic disenfranchisement. But as more and more blacks were able to register to vote, and their numbers on the electoral rolls began to approach those of white voters, concern of a black takeover of city government prompted citizens to lobby the state legislature.

The resulting bill replaced the city's previously square boundary with what the Supreme Court later described as an "uncouth twenty-eight-sided figure" that excluded nearly every black community from the city limits. Of the four hundred registered African American voters who had once resided there, only four now remained. The new boundaries also removed the Tuskegee Institute, a historically black college founded by Booker T. Washington in 1881, that would later go on to become Tuskegee University.

A professor from the college, Charles G. Gomillion, acting with the support of the NAACP, filed a federal lawsuit alleging that the redrawing of the city boundaries violated the Fifteenth Amendment to the U.S. Constitution. This Reconstruction-era provision had purported to guarantee equal access to the franchise for all Americans regardless of their race. The failure of the federal government to properly enforce the amendment for almost a century, opening the door for the widespread disenfranchisement of African American voters, remains one of the most devastating civil rights failures in the nation's history.

But with the plethora of progressive justices who had been appointed

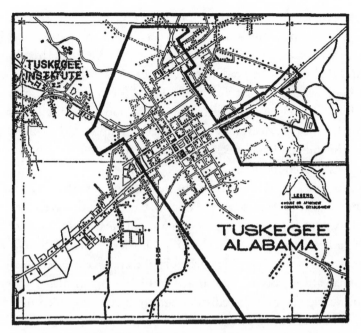

Map of the Tuskegee gerrymander, 1957.

by Presidents Roosevelt, Truman, and Eisenhower, the cause of civil rights now had a more sympathetic audience on the nation's highest court. "The [Fifteenth] Amendment nullifies sophisticated as well as simple-minded modes of discrimination," Felix Frankfurter had written in a 1939 case striking down Oklahoma's use of a grandfather clause—one that exempted whites from registration restrictions that were designed to make it harder for African Americans to vote—and he and his brethren were about to follow through on that promise. In 1960, they handed down their decision in *Gomillion v. Lightfoot* and in a unanimous ruling declared that the gerrymandering of the city's boundaries violated the Constitution.

Even Frankfurter found the allegations of racial discrimination in the case compelling enough to justify at least a minor detour into the political thicket. "Act 140 was not an ordinary geographic redistricting measure even within [the] familiar abuses of gerrymandering," he argued in his majority opinion. "If these allegations upon a trial remained uncontradicted or unqualified, the conclusion would be irresistible, tantamount for all practical purposes to a mathematical demonstration, that the legislation is solely concerned with segregating white and colored voters by fencing Negro citizens out of town so as to deprive them of their pre-existing municipal vote." On remand, the lower court permanently reinstated the original boundaries. Eleven years later, Johnny Ford, a thirty-year-old graduate of Alabama's racially segregated public school system, was elected as the first African American mayor of the city of Tuskegee. He defeated his white opponent, the incumbent mayor, Charles M. Keever, by only 124 votes. Ford would go on to serve eight nonconsecutive terms, totaling thirty-two years in office, before losing his reelection bid in 2016.

But precisely as doors seemed to be opening for African American candidates all over the South, the door to Curtis Graves's career in Texas politics was about to slam shut. His lawsuit, *Graves v. Barnes,* was heard before a three-judge panel of the U.S. District Court for the Western District of Texas in 1972. Even before the trial took place, his complaint had already become subsumed within the broader legal fight over the intricacies of the 1971 redistricting. Though he had filed the initial suit in Harris County, Graves's case was consolidated with three others that raised similar claims: a "one person, one vote" challenge to alleged population variances in the state house of representatives plan; a racial gerrymandering challenge to the use of multimember districts in Dallas County; and a similar cause of action in heavily Latino Bexar County, home to the city of San Antonio.

Graves fought hard against the consolidation. He petitioned the court to keep his case separate from the others, fearing that his claim might be eclipsed by the broader forces now at work. But his pleas were denied. "I preferred to have it separate, because to me it was a unique situation," he told me, "sometimes you get lost in the shuffle." And this early loss was merely a precursor of what was to come. After more than a decade of litigation, and following four rulings by the district court, one by the U.S. Court of Appeals for the Fifth Circuit, and two trips to the U.S. Supreme Court, Curtis Graves still had not received the relief that he so craved.

"We are once again in the Texas sector of the political thicket of legislative redistricting," began the ruling of the three-judge panel in *Graves I,* the opening salvo in the epic twelve-year legal saga that was about to play out, "and required to contour the condition of the individual trees as well as the physiography of the forest as we explore for 'crazy quilts,' 'groves,' contiguity, compactness, specie, motivation in planting, and other possible impedimenta to constitutionality in redistricting." And acknowledging the legal morass that had already been created by the Supreme Court's rulings during the reapportionment revolution, the court went on to lament that "in ten years of wandering about this political thicket, we have not yet found the burning bush of final explanation." But when they turned their attention to the alleged racial gerrymandering of the Eleventh District of the state senate, two of the three judges found insufficient evidence of racially discriminatory intent to justify ordering it redrawn and little legal merit in Curtis Graves's complaint. "Absent preponderating evidence," they concluded, "this Court can only conclude that the plaintiff in the Harris County case has failed to show that Harris County's single-member senatorial districts either operate or were designed to dilute the vote of that county's black minority."

In a majority opinion that ran for more than fifty pages, Graves's allegations were dismissed in four short paragraphs. Adding insult to injury, it was the testimony of his old nemesis, Barbara Jordan, that the court relied on in reaching this conclusion. "Indeed, State Senator Barbara Jordan, a Black," they wrote, somewhat condescendingly, "testified that she would not concede that she could not win from the new senatorial district because she believed that she could appeal to a broad base of the voters."

Only one of the three judges on the panel found any merit in Graves's complaint. The district judge William Wayne Justice, a Texas native who had been appointed to his position by President Lyndon Johnson, had not been fooled by the subterfuge that the Redistricting Board engaged in to conceal the intricacies of their gerrymander. Judge Justice was a jurist who more than lived up to his auspicious name, frequently standing up for the marginalized and the downtrodden in society, no matter the political cost. He drew the ire of segregationists in 1970 when he directed the Texas Education Agency to integrate its more than one thousand school districts, a sweeping order that impacted the lives of almost two million students. Later, he would further enrage the law and order crowd in ruling that the inhumane conditions in the state prison system constituted cruel and unusual punishment in violation of the Eighth Amendment to the Constitution. And now Justice smelled a rat in Austin. As it turned out, there had been bigger things at play than a mere attempt to deny the flamboyant and disruptive Graves a seat in the state senate. Both Graves and Jordan had been mere pawns in a larger game of political chess between the conservative and the liberal factions of the Texas Democratic Party. It was a game that Ben Barnes had been determined to win.

Ever since the passage of the Civil Rights Act in 1964, the Democratic Party had been at war with itself. "We have lost the South for a generation," Lyndon Johnson told an aide after signing the legislation into law. And while it took the Democrats more than a generation to finally lose the South for good, Johnson's embrace of the cause of civil rights drove the first cracks into the foundation of an electoral coalition that had held together since the New Deal. For generations, the party had relied on the votes of conservative southerners and liberal northerners to win elections at the national level, and with spectacular success. Between 1933 and 1973, Democrats enjoyed majorities in both the House of Representatives and the Senate for all but four years: two under Harry Truman, and two under Dwight Eisenhower. But in the 1968 presidential election, the Alabama governor George Wallace—a hard-core segregationist who had thrice sought the Democratic nomination for president, including against Lyndon Johnson in 1964—ran a third-party campaign under the banner of the American Independent Party. His slogan: "There's not a dime's worth of difference between the Republicans and Democrats."

Wallace's candidacy drove a wedge between the liberal and the conservative factions of the Democratic Party in the South. Conservatives loved his antibusing, law-and-order, blue-collar appeal, and he avoided overt discussions of race in favor of attacks on liberals, intellectuals, hippies, and pacifists. "If some anarchist lies down in front of my automobile," he told supporters at one campaign rally, "it will be the last automobile he will ever lie down in front of." When accused of harboring Nazi sympathies, he responded, "I was killing fascists when you punks were in diapers." In the election in November, Wallace performed alarmingly well, winning almost ten million votes in a three-way race with the Democratic nominee, Hubert Humphrey, and the Republican, Richard Nixon. He also captured the Electoral College votes of five states: Alabama, Arkansas, Georgia, Louisiana, and Mississippi. After maintaining their stranglehold on the "solid South" for almost a century, the Democrats won only one state of the former Confederacy in 1968. That state was Texas.

There's an old saying in Texas politics that the most powerful political office in the state is not that of the governor but that of the lieutenant governor. Elected separately rather than on a single ticket, the lieutenant governor serves as a member of not only the aforementioned Legislative Redistricting Board but also the Legislative Budget Board, as well as several other policy-making bodies. And most significantly, the LG serves as the president and presiding officer of the Texas Senate, controlling not only the agenda of the chamber but also

Ben Barnes (left) with campaign aide Dee Kelly, 1968.

the establishment of all standing and select committees, the appointment of their chairpersons and members, and the committee assignments for all pending legislation.

Ben Barnes, a card-carrying member of the conservative faction of the Texas Democratic Party, had been elected as the state's lieutenant governor in 1968. He was then able to use his authority in the senate to defeat numerous pieces of legislation favored by the party's liberal wing. According to the evidence presented at trial in *Graves I,* Barnes and the conservative Democrats in the senate saw in redistricting an opportunity to bolster their fragile majority. He was supported by the Texas Association of Taxpayers and the Houston Chamber of Commerce, who both lobbied heavily for the Harris County districts to be gerrymandered. "To accomplish this purpose," wrote Judge Justice, "the requisites of the situation demanded that liberal (black) voting precincts in the inner city be rearranged."

To comply with "one person, one vote," four state senate districts would need to be drawn in Harris County. "If conservatives were to succeed in electing conservative Democrats to the State Senate," testified Searcy Bracewell, a lobbyist who had been involved in the redistricting process, "it would be necessary, first, to devise two districts with a sufficient number of Democrats to defeat Republicans in the General Election; and, second, provide for a contingent of conservative voters in each district large enough to elect conservative candidates over liberal candidates in the Democratic Primary Elections." What he proposed was essentially a double gerrymander, one that rigged the results of the Democratic primaries in favor of conservative white Democrats while keeping the district as a whole sufficiently blue to prevent a Republican from triumphing in the general election.

It was a tough needle to thread, but that's precisely what the Redistricting Board did. Adopting almost without modification a map proposed by the Houston Chamber of Commerce, they redrew Harris County's senate districts to ensure that a conservative white Democrat, rather than a liberal African American Democrat like Curtis Graves, would be best positioned to win. And who was pulling the strings throughout this entire sordid saga? "The depositions of the members of the Legislative Redistricting Board indicate very clearly that Lieutenant Governor Barnes had effective control of the redistricting process." Judge Justice had seen enough. "I am of the opinion," he concluded his dissent, "that the evidence more than amply supports a conclusion that the Senate districts in Harris County designedly operate to dilute, minimize, and cancel out the voting strength of blacks."

Of considerably more interest to the other two judges on the panel than Graves's complaints about the senate plan, however, were the shocking racial disparities evidenced in the districting system that was put in place for the state house of representatives. It was this component of the case that would mire the judges in litigation for the remainder of the decade, long after *Graves I,* and indeed Graves himself, had been left in the rearview mirror. Under the house plan that was put in place by the Redistricting Board, Dallas County was consolidated into a single multimember district from which 1.3 million residents would elect 18 members of the state legislature. Meanwhile, in Bexar County, San Antonio's 830,000 inhabitants formed a similar district from which 11 representatives would be chosen. So effectively did this system sever the connection between members of the legislature and the communities they were supposed to represent that in the words of the court "it is entirely possible for each and every one of the district's eighteen representatives to reside in the same apartment complex."

That these two specific counties were singled out despite their clear wishes to the contrary, as expressed in polling evidence submitted to the Redistricting Board, was particularly suspicious to the court, given their large African American and Mexican American populations. Also telling was the clear evidence presented at trial that such consolidated districts frequently "operate to minimize or cancel out the voting strength of the minority." "While we are far from the Jeffersonian ideal or the modes of Grecian democracy," pondered the judges, in a brief detour into philosophical musing, "this voter anonymity, this contracting the voter to be a mere speck in a magnitudinous cosmos, takes us far from the founding fathers' concept of citizen participation." And, in concluding that both multimember districting arrangements violated the Fourteenth Amendment to the Constitution, the judges succinctly summed up the crux of the issue. "No political, racial or other interest group has any constitutional right to be successful in its political activities," they conceded. "However, a State may not design a system that deprives such groups of a reasonable chance to be successful."

On appeal, the nine justices of the U.S. Supreme Court agreed. "The District Court's order requiring disestablishment of the multi-member districts in Dallas and Bexar Counties was warranted," wrote Justice Byron White (more on him in chapter 9) for a unanimous Court, "in the light of the history of political discrimination against Negroes and Mexican-Americans residing, respectively, in those counties and the residual effects of such discrimination upon those groups." But things were far from over. In 1974, two years after their initial ruling in *Graves I,* the same three-judge panel reconvened to consider additional constitutional challenges to the use of multimember districts in nine other Texas counties.

"We have reviewed each county from a contemporary vista," they wrote in *Graves II,* unable to resist another philosophical detour, "while always remembering that our todays are the products of our yesterdays. Here as in many constitutional thickets it has been wisely said that a page of history is worth a volume of logic." Seven of the nine multimember districting systems, they concluded, also violated the Constitution. Two years later—after Gerald Ford's attorney general, Edward Levi, concluded based on his own authority under Section 5 of the Voting Rights Act that the Texas legislature's remedial plan still contained lingering discriminatory effects on the African American population of Tarrant County, home to the city of Fort Worth—the long-suffering panel of Judges Irving Loeb Goldberg, William Wayne Justice, and John H. Wood Jr. were back at it again.

In *Graves III*, they ruled that there was insufficient time to craft a solution before the 1976 election, punting on the issue for the time being and allowing an interim plan proposed by the state legislature to go into effect. Then, finally, in 1977, now six years and three elections removed from Curtis Graves's original lawsuit, the panel in *Graves IV* rejected the interim map and imposed a new set of districts for Tarrant County that had been proposed by the plaintiffs. Judge Wood, who had concurred in the Dallas and Bexar County rulings in *Graves I*, had by this point become thoroughly disillusioned with the direction the other two judges had taken as the case evolved. "Forewarned, but undaunted by our original judicial foray into the political jungle," he lamented, in a dissent reminiscent of Felix Frankfurter's a decade before, "the majority of this Court again sallies forth on another legislative reapportionment expedition. Contrary to my fellow travelers on the Panel, I do not find the scythe of the recent jurisprudence adequate to cleave a path through a myriad of thorny legal precepts. . . . The once simplistic course toward the goal of 'one man, one vote' now appears as elusive as the source of the Nile." It was a prescient preview of things to come at the Supreme Court.

The dissenting opinion in *Graves IV* turned out to be one of the final acts of John H. Wood Jr.'s tragically short career on the federal bench. On May 29, 1979, the sixty-three-year-old Nixon appointee, who had earned the nickname Maximum John for the harsh sentences he routinely handed out to federal drug offenders, was assassinated outside his San Antonio home, the victim of a single shot fired from a high-powered rifle. He was the first sitting federal judge to be murdered in the twentieth century. The gunman was a contract killer by the name of Charles Voyde Harrelson, the estranged father of the Hollywood actor Woody Harrelson. The hit had been put out by Jamiel "Jimmy" Chagra, a Lebanese American drug trafficker from El Paso who was scheduled to appear in Judge Wood's courtroom that very morning on charges of smuggling. After an extensive investigation by the FBI, Harrelson, his wife, Jo Ann, Jimmy Chagra, his wife, Elizabeth, and his brother Joe were all indicted by federal authorities over their role in the conspiracy. Harrelson died in prison in 2007 while serving two consecutive life sentences.

Now living in Washington, D.C., Curtis Graves had followed the case with interest, even though his own complaint no longer played a starring, or even supporting, role. Despite winning rulings in the litigation striking down the discriminatory multimember districts that were used to dilute the African American and Mexican American vote in numerous Texas counties, a landmark step in the broader fight against the pernicious harms of racial gerrymandering, he had lost the one that mattered to him the most: the challenge to the redistricting plan that shut him out of a run for the state senate. "It is what it is," he told me. "I thought the case should be filed and was glad that it went forward." And though the litigation had continued to bear his name all the way to the Supreme Court, the legal battle at play was no longer very much about Curtis Graves. The final ruling in the dispute, handed down by the Fifth Circuit Court of Appeals in 1983, concerned questions not of civil rights or racial gerrymandering but of how much the State of Texas would have to award in attorney's fees to the other side. At least the lawyers got paid.

In truth, the winds of jurisprudence had already begun to shift against Curtis Graves's cause even before his lawsuit had been filed. Richard Nixon's victory in the 1968 presidential election had been predicated, in part, on a promise to rein in the liberal excesses of the Warren Court. This appeal was framed most overtly in the area of the rights of criminal defendants, who Nixon believed were being coddled by the soft-on-crime liberals on the bench. But the coded language of the Southern Strategy, a concerted attempt to win over the conservative southern Democrats who had been abandoning the party in droves, also signaled a backlash against the cause of civil rights.

Nixon wasted no time following through on his promise after assuming office. He nominated Warren Burger to the vacant position of chief justice in 1969, followed by nominations at associate justice of Harry Blackmun in 1970 and Lewis Powell and William Rehnquist in 1971. That same year, the Court handed down a decision in the case of *Whitcomb v. Chavis,* in which they declined to strike down an alleged racial gerrymander of the Indiana state legislature. "Appellees' claim that the fact that the number of ghetto residents who were legislators was not proportionate to ghetto population proves invidious discrimination . . . is not valid," wrote Byron White for the 6–3 majority, in language that has certainly not stood the test of time, "and, on this record, the mal-proportion was due to the ghetto voters' choices' losing the election contests."

At the core of the judiciary's attempts to grapple with the issue of racial gerrymandering was the question of what burden of proof those alleging vote dilution should be required to meet. Specifically, could the effects of a given redistricting scheme alone be sufficient for conclud-ing that it was an unconstitutional racial gerrymander, or must those challenging the plan be required to demonstrate that those responsible acted with discriminatory intent when the districts were drawn? This distinction is not of mere academic concern. It strikes to the very core of whether disadvantaged minorities could rely on the courts to protect the constitutional right for their vote to count equally with those of the white majority. As the three-judge panel in *Graves I* had noted, "Racial motives are rarely stated openly nowadays."

In a 1964 case, *Wright v. Rockefeller,* the Court had placed this burden upon the state, rather than the plaintiff. They ruled that so long as the preponderance of the evidence was "equally, or more, persuasive that racial considerations had not motivated the State Legislature," the chal-lenged plan would be allowed to stand. Applying this precedent, lower courts invoked a balancing test. If a challenged redistricting scheme appeared to have a significant discriminatory effect upon a particular racial minority group, and the legislature could offer no plausible alter-native explanation for their actions that was at least as likely as a desire to dilute their votes, then the judge would conclude that the Constitu-tion had been violated. But as the 1980s approached, the Court was preparing to deliver another blow to the cause of minority voting rights. This time, however, a backlash from the public would produce a change of course.

The city of Mobile looms large and hulking on the horizon of Mobile Bay as you drive west on I-10, its smattering of skyscrapers framed by the container cranes of the only deep-water port in the state of Alabama. Right before reaching downtown, the highway plunges underground beneath the city into the cavernous George Wallace Tunnel, named for the aforementioned governor whose third-party presidential bid irreparably tore the southern Democrats asunder in the 1968 election. The last major city of the Confederacy to surrender to Union forces in the Civil War—three days after Robert E. Lee had laid down his own arms to Ulysses S. Grant at the Battle of Appomattox Courthouse—Mobile had been a colony of France, Britain, and Spain before joining the United States in 1813, part of the West Florida territory acquired by President James Madison.

More cosmopolitan and culturally diverse than its neighbors Birmingham and Montgomery, the city of Mobile was among the first in the state of Alabama to embrace desegregation. Its police force, public colleges, city buses, and lunch counters had all been voluntarily integrated by the end of the 1950s. Yet the city's public schools remained entirely racially segregated until 1964, a full decade after *Brown v. Board of Education* declared the practice unconstitutional. In 1963, a group of African American parents had filed a civil rights lawsuit against the school district, leading to the token admission of three black students to the previously all-white Murphy High School. But more effective remedies remained elusive. The case dragged on for more than twenty-five years, before finally being settled in 1988. It was not the only time that the city's racial politics triggered a protracted legal battle before the federal courts.

In 1911, the Alabama state legislature—pursuant to the recently ratified 1901 constitution—passed legislation permitting every large municipality in the state to form its own city commission for the purposes of home rule. These city commissions, presided over by a largely ceremonial mayor, exercised all legislative, executive, and administrative powers within their jurisdictions. As required under the law, the Mobile City Commission consisted of three commissioners serving four-year terms, each of whom was elected at large by the voters of the city as a whole. "This is the same basic electoral system," the Supreme Court later noted, "that is followed by literally thousands of municipalities and other local governmental units throughout the Nation."

Such methods had been used before for the purposes of gerrymandering. Recall, for example, the at-large and general ticket congressional elections that were popular in many states during the early nineteenth century. And just as those earlier systems had often allowed the majority party in the state to maintain control of all the available seats, the at-large method that was utilized for Mobile's City Commission elections operated to permanently entrench the city's white majority in power.

By 1970, more than a third of Mobile's 190,000 inhabitants were black. The minority population was also sufficiently concentrated geographically that it was "impossible to divide the city into three contiguous zones of equal population without having at least one predominantly black district." Still, no African American candidate had ever been elected to the city commission. Combined with the fact that "Mobile blacks were subjected to massive official and private racial discrimination"—namely, the poll taxes, literacy tests, and other assorted tools of systematic disenfranchisement that characterized Jim Crow–era Alabama—this had the effect of shutting the African American community out of the process of city governance entirely.

In 1976, with the assistance of the NAACP Legal Defense Fund, Wiley L. Bolden, a community activist who had spearheaded a campaign in the 1940s to persuade the state to allow African Americans to register and vote in the Democratic primary, filed a class-action lawsuit in federal court on behalf of all similarly situated black voters in the city of Mobile. The at-large system used for electing members of the city commission, he alleged, had the effect of diluting the voting strength of the black minority, in violation of the Fourteenth and Fifteenth Amendments to the Constitution.

By the time the case reached the Supreme Court in 1979, the four justices who had been elevated to the bench by Richard Nixon had been joined by another Republican appointee, John Paul Stevens, who was nominated by Gerald Ford in 1975 to replace the retiring William O. Douglas. And in a pair of cases decided in 1976 and 1977, it became abundantly clear how sympathetic an audience claims of racial discrimination would receive before the nation's highest court.

First, in *Washington v. Davis,* the justices by a 7–2 vote rejected a challenge to the hiring procedures used by the Washington, D.C., police department. These included a verbal skills component that was disproportionately failed by black applicants. Then, less than a year later in *Arlington Heights v. Metropolitan Housing Development Corp.,* a 5–3 majority concluded that a zoning ordinance in suburban Chicago that allowed for the construction of only single-family dwellings, pricing many of the city's African American residents out of the neighborhood, also did not violate the Constitution.

The logic of the decisions was the same. Even though the challenged policies had a racially disparate impact—in essence, they could be shown to disproportionately affect or disadvantage minorities compared with whites—this was perfectly legal absent clear and convincing evidence of discriminatory purpose or intent. The rulings effectively sounded the death knell for Bolden's class-action suit against the City of Mobile.

The Supreme Court held initial oral arguments in *Mobile v. Bolden* in March 1979. Joining the side of the civil rights attorneys representing the class-action plaintiffs were lawyers from the U.S. Department of Justice, including Deputy Assistant Attorney General James P. Turner, who represented the government at oral argument. Even with the combined might of the Justice Department and the NAACP in their corner, the plaintiffs immediately faced a skeptical audience from the nine justices on the high court. Representing the City of Mobile was Charles Rhyne, coincidentally the same attorney who had argued on behalf of Tennessee seventeen years earlier in *Baker v. Carr*. And after failing to reach a consensus during their post-argument deliberations, the Court scheduled a second set of hearings for later that same year.

There is a small but diligent cottage industry of political scientists and legal scholars who have built careers on analyzing the effect of events that occur during oral argument on the eventual outcome of Supreme Court cases. Among their findings: the attorney who is asked the most questions goes on to lose the case more often than not; the more the justices attempt to derail an advocate's focus on the core issues by bringing up threshold procedural questions, the greater the likelihood of an adverse ruling; and the more times the transcript indicates that laughter occurred in the courtroom during a lawyer's presentation—most often in response to a quip by one of the justices—the greater the probability that the side on the receiving end of that laughter is headed for defeat.

For those reading the tea leaves during the second round of oral arguments in *Mobile v. Bolden* in October 1979, the writing certainly must have appeared to be on the wall. Charles Rhyne delivers an opening monologue that runs for almost thirteen pages of the transcript before his first interruption for a question from the bench, and faces only fourteen questions in total. The unfortunate plaintiffs' attorney,

James Blacksher, makes it less than a page into his presentation before the circular firing squad of questioning begins. He is peppered by no fewer than sixty questions from the justices during his thirty minutes of advocacy. And while he performs admirably amid the barrage—the case notes of Justice Harry Blackmun, who rated the quality of the attorneys appearing before the Court on an 8-point scale, reveal that he graded Blacksher as a 6, the same rating assigned to Rhyne, and one better than the 5 he gave Turner, who managed to spit out only nine words before his first interruption for questioning—it appeared that the Court was finally ready to make up its mind.

On April 22, 1980, the justices released their decision, ruling 6–3 that "action by a State that is racially neutral on its face violates the Fifteenth Amendment only if motivated by a discriminatory purpose." The opinion was written by Justice Potter Stewart, by then the longest-serving member of the bench, having been nominated by President Dwight Eisenhower in 1958. Stewart had dissented in the landmark "one person, one vote" ruling in *Wesberry v. Sanders* in 1964. "Disproportionate effects alone are insufficient to establish a claim of unconstitutional racial vote dilution," he concluded. "Only if there is purposeful discrimination can there be a violation." Joining him in the majority were the four Nixon appointees, Rehnquist, Burger, Blackmun, and Powell, along with the Ford appointee, John Paul Stevens.

Only the three liberal justices dissented. All four of the "pragmatic" centrists, the swing votes on the Court at the time, sided with Mobile. "The American ideal of political equality, conceived in the earliest days of our colonial existence and fostered by the egalitarian language of the Declaration of Independence, could not forever tolerate the limitation of the right to vote to white propertied males," wrote Justice Thurgood Marshall, the first African American in the nation's history to sit on its highest court. "The Court's decision today is in a different spirit." But the story, it turns out, was not quite over, either for the class-action plaintiffs from Mobile or for the broader fight against discriminatory racial gerrymandering.

In their ruling, the justices remanded the case back to the lower court for further proceedings before the U.S. district judge Thomas Virgil Pittman. And before a new trial could even be held, a smoking gun emerged that proved the existence of discriminatory intent beyond any reasonable doubt. It came in the form of a 1909 letter to the Alabama legislature, during the debates over the home rule bill that had eventually passed in 1911. It was written by Mobile's former state senator, U.S. representative, and president of the Alabama Bar Association, Frederick G. Bromberg.

"In this letter to the Mobile legislative delegation," wrote Judge Pittman, "Mr. Bromberg was expressing support for a pending bill to amend the Alabama Constitution explicitly to outlaw black officeholding." And his support was not subtle, couched in racially coded language, or difficult to decipher. "Respectfully now recall to your mind that portion of my address," Bromberg mused, "which refers to the expediency of amending the state constitution so as to exclude negroes from holding elective offices in this state. We have always, as you know, falsely pretended that our main purpose was to exclude the ignorant vote, when, in fact, we were trying to exclude, not the ignorant vote, but the negro vote."

And lest there be any lingering traces of doubt regarding his intentions, coming as they did against the background of a series of lynchings that had occurred in Mobile between 1906 and 1909, Bromberg went on to hammer home the necessity of acting quickly. "The masses of the colored race are indifferent to the right to vote and still more indifferent to the right to hold office," he concluded. "By adopting remedial measures now we shall cause no discontent, because of the present apathy of our colored citizens." Case closed.

In April 1982, Judge Pittman issued his order, finding that the at-large system used to elect members of the Mobile City Commission unconstitutionally discriminated against its black residents, even under the stricter burden of proof now required by the Supreme Court. Rather than appeal the ruling, the city agreed to a settlement. In the next election, the commission would be replaced by a seven-member city council elected from single-member districts. In that election, held in 1985, three black candidates won their races, becoming the first African Americans to serve as elected representatives in Mobile since Reconstruction. Two decades later, Sam Jones, a U.S. Navy veteran who had served under the command of John McCain on the aircraft carrier USS *Forrestal,* was elected as the first African American mayor in Mobile's history.

The backlash against the Court's decision in *Mobile v. Bolden* was swift. "Justice Stewart's plurality opinion was subjected to perhaps the most vociferous protest of any Supreme Court civil rights opinion since *Brown*," wrote the historian J. Morgan Kousser in his book *Colorblind Injustice*. Criticism of the justices poured forth from the ACLU, the NAACP, and numerous other civil rights advocacy groups. *The Washington Post* described the ruling as a "major defeat for blacks and other minorities fighting electoral schemes that exclude them from office." *The New York Times* labeled it "the biggest step backward in civil rights to come from the Nixon Court." The legal community also pushed back, with the law professor Avi Soifer characterizing it as requiring an "overwhelming demonstration of the most blatant form of discriminatory motive, . . . proof far stronger than the standard of causation generally used in the common law, . . . proof akin to that required in a criminal context." The ACLU attorney Laughlin McDonald put it even more bluntly: "Nothing short of a body buried in a shallow grave will meet the *City of Mobile* test."

And on Capitol Hill, momentum began to build behind a push for congressional action to provide greater protection for the voting rights of minority citizens. The Voting Rights Act of 1965 had contained its own provisions attempting to outlaw racial gerrymandering and vote dilution, provisions that the Supreme Court had interpreted as being identical to those also found in the Fourteenth and Fifteenth Amendments to the Constitution. Certain sections of the act, most notably those requiring covered states to receive advance approval from either the Justice Department or the federal courts, known as preclearance, before making any changes to their election regulations, had been set to expire in 1970. Recognizing that more still needed to be done to combat the problem of racial discrimination in voting, Congress extended those provisions for another five years in 1970, and for an additional seven years in 1975. By the time the Court decided *Mobile v. Bolden* in 1980, the deadline for renewal was again approaching.

As debates over what form a new extension might take began to ramp up in the committees and subcommittees of the House and Senate, the NAACP organized an unprecedented lobbying campaign. Known as Operation Network, it deluged the offices of representatives and senators with phone calls, letters, and telegrams. Their message was a simple one. Merely renewing the existing provisions for an additional period of time was no longer sufficient. Congress must take proactive steps to amend the legislation to provide greater protection against vote dilution. The intent test that the Court had imposed in *Mobile v. Bolden* needed to be replaced with an effects test that made it easier for aggrieved parties to bring legal challenges.

After seven weeks of hearings in which more than a hundred witnesses testified, the vast majority in support of the NAACP's position, Congress finally relented. The legislation that emerged was, according to the report submitted by the Senate Judiciary Committee, "designed to restore the legal standard that governed discrimination cases prior to the Supreme Court's decision in Bolden." "The intent test focuses on the wrong question," the committee alleged, "and places an unacceptable burden upon plaintiffs in voting discrimination cases."

These 1982 amendments to the Voting Rights Act—which in addition to modifying the vote dilution test extended the legislation as a whole for another ten years—passed the House on a 389–24 vote and then the Senate by a similarly lopsided 85–8 margin. President Ronald Reagan, after initially opposing a new effects test, and then backtracking after the momentum against that position on the Hill became overwhelming, signed it into law on June 29, 1982.

The legislation was a stunning rebuke to the high court, effectively reversing their decision in *Mobile* only two years after it had been issued. It also unleashed a deluge of litigation against states' use of at-large elections, multimember districts, and other racial gerrymandering techniques that had the effect of reducing the strength of the minority vote. In the first of these cases to reach the Supreme Court, *Thornburg v. Gingles,* the justices ruled unanimously in 1986 that the multimember districting system used to elect members of the North Carolina General Assembly violated the newly amended Voting Rights Act.

Justice Brennan's majority opinion noted that, "from 1971 to 1982, there were, at any given time, only two-to-four blacks in the 120-member House of Representatives—that is, only 1.6% to 3.3% of House members were black. From 1975 to 1983, there were, at any one time, only one or two blacks in the 50-member State Senate—that is, only 2% to 4% of State Senators were black. By contrast, at the time of the District Court's opinion, blacks constituted about 22.4% of the total state population."

Under what became known as the "totality of circumstances test," whenever a redistricting plan diminishes the ability of a sufficiently large and geographically compact minority group to elect candidates of its choice, that plan must be invalidated. The results were dramatic. In 1970, there were only fifteen hundred black elected officials in the entire United States. By 1995, that number was more than eight thousand. The number of Hispanic and Latino elected officials doubled within a twenty-year period, from three thousand in 1984 to six thousand in 2014. The promise of the Voting Rights Act of 1965, and the Fifteenth Amendment a century before it, appeared to finally, albeit belatedly, be realized.

But right as the problem of racial gerrymandering appeared to have found its solution—although as chapter 11 discusses, there's more to that story as well—those bringing legal challenges to some of the most egregious partisan gerrymanders were about to receive a similar cold shoulder from the Supreme Court. On the same day that they released their decision in *Thornburg v. Gingles*, the justices also handed down another ruling, in a case involving a constitutional challenge to the gerrymandering of the Indiana state legislature. The confusing hodge-podge of opinions that resulted would lead the federal judiciary inexorably back into the tangled clutches of the political thicket. Three decades of litigation later, the nation was no closer to a solution to partisan gerrymandering by 2016 than it had been in 1986. And in the meantime, emboldened by the "one person, one vote" mandate that now required all fifty states to redraw their districts every ten years, the modern gerrymander began to slowly spread its wings.

7

A Blue Tide in the Golden State

Perhaps the greatest stumbling block to the effort to end gerrymandering in the United States is that opinion on the issue has become, like most other controversial topics in contemporary American political debate, intensely polarized along partisan lines. The simple fact is that since 2000, Republicans have done a much better job of using redistricting to boost their electoral fortunes than Democrats have, and quite dramatically so. As a result, active support for reform has come almost exclusively from politicians, interest groups, and rank-and-file voters who affiliate with Democrats and progressive causes while being met with virtually monolithic opposition from those on the right.

What should have been framed as a matter of democratic best practices, as a good government reform that protects the interests of all citizens, has instead become one more partisan political football, tossed around on the editorial pages of newspapers, cable news talk shows, and the discourse on social media. Republicans, many of whom still remember the experience of being under the jackboot of the Democratic gerrymanders of the 1970s and 1980s, are not about to surrender the power to do the same to their opponents, particularly so soon after finally being in a position to exercise it. After all, the Democrats did little to nothing to combat the harms of gerrymandering when they were the ones who were benefiting from it. Why should they be bailed out now that the jackboot is on the other foot?

Exhibit A in this narrative has, of course, been REDMAP. But the redistricting cycle following the 2000 census was similarly tilted in favor of Republican success stories. There are a couple of explanations for this trend, the first of which has been geographic. In the same way as the concentration of African American and Latino voters in certain neighborhoods made them an easy target for the racial gerrymanders of the 1970s, so too has the tendency of Democratic voters to cluster in urban areas, where their candidates run up huge majorities, made the task of cracking and packing them into neatly gerrymandered districts considerably more straightforward. Republicans, meanwhile, tend to be more dispersed across geographic space, with significant electoral strength in both suburban and rural areas, where they win by consistently smaller margins.

The second explanation has been political. Beginning in 1994, when Newt Gingrich and his "Contract with America" swept the GOP into power on Capitol Hill, Republicans have performed dramatically better in state legislative elections than they ever had before. With this growing influence over the working of state government has come the ability to control the redrawing of districts for state legislatures and the U.S. House of Representatives, after decades spent largely on the outside looking in.

Take 1984 as an example. Despite Ronald Reagan's landslide reelection in the presidential race that year, Republicans emerged with full control of only nine of the nation's statehouses, compared with twenty-seven for the Democrats. By 1994, that gap had narrowed to a twenty-to-seventeen edge for the Democrats. And in 2004, things finally flipped. Republicans now controlled twenty-one state legislatures; their opponents only seventeen. The continuing decline of Democratic hegemony in the South was a major driving force behind this development, but so too was the emerging Republican strength in swing states like Florida, Missouri, Michigan, Pennsylvania, and Ohio.

The party's appeal to working-class blue-collar voters in the Rust Belt, rural populations left behind by the effects of globalization, evangelical Christians, and middle-class suburban whites created a formidable coalition that consistently outpolled the Democrats' increasingly urban, educated, and minority constituency. They were not about to let the opportunity go to waste. The road map for the GOP's REDMAP-inspired gerrymandering successes of the 2010s had already been laid by a previous generation of Democratic line drawers. And for arguably the first example of the quintessentially modern gerrymander, we need look no further than the state of California.

No one was better acquainted with how the Democrats had behaved when they had been allowed to control redistricting than Thomas Hofeller. Hofeller was born in San Diego in 1943 and operated for more than four decades as the GOP's gerrymandering guru. He traveled around the country assisting Republican state legislators, first in their efforts to resist Democratic designs on gerrymandering and then later in the GOP's attempts to craft their own. "Tom was the father of Republican map-drawing, and also its grandfather, great-grandfather and great-great-grandfather," opined the Republican election law attorney Ben Ginsberg, a contemporary of Hofeller's during his time at the Republican National Committee. "He understood both the art and science of [redistricting] like no one else."

After graduating from Claremont McKenna College in California in 1965 with a bachelor's degree in political science, Hofeller served his country for four years during the Vietnam War aboard a navy destroyer in the Tonkin Gulf. But after this brief foray into military service, he would spend the remainder of his life in politics, becoming perhaps the most influential Republican operative of the last fifty years. Notably, however, this influence was exercised almost exclusively behind the

Thomas Hofeller with his daughter, Stephanie, sometime in the 1970s.

scenes, in the shadowy corners of the American political system where political influence is parceled out using spreadsheets of census data and sophisticated computerized mapping tools. Though well known among his contemporaries in the narrow and highly insular cabal of redistricting professionals, when Hofeller passed away in 2018, few Americans even knew his name.

On his return to California from Vietnam, Hofeller enrolled at the Claremont Graduate School, now Claremont Graduate University. It was here that his lifelong passion for the art and science of political line drawing was ignited. He earned a master's degree in government in 1975 and wrote his 147-page thesis on the history of redistricting in California, tracing the Golden State's conflicts over gerrymandering from statehood, through the malapportionment era of the early twentieth century, to the events that he himself was watching play out in Sacramento during the 1970s. What Hofeller discovered in that history would reinforce what became the central mantra of his entire political career. Democrats, if left to their own devices, would use every tool in the box to manipulate the electoral landscape in their favor. And so Republicans, if they hoped to compete on a level playing field, must be prepared to be equally dirty, underhanded, and devious as they were. "I define redistricting as the only legalized form of vote-stealing left in the United States today," Hofeller said in 1991, never one to mince words about the true nature of his chosen profession. And in a state that had recently surpassed New York as the most populous in the nation, not to mention its fifth fastest growing, there were a lot of votes out there ready to be stolen.

California's redistricting in the mid-twentieth century had been characterized by dueling gerrymanders put in place by Democrats and Republicans. Neither had been particularly successful. The GOP controlled the state government after the 1950 census and had used that control, in Hofeller's words, to "wield the gerrymander's knife to maintain or increase their seats in the face of a three to two Democratic registration [advantage]." But infighting between the state's three most powerful Republican politicians—Vice President Richard Nixon, Governor Goodwin Knight, and the U.S. senator William Knowland—ended up derailing their efforts to stretch that control into a second decade.

Things came to a head in the 1958 election. Knowland announced that instead of running for reelection to the Senate, he was challenging Knight in the Republican primary for governor, part of a plan to use the office as a springboard to seek the Republican presidential nomination against Nixon in 1960. Depending on whose version of events you believe, Knight then either volunteered, was coerced by Knowland, or agreed in a backroom deal under pressure from outside forces to step aside and instead run for Knowland's soon-to-be-vacated Senate seat, an office he had no particular desire to pursue. This would in turn clear the way for Knowland to be the Republican nominee to replace Knight as governor.

The "Big Switch," as it was termed by the Sacramento press corps, did not work out well for either man. Voters disliked the perception that the state's elected offices were being shuffled up and dealt like a deck of cards in a Vegas casino. In the end, both Knowland and Knight went down in flames in the wake of the switcheroo. Knowland lost his bid for governor to the Democratic attorney general Pat Brown, Knight lost the Senate seat that the Republican Party had held since 1900, and Democrats swept to large majorities in both the assembly and the state senate. This set the stage for them to enact their own gerrymander after the 1960 census. It was time, as Hofeller describes in a rare departure from the formulaic academic prose that characterizes most of his thesis, for the "same [map] that the Republicans had performed surgery upon in 1951 [to go] on the Democratic operating table."

But just as the Republican gerrymander had been thwarted by the Knight-Knowland conflict in 1958, so too would this new Democratic gerrymander end up being dismantled before a decade could pass. This time, however, it was because of factors entirely outside their control. In 1964, the U.S. Supreme Court ignited the reapportionment revolution, and with it pulled the Golden State right back into the political thicket. In 1967, all California's legislative districts would need to be redrawn again to comply with the constitutional mandate of "one person, one vote." And by now Ronald Reagan had defeated the incumbent Democratic governor in the 1966 election, meaning that divided government would once again be the order of the day.

What followed was a compromise plan that largely unwound the most egregious effects of the Democratic gerrymander—one that had been predicated in no small part on the creative use of the now-illegal practice of malapportionment—and returned as many incumbents of both stripes to office as possible. This particular flavor of gerry-mandering, perpetuated in service of bipartisan incumbent protection, rather than overt partisan manipulation, will be discussed in greater detail in chapter 10.

And by the time that Thomas Hofeller, budding scholar of the art and science of gerrymandering, enrolled at the Claremont Graduate School in the early 1970s, redistricting was once more on the state's political agenda. The GOP's hopes of controlling the process under the stewardship of Governor Reagan had been dashed in the 1970 election, when their razor-thin majorities in the assembly and senate were upended and replaced with equally hairline margins for the Democrats. Hofeller, busy at work on his thesis and in the early stages of developing one of the very first computerized mapping systems, known as REDIS, that could be used to quickly and easily redraw districts, served as a consultant to the assembly Republicans. Their goal was to negotiate a compromise plan similar to that which had passed in 1967.

"He started out in the days when we were doing redistricting with pencils and paper and very large erasers," recalled John Ryder, another RNC colleague and friend. But Hofeller, though new to the process in which he had now become embroiled, was about to revolutionize it. One of his graduate school professors, Alan Heslop, had been the founding director of the Rose Institute of State and Local Government at Claremont, cementing the informal ties between that institution and the state Republican Party, for whom Hofeller worked as a consultant. The institute supplied the technical and academic expertise to pair with the computing power of the GOP's technology firm, Compass Systems. But the bipartisan talks on redistricting in the legislature eventually broke down, leading to an attempted Democratic gerrymander that was swiftly vetoed by Governor Reagan, throwing the process to the courts.

Hofeller used his newly created mapping software to draw his own set of districts, which the Republicans hoped to persuade the state supreme court to adopt. Hofeller's map was an early preview of what was to come. He was able to use the power of computers to produce districts that to all outward appearances seemed to be compact, regularized, and pleasing to the eye yet that still contained a sufficiently pro-Republican bias to all but guarantee them a majority in the state legislature.

The seven justices on the supreme court, however, were not biting. Five of the seven had been appointed by the previous Democratic governor, Pat Brown. So it was not surprising that Hofeller's map, a wolf of a Republican gerrymander after all, albeit one in sheep's clothing, was rejected. But the court went on to hand the Democrats an almost total victory in the dispute. The legislature's proposed U.S. House plan was adopted almost without modification. And, after allowing the existing 1967 map to be used for the 1972 state legislative elections, the court also adopted a final plan for those chambers that bore a striking resemblance to the attempted Democratic gerrymander of 1971.

The outcome seared a lesson into the mind of the young Thomas Hofeller, who had now taken the first steps toward carving out a career in the GOP's redistricting machine. The courts could not be trusted to protect the integrity and fairness of the redistricting process, at least as far as the Republican Party was concerned. When judges redrew the lines, he reasoned, it was virtually the same thing as having Democrats redraw the lines. Republicans would have to fight tooth and nail to protect their interests and show the enemy no mercy, and to the victor would go the spoils. Redistricting was a zero-sum game: if you're not winning, then you're losing.

Hofeller eventually graduated from Claremont in 1980 with a PhD in government, later moving to Washington, D.C., to work as both the redistricting coordinator and the information technology director for the Republican National Committee. There would be scarcely a Republican gerrymander over the next forty years that did not have his fingerprints on it. But first, he had one more political score to settle in his home state.

When California began the process of redrawing its state legislative and congressional districts after the 1980 census, Hofeller was ready for battle. The twin Democratic gerrymanders of the 1960s and 1970s—one imposed by the state legislature and the other by the supreme court— had eclipsed the now-distant memory of the lone Republican success story of the 1950s, convincing him that the stakes could not be higher when it came to this latest decennial line-drawing exercise. "The GOP forgot the vital connection between success in state legislative elections and its future ability to regain and keep control of the U.S. House of Representatives," he later wrote in an RNC strategy memo, one of the thousands of documents that were discovered among the files that were turned over to Common Cause by his daughter, Stephanie, after his death. "It has all but forgotten the historical electoral disadvantage to GOP candidates caused by past Democratic gerrymanders resulting from their lock on the redistricting process." Hofeller would spend his entire career attempting to prevent those lessons from being forgotten a second time.

For now, though, he and his allies in the California legislature found themselves fighting another holding action. The Watergate scandal, which ended the presidency of the state's most famous Republican politician, had been devastating to the California GOP. Combined with the effects of the gerrymander that the Democrats had managed to ram through with the help of their allies on the state supreme court, it appeared to consign the California Republican Party to electoral oblivion. By 1976, two years after Nixon's resignation and the ascent to the presidency of his vice president, Gerald Ford, the prospect of the GOP ever regaining hold on the levers of power in the Golden State were looking dim indeed.

In that election, despite Ford's narrow victory in California over Jimmy Carter in the presidential race, Republicans were obliterated in the elections for the state legislature. Democrats won fifty-seven of the eighty seats in the state assembly, and twenty-eight of the forty in the state senate, good for a more than two-thirds majority in each chamber. But as had occurred with the Republicans in the late 1950s, political infighting threw a wrench into the emerging Democratic hegemony, spinning the orderly revolution of the political world in Sacramento off its axis. This shock to the system came from one of the unlikeliest of sources: a cigar-smoking, vodka-drinking Mormon by the name of Howard Jarvis.

"They said he was just an old coot," begins the political scientist T. Anthony Quinn's account of the events that led up to the 1980s California redistricting battle. "A perennial candidate for office not to be taken seriously. So it wasn't until well into the spring of 1978 that the political establishment awakened to the phenomenon of Howard Jarvis." But in less than a year, this seventy-five-year-old real-life Howard Beale— whose 1979 autobiography was quite appropriately titled *I'm Mad as Hell*—orchestrated the greatest tax revolt in American history.

Jarvis was born in 1903 in Magna, Utah, a tiny frontier agricultural hamlet that was in the process of becoming a copper-mining boomtown. He was the son of a Democratic state supreme court judge, often joining him on the campaign trail during his youth. His own politics, however, would end up diverging wildly from those of his father. He has been described in the media as a "right-wing political gadfly," "a burly and profane spud of a man," or alternatively, by those more in tune with his libertarian small-government philosophy, the "new hero to the U.S. taxpayer." Jarvis ran for office as a Republican on at least four separate occasions, but lost every time. This did not prevent him, however, from becoming perhaps the most consequential political figure in 1970s California.

In an early preview of his later pugnaciousness, Jarvis was a boxer during his younger years. He was also the first graduate of his tiny Utah high school to finish college and initially planned to follow his father into the law. Instead, he would end up charting his own path in life. And what a path it was. Shortly after graduating from Utah State University, Jarvis purchased a local newspaper, *The Magna Times*. Its success allowed him to acquire a chain of eleven Utah papers while still in his twenties. After unsuccessfully seeking a seat in the state legislature, he became involved in national politics, serving as press secretary for the western division of President Herbert Hoover's disastrous 1932 reelection campaign against Franklin Roosevelt. He also attended the 1934 Republican National Committee meeting in Chicago, where he made the acquaintance of an obscure young California district attorney by the name of Earl Warren. It was Warren who persuaded him to sell his newspaper holdings in Utah and move to the West Coast. And after settling in Los Angeles, Jarvis pursued a variety of business interests, with varying degrees of success.

In one of the more bizarre chapters, he became involved in a patent dispute with the manufacturers of the first American garbage disposal, which he claimed to have previously invented. "I should have held on to that garbage disposal," he later told *The New York Times*. "I didn't realize how big it was going to become." Other business ventures included the acquisition of a chemical company, the development of a device to silence office machines, the invention of a process to demagnetize the hulls of U.S. warships during World War II, making them less susceptible to German mines and U-boats, and the creation of a business that manufactured household appliances and aircraft subassemblies. Eventually, though, having retired from his manufacturing company at the age of fifty-nine, he settled into a career in real estate, ultimately being elected president of the Apartment House Association of Los Angeles. And it was there that he embarked on the mission that would consume the remainder of his life: the fight against California's skyrocketing property taxes.

After allegedly passing up an opportunity to purchase a mile of the Las Vegas strip for the bargain price of $5,000—that particular lucrative business venture having apparently met the same fate as his earlier garbage disposal prototype—Jarvis watched as his own home at 515 North Crescent Heights Boulevard in West Hollywood ballooned in tax-assessed

Howard Jarvis during the 1978 campaign for Proposition 13.

value. The house he had purchased for $8,000 in 1941 was by 1976, at least according to the tax authorities, worth in excess of $80,000. Jarvis, mad as hell at the perceived injustice, undertook a series of unsuccessful campaigns for mayor of Los Angeles, running on the single-issue platform of tax reform.

The same rapid population growth that had thrown gasoline on the redistricting debates of the 1950s, 1960s, and 1970s had also produced a surge in real estate and land prices that threatened to price many middle-class and lower-income Californians out of their homes. The public was primed to listen with open ears to an antitax, small-government message, and Howard Jarvis was about to give them a voice with which to express their dissatisfaction and anger. If he wasn't able to do so as a politician, then he would have to find some other avenue to achieve his goals.

California is one of a handful of states that allows for citizen initiatives. Policy proposals may be placed on the ballot by petition for a direct popular vote of the people, bypassing their elected representatives in the state government entirely. Decades later, this same maneuver would be used to create the California Citizens Redistricting Commission, which removed from the hands of politicians the responsibility for drawing district boundaries that had so divided the state's previous generations of political parties. Now, though, Jarvis and his antigovernment allies were preparing to use the same procedure to try to ease their crippling tax burden.

Their proposal, which became known as Proposition 13, called for property taxes to be cut by two-thirds; capped any future increases at a maximum of 2 percent per year, unless the property was sold; and, perhaps most radically of all, required a supermajority vote in the legislature for any subsequent increase in state taxes. It was a shoot-the-moon grab bag of libertarian dream reforms pulled straight from the playbook of Barry Goldwater's disastrous 1964 presidential campaign against Lyndon Johnson, a campaign in which he had lost the state of California by almost twenty points. But in these drastic times, Jarvis gambled that the voters were now ready for drastic measures.

Proposition 13 set the proverbial cat among the pigeons of the California Democratic Party. The state assembly Speaker, Leo McCarthy, decried the proposal as a "disaster," while San Francisco's mayor, George Moscone, alleged that "no matter how you slice it, our police, our libraries, our fire department and schools would be crippled." The state party chairman Bert Coffey was quoted in the *Los Angeles Times* in February as saying that passage of Proposition 13 would mean "turning the state over to the current-day anarchists." "If I were a Communist and I wanted to destroy America," wrote Pat Brown in a misguidedly hyperbolic letter to the state GOP, "I would support the Jarvis Amendment."

All of this was music to the ears of the Republicans. They rallied in support of the reform, making it the cornerstone of their 1978 campaign. After all, who ever looked bad when telling voters that they should pay less in taxes? "Jarvis had unleashed a political earthquake that rumbled across California and the nation," Quinn argues in his retrospective. "Before the year was out, Jarvis and his Proposition 13 had reduced the orderly political landscape of California to rubble. They also rescued from near oblivion one of California's two major political parties."

When the dust settled, Proposition 13 had passed by a landslide. Sixty-three percent of the state's voters endorsed the reforms. For Jarvis, it was a vindication of his life's work. The man who had failed on so many occasions to become a politician himself had now done more in a single year to blunt the expansion of the bloated state government, not to mention the power of the Democratic majority he so despised, than the entire California Republican Party had managed in decades. Jarvis became a media sensation, lapping up the attention that was lavished on him by the popular press. "This is a victory for freedom and liberty in the United States," he told reporters. "This is a new revolution against the politicians and insensitive bureaucrats whose philosophy is spend, spend, spend; . . . tax, tax, tax." Jarvis's supporters were no less jubilant. "You're damn right we feel like revolutionaries," gushed Dick Molinoy, a cigar-chewing swimming pool installer. "I'm here because this is American history being made. How do I feel about Howard Jarvis? He should be president. If he could cook, I'd marry him."

In the general election later that fall, eleven Democratic incumbents lost their seats. And while the lingering effects of the 1971 gerrymander were enough for them to keep their majorities, the party now found itself reeling. Assembly Speaker Leo McCarthy, who had been expected to spearhead the redistricting process after the 1980 census, was ousted from his position after a titanic power struggle against his own lieutenant, Majority Leader Howard Berman. The Republicans, seeking to destabilize things even further, backed the dark horse candidate, the flamboyant San Francisco assemblyman Willie Brown, allowing him to assume the speakership over Berman. Brown had been one of the few Democrats who had supported the redistricting compromise pushed by Hofeller and his allies in 1971, and the Republicans believed they would be better positioned to outmaneuver him during negotiations.

Then, in 1980, another bombshell dropped. Ronald Reagan defeated the incumbent, Jimmy Carter, by a landslide in the presidential election, becoming the second California Republican to occupy the Oval Office in less than a decade. Nine additional Democratic incumbents lost their seats, further cutting into their rapidly diminishing majorities. Crucially, however, the Democratic governor, Jerry Brown, the son of the former governor Pat Brown, was able to hold on to his position in the 1978 election. The Democrats had been battered and bruised by the fallout from Proposition 13, but they clung tooth and nail to their control of the state government. And with redistricting now fast approaching, they were spoiling for a fight. As Quinn puts it, "Nothing radicalizes politicians like losing."

"Political analysts often argue about when the modern-day conserva-

tive movement in America began," wrote the Cato Institute's Stephen
Moore in 1998. "Some say that it began with Barry Goldwater's campaign in 1964. Others say it began with the election of Ronald Reagan
in 1980. I believe that the conservative, anti-big-government tide in
America began 20 years ago with the passage of taxpayer advocate Howard Jarvis's Proposition 13 in California." For Jarvis, though, while the
battle over Proposition 13 had been won, the war was only beginning.
Fearful that the Democrats in Sacramento would attempt to thwart the
people's mandate, he formed the nonprofit Howard Jarvis Taxpayers
Association, which continues to lobby for tax reform to this day. In
1980, he made a cameo appearance in the movie *Airplane!* as the taxi
passenger who is driven to the airport by Robert Hays's protagonist, Ted
Striker, only to spend the entire film sitting in the parking lot with the
meter running.

Jarvis died in 1986, at the age of eighty-two, due to complications
from blood disease. Even while incapacitated by his final illness, he
never stopped fighting for lower taxes. And as for the home at 515 North
Crescent Heights Boulevard, the one whose skyrocketing property tax
assessment had begun this whole crusade? After Jarvis's widow, Estelle,
sold the house in 2008 for $822,000, more than one hundred times the
original 1941 purchase price, it was turned into the Nechung Dharma-

Howard Jarvis holding a copy of his 1979 autobiography.

pala Center, a nonsectarian Buddhist meditation institute. The irony would surely not have been lost on the man whose entire life's work was grounded in the acquisition, and retention, of material wealth. "Well, I'll give him another twenty minutes," Jarvis deadpans in the final line of *Airplane!*, delivered while still waiting in the taxi after the closing credits have rolled, "but that's it!"

If Thomas Hofeller and his Republican allies thought that they might be able to engineer another compromise redistricting with the Democratic majority in Sacramento, then they surely hadn't reckoned with Phil Burton. Howard Jarvis's Proposition 13 had sent the Democrats reeling. It had unseated numerous incumbent members of the state legislature, thrown the assembly caucus into a protracted and divisive leadership battle that brought down the Speaker, and mired Governor Jerry Brown in the political fallout of an almost 60 percent reduction in tax revenues. Things were looking bleak indeed. But into this power vacuum stepped Congressman Burton. The "hard-boiled San Francisco Democrat," populist advocate, and progressive reformer had in 1976 come within a single vote of being elected House majority leader, losing 148–147 to the Texas congressman Jim Wright. Now he made it his mission to save the California Democratic Party from itself.

Burton was born in Cincinnati in 1926, the son of Thomas Burton (originally Berger), a German American traveling salesman, and Mildred Burton, an Irish Catholic. He was later described by a Democratic colleague as "the most naturally gifted elected official or politician I have ever known or run across." The family moved frequently during his childhood, spending time in Ohio, Michigan, and Wisconsin. After originally enrolling at one Washington High School in Milwaukee, Burton eventually graduated from another, George Washington High in San Francisco, where his father had moved to pursue a medical degree. He worked initially as an attorney, establishing a law practice in San Francisco alongside his African American partner, Joseph Williams, and serving as a lawyer for the air force during the Korean War. But politics was always his first love.

In 1956, Burton sought election to the California state assembly. When his primary opponent, the incumbent Democrat William "Cliff" Berry, passed away a month before Election Day—too late for the ballots to be reprinted—he could have been forgiven for thinking that he had the election in the bag. The voters had other ideas. When the returns were in, Burton had lost to Berry, now interred at Holy Cross Cemetery, by a more than two-to-one margin. Devastated, he resolved never to allow the meat grinder of party-machine politics to get the better of him again.

By the time he ran for the assembly a second time two years later, Burton was prepared. Relentlessly canvassing his new district's neglected African American and Chinese American communities, he managed to defeat the thirty-two-year Republican Sacramento veteran, Tommy Maloney, by the narrow margin of 659 votes. When a seat in the U.S. House of Representatives opened up in 1964 with the departure of the Democratic incumbent John F. Shelley—who resigned after being elected mayor of San Francisco—Burton threw his hat into the ring. Throughout his entire political career, he never lost an election to a live human being.

Burton had a passion for conservation. In Congress, he was influen-

Congressman Phillip Burton during a tour of Alcatraz Island, 1974.

tial in the creation of the Golden Gate National Recreation Area, which at eighty-two thousand acres—more than twice the size of the city of San Francisco itself—is one of the largest urban parks in the world. He also advocated tirelessly for the National Park Service, believing that America's natural resources should be preserved and protected in perpetuity, available for the enjoyment of all, regardless of their socio-economic status. An opponent of the aggressive use of the U.S. military in the fight against communism, he was one of only three members of the House to vote against funding the Vietnam War in 1965. And in the early 1980s, he spearheaded legislation to promote scientific research into the AIDS epidemic in San Francisco.

Now Burton had set his sights on the California GOP. He was described by the press as "an invisible hand shaping the California congressional races this year that has not been quite invisible enough." The Golden State was about to witness its fourth consecutive decade of knock-down-drag-out gerrymandering. "What you find out in many of these races," said the RNC regional coordinator Harvey Hukari, "is that you're not fighting the incumbent so much as you're fighting Phil Burton."

The opening gambit in this game of redistricting chess was made by Hofeller. He and his former Claremont professor Alan Heslop, now serving as the director of the Rose Institute, were keenly aware that setting the agenda, and winning the public relations war, were key elements to seizing the initiative. With little movement from the Democrats throughout most of 1981, Hofeller set about using his REDIS mapping software to draw a proposed set of compromise districts that might serve as a starting point to avoid a protracted fight between the parties.

In June, the institute unveiled its map, marketed as a "model" plan for the state, featuring "compact, attractive districts that garnered much press attention, and more than a few laudatory editorials." The media ate it up. Described as a "practical benchmark" for the legislature's negotiations by the *San Francisco Examiner,* and the "honest computer plan" by the *Chronicle,* Hofeller's map would have preserved smaller Democratic majorities in the state legislature while allocating them twenty-four U.S. House seats compared with twenty-one for the Republicans. But it was a nonstarter. Speaker Willie Brown, upset at the changes made to his own district under the plan, lambasted it as a Republican plot, insisting that "the Rose Institute is totally skewed towards Republicans." Meanwhile, behind the scenes, Phil Burton began preparing his countermove.

"The most important thing you do, before anything else," Burton later said of his redistricting strategy, "is you get yourself in a position to draw the lines for your own district. Then you draw them for all your friends before anyone else's." For Burton to successfully maneuver himself through the minefield of California redistricting and craft an effective gerrymander, however, he would also need to keep his enemies happy. What he produced was a magnum opus. Howard Berman and two of his allies were placated with custom-drawn congressional districts. This also carried the added bonus of getting them out of the assembly, consolidating the Burton ally Willie Brown's power over the Democratic caucus. "You're in your mother's arms," Burton reassured them, his go-to catchphrase for when the creation of a safe, reliable district was a done deal.

The state's growing Latino population, long excluded from fair representation in Sacramento, was given additional minority-influence districts in the state legislature. Their representatives also signed off on Burton's plan, having previously threatened to join the Republicans in a lawsuit if their demands were not met. Realizing that the appearance of Republican participation would help bolster him against accusations of partisanship, Burton allowed the Republican representative Clair Burgener to draw the four San Diego–area districts, knowing full well that he would be forced to protect the three existing Republican incumbents, allowing the Democrats to snag the fourth seat.

In the Central Valley, where another new seat needed to be created, he appeased another powerful adversary, Tony Coelho, by completely bifurcating the city of Stockton. Half of it was assigned to a new Democratic seat in Fresno, connected by a long finger that skirted around the edge of Coelho's district, and the other half to a sprawling rural seat that snaked all the way to the Oregon border. Perhaps the most egregious affront to the state's geography came in the Bay Area, where Burton was determined to create another safe Democratic seat for his own brother, John, to run in. In what he later described to the media as "my contribution to modern art," Burton drew a district that attached the heavily Democratic city of Vallejo in the East Bay to two disconnected parts of Marin County and the city of San Francisco, creating

Phil Burton's bay-hopping 1981 "contribution to modern art."

what Quinn describes as "the only district in California history to cross the San Francisco Bay twice without the use of a bridge." "I just hope he swims well," quipped William Campbell, the Republican leader in the senate. Thomas Hofeller was somewhat less sanguine in his own reaction to the plan. "This is gerrymandering at its most acute level," he told *The New York Times*. "They probably should award Phillip Burton the 'Gerrymander of the Year Award.'"

But the line-drawing shenanigans in the Bay Area were merely the appetizer for what Burton had in store for Los Angeles. Sensing the opportunity to pick off no fewer than three vulnerable Republican incumbents, he took a hacksaw to the City of Angels. First on the chopping block was the district represented by Bob Dornan, a conservative firebrand who once personally swam the channel between Chappaquiddick and Edgartown in Massachusetts just to prove that Ted Kennedy had lied in his account of the famous accident that killed his female companion, Mary Jo Kopechne. His district was cleaved in two, with the northern areas around Malibu and Santa Monica joined with parts of west-central L.A. to form a district designed to elect an African American Democrat, and the southern Manhattan and Redondo Beach sections shoehorned into an absurdly shaped Republican supermajority district that packed together every GOP neighborhood in and around the city of Long Beach.

Another Republican House member, Bobbi Fiedler, had her home drawn out of the moderately Democratic district she had captured in 1980 and into the neighboring, far more conservative district represented by Barry Goldwater Jr. Since Goldwater was retiring, Fiedler now had an easy task of running for reelection in her new district, allowing the Democrats to recapture her old seat, now denuded of its only Republican neighborhoods, as well as its incumbent.

The final indignity was reserved for Burton's archenemy John Rousselot, the Republican whom he suspected of funneling money to his opponent in his previous reelection campaign. Earlier in the year, Burton had cornered Rousselot during a cruise on the Potomac in Washington, D.C., that had been organized for the California delegation and berated him. "I had no choice but to listen or jump," Rousselot recalled of the incident. "He said, 'You've been bad for California. You're in trouble.'" It was no empty threat. Rousselot's L.A.-area district was destroyed, with parts of it drawn into a packed GOP seat that also paired two other Republican incumbents together, and the rest parceled out among several surrounding Latino-influence districts. Rousselot was forced to choose to either run against two other incumbent GOP congressmen in the San Gabriel valley seat or seek election in one of the heavily Democratic seats that surrounded it. "Everyone north of the Tehachapi is in their mother's arms," Burton told Bill Thomas, his GOP counterpart. "Los Angeles is dog meat. And San Diego takes care of itself."

Outrage from the Republicans and the media swiftly poured forth as soon as Burton's plan was unveiled to the legislature. "It resembles nothing so much as a jigsaw puzzle designed by an inmate of a mental institution," declared *The Sacramento Union*. "Districts dip and swirl around, picking up a few votes here, and a few more there." "We believe that what the Democrats are up to is a major form of ballot box stuffing," opined the senate Republican leader William Campbell. His counterpart in the assembly, Robert Naylor, put it even more bluntly: "Reapportionment is the closest we come in this country to lining people up against the wall with a firing squad." It was a gerrymandering master class that drew from every page of Burton's encyclopedic knowledge of California politics. No stone in the political landscape was left unturned, no petty squabble or half-forgotten grudge too small, no minor partisan advantage that might be eked from the map too insignificant to escape his notice.

Every traditional districting principle that you could think of, from the preference for compact, regularly shaped districts, to the desire to avoid dividing cities, counties, communities, and neighborhoods, to even the quaint notion that the disparate parts of an individual district be in some way connected or even related to one other, was jettisoned if it provided the Democrats with even the slightest edge in the battle for control. Gone were the colorful cartoon creations of Ohio in the 1840s and Massachusetts in the second decade of the nineteenth century, the neatly regularized conglomerations of counties that were easily satirized in the pages of the popular press. Burton's districts were so convoluted, so outrageously misshapen and contorted into bizarre splotches, dribbles, and brushstrokes on the canvas of the state that even visualizing them on a map presents a considerable challenge. What Burton had created was arguably the first quintessentially modern gerrymander in American history, replete with all of the same underhanded manipulation of the electoral playing field, ruthless targeting of opposing incumbents, and outright disdain for the norms of democratic accountability that characterized the Republicans' later REDMAP project.

Burton himself was singularly unapologetic. He was on a crusade. "I trust visceral reactions, and I trust workers' reactions," he told *California* magazine in November 1981, in a story appropriately titled "Boss." "I like people whose balls roar when they see justice. . . . I'm determined to make the universe a better place. Not the world, the universe." For Burton, securing justice for the marginalized communities of California meant that the Democrats had to win, at any cost.

In 1982, the first election to be held under his newly gerrymandered congressional boundaries, he and his colleagues were firmly in their mother's arms. They turned what had been a narrow twenty-two-to-twenty-one-seat edge into a twenty-eight-to-seventeen romp, picking off numerous Republican incumbents, forcing others into retirement, and establishing a stranglehold that they have yet to relinquish to this day. The Republican Party would never again control a majority of the House seats in the state of California. And barring a brief period from 1995 to 1997 when they held the assembly, they were perpetually shut out of control of the state legislature as well. Though moderate Republicans have achieved some successes in governor's races, Burton's gerrymander effectively consigned the party to permanent minority status.

Things were no less fiery in the negotiations between Democratic and Republican leaders in the legislature, although Burton, persona non grata in Sacramento following his evisceration of the GOP's Congress members, wisely took a backseat to Speaker Willie Brown and President Pro Tempore David Roberti. "The congressional redistricting was dropped on a Legislature already torn apart by its own line-drawing," writes Quinn. "Soothing promises of an 'easy' redistricting had given way to a nasty battle one reporter called 'a cat fight that (shows) the Legislature at its very worst.'"

First on deck was the senate plan. The initial goal of Roberti, who spearheaded the process along with the Appropriations Committee chairman, Daniel Boatwright, was a simple one: to protect the seats of all twenty-three Democratic incumbents. That part of the plan, at least, went off without a hitch. When the initial version of the map was unveiled to the Democratic caucus that summer, most liked what they saw. But the Democrats were unable to resist the temptation to stick it to some of their least favorite members on the opposite side of the aisle, and it was from there that the fireworks began.

Elections to the California Senate, like those for the U.S. Senate, are staggered, with only a portion of the seats going up for reelection during each two-year cycle. Its forty members are elected to four-year terms, meaning that those incumbents who represented even-numbered districts were scheduled to face the voters in 1982, while those in odd-numbered seats would not have to do so until 1984. This presented the Democrats with a unique opportunity. By manipulating the numbering of senate districts, switching odd districts to even and even districts to odd, they could ensure that their own incumbents would remain safely in office until 1984, while vulnerable Republicans could be forced to run for reelection in 1982, putting their seats in jeopardy. The threat of a numbering switcheroo could also be used as a bargaining chip in the negotiations, something to hang over the heads of the GOP caucus members to force them to accede to other changes that benefited the majority.

One of the most prominent renumbering victims was John Doolittle, the Sacramento Republican who had ousted the popular Democratic incumbent Albert Rodda in the previous election. And to add insult to injury, his district was also redrawn to bring in additional Democratic areas in the city's urban core while removing some of the more conservative suburbs. "Not only would Doolittle find it nearly impossible to survive," Quinn writes, "but he would not even be allowed to serve out his term before facing the voters again."

Another victim, Dan O'Keefe, was paired in a district with a fellow Republican incumbent that was also renumbered. It was an outrageous and unprecedented subversion of the norms and conventions of the redistricting process by the Democrats, one that only added further fuel to the partisan fire that Burton had already ignited. Never before in California history had a party used the renumbering of senate districts as a strategy for crafting a gerrymander. And quite predictably, it did not go down well within the ranks of the GOP senators. What had begun as a good-faith effort to preserve the existing incumbents on both sides had devolved into yet another round of partisan chicanery, and things would only go from bad to worse as the year progressed.

Bill Richardson, the leader of the Republican faction in the senate that had proved most intransigent to the Democratic majority, was singled out for special treatment. His neatly compact San Gabriel valley district was enlarged into a mostly uninhabited desert monstrosity that spanned an area larger than the entirety of New England. Merely canvassing this sprawling wasteland, which included both Death Valley and Mount Whitney, would keep him occupied for most of the next two years. "Amused Democrats claimed their nemesis would be happy in the desert," Quinn reports. "He was after all an active gun-owner and would surely enjoy shooting rabbits." All Republican efforts to resist the gerrymander proved futile. The Democrats were simply not prepared to compromise. On September 3, the senate redistricting bill passed by a 26–11 majority, with three Republicans crossing the aisle to vote for it under the threat of a numbering switch.

GOP-affiliated media were already manning the barricades. *The*

Sacramento Union, a conservative paper, published photos of the three defectors under the headline "Roll of Dishonor." The *San Jose Mercury* railed against "the audacity of the decision by Democratic Senators to strip more than a million Californians of representation in the State Senate for two years." The *Los Angeles Herald Examiner* called the gerrymander a "brand of quack surgery that warrants criminal prosecution."

Meanwhile, in the senate itself, the Republicans who had broken ranks to support the plan, including Bob Beverly, a pragmatic and popular centrist who was well liked even among his Democratic opponents, found themselves pariahs. Gerald Felando, one of the L.A.-area representatives whose previously comfortable district had been collapsed into oblivion, "took the picture of Beverly off the wall in Minority Leader Hallett's office where it hung with other GOP Minority Leaders and stomped on it, breaking the glass. He then left the office, muttering about finding Beverly in a local bar and punching him in the face."

Over in the assembly, the prospects of a bipartisan compromise on the new districts initially looked brighter. "Speaker Brown had no desire to punish anyone in redistricting," members were told, "he assured his colleagues that everyone would have a district in which to run." But the demographic realities made it virtually impossible for him to keep that promise. The preceding decade had seen the population in the areas around Los Angeles grow at a slower rate than the rest of the state, meaning that to remain in compliance with "one person, one vote," two assembly districts in the region would need to be eliminated and reconstituted elsewhere. And with none of the incumbent representatives on either side planning to retire, someone would be left out in the cold. As negotiations progressed, it became increasingly clear that those sacrificial lambs would not be led to the slaughter from the Democratic side of the aisle.

This time, though, the Republicans were not caught setting foot on the battlefield unprepared. Pulling the strings behind the scenes, once again, was Hofeller and the Rose Institute. They used their extensive database and mapping software to draw up the Republican plan that would be deployed for negotiating purposes. To avoid tipping their hand, the full plan was not unveiled to the public or the Democrats, as had been done in 1971, but instead released piecemeal as "sizzle packages." These were intended, in the words of Assemblyman Ross Johnson, to "sell the sizzle, not the steak."

Their strategy was to appeal to vulnerable Democrats by floating sizzle packages that promised to shore up their districts, as a carrot to be dangled in return for preserving those of GOP incumbents in Los Angeles. The Rose Institute softened the ground further by hosting propaganda sessions to "educate" the Sacramento press corps about the process. Many of those journalists then dutifully reprinted the sizzle packages that were strategically leaked to them by the GOP caucus.

But L.A. remained a sticking point, particularly when word leaked that Burton was drawing tailor-made districts for the area assemblymen Howard Berman and Mel Levine to run for Congress. Why save their districts, the GOP wondered, when neither of them was going to be around to run in them? The Republicans smelled a rat. Formal negotiations ground to a halt, and based on information gleaned informally during hushed late night conversations at Sacramento bars, it appeared that a plan was afoot to wreak havoc with the GOP incumbents in Southern California.

"It was hard to say just when the Speaker's resolve to effect a bipartisan reapportionment went out the window," Quinn muses, but when rumors started swirling in the press about an alleged plot, denied by all parties, to unseat Brown and replace him with Howard Berman—a highly implausible notion considering that Berman was planning to run for Congress—any veneer of bipartisanship that still remained was stripped away. Many believed that Berman had planted the rumor himself, hoping to undermine Brown's leadership in retaliation for being denied the speakership the previous year. Whatever the genesis, everyone had now retreated to their various camps. Any incentives there might have been for Brown and Richard Alatorre, the chairman of the Elections and Reapportionment Committee, to compromise had evaporated.

Which isn't to say that there were not occasional moments of levity among the bickering. Quinn recounts one incident in which two Republican assemblymen, Gilbert Marguth and Bill Baker, "borrowed a coat from a large member of the Assembly staff and entered Alatorre's office with both of them wearing it, symbolizing the fact that they were both in the same district." The district of the senior Democratic assembly member Tom Bane, whose shape resembled "a well-known obscene gesture," was nicknamed the "Bane finger" by his amused colleagues. Other jokes were not so well received. "Some Republican Assemblymen were passing around the line that Alatorre, of Hispanic descent, was drawing district boundaries with spray paint. Alatorre did not find that funny at all."

Some revelations provoked a much angrier reaction. When Cathie Wright, another GOP incumbent, was "escorted into Alatorre's office to see her new seat, she found her formerly compact district had been stretched from Vandenberg Air Force Base in Santa Barbara County to Lancaster north of Los Angeles." "A woman of short fuse anyway, [she] took the map and threw it on the floor, telling Alatorre that he could put the district 'where the sun doesn't shine.'" "A Republican staff member remarked that the Air Force could fire a missile from Vandenberg and it would run out of fuel before it left Cathie Wright's district; and the closest thing to a community of interest in the far-flung district was the fact that it united all of the state's condor refugees." When Brown entered Alatorre's office one day, according to reporting from the *Los Angeles Times,* he asked, "Richard, what's your justification for a seat that looks like that?" "It's very simple," Alatorre responded, "the bird people said we should unite the condors."

As the end of the legislative session approached, tensions between the two sides reached a breaking point. Assembly Republicans announced that they would block all bills that required a two-thirds majority to pass. Under Howard Jarvis's Proposition 13, this included any legislation that increased the government's revenues. Senate Democrats then announced a counter-boycott of all such bills originating in the assembly. Most distressingly of all, at least in the minds of the politicians, the logjammed legislation included a bill giving legislators a 10 percent pay raise in their next session. The world's tiniest violin orchestra most surely struck up a somber symphony in lament for their loss. "Since they injected unorthodox and outrageous games in the process," whined one senate Democrat, apparently conceding that playground rules were now in full effect, "we felt we had no choice. Obviously there is no place for that kind of tactic, but at the same time we can't reward them by ignoring it."

"The most interesting moment in the Assembly debate came when one Republican compared the Democratic remapping to the Holocaust," Quinn relates, "and said what the Democrats were doing to Jerry Felando matched what the Nazis had done to the Jews." A Democratic colleague retorted, "He can always go back to dentistry: it's not quite the same as it was in Germany." In an apparent attempt to one-up his cohort's unfortunate invocation of Godwin's law, the Republican Bob Naylor "bitterly compared Speaker Brown to the Ayatollah Khomeini, the only difference being that the Ayatollah lined his enemies up against the wall, not his friends." With both sides rending their garments in faux outrage, and toys being thrown from strollers in all directions, there was little left for anyone to do but vote. By September, with the deadline fast approaching, Brown decided to go ahead and pass Alatorre's plan, Republican outrage be damned. The assembly redistricting bill was enacted on a party-line vote, 44–35, on the final day of the legislative session.

When it was over, Alatorre took a well-deserved victory lap on the assembly floor. Literally. "He rose," reported the *San Francisco Examiner,* "performed an exaggerated strut to the podium, spread his arms in a gesture of success, and sauntered back to his seat without saying a word. One of his colleagues later remarked that it was the most eloquent speech he had witnessed in weeks." In the 1982 elections, the Democrats increased their seat total in the assembly to forty-eight. The blue tide had well and truly rolled.

The postscript to the Great Golden State Gerrymander of 1981 was a rosy one for the Democrats. But even then, it was not without its stumbling blocks. Republican dissatisfaction eventually coalesced into a campaign to force a popular referendum on the redistricting plans during the 1982 primary election. After the requisite number of signatures had been collected—including that of President Ronald Reagan, who remarked, as he signed the petitions in the White House Rose Garden, that "the situation in California seems to have gotten out of hand"—the fate of the Democratic gerrymander was now in the hands of the voters. And they did not like what they saw one bit. In the election that June, the people of California roundly rejected the Democratic plans. But just when it appeared that the work of Burton, Brown, Alatorre, Roberti, and Boatwright would be undone, their allies on the state supreme court stepped up once again to save the day.

With the November general election fast approaching, the court faced the tricky question of what districts would be used to elect members of the U.S. House, state senate, and state legislature. On the House plan, they were unanimous. Since the Burton gerrymander was the only one that accounted for the increase in seats from forty-three to forty-five, the justices ruled that it must be used. But the Republicans were hopeful that they might still be able to convince a majority of the seven justices, six of whom were Democratic appointees, that the old districts for the state legislature should be temporarily left in place. Those hopes too were swiftly dashed. The court ruled 4–3 that the Democrats' gerrymandered districts must also be used for those elections. "A bare majority of this court have become entangled in the 'political thicket,'" wrote the dissenters, "by ignoring their obligation of neutrality on a partisan issue, a neutrality that can be observed only by a maintenance of the status quo in legislative districting until the people speak at the upcoming election."

And speak they did. While the gerrymander was sufficient to preserve the large Democratic majorities in the legislature—despite their winning less than 50 percent of the popular vote—they lost both their U.S. Senate seat and the governorship. But there was still time, during the lame-duck session between the election and the arrival of the Republican governor-elect, George Deukmejian, in early 1983, for the Democrats to thwart the will of the voters one last time. The outgoing governor, Jerry Brown—whose own political career appeared to be over after his Senate defeat to the Republican Pete Wilson—called an extraordinary session of the legislature in January 1983 to pass new plans. While the harshest edges of the previous year's gerrymander were somewhat softened, what emerged from that session was a set of maps that were still heavily tilted in the Democrats' favor. Brown signed the bills into law mere hours before leaving office.

But what to nickname this latest affront to representative democracy? There was no need for the Sacramento press corps to procure the services of a Hollywood screenwriter: the script wrote itself. Just as another Governor Gerry had inspired eponymous infamy with his reluctant redistricting scheme almost two centuries earlier, Governor Brown now had his own unfortunate legacy: the Jerrymander.

The 1980s, now two decades removed from the reapportionment revolution, were the first time the quintessentially modern gerrymander fully spread its wings and took flight. Gone were the relatively simple pencil-and-paper creations of bygone eras, replaced with complex and abstract multisided polygons, exquisitely tailored and manipulated down to the individual city block level. The 1980s were also the first decade in which both sides came to the fight armed with sophisticated computerized mapping systems and reams of electoral data. The Republicans had Hofeller's REDIS software and the power of Claremont's computers, while the Democrats had spent much of 1981 developing their own parallel technology, deploying it to full effect in the creation of their gerrymander. The redistricting wars had seen the creation of their very own weapons of mass destruction. And once those weapons were within their arsenal, neither side could afford to unilaterally disarm.

Hofeller himself, exhausted from a second consecutive decade of fighting in vain to prevent the Democrats from committing wanton acts of brutality against the political landscape of his home state, left for Washington to take up a position in the Census Bureau under President Ronald Reagan. But his departure from the redistricting battlefield was merely a temporary one. As chapter 11 discusses, he would return in 1991 to help ensure that Republicans would not find themselves on the losing end of the fight yet again. And while Jerry Brown eventually resurrected his political career—serving as the chairman of the California Democratic Party, mayor of Oakland, and the state's attorney general before once again returning to the governor's mansion in 2011—the 1982 election proved to be Phil Burton's last rodeo.

Having given up the juiciest precincts in his own district to craft the absurd bay-hopping monstrosity for his brother, Burton found himself in a closely contested reelection battle against the Republican Milton Marks. Though he won the race with 59 percent of the vote, that was still seven points worse than Jimmy Carter had performed in the district during his landslide defeat to Reagan in 1980. Already in poor health, Burton passed away at his San Francisco home on April 10, 1983, from a ruptured aortic aneurysm. He was fifty-six. "One observer surmised that Burton's body had finally exploded from the intense pressure of his personality." "More than a hundred members of Congress flew to California for his funeral," Quinn wryly observes, "although some may have come just to make sure that the crafty Burton was actually in his grave." When the Democrats somehow hung on to their twenty-eight-to-seventeen House majority in the 1984 election, despite Reagan's eighteen-point landslide in the presidential race, the DNC chairman, Charles Manatt, was asked how they had managed it. "God and Phil Burton," he replied.

8

The Prisoner's Dilemma

M y first encounter with American gerrymandering came before I was
even familiar with the term, or the concept for which it stood. I
observed it every day when, as a young graduate student at the University at Buffalo in upstate New York, I climbed in my car to make the
twenty-five-minute drive from my tiny duplex apartment—located in
the town of Alden in the rural eastern part of Erie County—to the UB
campus in Amherst, northeast of downtown.

Right along the street from where I lived were no fewer than three
penitentiaries: the minimum-security Buffalo Correctional Facility,
for some reason located fifteen miles outside the city of Buffalo; the
Erie County Correctional Facility, whose website boasts of its "'New
Generation Jail' pods and open bay construction," whatever those are;
and a maximum-security state prison, the Wende Correctional Facility, whose most famous inmates include Mark David Chapman, who
murdered John Lennon in 1980, and Harvey Weinstein, the disgraced
former media mogul. Most American prisons, especially those housing
dangerous and violent criminals, are located away from major population centers. In Illinois, for example, 60 percent of inmates in the state
correctional system are from Chicago, but 99 percent of them are serving their sentences elsewhere in the state.

In his 2017 book, *Big House on the Prairie*, the University of Wisconsin sociology professor John M. Eason estimates that 70 percent of the
prisons constructed in the United States since 1970—a period that saw
the number of correctional facilities more than triple—were located

in rural communities. In that same time, the number of Americans incarcerated in prisons or jails also skyrocketed, from fewer than half a million to almost 2.5 million. When approximately 1 percent of your population is behind bars at any given time, the question of how to count those people for the purposes of political representation, and the distribution of federal funding and benefits, becomes a substantially more pressing one. Traditionally, both the U.S. Census Bureau and the governments of individual states have counted incarcerated persons not as residents of the counties, districts, cities, and towns where they lived prior to running afoul of the criminal justice system, and to which they will presumably return, but as residents of the facilities where they are being held.

The resulting overpopulation of rural areas, to which prisoners are disproportionately sent, and corresponding underpopulation of urban areas, from which they disproportionately originate, has profound implications for the division of political power. Exactly like the creeping gerrymanders of the early twentieth century, it creates a situation where citizens in rural areas have a much louder voice in the making of government policy than is justified by their numbers.

What I didn't realize as I drove to campus those many years ago was that the more than two thousand inmates of the three correctional facilities I passed during my commute, despite not enjoying the right to vote themselves, represented 19 percent of the population of the town of Alden; 1 percent of the population of the 142nd State Assembly District; and together with those housed in other rural western New York facilities, 4 percent of the population of the Fifty-Ninth State Senate District. This phenomenon, whereby phantom constituents pad the populations of seats represented by rural politicians at the expense of their urban counterparts, is known as prison gerrymandering.

Danny Young won the 2005 election for the Ward 2 seat on the Anamosa City Council in Iowa by a single vote. This would be an unusual occurrence in any political race, even in a small town like Anamosa, which covers just 2.2 square miles and has only fifty-seven hundred residents. But it becomes even more remarkable when you consider that Danny, a fifty-three-year-old backhoe operator with no political experience, not only was never a candidate for the seat but raised no money, ran no campaign, and his name did not even appear on the ballot.

There were three reasons for his unexpected success. The first is that despite boasting a population of almost fourteen hundred people according to the 2000 census, Ward 2 contained only fifty-eight eligible voters, and most of them failed to turn out that November. The second is that the twelve-year incumbent, Bernie Keeney, had declined to run for reelection. Since no candidates had filed to replace him, this meant that write-in votes alone would determine who won. And the third is that only three ballots were cast in the Ward 2 contest: two for Danny, one of which was from his wife, the other from a neighbor; and one for Marty Seeley, his nominal opponent. Danny, now the city counselor elect, couldn't even be bothered to vote for himself.

In the southeast corner of Ward 2 sits Anamosa State Penitentiary,

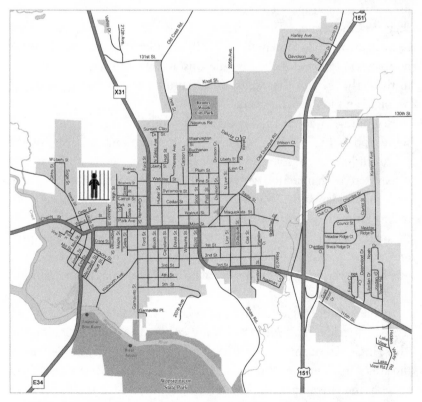

Map of Anamosa, Iowa, showing the location of Anamosa State Penitentiary.

the largest in Iowa. Its 1,321 inmates now represented 96 percent of Danny's constituents. Or at least they did in theory. But with incarcerated persons being disenfranchised in all but two states, Maine and Vermont, there's very little incentive for the politicians who represent districts whose populations are artificially inflated by the inclusion of prisoners to pay any heed to their liberty-challenged inhabitants.

"Do I consider them my constituents?" Danny pondered in an interview with *The New York Times,* before amply summarizing the representational deficiencies that prison gerrymandering creates: "They don't vote, so, I guess, not really." The man he replaced as Ward 2's representative on the city council gave a more polished politician's answer when asked the same question. "A lot of the things we do in the community does affect them," Bernie Keeney told *The Anamosa Gazette.* "We have to serve all citizens."

Anamosa is by no means an isolated example. In almost every state, prisoners are routinely counted as residents of the institutions where they are incarcerated. The resulting representational discrepancies have been extensively documented by the Prison Gerrymandering Project, a nonpartisan effort launched by the Prison Policy Initiative think tank in the early years of the twenty-first century to raise awareness of the problem and lobby for reform.

Beginning in 2002, the organization produced a series of state-by-state reports highlighting some of the most dramatic effects of the prison-industrial complex on America's legislative elections. What they discovered is that prison gerrymandering, which had largely flown under the radar as the War on Drugs precipitated the escalating mass incarceration crisis—one that every year sees 600,000 individuals pass through the gates of the nation's two thousand federal and state prisons, and 10.6 million occupying cells in its three thousand local jails—was having very real effects on the allocation of resources and political power.

In New York, for example, the 2000 census saw some forty-four thousand residents of New York City counted in rural upstate areas. These included the more than two thousand inmates who resided down the street from my apartment in Alden. The imbalance was sufficient to deny the city an additional state senate seat, which the Republican majority was instead able to relocate to an upstate area where they could be reasonably assured of controlling it. Two of the politicians whose districts boasted the largest populations of prisoners, "representing" fully 23 percent of the total incarcerated persons in the state, were the Republican senators Dale Volker and Michael Nozzolio. These men also happened to chair the two committees in charge of criminal justice policy. Whenever momentum began to build in Albany to repeal the state's harsh drug laws—laws that sent a constant parade of nonviolent offenders, and taxpayer dollars, to their districts—Volker and Nozzolio managed to short-circuit it.

The most extreme example, however, was New York's 114th State Assembly District. Located in the far northern reaches of the state along the Canadian border, it is home to two large maximum-security prisons: the Upstate Correctional Facility and the Clinton Correctional Facility. Fully 7 percent of the district's inhabitants at the time of the 2000 census—including 83 percent of its African American adult residents and 74 percent of its Hispanic residents—were disenfranchised prisoners.

By decade's end, the prison population of the 114th would also include its state assemblyman, the Republican Chris Ortloff. In 2008, the Vietnam veteran who had represented the seat since 1986 was arrested by federal authorities at a motel in Colonie, New York, on felony charges of soliciting sex with a minor. The indictment alleged that he had made arrangements to meet two sisters, aged eleven and twelve, whom he believed he had been grooming online. In reality, he was chatting with an undercover state police officer. At least he was spared the indignity of being incarcerated in his own district. After pleading guilty, Ortloff was sent to the federal correctional facility in Danbury, Connecticut, to serve a minimum ten-year sentence. He was also forced, somewhat ironically, to resign his $110,000-a-year positions on the state parole board and the legislature's redistricting taskforce. As will be discussed in chapter 10, he was far from the only member of the New York legislature to find themselves entangled in the criminal justice system.

Then take the case of Michael Cady, a longtime vagrant who in the fall of 1893 was convicted by the state of illegally registering to vote. Cady had an unusual habit. Every six months or so, he would visit the local police constabulary and confess to the crime of vagrancy. Under New York law at the time, this offense did not lead to a loss of voting rights. But it did allow a magistrate judge to commit the offender to a correctional facility for a set period of time. Cady would then be sent to

the Tombs—the colloquial name for what is now the Manhattan Detention Complex, and what was then the New York City Halls of Justice
and House of Detention—the notorious city jail in the Five Points
neighborhood of lower Manhattan. There he would be provided with
room and board, and the warden would employ him to run errands,
sometimes even outside the prison walls. Cady had been doing this for
seven years and apparently had no intention of stopping anytime soon.

Despite his unusual lifestyle, Cady evidently still felt a sense of civic
responsibility, for he registered to vote at what he at least considered
his primary residence: the Tombs. But the authorities saw things differently. Even though the federal census, which the state used to draw
its legislative districts, counted him as a resident at the location where
he was incarcerated, the state constitution, which provided that "no
person shall be deemed to have gained or lost a residence, by reason of
his presence or absence . . . while confined in any public prison," did
not. Cady was convicted of illegal registration, and the New York Court
of Appeals unanimously affirmed. The court documents unfortunately
make no reference as to whether he was permitted to serve his sentence
at the Tombs.

Outside New York, a quick perusal of the results of the 2000
census—subsequently used by all fifty states to redraw their legislative
districts—reveals some additional disturbing abnormalities. There were
twenty-one U.S. counties, eight in Texas alone, where more than one-
fifth of the reported residents were incarcerated prisoners. Those behind
bars made up 33 percent of the population of Concho County, Texas
(which, in addition to having the fourth-lowest per capita income in the
nation, is home to what was then Eden Detention Center, since closed
and repurposed as an Immigration and Customs Enforcement facility);
33 percent of the population of West Feliciana Parish, Louisiana (location of the Louisiana State Penitentiary, the largest maximum-security
prison in the United States, also known as the Alcatraz of the South);
and 35 percent of the population of Crowley County, Colorado (site of
the privately owned and operated Crowley County Correctional Facility, which in 2013 paid $600,000 to settle a class-action lawsuit filed by
a group of prisoners who were injured in a 2004 riot that the chronically
understaffed facility had failed to adequately respond to).

Number one on this list would be Union County, Florida. Thirty
percent of its 5,500 residents were inmates at the Union Correctional

Institution, part of the sprawling Florida State Prison complex where the state's death row is located and Ted Bundy was executed by lethal injection in 1989. But the property is bifurcated by the New River, placing about half of the inmates across the border in Bradford County, where they also find themselves in an entirely different congressional district. Fifty-six counties whose populations declined between 1990 and 2000 appeared to be growing according to the census numbers, solely by virtue of their increasing prison populations. Jones County, Texas, which lost 355 actual residents, saw its census population rise by 26 percent, thanks to the 4,650 additional inmates sent their way by the Texas Department of Corrections.

Unlike the gerrymanders discussed in chapter 6, the phenomenon of prison gerrymandering was not a product of overt racism. Nor was there any deliberate attempt among policy makers to distort the populations of legislative districts, at least initially. Instead, it came about largely as an accident of history. When the very first federal census was conducted in 1790, counting prisoners at their place of incarceration was not unreasonable. "While incarceration rates were low, prisons were in or near prisoners' home communities, and census data was used solely to allocate congressional seats, prison gerrymanders generate[d] little controversy," writes the DePaul University political science professor Christina Rivers. "They also had minimal influence on representational outcomes."

But the policy of counting prisoners at their "usual residence," defined by the Census Bureau as "the place where a person lives and sleeps most of the time," has become considerably more problematic in the era of mass incarceration. "Current census residency rules ignore the reality of prison life," argues Kenneth Prewitt, a former director of the Census Bureau under President Bill Clinton. "Incarcerated people have virtually no contact with the community surrounding the prison. Upon release the vast majority return to the community in which they lived prior to incarceration."

Nevertheless, while fully 62 percent of the public comments received in response to the proposed residency rules for the 2010 census related to the counting of prisoners, the Obama administration declined to adjust its formula. In the lead-up to the 2020 census—citing the "major operational issues for both the correctional facilities and the Census Bureau" that would result from a change in policy—the Trump administration followed suit. One wonders whether those "major operational issues" might be solved, to throw an idea out there, by simply asking those who administer the nation's jails, prisons, and detention centers for the last known address on file for each of their inmates. The handful of states that on their own initiative have opted to adjust the census data to count prisoners at their homes, rather than their cells, did not appear to have any significant difficulty overcoming the logistical challenge.

The negative antidemocratic effects of prison gerrymandering cannot be ignored. Not only does it create urban-rural imbalances in the comparative level of representation that different communities receive in state and federal government, but these in turn affect the allocation of federal and state tax dollars and other resources. In Maryland, for example, a report by the Prison Gerrymandering Project documented that "18% of the population currently credited to House of Delegates District 2B (near Hagerstown) is actually incarcerated people from other parts of the state. In effect, by using uncorrected Census data to draw legislative districts, the legislature granted every group of 82 residents in this district as much political influence as 100 residents of every other district." The result: both power and money flowed away from the city of Baltimore and into the sparsely populated Appalachian counties of western Maryland.

Things were even worse in Somerset County, located along the Eastern Shore of the Chesapeake Bay. "A large prison is 64% of the 1st County Commission District," the report continues, "giving each resident in that district 2.7 times as much influence as residents in other districts. Even more troubling is that by including the prison population as 'residents' in county districts, the county has been unable to draw an effective majority–African American district and has had no African-American elected to county government, despite settlement of a vote dilution lawsuit in the 1980s."

That lawsuit had ended the practice of at-large districting, which had prevented the county's African American residents—who make up 42 percent of its population—from being able to elect even a single black commissioner. But soon after the lawsuit had settled, the brand-new Eastern Correctional Institution opened its doors. The resulting impact on the 1990 census numbers turned what appeared to be a majority-minority district into one that, once disenfranchised felons were excluded, actually had a sizable white majority.

"Another problem with prison gerrymanders," Rivers writes, "is that of 'ghost' constituents. Electoral district populations are not adjusted with the release or relocation of incarcerated individuals. Because newly released individuals are not counted at their new address until the next census, their political presence remains incarcerated at their former prison address. The same would go for those who are transferred from one institution to another." So whatever inequalities are created by the counting of imprisoned persons at the time of the census are frozen in place for the remainder of the decade. An entire prison may be closed down, and every inmate relocated out of both the county and the districts of which it is part, while the remaining residents continue to reap the benefits of its inflationary effect on their numbers. "Consequently, though no longer physically present in that district," she continues, "these 'phantom' constituents continue to enhance the political power of the communities that count them in their districts for many years."

All of this would be disturbing enough even if the demographics of the incarcerated population perfectly matched those of the public at large. At least then the negative effects of prison gerrymandering would be equitably distributed across different demographic subgroups. But the problem is far worse than that. As the Somerset County example illustrates, the effects of prison gerrymandering are felt most acutely not by the nation's white citizens but by its more vulnerable and marginalized minority populations. The downstream effects of the shocking racial inequities that exist within the American criminal justice system—themselves a product of systemic racism and a lack of access to educational and other resources that contribute to the lower socioeconomic status of many minority communities—have been a massive overrepresentation of African Americans and Latinos in the U.S. prison population. And with prisoner disenfranchisement being the norm, the sum effect of prison gerrymandering has been a decades-long transfer of political power away from America's African American and Latino residents and into the hands of the white majority.

Take rural Brown County, Illinois, located west of Springfield between the Illinois and the Mississippi Rivers. According to the 2000 census, Brown County's population was 18 percent black. But all but five of those 1,265 African American residents, 99.6 percent of the total, were inmates at the Western Illinois Correctional Center. The facility's 2,000 prisoners made up almost a third of the county's population. In the nation as a whole, there were 173 counties where more than half of the black population was incarcerated at the time of the 2000 census.

As mentioned earlier, the origins of prison gerrymandering were largely a historical accident, a product of decisions made during the very earliest years of the Republic that became entrenched due to bureaucratic inertia and governmental convention. And while that remains true, in more recent decades politicians have also embraced prison gerrymandering as a deliberate strategy. In a 2012 study, the Princeton University political scientist Jason P. Kelly analyzed what happened to prison populations in states where control of redistricting had flipped from one political party to the other. Recognizing that these situations provided the most fertile opportunities for politicians to manipulate prison populations for political gain, he hypothesized that "by shifting a significant proportion of these phantom constituents into districts that lean heavily toward the majority party, legislators can free up an equal number of citizens from those districts to be distributed among neighboring marginal ones, thereby increasing that party's likelihood of picking up additional seats in the state legislature."

"Alternatively," he continues, "prison populations in relatively safe districts controlled by the out-party can be swapped with citizens in marginal districts, who are more likely to vote for the opposition, in hopes of flipping the marginal district." In effect, in the redistricting game incarcerated persons act like jokers in a deck of cards. Nominal constituents who can be shuffled around between districts for strategic advantage, but whose lack of voting rights denies them any opportunity to influence subsequent election outcomes. This allows them to be deployed in a way that strengthens the hands of the majority party's candidates while weakening the cards held by their opponents.

"To the extent that such gerrymandering does occur," Kelly continues, "we should expect to see a movement of prison populations from marginal districts and safe seats held by the out-party to safe districts controlled by the majority party, particularly after a switch in partisan control." And that's precisely what the study's results showed, although there were some inconsistencies in the extent to which line drawers in different states had been prepared, or able, to utilize this tool. The two most aggressive prison gerrymanders were created by the Republicans in Texas and Florida. There, tens of thousands of incarcerated persons were shifted from competitive Democratic districts into safe Republican ones. The net effect of these changes was sufficiently large to flip control of several state senate seats.

In contrast, Democrats in California and Republicans in Michigan, though presented with opportunities similar to those of their southern counterparts, declined to push the envelope. Kelly credits this to a desire among California Democrats to implement a plan that protected existing incumbents, in the hopes of forestalling an effort to create an independent redistricting commission (they were unsuccessful), and stricter legal constraints on the redistricting process in Michigan. Across the nation, in situations where a party took control of the redistricting process when they had not held it during the prior decade, an average of five thousand prisoners per state were shifted into seats that party held. Prison gerrymandering had now become more than a mere historical oddity. It was a new weapon in the gerrymandering arsenal.

Why has there not been a concerted legal effort to end prison gerrymandering? After all, the same "one person, one vote" arguments that proved so successful at the Supreme Court in the 1960s are equally applicable to the malapportionment of districts created by the misallocation of prisoners. And the disproportionate burden that prison gerrymandering places on racial minority groups might also lend itself to a challenge under the Voting Rights Act.

Part of the explanation must surely lie in the fact that for most of U.S. history—until the War on Drugs and subsequent profusion of mandatory minimum sentences created the mass incarceration crisis of today—prison gerrymandering wasn't really that big of a problem. And when it did become one, things happened slowly, like the proverbial frog crouching unsuspectingly in a pot of water on the stove, gradually being brought to a boil. But the truth is that prison gerrymandering also represents the largely ignored and forgotten stepchild of the gerrymander family. It lacks the wildly contorted and misshapen districts that can be easily satirized in the pages of the popular press, and the backing of moneyed interests and aggrieved politically connected plaintiffs that might provide the impetus to spur on litigation. And on the political side, both mass incarceration and prisoner disenfranchisement have to date been largely bipartisan problems, lending neither side much incentive to rock the boat by pushing for reform. But creepingly, agonizingly slowly, things have finally begun to change.

The first big push to end prison gerrymandering came in New York. The charge was led by the Prison Policy Initiative, whose very first published report in their Prison Gerrymandering Project series, released in 2002, had focused on the state. They partnered with the National Voting Rights Institute and Demos, the New York City–based progressive think tank, to file an amicus brief in a 2005 case that was pending before the U.S. Court of Appeals for the Second Circuit.

In that litigation, Jalil Abdul Muntaqim, who had been convicted of the 1971 murder of two New York City police officers and was serving a life sentence, attempted to mount a vote dilution challenge under the VRA to the state's felon disenfranchisement laws. The lawsuit was eventually dismissed for lack of standing. Muntaqim was unable to convince the court that the proximate cause of his inability to register to vote was actually the state's policy toward convicted felons, rather than his lack of residency there (he had previously resided in California and expressed an intent to live with family in Georgia if paroled). But this was still the very first case where arguments against prison gerrymandering had been raised before a federal appellate court.

The lawsuit caught the interest of the New York state senator Eric Schneiderman, who that same year introduced a bill proposing to count incarcerated persons at their home addresses for the purposes of redistricting after the 2010 census. Though his bill stalled in committee, momentum was now gradually beginning to build behind the cause. Similar proposals were introduced in Illinois and Texas, again without success. But as the census grew closer, and the sense of urgency began to increase, change belatedly started to happen.

Maryland was the first state to break through the logjam. In April 2010, with the census in full swing, the general assembly passed, and Governor Martin O'Malley signed into law, the No Representation Without Population Act. It required the state to count prisoners as residents of their home districts for the 2011 redistricting. With the stroke of a pen, the city of Baltimore regained almost six thousand inhabitants that the census had counted as residents of correctional facilities elsewhere in the state, a 1 percent population increase over the numbers that the federal government had supplied. Soon thereafter, the residents of

Somerset County elected the first African American city commissioner in their history.

Later that same year, New York finally followed suit. In August, the legislature passed the latest version of Schneiderman's bill, and Governor David Paterson signed it into law. The next month, Delaware enacted a similar law, followed by California in October 2011. Their legislation, however, came too late for the 2011 redistricting cycle and would instead go into effect following the 2020 census.

But almost immediately, the celebratory champagne had to be put back on ice. A group of African American Maryland voters—represented, the Prison Gerrymandering Project alleged, by "Republican Party attorneys" engaged in "a partisan power grab under the guise of an African-American voting rights lawsuit"—filed suit in federal court claiming that the No Representation Without Population Act violated the Constitution. The three-judge federal panel was having none of it. In their unanimous ruling in *Fletcher v. Lamone,* they declared, "We find no support in the record for this contention." "Because some correction is better than no correction," the judges reasoned, "the State's adjusted data will likewise be more accurate than the information contained in the initial census reports, which does not take prisoners' community ties into account at all."

Around the same time, a state court in New York also upheld their law against a lawsuit claiming that it violated the state constitution. And in 2012, without argument or noted dissent, the U.S. Supreme Court summarily affirmed the lower court decision in the Maryland case. With that decision states were finally given free rein, should they choose to do so, to end prison gerrymandering within their own borders.

The last few years have brought even further progress. In 2019, Washington and Nevada passed legislation pledging to count prisoners at their home addresses for the purposes of redistricting after the 2020 census. In early 2020, New Jersey, Colorado, and Virginia did the same, followed by Connecticut and Illinois in 2021, bringing the total number of states that have adopted such laws to eleven, although Illinois's will not take effect until after the 2030 census. In addition, according to data collected by the Prison Policy Initiative, literally hundreds of individual counties, cities, and towns in almost every state in the nation have taken similar steps to end prison gerrymandering in their local elections. The strength of the momentum behind reforming the counting of incarcerated persons for redistricting has a clear relationship, in my opinion, to the fact that there really aren't any particularly compelling arguments against it.

Opponents will contend that the last known addresses of some prisoners might not be 100 percent accurate, or that not every individual who is incarcerated will return to their home community after their release. And while both of these things are undoubtedly true, they ignore the fact that this adjusted method of counting prisoners is, at the very least, no less inaccurate than what the Census Bureau already does. And as the court concluded in *Fletcher,* it is in all likelihood substantially more accurate.

Using the federal census numbers for redrawing districts will always produce such effects. As people are born, die, and move from one location to another, actual district populations will inevitably deviate from the mathematical ideal of population equality on which they were drawn. This is particularly true later in the decade, by which point the census numbers are almost ten years out of date. This is not an indictment of the movement to end prison gerrymandering. It's an indictment of our entire district-based electoral system.

One of the local jurisdictions that decided to implement reform was Anamosa, Iowa. The election of Danny Young in 2005 had revealed the staggering inequalities in voting-eligible population between the various wards that were used to elect the city council. These revelations prompted Bertha Finn—"a retired journalist and county clerk as well as an accomplished amateur historian," according to a 2015 obituary—to organize a petition drive to place a referendum on the 2007 ballot to replace the existing ward system with an at-large selection method. Sixty-four percent of Anamosa voters supported the change.

And as for Danny Young, the accidental politician whose one-vote victory had made him the poster child of the prisoner's dilemma? He finished tenth in the 2009 city council election, held under the at-large system approved by the voters in the earlier referendum. And while, with only six seats up for grabs, this meant that he would lose his incumbent position on the city council, he did at least have the satisfaction of improving significantly on his 2005 showing. This time he received twenty-two votes.

9

Win One for the Whizzer

I n addition to witnessing the birth of the modern gerrymander, the 1980s marked the beginning of what would prove to be a largely futile thirty-year fight to persuade the federal courts to step in and police the practice. In truth, it was an uphill battle before it had even begun. In contrast to racial gerrymandering—where those bringing legal challenges could point to decades of precedent applying particularly aggressive scrutiny to government policies treating citizens differently on account of their race—judges and litigants alike were largely flying blind, attempting to shoehorn existing doctrines of equal protection and freedom of association into as-yet-uncharted areas of legal inquiry.

Courts as institutions are generally conservative in temperament, looking backward through the lens of well-worn concepts like tradition, history, text, and jurisprudence rather than pushing forward into new frontiers of social change. But courts also have a fundamental role to play as the watchdogs and guardians of democracy. The only champions of the downtrodden, the oppressed, and the powerless whose interests the regular machinery of democracy is not well-equipped to protect. Perhaps the most frustrating element of the legal fight against gerrymandering is the insistence by so many robed jurists that the courts have no place on this playing field at all. Those like Felix Frankfurter who contend that the proper remedy for unfairness in elections is to vote for politicians who will make those elections less unfair. But when the courts abdicate this responsibility, there's often nothing left standing between the foxes and the henhouse.

As chapter 7 discussed, one major flash point in the evolving redistricting wars was the state of California. The legal battle over the Democratic gerrymander would stretch on for most of the decade, eventually reaching the Supreme Court in 1988. Another was the state of Indiana. And here, the proverbial jackboot of oppression was very much on the other foot. The Hoosier State's Republicans, in a manner reminiscent of their Golden State Democratic counterparts, set about gerrymandering the state's legislative districts after the 1980 census. In 1984, a divided panel of the U.S. District Court for the Southern District of Indiana ruled that those districts violated the Constitution.

Only a year earlier, in the case of *Karcher v. Daggett,* a similarly divided Supreme Court had held that a Democratic gerrymander by the New Jersey legislature was also unconstitutional. And though their decision was based primarily on violations of "one person, one vote," rather than the unfairness of the gerrymander itself, a majority of the justices appeared to indicate that the modern gerrymander might pose an even greater threat to fair representation than the creeping gerrymanders it had replaced. Things came to a head in 1986, when the appeal of the Indiana decision reached the Court. Many expected a ruling setting a strong precedent against partisan gerrymandering. But it was not to be. The justice who had written the dissenting opinion in the New Jersey case, one that hinted at evils that gerrymandering could still produce even when district populations were equal, would also write the controlling opinion in the Indiana dispute. His failure to articulate a workable solution to the problem represents perhaps the greatest missed opportunity in the entire history of the Court's adventures in the political thicket.

Few Americans can boast on their résumés of serving as a justice on the U.S. Supreme Court, earning two Bronze Stars in active combat, or leading the National Football League in rushing yards as a rookie. But Byron White was not like most Americans. He achieved all three. Nicknamed Whizzer by a newspaper columnist during his time as an all-American halfback for the Colorado Buffaloes—a moniker that, much to his chagrin, followed him for the remainder of his life—White was born in Fort Collins, Colorado, in 1917. He was the son of a poor frontiersman, Alpha Albert White, and his wife, Maude, neither of whom attended high school. White's grandfather fought with distinction on the Union side during the Civil War, before returning to Iowa to father fifteen children. He had died in poverty and obscurity before Byron was born. But from these humble western roots blossomed a quintessential story of the American dream.

"He has had a truly remarkable life," reflected President Bill Clinton on March 9, 1993, the day that White announced his retirement from the nation's highest court after thirty-one years of service. Some version of this phrase appears in almost every postscript of his career. "Justice White may have enjoyed fame, honor and (briefly) riches in youth, but he paid for it, often in subtle ways, the rest of his career," wrote his former law clerk Dennis Hutchinson. "To the extent that the legend distorts our appreciation of the public service, it would be a courtesy to clarify where myth and man depart, and why he loathes the sobriquet that made him famous long ago." White never allowed himself to give in to the temptation of concluding that he was anything other than ordinary. But throughout his career he could never quite manage to extricate himself from the shadow that was cast by his own astonishing CV, and of course the nickname that he so despised.

Despite their lack of formal schooling, White's parents believed firmly in the value of education for their own children. In the tiny town of Wellington, Colorado, dominated by the sugar beet industry, this meant that Byron and his older brother, Sam, attended the tiny Wellington High School, from which each of them graduated as valedictorian. Byron's entire 1934 high school class totaled only six students. The family's economic travails forced White to work from a young age, beginning with his first job in the beet fields of Wellington at the age of six. "He also did odd jobs," wrote another former law clerk, Leon Irish, "such as unloading lumber from trains and trucks, shoveling coal, sweeping out buildings, swinging a sledgehammer for the railroad, and hashing a fraternity. [But] the work in the sugar beet fields was his most consistent job. Cultivation of sugar beets, at that time, was backbreaking labor."

Initially earning $1.50 an hour for their work, White and his brother, Sam, eventually moonlighted in the beet-growing business themselves, renting a twenty-five-acre tract in town and contracting with local growers to cultivate the crop. "There was very little money around Wellington, and I suppose you could say that by the normal standards of the day we were all quite poor," he later said of his upbringing, "although we didn't necessarily feel poor because everyone was more or less the same. Everybody worked for a living. Everybody."

A star on the gridiron, the track, the baseball diamond, and the basketball court in high school, White was offered athletic scholarships by five different schools after graduation. He chose to play football at the University of Colorado, turning down a $5,000 signing bonus offered to him by the St. Louis Cardinals to turn pro in baseball, instead waiting tables on the side to earn some extra cash. In spite of his talent, things got off to a slow start. White failed to make the starting lineup as a freshman and blew out his knee early in the first game of his sophomore season.

"White's junior year was the first step on his road to national prominence," writes Hutchinson, "he played well enough to receive all-conference honors, and his stature as a three-sport star (basketball and baseball, too), combined with a straight-A average, made him the most famous man on campus and the logical choice for the faculty committee who annually selected the President of the Student Body." Despite his athletic prowess, academics were always White's primary passion. *The New York Times* reported one story of a time when the Buffaloes' coach, Bunny Oakes, discovered him reading a textbook on the Boulder campus and chastised him to study the team's playbook instead. "You take care of the football," his young halfback responded, "I'll take care of the books."

Expectations were understandably high when White returned to Boulder for his senior year in 1937, and he did not disappoint. Already identified as a potential all-American by the famed sportswriter Grantland Rice—"'Whizzer' White is the ideal moniker for a triple threat tailback," Rice declared on his radio show; "the man with that name [is] going to live up to it"—he proceeded to put together one of the greatest statistical seasons in college football history. The Buffaloes went undefeated in the regular season, scoring an invitation to that year's Cotton Bowl in Dallas. White led the nation in both rushing yards and points scored, was named an all-American at halfback, and finished runner-up for the Heisman Trophy to the Yale halfback Clint Frank. And though the seventeenth-ranked Buffaloes lost their Cotton Bowl matchup 28–14 to Rice (White scored all fourteen of their points and

LEFT Byron White during practice with the Colorado Buffaloes, 1938.

BELOW Byron White (*center*) with his father, Alpha Albert "Al" White (*right*), and brother, Sam (*left*), in Wellington, Colorado, circa 1924.

was named MVP), he had quickly established himself as a national sensation.

As "Whizzer-mania" spread like wildfire through the college football universe that fall, White emerged as a consensus top-five pick for the upcoming 1938 NFL draft. Amid the sudden glare of the media spotlight, he still found time to lead the Colorado basketball team to the

1938 National Invitation Tournament at Madison Square Garden and receive further pro-baseball contract offers from the Cardinals, Browns, and White Sox. But he was also wary of allowing his newfound fame to distract from his primary focus: academics.

After graduating first in his class of 267, White received a prestigious Rhodes scholarship to study at the University of Oxford in England, intending to apply to law schools in the United States upon his return. But the decision as to his future became substantially more complicated in December, when he was selected fourth overall by the Pittsburgh Pirates (now Steelers) in the NFL draft. The Pirates owner Art Rooney then offered him a $15,800 annual contract to play for the team. This would make him, as a rookie, by far the highest-paid player in the league. After initially deciding "to forgo the money and go to Oxford, a choice celebrated editorially in state newspapers," White discovered that he could delay his graduation from Colorado until 1939. This enabled him to defer the Rhodes scholarship and join the Pirates when their training camp opened that summer. It also marked the beginning of a period during which he attempted to juggle, with admirable aplomb, the responsibilities of being both a star athlete and a star academic.

White's rookie season in the National Football League was perhaps even more impressive than his senior year at Colorado had been. Though his team struggled, finishing the year 2-9 and dead last in the league standings, White led the NFL in rushing yards, finished second in rushing touchdowns, and was named an All-Pro. He left the team in early 1939 to sail to England, but not before earning the admiration of Art Rooney, who said of him, "Of all the athletes I have known in my lifetime, I'd have to say Whizzer White came as close to anyone to giving 100 percent of himself when he was in competition."

"I had never seen anyone work as hard as he did," recalled his teammate Bill Radovich. "And after practice was over, he was still out there, practicing punt returns—catching them on the fly—or kicking, and always taking extra laps." Opponents too could not help but respect White's hustle on the field. The Washington Redskins star Sammy Baugh recalled, "He didn't quit, even for one play, all day long, both ways. He was no fun to tackle, I'll tell you. Others were faster, but listen, he was a hard man to bring down. A hard man." White himself perhaps put it most succinctly. "I hate to lose right down to my heels," he told a reporter in 1938.

That extraordinary work ethic was now about to be unleashed on some of the world's finest institutions of higher learning. Oxford came as a welcome opportunity to remove himself from the media spotlight, something that White would attempt to do for the remainder of his life. "I was so tired of athletics," he later said, while reminiscing on his arrival in England. "It was just like coming out into the sunshine, to go to school and not have to go out and knock your damn brains out at three o'clock every day."

While traveling in Munich during the summer break, he made the acquaintance of another young American with a famous name, John F. Kennedy, who was jaunting around Europe on a grand tour while his father served as the U.S. ambassador to Great Britain. Though their initial meeting was inauspicious ("I think we mostly sat around and had a few beers," White said in 1964), twenty-three years later Kennedy would nominate White to a seat on the U.S. Supreme Court.

The outbreak of war in Europe brought his time at Oxford to a premature end, because all the American Rhodes scholars were sent home when Britain declared war on Germany in September 1939. But the return to the United States gave White the opportunity to continue the double-dip indulgence of his twin passions: football and law. He signed with the Detroit Lions for the 1940 NFL season, again leading the league in rushing yards as an All-Pro while simultaneously studying at Yale Law School, earning the highest grades of any student in his first-year class.

Law school was a revelation for White, whose academic career so far, while stellar, had largely lacked direction or focus. He later described that first year at Yale as "the most stimulating intellectual experience I had had up to that time." But after a somewhat disappointing 1941 season with the Lions—one that would turn out to be White's final year in the NFL—his burgeoning careers both as an athlete and as an attorney were placed on the back burner in December 1941, when the Japanese bombed Pearl Harbor.

As a good all-American boy, White's patriotism was beyond reproach. There was never any question as to whether he would heed the call of duty. After attempting to enlist in the U.S. Marine Corps, and being rejected on account of his color blindness, he instead joined the naval intelligence services and was quickly shipped out to the South Pacific to serve in the PT boat organization. There he found himself once again alongside Kennedy, whom he met while the future president was recovering from his exploits aboard PT-109 in 1943.

When the vessel was cut in two by a Japanese destroyer, Kennedy swam three and a half miles from the ruined boat to the safety of a nearby island, pulling a severely wounded crewmate by a life-vest strap clenched between his teeth. White conducted the naval intelligence investigation into the incident and quickly struck up a friendship with the young and gregarious lieutenant, occasionally joining him on PT boat patrols when Kennedy returned to active duty. White served with admirable distinction during the war, although in typically understated and self-deprecating fashion, he downplayed the occasionally heroic nature of what the newspapers back in Colorado fervently serialized as "Whizzer White's Exploits in the South Pacific."

His own mother, "Ma" White, only learned of his heroism aboard the USS *Bunker Hill*—where, after the ship was struck by two Japanese kamikaze planes, White and another officer, E. Calvert Cheston, pulled numerous men from the flames belowdecks—when asked about it by a reporter. Beaming with pride, she responded, "My son never talks much about his experiences." The press lapped it up. White's reticence and humility only made him more attractive fodder for the tabloids. "Whizzer White Survives Bunker Hill," blazed the headline in the local paper after the incident. But it was the caption that told the real story: "Ex-buff grid great fails to mention heroic role in attacks." The sailors who served with White on the *Bunker Hill* held him in no less regard. "He was absolutely focused on the fires and on the men," Cheston later recalled. "A shell would go off or an explosion would occur, but there was Byron—locked in on the man who needed help or on the hose that needed to be manned. I don't think he ever thought about himself. We were all working frantically, but he stayed so cool it was almost unnerving. And he never took a rest."

Perhaps it was these experiences in combat, for which he was awarded two Bronze Stars, that had the effect of clarifying his life goals. For when White's four years of military service came to an end after the war, he expressed little interest in rekindling his NFL career. "There's little doubt that 'Whizzer' could have been a Hall of Famer had he been able to concentrate solely on football," wrote the Detroit sports historian Dan Holmes. "But he had different interests and goals in mind." White threw himself back into his studies at Yale full time, graduating first in

Byron White during his Supreme Court clerkship, 1946.

his law school class in 1946 and securing a prestigious clerkship with the U.S. Supreme Court chief justice Fred M. Vinson. It was during this time that he began to hone the philosophy of pragmatic, centrist nonconformity that would later make him such an enigma as a judge.

At the conclusion of his clerkship, keen as always to remove himself from the public spotlight, White eschewed all opportunities that had now opened up for him in the nation's capital to return to Denver and enter private practice. "I retired from the fray and went out to practice law in my home state," he recalled in a 1964 interview, "which was very enjoyable, so enjoyable that I really didn't pay too close attention to all the details and events concerning various people in Washington."

But when his old friend Jack Kennedy announced his candidacy for president in 1960, White once again answered the call of duty. "How many people do you know well who ask you to help them become president of the United States?" he told friends. "Whizzer Carries the Ball for Kennedy," proclaimed the headline in the *Rocky Mountain News* on November 22, 1959. The decision catapulted him back into the world of politics, the full glare of the limelight that he had always shunned, and to a job on the high court that he had never sought, or even particularly desired.

As had been the case with Felix Frankfurter several decades earlier, Byron White joined the bench at a time of considerable transition. The legacy of FDR's eight appointments between 1937 and 1943 had been a Court that was dramatically more progressive on issues of economic policy, but was still largely unwilling to take on the causes of civil rights, civil liberties, and social justice. The landmark 1954 school desegregation ruling in *Brown v. Board of Education* had been followed, a year later, by a tepid remedy in *Brown II* that directed school districts that practiced racial segregation to act "with all deliberate speed" to rectify those constitutional violations. It was a wishy-washy mandate that gave states cover to drag their feet on desegregation for more than a decade. Five years before that, in *Wolf v. Colorado,* the Court had also dealt a blow to those advocating for fairness and equality in the criminal justice system, ruling 6–3 that evidence obtained illegally by law enforcement could still be used to prosecute defendants in court. Frankfurter wrote the majority opinion.

But with the nominations of Earl Warren and William Brennan by Dwight Eisenhower—the beginning of a procession of apparently conservative Republican nominees who turned out to be surprisingly liberal as justices—those causes now had their champions. And soon, by virtue of the four appointments to the Court during the 1960s by Kennedy and his successor, Lyndon Johnson, they also had their majority. Notably, however, that majority would not often include Byron White.

The issues confronting the line drawers in Indiana were the polar opposite of those facing Phil Burton and his Democratic colleagues in California. While booming population growth brought with it extra congressional districts that had to be incorporated into the Golden State's political map, Indiana's population had stagnated. The 1980 census saw its U.S. House allocation reduced from eleven seats to ten. Nineteen eighty had also been an extremely bad year for the state's Democrats. Their candidate for governor, John Hillenbrand, failed to capitalize on the opportunity created by the retirement of the GOP incumbent, Otis Bowen, losing handily to the Republican Robert Orr. The Democrats also suffered a heavy defeat in the state legislative elections that year. The GOP emerged with a sixty-three-to-thirty-seven majority in the state house, and a thirty-five-to-fifteen edge in the state senate.

So when the legislature turned its attention in 1981 to the redrawing of districts, the Republicans now had unilateral control over the process. From the moment they convened, it was clear that secrecy and partisanship were to be the order of the day. The Republicans majority contracted with a Detroit computing firm, Market Opinion Research, which was paid $250,000 for supplying the technology to draw the maps. The redistricting committee consisted of four Republicans and four Democrats, but only the Republican members were permitted to vote. The four Democrats were excluded from its deliberations entirely. The final plans were approved by the full legislature on a strict party-line vote on the final day of the 1981 session. This was also the first time that the Democratic minority was able to see what was in them.

Under previous redistricting plans in the state, the fifty members of the senate had been elected from single-member districts, while the hundred members of the house were chosen from a combination of single-member and multimember districts, nested within the boundaries of the senate districts. That convention, however, much as had occurred with the creative renumbering of senate districts by the Democrats in California, was swiftly jettisoned in the service of partisan politics. The new Republican house map created sixty-one single-member districts, nine two-member districts, and seven three-member districts, creatively arranged to ensure that the maximum number of Republican candidates would be elected.

On the congressional side, things were similarly skewed. Three of the six Democratic incumbents were drawn into the same district, while a fourth saw his constituency carved to pieces, the remains dispersed among four surrounding Republican seats. The goal was to turn the six-to-five Democratic edge into a safe seven-to-three Republican advantage, removing the last bastion of Democratic strength from the electoral landscape. The results were phenomenally successful. Despite winning 52 percent of the popular vote in the 1982 midterms, the Democrats picked up only 43 percent of seats in the house and 36 percent in the senate. It was no surprise, then, that the gerrymander was immediately met with legal action. A group of Democratic voters, led by Irwin C. Bandemer, along with the NAACP, filed suit in federal court in early 1982 against Susan J. Davis, a member of the state election board. The court's conclusions, at least initially, were highly promising.

"There is no evident pattern to the redistricting plan," wrote the panel of federal judges in their 1984 ruling in *Bandemer v. Davis,* which struck down the state legislative maps. "No clear policy statements are evident to the Court from either the debate on the bills or the documents presented." The evidence at trial had demonstrated a cavalier lack of respect for Indiana's communities on the part of the GOP. Districts frequently divided counties, townships, and cities, cramming together precincts that shared little in terms of demographics, political culture, or identity. "For instance," the court mused, "it is difficult to conceive the interests shared by blacks in Washington Township and white suburbanites in Hamilton and Boone counties, or the shared interest of Allen and Noble county farmers with residents of downtown Fort Wayne." The judges also flagged the unusual nature of the procedures used to draw the maps. "The process underlying the reapportionment proceedings was fiercely competitive and unashamedly partisan," they continued. "The result of that attitude is revealed in the remarkably candid statements of both Speaker Dailey and Senator Bosma in their deposition testimony."

Under questioning from the attorney representing the plaintiffs, J. Roberts Dailey had been asked what the motivation was for creating the odd arrangement of single- and multimember districts for the house plan. "Political," he replied. "We wanted to save as many incumbent Republicans as possible." When quizzed about newspaper reporting suggesting that the Democratic "advisors" to the conference committee were informed that any potential map they generated would not even be considered by the Republican majority, Charles Bosma was similarly candid. "That's accurate," he responded. "I might add that I don't make goals for the opposite team." There seemed to be an attitude among the Republican majority, also on display in the antics of Burton and his Democratic allies in California, that so long as they complied with "one person, one vote," everything else was fair game.

This is the essence of the modern gerrymander, the supreme irony of the Court's efforts to institute greater electoral fairness during the reapportionment revolution. By entering the political thicket, and striking down the creeping gerrymanders that had been prevalent in the first half of the twentieth century, they created a situation where redistricting was now constitutionally mandated in every state at least once per decade. This created powerful and perverse incentives for politicians, now emboldened by their compliance with "one person, one vote," to manipulate the process to their advantage in whatever ways they could.

And now, as the judges keenly recognized, they finally had the tools to be able to do so effectively. "The Court acknowledges the historical existence of so-called 'gerrymandering' of districts, a device which has been used by both major political parties and which is claimed to have occurred in this case by the Bandemer plaintiffs," the ruling continued. "The approach used by the majority party in this instance presents a new twist, however, in that sophisticated computer equipment obviously provided more flexibility to the mapmakers."

The effects of this computer manipulation were on display in the bizarre and unusual shapes of some of the Indiana districts. Most notable was District 48, which in the minds of the reviewing judges "presents the most grievous example of the political cartographer's handiwork in this case." The district snaked around downtown Indianapolis, collecting "portions of the urban southwest side of the city, the airport and suburban area around Ben Davis High School on the west side, and the Meridian Hills area at the northern part of the county. There is simply no conceivable justification for this kind of district." Also suspicious was the unusual configuration of multimember districts. The discriminatory burden of these, the court concluded, "falls particularly hard and harsh upon black voters in the state." While African Americans made up a mere 8 percent of Indiana's population, more than 80 percent of them were drawn into multimember districts under the Republican plan.

"Multi-member districts are confined to urban areas," the judges noted, "but there is no particular pattern which is applied consistently." "The history of multi-member districts in Indiana is sketchy," they concluded, observing that while similar districts had been used selectively throughout the twentieth century, it was not until 1972 that they had incorporated areas larger than a single county. In one such district, encompassing Marion and Allen Counties, Democrats won 46.6 percent of the vote in the 1982 election, but Republican candidates captured 86 percent of the available seats. "The Court feels that such a disparity speaks for itself."

The question, however, was what to do about it. Recognizing that "the Supreme Court has yet to address directly the constitutional ramifications of a political gerrymander," the three-judge panel instead turned to the racial vote dilution cases discussed in chapter 6. In particular, the *Mobile v. Bolden* intent and effects test, while superseded by the Voting Rights Act Amendments of 1982 in racial gerrymandering cases, was seen as an ideal vehicle to adjudicate the equal protection questions here. "The same standard," the court concluded, "applies where political gerrymandering is alleged."

But the decision, in a preview of how significantly the issues involved would divide the justices of the Supreme Court two years later, was not unanimous. Two of the judges on the panel, one appointed by Jimmy Carter and the other by Lyndon Johnson, believed that the Indiana gerrymander violated the Constitution. The third, an appointee of Richard Nixon, did not. Already, even in the judicial branch, opinions on gerrymandering had become impossible to separate from the partisan attachments of those being asked to adjudicate it.

When the Kennedy administration assumed office in early 1961, the young and largely green incoming attorney general, Bobby Kennedy, was looking for an experienced hand to help staff the Justice Department. He turned to Byron White, the new deputy attorney general, whom he tasked with assembling a collection of young legal talent to help implement the president's New Frontier agenda. White put together a star-studded team of attorneys at DOJ, including the famed Harvard Law professor and future Watergate special prosecutor, Archibald Cox, as solicitor general and the future LBJ attorney general Nicholas Katzenbach to head the Office of Legal Counsel. "It was reassuring to know that prior political connection wasn't the exclusive formula for entitlement," White said of his team. "Most of the people that were brought in hadn't been soldiers in the campaign. They were good, competent lawyers that Bob thought could fill these positions."

As was befitting the administration of the youngest elected president in U.S. history, the Kennedy DOJ was characterized by its youthful energy and vigor. Cox, at forty-eight, was the old hand in the office, with White at forty-three the next most experienced. Katzenbach, thirty-nine, and RFK, thirty-five, rounded out the crew. One evening early in their tenure, Bobby and Byron were walking the halls of the Justice Department, tossing a football back and forth as they discussed legal affairs, when a suspicious staffer, not recognizing the two men, accosted them. "Anything I can do for you?" the staffer asked warily. "Yes," came the reply, "I'm Bob Kennedy and this is Mr. White. We're looking for a gym."

White was also tasked with recommending candidates to the Kennedy brothers for appointment to the lower federal courts. Kennedy named no fewer than 125 federal judges to life terms during his short tenure in office, almost as many as his predecessor, Dwight Eisenhower, had managed in a full eight years. This was largely a product of legislation passed by Congress early in his presidency creating fifty new federal judgeships, placing a great deal of responsibility on White to identify suitable nominees. "In my own mind the primary concern was not so much whether Democrats or Republicans were put on the bench," he recalled, exhibiting the commitment to judicial independence and nonpartisan administration of justice that would characterize his own judicial career, "but whether they were honest men of acceptable competence."

White also took a front seat in the new administration's efforts to enforce civil rights. He led a delegation of four hundred U.S. marshals and deputies to Alabama to keep the peace after violence erupted in the wake of the Freedom Rides in 1961. After tense negotiations with the state's segregationist governor, John Malcolm Patterson, White was typically understated in his account of the meeting. "There were strong words," he reported, "spoken strongly." But he also had a keen recognition of the momentousness of the events that were playing out. "This is how you are measured," he told John Doar, an attorney in the Justice Department's Civil Rights Division, when discussing how the president's order would be enforced. "This will test us."

When Justice Charles Evans Whittaker announced his retirement on March 30, 1962—Whittaker, you may recall from chapter 5, was the justice who suffered a nervous breakdown in the middle of the Court's deliberations in *Baker v. Carr,* before recusing himself from both the case and, soon thereafter, the bench itself—White expected to be heavily involved in the search for his successor. This would be the most con-

Byron White with John F. Kennedy at a 1959 college football game
between the University of Colorado and the Air Force Academy.

sequential decision of the Kennedy administration to date. The liberal
contingent of Warren, Brennan, Black, and Douglas were, at the time,
still outnumbered on the Court by the center-right coalition featuring
the moderates Stewart, Clark, and Whittaker, along with the conservatives Frankfurter and Harlan. Whomever Kennedy chose would tip the
balance in one direction or the other, potentially for a generation or
more.

"My participation was to talk to the attorney general about the qualifications of various people who were suggested," White recalled. "I
was not aware that I was being seriously considered until the president
called me and asked me if I wanted the job." It was a risky move for the
administration. Kennedy passed on a plethora of well-qualified candidates in favor of White, a wild card whose loyalty to the family was
unquestioned but who had never held elected office, who had no judicial experience, and whose policy preferences and judicial philosophy
were largely unknown.

Though he had mixed feelings about the nomination—he was later quoted in the *Los Angeles Times* as describing the job to a colleague as like being "put out to pasture early," and when Katzenbach called him to inform him that he was on the short list, his response was, "I think the President can do much better than that"—White felt duty-bound to accept the president's call to serve his country. There was also an upside to service on the high court: it allowed him to shutter himself away from the constant media scrutiny. Unlike those in the political branches of government, judges have the luxury of no longer having to make themselves available to the press.

Even then, it was touch and go. Here's Arthur Schlesinger's recollection of the telephone call in which Kennedy offered White the job: " 'Well, Byron,' Kennedy said, 'we've decided to go ahead on you.' There was a moment's silence, and the President said, 'We want to get the announcement out in twenty minutes, so we need an answer right away.' Another silence, and the President said, 'All right, we'll go ahead.' " But for those who had known him only as Whizzer, the appointment was a moment for celebration. "President Kennedy couldn't have appointed a greater man," opined Art Rooney. The *Washington Post* columnist Shirley Povich, who had covered White during his time in the NFL, perhaps said it best of all: "For every professional football player whose nose has been ground into the dirt or whose calling has been scorned as primitive by politer society, there now must be a glow of pride. One of their boys has made it all the way to the Supreme Court of the United States."

Byron White took the oath of office as the eighty-third associate justice of the U.S. Supreme Court on April 12, 1962. Almost immediately, he was a disappointment to his backers in Camelot. In contrast to the liberal activism of Arthur Goldberg, who left a cabinet position to replace Felix Frankfurter when he retired that same August, White was cut from very different ideological cloth. "He was a man who knew himself and knew his convictions and didn't care too much what others thought," wrote the University of Colorado law professor Ira C. Rothgerber, in reference to White's somewhat enigmatic brand of judicial restraint.

"Being non-ideological and non-doctrinaire is clearly very important to White, just as is being his own person and not worrying about his place in history," explained a former clerk. "He recognizes that being a justice who believes in a more limited Constitution is not the way to gain historical notoriety. Whether it's because he gained such fame as a young man in sports or whether it's just his natural disposition, I think he cares a lot more about doing what he thinks is right than whether it will make him a famous figure in history." But throughout his tenure on the Court, doing what he thought was right often placed White at loggerheads with the emerging liberal activist wing. With the appointment of Goldberg, that wing now represented a majority of the justices for the very first time.

Only two years into his tenure, the Court ignited the reapportionment revolution with its decisions in *Wesberry v. Sanders* and *Reynolds v. Sims*. Like Frankfurter before him, White was already in danger of being left behind by the locomotive of history. Though he joined the majority opinions in each of those cases, it was as far as he was prepared to go along the path into the political thicket. White was in the majority for less than 50 percent of the 5–4 decisions issued by the justices during the 1960s, and he began to cultivate a reputation for his dissents against the perceived excesses of the Warren Court. The Yale Law School professor Kate Stith, another former clerk, described White in a 1993 law review article as "the last of the New Deal liberals." There has probably been no more apt description of his judicial legacy. Only forty-four years old at the time of his nomination, his approach to jurisprudence would have been more at home on the economically progressive Courts of the 1940s and 1950s than among the social justice warriors who were now warming the bench.

"A recurring theme of his opinions," Stith writes, "was that the judiciary undermines its own legitimacy when it insists upon social or political objectives not rooted in the Constitution and resisted by the democratic institutions of society." White's confidence in the people's elected representatives, whether federal, state, or local, to do the right thing, even in the face of glaring evidence to the contrary, would lead to his being described by the time of his retirement in 1993 as "a card-carrying member of the conservative bloc."

White's reluctance when it came to flexing the muscles of judicial power was on display in the very first opinion he wrote as a justice, a dissent in the Court's 6–2 ruling in *Robinson v. California*. In that case, the majority struck down as a violation of the Eighth Amendment's prohibition of cruel and unusual punishment a California law allowing for the imprisonment of individuals with drug addictions. The majority likened it to an "attempt to make it a criminal offense for a person to be mentally ill, or a leper, or to be afflicted with a venereal disease." "I fail to see why the Court deems it more appropriate to write into the Constitution its own abstract notions of how best to handle the narcotics problem," White countered, in an opinion joined by none of the other justices, "for it obviously cannot match either the States or Congress in expert understanding."

Four years later, White also dissented in one of the most famous criminal procedure decisions in the Court's history, *Miranda v. Arizona*. In a 5–4 ruling that catapulted into public consciousness the ubiquitous "*Miranda* warning," a trope of just about every police procedural of the last fifty years, the Court determined that the Fifth Amendment right against self-incrimination requires law enforcement to inform suspects of their constitutional rights at the moment of arrest. "The proposition that the privilege against self-incrimination forbids in-custody interrogation without the warnings specified in the majority opinion and without a clear waiver of counsel," he began his blistering dissent, "has no significant support in the history of the privilege or in the language of the Fifth Amendment."

"The real concern is not the unfortunate consequences of this new decision on the criminal law as an abstract, disembodied series of authoritative proscriptions," he continued, "but the impact on those who rely on the public authority for protection, and who, without it, can only engage in violent self-help with guns, knives and the help of their neighbors similarly inclined." It was the first of a series of cases where White sided consistently with law enforcement and in opposition to his brethren's expansion of the rights of the criminally accused.

But perhaps his most notable dissent, and the one that drew the greatest ire from proponents of individual liberty, personal privacy, and reproductive choice, would come in the case of *Roe v. Wade*. In 1969, a twenty-one-year-old Texas single mother named Norma McCorvey became pregnant with her third child. At the time, state law allowed for a pregnancy to be terminated by a physician only "for the purpose of saving the life of the mother." With the assistance of the attorneys Linda Coffee and Sarah Weddington, and using the alias Jane Roe, McCorvey filed a federal lawsuit against the Dallas County district attorney, Henry Wade, alleging that the state's criminalization of elective abortions was a violation of her constitutional right to privacy.

In 1970, a three-judge federal court panel that included Irving Loeb

Goldberg, who also presided over Curtis Graves's lawsuit, ruled unanimously for Roe. "Plaintiffs argue as their principal contention," the court wrote, "that the Texas Abortion Laws must be declared unconstitutional because they deprive single women and married couples of their right, secured by the Ninth Amendment, to choose whether to have children. We agree." This ruling, and the Supreme Court decision that followed, were far from the unprecedented bombshells that their later infamy might suggest. "Freedom to choose in the matter of abortions," the panel noted, "has been accorded the status of a 'fundamental' right in every case coming to the attention of this Court where the question has been raised."

On appeal, the nine justices of the Supreme Court did not find the question all that controversial either. By the time they issued their ruling in January 1973, McCorvey had long since carried her pregnancy to term and had placed her child up for adoption. But both within the Court itself and among the broader public, the abortion issue did not produce the kind of heated divisions and polarized rhetoric that it does today. In a 7–2 decision written by Justice Harry Blackmun, who had formerly been the general counsel for the Mayo Clinic, they concluded that the interest of the state in protecting the life and welfare of the unborn must be balanced against the reproductive privacy rights of the mother. Crucially, Blackmun and the majority viewed the issue not as a moral or political question but as a medical one, best resolved in consultation between the individual patient and her physician. The seven-justice majority consisted of five appointees of Republican presidents and two who were appointed by Democrats.

For White, though, this was another example of an issue that should be left to the wisdom of the people's elected representatives to resolve. "I find nothing in the language or history of the Constitution to support the Court's judgment," he began his dissent. "The Court simply fashions and announces a new constitutional right for pregnant mothers and, with scarcely any reason or authority for its action, invests that right with sufficient substance to override most existing state abortion statutes." For White, the question of how abortion, as a sensitive issue "over which reasonable men may easily and heatedly differ," should be treated under the law was one that "should be left with the people and to the political processes the people have devised to govern their affairs." It was an opinion that could have been written by Felix Frankfurter, replete with references to the exercise of "raw judicial power," "improvident and extravagant" overreach, and, somewhat bafflingly given his contention that the justices should steer clear of injecting their own biases, uncharitable references to the "convenience, whim, or caprice of the putative mother."

It was not the last time that White placed himself on the opposite side of a contentious social issue from advocates for privacy and sexual autonomy. In 1986, toward the end of his time on the bench, the Court agreed to take up the case of Michael Hardwick, a Georgia man who had been arrested for violating the state's prohibition against "homosexual sodomy." At the time, twenty-four states and the District of Columbia still had laws on the books that criminalized private sexual activity between consenting gay and lesbian adults, and the ACLU had been searching for a test case with which to bring a legal challenge.

The circumstances of Hardwick's case—he was arrested by a police officer who entered his home without a warrant, apparently as retaliation for the "attitude" Hardwick had shown him during a prior incident between the two men—made it an ideal vehicle for such a suit. And while the court of appeals had ruled in Hardwick's favor based on the existing line of privacy cases, the Supreme Court reversed that decision 5–4. The majority opinion in *Bowers v. Hardwick* was written by none other than Byron White.

"This case does not require a judgment on whether laws against sodomy between consenting adults in general, or between homosexuals in particular, are wise or desirable," he began. "The issue presented is whether the Federal Constitution confers a fundamental right upon homosexuals to engage in sodomy, and hence invalidates the laws of the many States that still make such conduct illegal, and have done so for a very long time." It was more textbook deference to the wisdom of legislators. And once again, some of the rhetoric in White's opinion belies the contention that his views on the underlying conduct do not factor into the decision.

"It would be difficult, except by fiat, to limit the claimed right to homosexual conduct," he argued, "while leaving exposed to prosecution adultery, incest, and other sexual crimes even though they are committed in the home. We are unwilling to start down that road." The ruling in *Bowers,* like that in *Roe,* produced a significant backlash and was eventually overturned by the Court in 2003. But it also further alienated those who had come to see White as an anachronism, a justice whose progressive tendencies were more in line with FDR's economic populism than with JFK-style counterculture.

"Is it possible to trade in a Supreme Court justice? If so, I'd like to offer Byron White," wrote *The Denver Post* in 1988. "Anything of value will be considered. An engine from a '37 Buick. A bushel of buttered popcorn. A person in touch with individual dignity and privacy. Yes, someone who values privacy would be nice." It was a stinging rebuke from the paper that had once celebrated Whizzer-mania and lauded White as a hometown hero when he was first nominated to the Court.

And on the very same day that *Bowers* was decided, June 30, 1986, the Court also released another ruling, again written by White. It came in a case that cut to the very heart of the debate over gerrymandering and electoral fairness: *Davis v. Bandemer,* the appeal of the lower court decision striking down Indiana's state legislative districts. Now presented with the opportunity to nip the modern gerrymander in the bud, before it further spread its monstrous wings and sank its claws ever deeper into the raw underbelly of democracy, the justices balked.

For those reading the tea leaves, it certainly appeared as if the Supreme Court were about to deliver a decisive blow, or at the very least a substantial and stern rebuke, against the growing threat of partisan gerrymandering to the nation's political institutions. The signs had been present three years earlier, in the aforementioned case of *Karcher v. Daggett.* There, the justices had confronted a lawsuit against the State of New Jersey. Like Indiana, the Garden State experienced anemic population growth over the prior decade, leading to a reduction in its U.S. House representation from fifteen seats to fourteen. The 1980 election had this time seen the Democrats win majorities in both chambers of the state legislature, right as the Republicans were seizing power in Indiana. Already in control of the governorship, they had free rein to gerrymander the districts at will.

But after much deliberation, and amid concerns that minority voting strength in the city of Newark was being diluted, the Democratic majority failed to pass a satisfactory redistricting scheme by the end of 1981. The incumbent Democratic governor, Brendan Byrne, was then defeated in his reelection bid by his Republican opponent, Thomas

Kean. The legislature, in a move reminiscent of their colleagues in California, hurriedly passed a plan that was clearly drawn to maximize Democratic power. It was signed into law by Byrne shortly before he left office in January 1982. In their haste, though, they failed to adequately ensure that the congressional districts they were creating were substantially equal in terms of their populations, opening the door for a Republican legal challenge.

When the case reached the Supreme Court, the main thrust of the arguments on both sides was focused on this alleged violation of "one person, one vote." Though the population discrepancies were orders of magnitude smaller than those the Court had confronted during the 1960s, with the largest district containing only four thousand more people than the smallest, the justices nevertheless determined that the Constitution "requires that the State make a good faith effort to achieve precise mathematical equality." Though White dissented, his opinion also contains much discussion of the cover that strict compliance with "one person, one vote" might provide for a state to impose a severe partisan gerrymander.

Noting that "the rule of absolute equality is perfectly compatible with gerrymandering of the worst sort," he went on to lament that the majority's approach "downgrade[s] a restraint on a far greater potential threat to equality of representation, the gerrymander." The result: "Even more than in the past, district lines are likely to be drawn to maximize the political advantage of the party temporarily dominant in public affairs." With this language, in which White was joined by three Republican justices, all Nixon appointees, hopes were high that when confronted with that very question in *Davis v. Bandemer,* a favorable ruling for the challengers might be forthcoming. It was not to be.

There's a saying among those in the business that redistricting makes for strange bedfellows. Depending on which way the political winds are blowing, what might be in the interest of Democrats in one state might be antithetical to the political goals and priorities of Democrats in another, yet firmly embraced by that state's Republicans. Such unusual alliances had occurred in redistricting litigation before. In *Thornburg v. Gingles,* a team of RNC lawyers that included Thomas Hofeller had filed an amicus brief in support of the Democratic African American plaintiffs. "The new districts gave blacks entree into a political system that had been closed to them—and made surrounding districts more white and more receptive to Republican candidates," claimed Hofeller's RNC colleague Mark Braden in his 2018 *New York Times* obituary. "Mr. Hofeller convinced black politicians that they had a common cause against white Democrats, who he said had rigged the system against both them and Republicans." This counterintuitive pattern of support from white conservatives for redistricting reforms designed to benefit African American Democrats will be revisited in chapter 11.

A similarly odd pattern of alliances of expediency, if not political philosophy, was also in evidence in *Davis v. Bandemer.* The RNC was the first to get in on the action, filing a brief in support of the Democratic voters who had challenged the Indiana gerrymander. "The Republican National Committee argues in support of the Democratic Appellees because gerrymandering is a two-edged sword with which members of a political party may either carve or be carved," they wrote. "It is the belief of the Republican National Committee that egregious partisan gerrymandering in several states dilutes the opportunities for Republican candidates for Congress and state legislatures. Of course, as in the instant case, the tables can be turned." Among the authors listed on the brief is Mark Braden.

And if there were any doubts about which of the "several states" he was referencing in the above quotation, those were quickly assuaged when the Democratic majorities in both chambers of the California legislature chimed in with their own briefs in support of the Indiana Republicans. "The Assembly knows that such claims can only bring disruptive litigation which distracts legislators from their duties and undermines the legitimacy of elected representatives," they wrote, no doubt keenly aware that a ruling for the Democratic plaintiffs would open the door for a Republican legal challenge to their own gerrymander in California.

For Byron White, the questions presented in *Davis v. Bandemer* also posed a challenge. Though he had expressed significant reservations about the gerrymander in his dissent in the earlier New Jersey case, those concerns ran directly counter to his underlying philosophy of deference to the wisdom of the people's elected representatives as the primary guardians of liberty. It was this principle upon which the Indiana Republicans would hang their hat. And ironically, they turned to Justice Brennan's majority opinion in *Baker v. Carr,* the case that had

Justice Byron White, 1976.

ignited the reapportionment revolution and catapulted the judiciary
into the political thicket in 1962, for their inspiration.

In that decision, to justify judicial intervention into the malapportionment of state legislative districts, Brennan had outlined six criteria
that framed the basic contours of what became known as the political question doctrine. This convenient mechanism provides an escape
hatch, known as justiciability, for courts to extricate themselves from
the most controversial and politically charged legal questions of the
day. Fifty-seven years later, it would serve as the justification for the
Roberts Court, in the case of *Rucho v. Common Cause,* to declare that all
disputes involving partisan gerrymandering are nonjusticiable political
questions that may not be litigated in federal court. For now, though,
the justices in *Bandemer* faced two questions. First, did they have the

power, as the three-judge panel of the lower federal court had done, to rule on the constitutionality of Indiana's adventures in partisan gerry-mandering? And second, if they did, under what standard would that constitutionality be judged?

Oral arguments in the case took place on October 7, 1985. From the beginning, the justices appeared to be grappling with the implica-tions of the state's position. "But if you say it's not justiciable," one justice asked, "[doesn't] that mean that even the most extreme example of gerrymandering would not be subject to any judicial review?" And if the Court were to make such a ruling, another justice chimed in, wouldn't it be true that "by gerrymandering, one party could put the other party entirely out of business, entirely, if you were using the com-puter, without discriminating against the voters in the other party?" William Evans, the attorney representing Indiana, was forced to admit that this was indeed the case. "I believe that is true," he conceded.

But when the turn came of the attorney representing the Demo-cratic voters, Theodore Boehm, the justices seemed equally concerned about the implications of his position, particularly the contention that policing gerrymandering would require the courts to impose a form of proportional representation. "Under your theory," questioned a justice who is identified in unofficial transcripts as Byron White, although I cannot vouch for their veracity, "it seems to me that almost any time a reapportionment or redistricting by a state legislature occurred and the result was not close to perfect proportional representation, that there would be a violation?" Though Boehm parried the question by pointing to the inarguable evidence of discriminatory intent in the case record, it was a warning sign for what was to come.

When the justices released their opinions, the ruling was, to put it charitably, a mess. On the question of justiciability at least, a clear majority did emerge. "None of the identifying characteristics of a non-justiciable political question are present," White declared, in a holding that was joined by Brennan, Marshall, Blackmun, Powell, and Stevens. But it was there that the agreement ended. Only two justices, Powell and Stevens, believed that the Indiana plan was an unconstitutional partisan gerrymander. Four, including White, conceded that while gerrymandering could violate the equal protection clause under some circumstances, those criteria had not been met here. Three justices (O'Connor, Burger, and Rehnquist) believed that such disputes should never be justiciable. The lack of a clear majority opinion was unfortunate. After all, lower courts would be the ones who would have to apply this precedent in future gerrymandering lawsuits. If the justices themselves had no real clue about how to proceed, what were those judges supposed to do?

Perhaps most lamentable about White's opinion in the case—aside from what most legal scholars consider the impossibly high bar he set for finding a gerrymander unconstitutional—was his focus on actual election outcomes as the sole yardstick by which the discriminatory effects must be measured. Boehm had specifically cautioned against this in his arguments. "We contend that you judge a map not by hindsight," he implored, "but what does the map look like on the basis of the data that is available as of the time this map was drawn." The problem with White's approach, of course, is that while the harm from a gerrymander is suffered immediately, when the electoral playing field is systematically tilted against one of the teams, the real-world effects of that harm can be observed only retrospectively, when it is already too late for it to be corrected.

This was precisely the concern that had been expressed by the Republicans in California. By allowing the 1982 elections to proceed under a gerrymandered set of boundaries that the people of the state had already rejected, the California Supreme Court was essentially guaranteeing that the beneficiaries of that gerrymander would be the ones responsible for "correcting" it. A far better standard, I would argue, is to judge the severity of a gerrymander based on facts in evidence at the time of the gerrymander itself. Only then can the perpetrators be prevented from profiting from their misdeeds. But this was not the approach the Court took.

"Although we find such political gerrymandering to be justiciable," White wrote, "we conclude that the District Court applied an insufficiently demanding standard in finding unconstitutional vote dilution. Consequently, we reverse." He went on to outline a two-pronged test, under which challengers would be "required to prove both intentional discrimination against an identifiable political group and an actual discriminatory effect on that group." And while the justices, at least those who were willing to entertain the question, had no problem concluding that there was sufficient discriminatory intent on the part of the Indiana Republicans, it was on the severity of the effects that they parted ways with the lower court. It was an odd reversal of the Court's logic in *Mobile v. Bolden*. There, the racial effects of the Alabama gerrymander had been largely uncontested, but the inference of discriminatory intent had been a leap too far.

"As long as redistricting is done by a legislature, it should not be very difficult to prove that the likely political consequences of the reapportionment were intended," White wrote, in an almost hand-waving dismissal of the intent prong. But "the mere fact that a particular apportionment scheme makes it more difficult for a particular group in a particular district to elect the representatives of its choice does not render that scheme constitutionally infirm." Instead, the party challenging such a scheme would have to prove that "the electoral system is arranged in a manner that will consistently degrade a voter's or a group of voters' influence on the political process as a whole."

To prevail, those challenging a gerrymander would have to show that they had been effectively shut out of contention entirely, consigned to minority status over multiple elections, and perhaps even an entire decade. Or at least that appeared to be the implication. But White's effects prong is so hopelessly vague, so lacking in clearly defined standards of adjudication, that it's almost impossible to extract from it the circumstances under which a partisan gerrymander even *could* violate the Constitution. Justice Powell's opinion, joined only by Justice Stevens, is much more straightforward.

He argues that the Constitution categorically protects against "deliberate and arbitrary distortion of district boundaries and populations for partisan or personal political purposes," outlining four factors that courts should use to identify whether districts were intentionally manipulated without legitimate justification. These include "whether the legislative process itself exhibited partisan motivation, disregard of traditional political boundaries, irregular shaped districts, and the absence of any considerations beyond partisan advantage." Applying them to the Indiana gerrymander, he agrees with the district court's determination that the Republican plan fails to meet constitutional muster.

The outcome in *Davis v. Bandemer* is hard to explain. Why did Justices Brennan, Marshall, and Blackmun—all part of the majority coalition that had insisted on strict enforcement of "one person, one vote" in the earlier New Jersey case—sign onto White's milquetoast muddle of a standard, rather than Powell's clear and concise test? These were the three most liberal justices on the Court at the time, those most insistent on protecting voting rights against government infringement. Could the decision have been strategic? Might concern over how a crackdown on gerrymandering would influence progressive causes at the ballot box have factored into their calculus? After all, at the time, it was the Democrats who were benefiting the most from the practice. Did they see the ruling as an opportunity to get a foot in the door, with the goal of fleshing out the constitutional test in subsequent cases once the lower courts had been put on notice? That was certainly the opinion of many legal scholars, who cautioned that the gap between White's and Powell's opinions was not that great and that their approaches would almost certainly meld once the Court heard additional cases on the issue. That prediction, however, was not borne out by the events.

Whatever the explanation, *Davis v. Bandemer* will go down in history as a missed opportunity to nip the modern gerrymander in the bud. Less than a year after the ruling, Justice Powell announced his retirement from the Court, and any opportunity for the melding of his approach with that of White was lost. And within eight years, before a new redistricting cycle could bring a fresh batch of cases to work out the details of how gerrymandering would be policed, Brennan, Marshall, Blackmun, and White himself were also gone. A new majority had emerged on the Court, and their redistricting priorities, as chapter 11 discusses, lay elsewhere. Any momentum that might have existed for serious democratic change amid the muddled hodgepodge of opinions that emanated from the Court in 1986 had been lost.

The California Republicans were also left out in the cold. Their own lawsuit challenging the 1982 Democratic gerrymander, *Badham v. Eu,* had been put on hold in anticipation of the Supreme Court's ruling in *Bandemer.* In 1988, the three-judge panel of the U.S. District Court for the Northern District of California dismissed their claim, finding insufficient evidence of discriminatory effects to meet the two-pronged test.

"As an initial matter, it is clear that the complaint sufficiently alleges a discriminatory intent," they wrote. "However, we also may take judicial notice of other facts which demonstrate that California Republicans are far from being effectively 'shut out' of the political process. Instead, California Republicans represent so potent a political force that it is unnecessary for the judiciary to intervene." On appeal, and without written opinion or explanation, the Supreme Court affirmed. It was another eighteen years before they would once again take up the mantle of partisan redistricting. During that time, not a single gerrymander was ruled unconstitutional by the lower courts under the *Bandemer* precedent.

10

The Handshake Deal

I n its essence, the contemporary process of redistricting in New York boils down to this," wrote Edward Schneier and Brian Murtaugh in their book, *New York Politics: A Tale of Two States:* "The Democrats, who control the assembly, draw the assembly district lines; the Republicans draw the state senate lines." *Sic semper erat, et sic semper erit*—thus has it always been, and thus shall it ever be. Or so everybody thought.

The Empire State's politics have long been defined by an inherent tension. Between the interests of the New York City metropolitan area, which contains almost two-thirds of the state's residents and tends to vote for Democrats, and the geographically larger upstate regions, where Republicans, at least outside other major urban centers like Buffalo, usually dominate. These types of regional and cultural cleavages are, after all, not unusual, conflict between urban and rural interests being a staple of political debates for time immemorial. But the state's geographic divide also obscures another, far more pernicious one. Since the mid-1970s, the Republican Party has consistently controlled the state senate, while the Democrats have maintained a stranglehold over the state assembly.

For fully thirty-four years, this pattern held, weathering every wave, every cyclone, every short-term shift in the direction of the political climate. Even when the election of Barack Obama in 2008 temporarily broke the logjam, carrying the Democrats to a narrow majority in the senate, the respite was only temporary. Scandals have come and gone, politicians have been indicted, convicted, and jailed, while others have

232 ONE PERSON, ONE VOTE

resigned in disgrace. What was once a swing state became a Democratic stronghold, and yet still the streak remained unbroken.

At no other time in U.S. history has a state experienced such a prolonged period of divided party control of its legislative branch. New York has voted for both Republicans and Democrats for president, U.S. Senate, governor, lieutenant governor, attorney general, and comptroller. In both the best of times and the worst, the cycle has continued. Every decade, the needle returns to the start of the song, and the band plays along like before. "New York State is governed, in effect, by a single Incumbency Party," wrote the *City Journal* in 1995, "dedicated above all to preserving its own power and privileges. The policy stasis, in other words, is part and parcel of a profound entrenchment of power. The Legislature has striven to keep its membership as unchanging as its policies."

But how could this possibly be? How could the voters of one of the nation's largest and most diverse states consistently place two opposing political parties in control of its legislature? The answer to this political riddle lies in a variety of gerrymandering that has so far not been discussed. But its undemocratic effects rival, or perhaps even exceed, those of the modern partisan gerrymander. I'm referring to what political scientists have termed the "incumbent gerrymander," the "bipartisan gerrymander," or alternatively, as is befitting of the backroom negotiations that often produce it, "the handshake deal."

Such gerrymanders reflect a situation, in the words of the political scientists Peter Miller and Bernard Grofman, "in which the existing balance of party seat share in the legislature (or in a state's congressional delegation) is 'glued' into place by creating districts that are 'safe' for the incumbents of both parties." "A special case of such a sweetheart deal," they continue, "is when each of the two chambers of a legislature is controlled by a different party, and a deal is cut between the chambers that allows each branch to draw its own map."

And that, of course, is what happened in New York. Since 1981, when the first handshake deal was put in place, the state has experienced some of the least competitive legislative elections in the nation. According to a study by the Brennan Center for Justice at New York University Law School, over one ten-year period as many members of the state legislature died in office as were defeated at the polls. More than 99 percent of the incumbents who contested either a primary or a general election during that time ended up winning their races, the vast majority by lopsided margins.

Such a lack of accountability to the will of the voters is a recipe for corruption, dysfunction, and gridlock. And New York has certainly experienced more than its fair share of these evils. The Albany press corps devised their own nickname for the scheme: "The Redistricting Cartel." This chapter is the story of how a handshake deal on gerrymandering turned the state of New York into a criminal oligarchy.

"Constitutionally Republican." That was how Al Smith, first elected as the governor of New York in 1918, and later the Democratic nominee for president against Herbert Hoover in 1928, described the politics of the Empire State's legislature. New York had been gerrymandered by design. The disproportional allocation of power to the heavily Republican upstate regions, at the expense of Tammany Hall's Democratic political machine in New York City, had been written into the very text of the state's constitution.

In 1894, the Republicans who controlled the constitutional convention were acutely aware of the threat that the growing population of the Big Apple—and in particular the seemingly never-ending flow of immigrants through Ellis Island—might have on their ability to continue to control the state's democratic institutions. So, they wrote into Article III a heavily convoluted system of reapportionment provisions designed to ensure that it could never happen.

Districts in the state legislature would be allocated among the individual counties based not on their total populations but on their citizen populations, thus excluding recently arrived immigrants from the count. And the deck was further stacked, in the form of a complex seat allocation formula, so that no matter how the cards were dealt by any particular census, upstate areas would always emerge with a number of assembly and senate districts far in excess of their share of the overall population.

"The more sparsely populated portions of the state have diverse interests and, therefore, should have relatively more legislators to represent those varied interests," helpfully explained the Republican delegate

Elihu Root. "Although a great city may have more inhabitants, it has a unified interest and, consequently, requires fewer legislators to represent that interest in Albany." Though the formula itself is too complicated to summarize here, it was described in one study as "a graphic illustration of how to use apportionment to resist the passage of time." And it worked like a charm.

Al Smith's frustration with this system was certainly understandable. Despite being elected to serve four terms as the Democratic governor of New York—even defeating Teddy Roosevelt Jr., the eldest son of the former president, in one of those races—his party never controlled the senate during his tenure, and held a narrow one-seat majority in the assembly for only two years of his second term. He was not the only Democratic governor to meet a similar fate. In the seventy years that these 1894 constitutional provisions were in effect, before the Supreme Court's reapportionment revolution changed everything, the Republican Party controlled the state assembly for sixty-six years and the state senate for fifty-seven. It was a virtually unbroken streak of single-party rule that many a dictator would have been proud of. And in the early 1960s, with their control of the state legislature securely entrenched by the 1894 constitution, or so they thought, the Republicans set their sights on the state's congressional districts as well.

In November 1961, the state's Republican governor, Nelson Rockefeller, called a special session of the state legislature. Because New York had lost two seats in Congress after the 1960 census, redistricting was required, even without the mandate of "one person, one vote." And the Republicans were in no mood to compromise. The session lasted a mere two days, leading more than one observer to wonder whether a fait accompli was in progress. "On November 10, in broad daylight," wrote *The New Republic*, in an article somewhat cryptically titled "Camel Bites Dachshund" (more on that in a moment), "the New York State Legislature, meeting in a special session called by Governor Nelson Rockefeller, stole away enough Democratic congressional districts to give the GOP an added margin of 10 to 12 seats from New York in the next Congress."

The line drawing itself had been done beforehand, entirely in secret. The results were not released either to the public or to the legislators themselves until the day the bill was introduced. It passed the very next day. The state senator Robert C. McEwen, who had chaired the redistricting committee, explained the lack of transparency by framing it as "strictly a technical subject." "No argument offered at a public hearing," he claimed, "no matter how emotional, political, or impassioned it might be, can change a census statistic."

Thomas Hofeller would have been proud. After all, his PowerPoint presentation to GOP redistricting officials, appropriately titled "What I've Learned About Redistricting—the Hard Way!," contains frequent warnings about the need for confidentiality and secrecy. He cautions his charges: "Treat every statement and document as if it was going to appear on the FRONT PAGE of your local newspaper"; "Trust but verify"; "Emails are the tool of the devil"; "Anything you say may be used against you in a court of law"; and "Loose Lips, Sink Ships."

"After the outlines of the gerrymander were made public," the article continued, "it was easy to understand the Senator's reluctance to face a public hearing over the projected larceny." The plan collapsed three Democratic districts entirely, injected four marginal ones with a transfusion of Republican voters, drew two new Republican districts on Long Island, and made an additional three New York City seats more hospitable to Republican challengers. Rockefeller himself, apparently attempting to wash his hands of the entire enterprise in a manner eerily reminiscent of Elbridge Gerry, never openly associated himself with the process. His sole formal actions were to call the special legislative session and then sign the resulting legislation into law. He refused to even be photographed at the bill signing. But in the plan that bore his signature, all of the now-familiar tropes in the gerrymandering handbook were on display. Including a throwback to the Midwest Menagerie of 1840s Ohio.

"A brief glance at the shapes of some of the new districts is enough to make a drinker go on the wagon," *The New Republic* reported soberly. "The map on page 10 reveals a zoo-full of fantastically shaped creatures slithering through the streets of New York City." "Among the Brooklyn fauna," the article notes, "are a camel biting the tail of a barking dachshund (the 14th CD), a mechanical dinosaur with key attached (the 15th CD), and a vulture (the 16th CD)." But, as the attached maps make clear, an almost Richland Roarer–sized leap of the imagination is required to see any such resemblance. "The vulture is flying towards its new laid egg," they explain: "Staten Island." No word on why the vulture appears to be separated from her egg by the Twelfth, Thirteenth, and Fifteenth Districts, but that particular burning question may be, in the words of Senator McEwen, "strictly a technical subject."

"Also in Brooklyn one finds an X-ray of a badly-shattered elbow (the 10th CD), an accusing finger (the 12th CD), and silhouette of General Washington in uniform (the 11th CD)." At exactly what or whom the finger is pointing accusingly, no further information is given. But it's probably safe to assume that it's not General Washington, given that his district is safely located behind the knuckle. The general certainly has some questions to answer about the shattered elbow, however. Visual cues would seem to suggest that the finger is pointing at either the camel or the dachshund, or possibly even at the dinosaur's key, but the true identity of the guilty party remains frustratingly elusive.

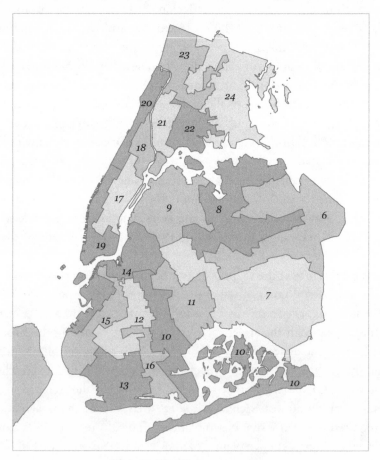

The 1961 New York gerrymander.

Moving into the outer boroughs, the assortment of beasts become even more bizarre, and the imaginations of the article's authors ever more questionable. They are Gus Tyler and David Wells, who according to the somewhat baffling byline, are writing in their capacities as the director and assistant director of the Political Department of the International Ladies' Garment Workers' Union. "Up in The Bronx," they continue, "the Legislature has carved out a fiery dragon (the 24th GD) and a snake suffering from indigestion after having swallowed a giraffe (the 23rd CD)." The latter of these is particularly difficult to infer from the attached map, leaving one to wonder whether at this point the garment factory fumes might have started going to their heads. The dragon, though, really does look like a dragon.

"In the Queens cages are a chicken with its head being cut off (the 6th CD), a shmoo (the 7th CD) and an upside-down pregnant crocodile (the 8th CD)." A "shmoo," according to the frantic Google search I just performed, is either a fictional cartoon character created by Al Capp in 1948 or an electrical engineering chart designed to graphically display the response of a component over a range of conditions or inputs—choose your own adventure. And as for the alleged upside-down pregnant crocodile? I've got nothing. "Upstate New York has been spared from the beasts," they conclude, which I'm sure comes as a great relief to its inhabitants. "But the 55th CD is clearly a submarine extending from Schenectady to Rochester, with a periscope poked into Lake Ontario—apparently about to torpedo Toronto." Clearly.

Unfortunately, while they did endure somewhat longer than the mythical beasts of the Midwest Menagerie—which, you'll recall from chapter 3, were never used for even a single election—the New York City Congressional Menagerie did not last the full decade. Nor was the gerrymander even particularly successful. In the 1962 elections, the Republicans won only twenty-one of the state's forty-one seats in Congress. Then, in 1964, LBJ's coattails carried the Democrats to an improbable victory. They woke up the morning after to find themselves in control of both houses of the legislature, and with a twenty-seven-to-fourteen-seat edge in the U.S. House delegation. "They were so stunned by this development," wrote the former assemblyman Alan Hevesi, "that they divided into bitterly competing political factions and failed to elect party leaders for five weeks."

Then came "one person, one vote." Suddenly the entire electoral map of the nation's most populous state, not to mention the key provisions of its constitution that had institutionalized the widespread malapportionment, had been rendered unconstitutional. In 1967, a federal court also ruled, in the case of *Wells v. Rockefeller,* that the gerrymandered congressional districts would have to be redrawn, containing as they did significant discrepancies in population. The largest district contained 470,000 people, while the smallest contained 350,000. And not surprisingly, the average population of the Democratic seats that made up the menagerie (439,000) was considerably higher than those held by Republicans (382,000).

But the GOP was undeterred. Under the continuing leadership of Governor Rockefeller, they set out to replace their constitutionally mandated gerrymander with what they hoped would be an equally effective legislatively created version. No longer under the state constitutional mandate to allocate seats among counties according to the 1894 formula, the legislature's plan represented "a wholesale abandonment of county and township lines as district boundaries." As was the case in California, the New York Republicans concluded that so long as they produced districts that were equal enough in terms of population to satisfy "one person, one vote," everything else was chopped liver.

But any gerrymander, no matter how well constructed, can only hold up for so long in the face of a sufficiently large electoral wave. And the Republicans were about to get hit with a deluge. Though they maintained their comfortable control of the legislature through the 1972 elections, the fallout from the Watergate scandal left them frantically attempting to bail out their sinking ship. And at least in the assembly, Democrats were prepared to capitalize. Through diligent recruitment efforts, they put together a lineup of young, well-qualified, aggressive candidates to run in upstate and suburban districts currently held by vulnerable Republican incumbents.

It paid off, to spectacular effect. The previous eighty-four-to-sixty-six Republican majority was flipped on its head, and the Democrats emerged with a resounding eighty-eight-to-sixty-two victory. They would never find themselves in the minority again. On the senate side, the Republican gerrymander held up better. Though three GOP incumbents were ousted, narrowing their majority to eight seats, the damage had been done. Their seventy-year mortal lock on control of the state legislature had finally been broken, once and for all. But the 1970s did not mark the end of the modern gerrymander's sordid influence over the Empire State's democratic institutions. In fact, it was only the beginning.

The First Handshake: Stanley Fink, Warren Anderson, and Hugh Carey

"You don't quarrel with the way that I draw the Assembly and I won't quarrel with the way that you draw the Senate," the Democratic Speaker Stanley Fink told his Republican counterpart, the senate majority leader, Warren Anderson. "I will pass a bill that has your version of the Senate if you will pass the same bill that has my version of the Assembly." It was 1981, and New York was about to embark on its first adventure in bipartisan redistricting. Things were not going well. For most of the year, talks between the chambers, and inside the bipartisan Legislative Task Force on Demographic Research and Reapportionment (for some reason abbreviated as LATFOR), had stalled. The two sides were unable to agree on a redistricting plan for the state legislature that would satisfy both their own caucuses and the courts.

To be fair, there were a lot of balls in the air that needed to be juggled. For the first time since the 1940s, when the Democratic governor Herbert Lehman had stared down Republican majorities in both houses of the legislature, the state had divided government during redistricting. The Supreme Court's "one person, one vote" jurisprudence had progressively narrowed the range of population deviations that were permitted between the most and the least populous districts, and the inherent tension between these rulings and the county mandate contained in the 1894 state constitution was very much on the minds of the powers that be in Albany.

Fink was a mere two years into his tenure as Speaker and was attempting to corral a Democratic caucus that was restless to capitalize on their hard-won control after so many decades in the wilderness. Anderson, meanwhile, was the old hand, almost a full decade into his own stewardship of the Republican senate majority. Neither man wanted to be the one who would blink first.

There's a saying in New York politics that all of the deal-brokering, horse-trading, and sausage-making machinations of the state's dysfunctional government can be boiled down into one simple phrase: "three men in a room." Everything from the budget to redistricting is hashed out through informal negotiations in the back rooms of Albany, whether smoke filled or not, between the governor, the assembly Speaker, and the senate majority leader.

By now, the special legislative session of 1981 had expired without a solution to the impasse. Nineteen eighty-one swiftly turned into 1982, and still no real progress had been made. Court-imposed deadlines came and went, and the specter of the judiciary stepping in to relieve the legislature of its responsibilities was looming large on the horizon. If a deal were to be struck to reach a compromise between the opposing factions in time for the 1982 elections to be held, these three men were going to have to be the ones who would strike it.

Before he became the first Democratic governor of the Empire State to successfully win reelection since the 1930s, the Brooklyn native Hugh Carey was also known as "the man who saved New York City." In 1975, the nation's largest and wealthiest metropolis found itself on the brink of financial collapse. On the night of October 16, more than seventeen hundred politicians, philanthropists, celebrities, and other dignitaries gathered at the Waldorf Astoria hotel in midtown Manhattan for the annual Al Smith Dinner, a white-tie Catholic fundraiser named for the former governor and the first Catholic candidate to appear on a major-party ticket for president. The mood was somber.

The Teachers' Retirement Association, by this point the only organization seemingly willing to purchase New York's municipal bonds, had just announced that it was reneging on that promise. At 4:00 p.m. the next day, more than $450 million of the city's mounting debt was scheduled to come due. And with only $34 million on hand in the coffers, the embarrassing prospect of insolvency appeared to be almost inevitable. The lawyers at city hall were already preparing for such an eventuality. In the middle of the night, they had drawn up a bankruptcy petition to be filed in court the next day. It began with an ominous statement of the grim nature of the circumstances: "The City of New York is unable to pay its debts or obligations as they mature."

There was still hope that the federal government would step in and provide a loan to safeguard their long-term financial future. But President Gerald Ford proved to be in no mood for handouts. "This is not a natural disaster or an act of God," argued his press secretary, Ron Nessen, the morning after the dinner. "It is a self-inflicted act by the people who have been running New York City." Days later, Ford delivered his infamous speech, immortalized by the headline that blazed across the front page of the *Daily News* the next day: "Ford to City: Drop Dead."

"I can tell you, and tell you now," he informed the American people, "that I am prepared to veto any bill that has as its purpose a federal bailout of New York City to prevent a default." Eventually, though, he did sign legislation to provide $2.3 billion in federal loans, in return for massive cuts in the city's budget, widespread layoffs of public employees, and a substantial increase in charges for city services. But the damage was done. A year later, Ford would narrowly lose the state, and with it the presidential election, to his Democratic challenger, Jimmy Carter. He later claimed that the *Daily News* headline had cost him the presidency.

In truth, the Big Apple's financial wounds had not been entirely self-inflicted. The economic stagnation of the early 1970s stretched the city's pension, welfare, and other fiscal obligations to the brink. Rates of violent crime were soaring, manufacturing and industry were in decline, and the flight of many middle-class white residents to the suburbs left a gaping hole in tax revenues, forcing the government to borrow more and more to make up its shortfalls. Mayor Abraham Beame had spent much of his time in office since being elected in 1973 attempting to ward off the looming financial catastrophe. He slashed city workforces, froze salaries, cut funding to hospitals, and hiked public transportation rates, but all to no avail.

Hugh Carey had already ridden to the city's rescue on one occasion. In April, the first time that bankruptcy appeared imminent, he agreed to advance funds to keep the lights on, in return for an agreement that the city would turn over the running of its financial affairs to the state. But this was little more than a Band-Aid on the gaping fiscal wound. And as banks began declining to make any more loans as the risk of default skyrocketed, things once again reached a crisis point.

Then, only two hours before the 4:00 p.m. deadline, the Teachers' Retirement Association had a change of heart. Amid frantic negotiations with Beame and Carey, they agreed to purchase the bonds. "No one else was coming forward to save the city," explained Al Shanker, the head of the teachers' union. But less than six years after saving the city from bankruptcy, Carey would find himself in the middle of yet another political crisis, once again frantically attempting to broker a deal between opposing political factions while the clock was ticking.

Stanley Fink also hailed from Brooklyn. The forty-five-year-old Speaker, a graduate of New York University Law School who had served with distinction in the U.S. Air Force's Judge Advocate General's Office during the early 1960s, had first been elected to the assembly in 1968. Anderson, as befitting the Republican Party's upstate electoral base, was born in the tiny village of Bainbridge, halfway between Binghamton and Oneonta in the state's rural Southern Tier. Two decades Fink's senior, he was also a JAG veteran, this time on the army side, and had been an attorney in private practice before seeking election to the state senate in 1952. He had already partnered with Carey once, helping to negotiate the first rescue package for New York City in April 1975.

Now the three men in the room faced the prospect of hammering out a deal to redraw the state's districts in time for the 1982 elections. Tensions were running high. "For 88 years, the Republicans drew the district lines, cutting up cities," complained Mel Miller, the Democratic co-chair of the Legislative Task Force. "This is the first time in almost a century that the Democrats have a real role." "I go into this with the idea of extracting fair representation for minorities," countered Donald Zimmerman, the Republican attorney who had been drawing districts for the party since the 1960s. "And in New York City one of those minorities is Republicans."

The Big Apple's districts were a major sticking point in the negotiations. The city's white flight had caused it to grow more slowly than the rest of the state, necessitating a reduction in assembly seats from sixty-five to sixty. On the senate side, that problem could be fixed by increasing the number of seats, something that the 1894 constitution permitted the legislature to do. The Republicans produced maps that boosted the number of districts located outside the city, hoping to safeguard their majority should the downstate political tides continue to turn against them.

The Democrats in the assembly did the opposite, drawing safe new city districts to lock up their control there for the foreseeable future and gerrymandering upstate boundaries to at least create battlegrounds on which they had a reasonable chance of being able to compete. The division of labor that allowed the senate Republicans free rein to redraw the senate districts while conceding hegemony to the Democrats in the assembly finally produced a workable compromise. On July 2, 1982, the final plans passed the legislature, and Governor Carey had already pledged to sign them into law. The first handshake deal had been completed.

It must be emphasized that the mere fact that the redistricting process was bipartisan did not in any way, shape, or form make what emerged from the special legislative session in Albany any less of a gerrymander. The maps embodied all of the same underhanded tactics that had characterized the 1960s Republican gerrymander: irregular shapes, crossing of county and township boundaries, and targeting of opposing incumbents. The difference was merely one of responsibility, rather than of kind. And the results spoke for themselves. The Republicans held on to control of the senate for the remainder of the decade, their majority never dipping below a seven-seat margin. Meanwhile, the Democrats in the assembly cleaned up, turning the eighty-eight-to-sixty-two majority they had enjoyed prior to redistricting into a ninety-eight-to-fifty-two landslide.

Things were working exactly as intended. The blueprint for how to turn a bitterly divisive fight over redistricting between two diametrically opposed chambers into a mutually beneficial black eye on the face of representative government and democratic accountability was established. The winners congratulated themselves on a job well done, a negotiated peace that had averted any further extension of hostilities. The losers, as is seemingly always the case in the redistricting wars, were the voters.

The Second Handshake: Saul Weprin, Ralph Marino, and Mario Cuomo

Mel Miller believed that he would be the one to shepherd the Democrats through the 1991 redistricting process. After all, the Brooklyn assemblyman had the experience. He'd played a key role a decade earlier as the co-chair of LATFOR, helping to draw the assembly lines during the first handshake deal. And now he also held the reins of power. When Stanley Fink had declined to run for reelection in 1986—citing a desire to spend both more time with his family and more money than his state salary would allow for—Miller had been his natural successor.

Known as a strong voice for liberal and progressive causes, the son of a milk truck driver assumed the speakership in January 1987 and quickly carved out a role as an independent voice among the state's political leadership.

As negotiations ramped up following the release of the 1990 census data, a repeat screening of the prior decade's feature presentation appeared to be firmly enshrined on the marquee. Politicians pontificated, mapmakers map made, and lawyers geared up to litigate the inevitable lawsuits that would surely follow. But the redistricting sideshow would be forced to take a backseat to another three-ring circus that was playing out elsewhere, in the not-so-friendly confines of a Brooklyn courtroom. Before the year was over, Mel Miller became the first in a long line of Albany legislative leaders to be convicted on federal felony charges.

Unlike most of the politicians who followed him through the revolving doors between the Albany establishment and the criminal justice system, Miller was not corrupt. In fact, the nineteen-count indictment that was issued against him in December 1990 by the Republican prosecutor Andrew J. Maloney had nothing whatsoever to do with his work in the state government, at least directly. Along with his business partner and top legislative aide, Jay Adolf, Miller stood accused of defrauding numerous clients, part of a real estate scheme they concocted to enrich themselves on the side.

While purportedly representing the purchasers, the pair had been secretly buying up apartments themselves and then selling them later, collecting some $300,000 in profits on top of the $238,000 the clients had paid them in legal fees. This violation of their fiduciary duty, according to the prosecutor, amounted to criminal fraud and conspiracy. Miller denied all wrongdoing. But the trial kept his attention away from Albany for most of 1991. And with New York law requiring mandatory expulsion from the legislature upon conviction for a felony, the prospect of a second handshake deal being reached while the charges hung over him were remote. Once again, negotiations on redistricting stalled.

In December, the jury convicted Miller on eight of the nineteen felony counts, ending his career as assembly Speaker and throwing the redistricting process into further chaos. "I think it's a disgrace," he said of his prosecution. "I think it was a political witch hunt." Maloney denied that political motivations were involved, citing the fact that the investigation had originated with the Democrats in the Brooklyn district attorney's office. Miller also mounted a spirited legal fight to complement the PR battle, hiring the big-time criminal defense attorney Gerald Lefcourt to pursue an appeal.

Two years later, a federal appellate court unanimously sided with Miller, overturning his conviction on the theory that his actions did not constitute a crime under the relevant federal statutes. "Miller and Adolf's dealings with the Group may not have been a model of candor and disclosure," the court conceded, "but they did not constitute felonies. The judgments of conviction are reversed." Miller never served a single day in jail. But the damage to his political career and reputation was already done. Someone else would have to lead the assembly Democrats through the remainder of the negotiations, and once again the clock was ticking.

Whoever succeeded Miller as Speaker would have to deal with Ralph Marino. The sixty-four-year-old Republican senate majority leader was something of a rarity in his own caucus; he represented a district in the New York metro area, rather than upstate. A native of Long Island, Marino was also considerably more moderate than many of his colleagues and was branded a Rockefeller Republican when he replaced Anderson as majority leader in 1989. Now he was facing pressure from high places to prevent the assembly Democrats from targeting more GOP incumbents, further entrenching their rapidly expanding majority.

At a 1990 Republican fundraiser in New York, President George H. W. Bush had singled out Marino in his remarks, emphasizing both the "importance of keeping control of this senate" and "the tremendous opportunity to fight the Democrat gerrymander" in the assembly. And there would now be a new Democrat sitting on the opposite side of the negotiating table. On December 16, Saul Weprin, the Queens Democrat who had campaigned for the speakership in 1986 but lost out to Miller, took over the leadership of the assembly. "This is not the way I wanted to become Speaker," he told his colleagues.

He was a very different species of political animal from the man he replaced. "The tenure of the brash, loquacious, often combative Mr. Miller is expected to give way to a markedly different Weprin era," wrote *The New York Times,* "led by a man who is understated, taciturn and who appears to place conciliation high in the pantheon of political virtues." But just as Marino and Weprin appeared poised to shake hands on another bipartisan redistricting deal, the other man in the room stepped up and demanded a seat at the table.

"This year you've got a third player in reapportionment and that's yours truly, and I'm not signing off in advance on anything," Mario Cuomo told reporters at a press conference in December 1991. "I'm going to insist that it be constitutional, and I'm going to insist that it be fair." Cuomo was not a fan of gerrymandering. The gregarious fifty-nine-year-old Democratic governor had been elected to succeed Hugh Carey in 1982 on a platform of progressive reforms. He later called for the establishment of an independent commission to take over the state's redistricting responsibilities. But like generations of politicians before him, all the way back to the unfortunate Elbridge Gerry, for whom grand declarations of fair play inevitably gave way to the grim reality of winning elections, he would learn to tolerate the gerrymander's political necessity, if not love its misshapen contours. In the meantime, though, he used the looming deadline as a bargaining chip, threatening to veto the legislature's redistricting bills unless he received both budgetary concessions and sweeping changes to the state's electoral laws. Neither Weprin nor Marino, however, was prepared to play ball.

Each chamber set about diligently crafting maps that would preserve their own incumbents while undermining those on the other side of the aisle. Marino's senate plan drew ten Democratic incumbent senators into five districts, ensuring that at least five of them would be forced to either retire, move, or face the prospect of defeat in a primary election against a member of their own caucus. The state constitutional requirements that districts be compact, be regularly shaped, and avoid crossing county lines were entirely ignored.

Under Weprin's assembly plan, for example, District 147, located outside the city of Buffalo, contained parts of six different counties, far in excess of what was necessary to comply with the federal constitutional requirements that the task force used to justify it. On the senate side, fully 46 percent of the districts crossed county lines, dividing twenty-three of the state's sixty-two counties among multiple seats. And not to be outdone by their senate brethren, the assembly plan also paired eight Republican incumbents in four districts. No norms were left unbroken, no unwritten rules too sacrosanct that they could not be jettisoned in service of preserving the status quo. As Marino later described the process, "You take care of your house, and you leave us alone."

By early March 1992, both chambers had voted to adopt their new plans. And those minority members whose seats had been preserved in the shuffle were falling over one another to throw their less fortunate colleagues under the bus. Seven Democrats crossed the aisle to vote with the Republicans in the senate, while in excess of twenty Republicans did likewise in the assembly. Cuomo dragged out the negotiations for another two months, complaining bitterly about Marino's senate plan in particular, while largely sparing Weprin's equally egregious assembly gerrymander from similar criticism. But time was his enemy. With little prospect of forcing changes to the bills, and the filing deadline for the state's primary elections rapidly approaching, he grudgingly signed them into law on May 4. He would not be the last governor named Cuomo to threaten such a veto, only to back down and accede to the legislature's handshake deal.

Cuomo's justification for the capitulation was weak, at best. A less charitable observer might have described it as self-serving twaddle. In a highly unusual "memorandum of explanation" accompanying his signature, he framed the decision as a kind of Sophie's choice, between signing a defective bill into law and allowing the elections to proceed under either the old boundaries or a court-ordered plan. "If our Legislature does not draw them, they will be drawn by strangers whom we did not elect and who are not directly accountable to the citizens of the State for their judgments," he lamented. "On that basis alone, I am signing these bills."

In return, the senate passed a watered-down version of his electoral reform bill that had already passed the assembly earlier in the year. Cuomo, of course, claimed the credit. "Why did they do it this year?" he mused, tongue firmly planted in cheek. "My guess? They somehow got the impression it would help them with the redistricting bill. That's only a guess." Handshake deal number two was officially in the books.

The majorities in the New York State Assembly and Senate proved remarkably resilient in the face of the turbulent national electoral climate of the 1990s. Perhaps the best illustration of the perniciousness of the bipartisan gerrymander can be gained by zooming in on one particular county. According to 1994 registration figures, the electorate of Westchester County, situated along the banks of the Hudson River north of New York City, consisted of 39 percent Democrats, 33 percent Republicans, and 25 percent independents, making it one of the most evenly divided in the state. One might expect, therefore, that it would return a roughly balanced slate of Democrats and Republicans to the state legislature. This was not the case.

Saul Weprin's assembly gerrymander packed as many Republican voters as possible into the supermajority Eighty-Seventh District, in which the GOP incumbent, Michael Spano, consistently ran unopposed. The remaining Republican populations in the county were cracked among the other six districts, all of which the Democrats won, although one of those seats would revert to Republican control in 1994. On the senate side, things were equally egregious. "By connecting the heavily Democratic areas of Mt. Vernon to the South Bronx; building a donut-shaped, largely white, North Bronx/Westchester district around it; and by extending part of another district into heavily Republican areas of Putnam and Dutchess counties," one study concluded, "the Republicans are nearly as solid in their control of the Westchester senate delegation as are Democrats in the assembly." The same voters returned a slate of candidates to Albany that was 86 percent Democratic for the assembly and 75 percent Republican for the senate. And the band played on.

The Third Handshake: Sheldon Silver, Joseph Bruno, and George Pataki

Before he was known as Inmate 71915-054, Sheldon Silver also answered to Mr. Speaker. An Orthodox Jew born into a family of Russian immigrants in 1944, Silver lived his entire life on Manhattan's Lower East Side. His father ran a successful chain of wholesale hardware stores, allowing the family to move from the tenements of Henry Street to the somewhat more upscale Hillman development on Grand Street by the time of his fifth birthday. Politics had been a dream of his from a young age. "He'd always say that he wanted to be president of the United States, even at 10, 11 years old," recalled Lenny Greher, a childhood friend, in a 2008 *New York* magazine profile. "If he wasn't an Orthodox Jew, who knows? Maybe it could have happened."

The knowledge of the art of the deal that would later facilitate his rise through the ranks of the Albany power-broking establishment had been instilled in Silver from the earliest stages of his upbringing. "My father taught us the value of a dollar," he said, "and the rules of the game." Those rules were elegant and above all simple: "Never negotiate against yourself," and "You have to be able to walk away." He also liked to play his cards close to the vest, developing the signature tic of lowering his voice to a largely unintelligible mumble at critical stages of conversations to conceal his intentions and allow himself to formulate a counterstrategy. "Some people call it playing games or telling you half of the story," recounted a former legislative aide. "Really, all the low talk, it's just a way to buy time, so he can figure out the best possible deal."

Silver's first love was the law. He enrolled initially at Yeshiva University, earning a bachelor of arts degree in 1965, before pursuing a law degree at Brooklyn Law School. His intention, spurred on by the encouragement of his father, was to pursue a career as a judge, but the appointments to New York City's judgeships were controlled by the political machine. He would have to forge those connections first before even being considered a candidate. Silver's initial foray into electoral politics came when he ran for the city council in 1974, losing by the agonizingly slim margin of ninety-five votes. Undeterred, and buoyed by the strong support he received from his Lower East Side community, he turned around and ran for the state assembly three years later. This time he won.

"I figured I'd spend a few years in public service, then become a judge," he explained. But the inside baseball of the Albany sausage factory proved far more compelling than the siren song of the judiciary. Silver ended up spending the next thirty-eight years as a member of the assembly, twenty-one of them as Speaker. He did, however, find time to moonlight as a personal injury lawyer at the Manhattan firm of Weitz & Luxenberg, much to the consternation of his critics, of whom there have been many over the years. Under New York's criminally lax governmental ethics laws, he never had to publicly disclose how much he earned from this side gig. Put a pin in that one.

A protégé of Saul Weprin, who took him under his wing when he assumed the speakership after Mel Miller's expulsion in 1991, Silver proved himself adept at greasing palms, trading favors, and negotiating his way through the high-stakes games of no-limit political hold 'em that frequently played out in the corridors of the state capitol. Weprin, seeking to consolidate his own power base, swiftly named him the chairman of the influential Ways and Means Committee. That committee oversees the state's budget negotiations, making him the second most powerful member of the chamber.

"My father saw a lot of himself in Shelly," explained David Weprin, son of Saul and today a member of the state assembly himself. "My father was a low-key guy, not flamboyant, not looking for higher office, always trying to protect the members and protect the institution of the Assembly." But two years into Saul Weprin's term as Speaker, tragedy struck. He suffered a debilitating stroke and died suddenly at the age of sixty-six, creating yet another power vacuum at the center of the Democratic caucus. Sheldon Silver sensed his opportunity. On February 11, 1994, he was elected the 119th Speaker of the New York State Assembly.

That same year produced a changing of the guard for all three of the men in the room. Nine months after Weprin's death, both Mario Cuomo and Ralph Marino also found themselves out of a job, one by virtue of a palace coup and the other at the hands of the voters. The instigator of both of their demises was George Pataki.

Pataki entered the decade as a relative unknown ("I prefer the chicken pataki to the beef pataki," David Letterman later quipped on the *Late Show*). But the Yale- and Columbia-educated lawyer's spectacular ambition, not to mention unbelievable chutzpah, would quickly catapult him to the very top of the state's political hierarchy, leaving a trail of bodies in his wake.

In 1980, at the age of thirty-five, Pataki was elected as the youngest ever mayor of the small town of Peekskill in Westchester County, unseating the incumbent Democrat Fred Bianco in a 70–30 landslide. He then challenged another Democratic incumbent, Assemblyman William Ryan in 1985, and beat him too, becoming one of the few Republicans to represent a district in the New York metro area. But the 1991 Weprin-Marino handshake deal was not kind to him. His district, which had reelected him with more than 90 percent of the vote in 1990, found itself on the gerrymandering chopping block. Choice GOP precincts in Orange, Rockland, and Putnam Counties were drawn into surrounding Democratic seats in service of Weprin's assembly gerrymander and replaced with more liberal enclaves in Westchester.

Pataki was unfazed. Rather than running for reelection in the newly redrawn district, and already harboring ambitions for a run for governor, he decided to jump ship to the senate to better position himself. There was one problem, though. His home district already had a Republican candidate in it—the seven-term incumbent Mary B. Goodhue. To complicate things further, Pataki had worked for Goodhue as a senate staffer in the early 1980s and considered her a friend. She was also the only woman in the entire GOP senate caucus. Marino discouraged him from challenging her, but his pleas fell on deaf ears. Pataki was going places, and neither Marino nor the Republican U.S. senator Al D'Amato, who would later attempt to derail his campaign for governor, was going to stand in his way.

"If George Pataki had been scared of Ralph Marino, and the Republican establishment," gushed the Albany GOP lobbyist James Featherstonhaugh, "there wouldn't be a Governor Pataki. By and large you don't get to be governor unless you've got some starch in your spine." Opponents saw him somewhat differently. "George Pataki is whatever you want him to be at the moment," said William Ryan, his former assembly opponent. "He's an empty vessel." "He did nothing," echoed Fred Bianco, now the former mayor of Peekskill. "Absolutely nothing. That's why he has to keep running for new offices so people won't catch on." "George uses people, and when they're no longer useful to him, he sticks in the knife," complained Mary Goodhue. "He made me look like a felon. He told everybody I was sick and old, I was dotty. Smearing is what he does."

And it kept working. Pataki defeated Goodhue 52–48 percent in the 1992 Republican primary, then cruised to victory in the general election. Chalk these critiques up to sour grapes if you will, but even the plucky underdog account of Pataki's very first electoral triumph, in the race for Peekskill High School senior class president, generated similar allegations of revisionist self-promoting puffery. "That's pure Pataki mythology," claimed Chris Stewart, a local journalist, when hearing his account of the events. "It was the start of a career-long political calculation," wrote the *Times Herald-Record*. "He was the insider who ran as an outsider."

While he would serve in the senate for less than a year, there was still time for Pataki to attempt another audacious act of political backstabbing. In cahoots with Joseph Bruno, the veteran upstate Republican senator, he mounted a challenge to Marino's senate leadership. And though the attempted coup resulted in abject failure, both Pataki and Bruno would end up having the last laugh.

Next on the agenda was the scalp of the most famous and powerful politician in the state, and things had not been going well for Mario Cuomo. After he reneged on his threat to veto the 1991 redistricting bill, both his ability to influence the legislature and his approval ratings began to drop precipitously. During his 1992 state of the state address, Anthony Seminerio, a fellow Democrat, actually heckled him from the floor of the assembly. Cuomo's almost comical vacillations over whether to seek the Democratic nomination for president in 1992 also earned him the nickname Hamlet on the Hudson.

Meanwhile, rising unemployment and the anemic economic recovery from the early 1990s recession began to stretch the pocketbooks of the Empire State's residents. But it was perhaps Cuomo's continued opposition to the death penalty in the face of unprecedented rates of violent crime (more homicides occurred during his third term than in any other four-year period in New York's history) that made him uniquely vulnerable to challenge. When combined with the disastrous decision by state officials to parole the convicted child killer Arthur Shawcross—who went on to murder twelve more people in a two-year rampage that earned him the nickname the Genesee River Killer—Cuomo was courting a dangerous reputation as being soft on crime.

Still, Marino and D'Amato did not want George Pataki to be the one who challenged him. "Marino doesn't want you," D'Amato told Pataki, according to reporting from *New York* magazine, "and I don't want a feud." "Fine," Pataki replied, "I'm running for governor." In truth, it was Marino who was leading the crusade against the junior senator from Westchester County, with D'Amato along for the ride by virtue of the stark discrepancy in power between the two men in Albany. That discrepancy was about to be reversed. Though Marino tried in vain to find an alternative candidate to challenge Pataki in the Republican primary—with names like Donald Trump, the jewelry and telemarketing magnate David Cornstein, and the insurance CEO Frank Zarb all floated as possibilities in what Pataki derisively called his game of "millionaire of the week"—none of them stuck.

The Republican assembly leader Clarence Rappleyea eventually called Pataki and told him, "You're going to be the candidate." "But they're floating Zarb now," Pataki replied. "Think about it," came the response. "They've gone through the Rolodexes, and they're already up to Z. You've got it." Pataki won the Republican primary with more than 75 percent of the vote, and D'Amato quickly threw his support behind him. Marino, still bitter about the unseating of Mary Goodhue, refused to endorse him. It was a decision he would pay for with his career.

Pataki's timing could not have been more fortuitous. The state as a whole had been trending Democratic for some time, and would continue to do so. When Al D'Amato lost his 1998 Senate election to the Democrat Chuck Schumer, Pataki became the only Republican to occupy an elected statewide office, and the last one to do so to this day. But 1994 was a good year to be running as a Republican, even in New York. The party swept into power in Washington, and the crest of the national GOP wave proved sufficiently high to carry Pataki into the governor's mansion. He defeated Cuomo 49–45 percent in the general election, largely on the basis of his upstate support. While Cuomo ran up huge margins in New York City, he won only one county outside the five boroughs, and that was Albany County, home to the state government. The entire race was amply summed up by Pataki's campaign slogan: "It's Mario's Fault."

On Thanksgiving, less than a month after the election, Pataki exacted his revenge on Marino. A group of GOP senators loyal to the new governor launched a coup against Marino's leadership, the second attempt to unseat him in less than a year. This time, though, it was successful. With twenty-four of the thirty-six members of the Republican senate caucus—led by Dean Skelos, who convinced his fellow Long Island Republicans that Marino was expendable—signaling that they no longer supported him, Marino stepped aside. His lieutenant, Tony Colavita, was also delivered a welcome message from Pataki, courtesy of Senator Nick Spano, another one of the ringleaders of the coup: "Tony, I'm here to offer you the chance to chair your retirement party." Pataki's ally Joseph Bruno, who had joined him in the earlier revolt and was an early endorser of his gubernatorial campaign, was installed as majority leader. Three entirely different men from those who had been there at the start of 1994 now occupied the room.

As redistricting approached, Sheldon Silver was facing his own set of problems. Now six years into his speakership, his brash, insular leadership style had ruffled quite a few feathers among his Democratic colleagues in the assembly. One of his first moves had been to nar-

row the Speaker's inner circle, declining to appoint a chief counsel—
"Apparently, he fancied himself as his own best lawyer," speculated
Kenneth Shapiro, an Albany lobbyist and former chief counsel to the
then Speaker, Stanley Steingut—and installing his protégé, the county
boss Herman "Denny" Farrell Jr., as the chairman of the Ways and
Means Committee.

He also paid close attention to history, cognizant of how the trappings
of leadership could distract a Speaker from the needs of his constituents.
"Stanley forgot about home," recalled Shapiro, referencing Steingut's
shocking 1978 primary defeat to the then-unknown challenger Murray
Weinstein. "Shelly paid special attention to that lesson: Never forget
about home." Silver's later downfall, though, would come from failing
to learn the lesson of another former Speaker, Mel Miller, not to let his
shady business dealings provide grist for his political opponents and
eager prosecutors sniffing around for a trophy scalp. That particular
story, however, will have to wait.

Before he could turn his attention to the post-2000 census line drawing, though, Silver would have to fend off his own attempted palace
coup. Disgruntled elements within the Democratic caucus, frustrated
by the perception that their needs were being neglected, launched an
effort in May 2000 to unseat him. "You could not get five minutes with
him, it was that bad," complained Nelson Denis, who represented East
Harlem. "My constituents were some of the poorest people in this city.
We needed his help." The coup was led by Silver's own deputy, Majority
Leader Michael Bragman, who on May 17 announced that he had the
votes to remove the Speaker. "This is not going to fail, I'm absolutely
confident," he told reporters. The plot had been hatched at a Knicks
game at Madison Square Garden earlier in the year, attended by Bragman and about a dozen Democratic colleagues.

"I knew it was coming, but I didn't think he would do it so soon.
I figured he would wait until after the elections," Silver recalled. But
even caught by surprise, he was not about to allow his upstart lieutenant to scuttle his career. It turned out that Bragman's vote count was
not quite as secure as he had thought. Diligently working the ears of
his disgruntled charges, Silver fought back hard, stripping Bragman
and his allies of their committee chairs, and even locking him out of
his assembly office. His efforts were successful; thirty-three Democrats
who had previously expressed support for Bragman jumped ship. The

speakership was safe. Silver denied allegations that he had threatened the districts of the coup participants in order to bring them back in line. But it's hard not to surmise that the upcoming redistricting effort, and Silver's virtually unfettered control of it, played a role in heading off the uprising. As will soon be clear, he was not above using redistricting as a vehicle for exacting retribution against his enemies.

The third handshake deal, between Silver, Bruno, and Pataki, proceeded much more smoothly than the previous two had done. Pataki, unlike Cuomo, had no interest in rocking the boat, effectively giving the two legislative leaders free rein to draw their own maps. And while the growing Democratic strength in the state made Silver's job straightforward, Bruno would have to work a lot harder to preserve his own majority. Doing so would require a far more audacious gerrymander than had previously been attempted.

"Because there are so many more Democrats than Republicans in New York State," wrote Daniel Feldman and Gerald Benjamin in their

"Abraham Lincoln riding a vacuum cleaner."

book, *Tales from the Sausage Factory,* "the task of producing comfortable majorities without wasting supportive votes was particularly challenging for the Senate." Bruno was more than up to the task. First on the agenda was to stretch the population deviation safe harbor allowed by the Supreme Court under its "one person, one vote" jurisprudence to the very limit. The senate districts drawn after the 1970 census had had an average population difference of 1.8 percent. To make his map work, Bruno was forced to push that to almost 10 percent, systematically shrinking the upstate Republican districts while enlarging the Democratic ones around New York City. But even that wasn't enough.

To crack and pack the growing populations of Democratic voters, he was forced to resort to some truly outrageous distortions of the district boundaries. District 51, said to resemble "Abraham Lincoln riding a vacuum cleaner," stretched half as tall and a third as long as the entire state, including all or part of seven different upstate counties. District 60, designed to capture every Democratic area in and around the city of Buffalo, consisted of two disconnected parts, one to the north that included Niagara Falls and a bifurcated segment of the city of Tonawanda, and the other to the south that shoehorned in Buffalo's heavily African American precincts, creating a monstrosity in which Democrats outnumbered Republicans by a five-to-one ratio. The two sections were connected only by a one-mile stretch of the Niagara River, in a manner reminiscent of Phil Burton's bay-hopping creation in Northern California.

District 49, centered on Syracuse, contained a meandering spiral arm that reached all the way to Lake Ontario, along with an added appendage to connect the city of Rome. It divided three counties and three towns. Twenty-seven of the sixty-two districts contained in excess of forty thousand more Democrats than Republicans, while none had a similar imbalance in the other direction. The map was described by *The New York Times* as "an inkblot that would confuse even Hermann Rorschach."

On the assembly side, Sheldon Silver had two goals. The first was to bolster his already ample majority. This he achieved by shoring up the districts that were already held by Democratic incumbents while undermining those held by Republicans. The 131st District, for example, outside Rochester, was currently held by the Democratic assemblywoman Susan John. But the suburban and rural areas of her district had

become increasingly Republican. So Silver added a hook-shaped protu-
berance to draw in some of the heavily Democratic precincts in the city
itself, turning her marginal district into a safe Democratic seat. Problem solved. Silver's map included sixty-eight districts where Democrats
outnumbered Republicans by more than twenty thousand; there were
only four such seats in which the reverse was true. It was essentially the
opposite of what Bruno had done in the senate, where enough competitive districts, more than 20 percent of the total, had to be drawn to give
the GOP a path to victory. Silver created only six competitive assembly
districts, representing a mere 4 percent of the overall seats. He didn't
need to: there were already more than enough Democratic incumbents,
and registered Democratic voters, to preserve his majority.

His second goal was to eliminate potential challengers to some of his
assembly cronies. One of these was Roger Green, who had faced a significant primary challenge for his Brooklyn seat in 2000 from the attorney Hakeem Jeffries. The race had been a contentious one. At a debate
between the candidates, Jeffries drew the ire of Green by referring to his
opponent's religion. "The issue in this race is not age—yes, the assemblyman is older, I'm younger," Jeffries began. "It's not religion—yes,
the assemblyman is a practicing Muslim and I grew up in the Cornerstone Baptist Church." Green interjected heatedly, "Practicing Muslim?
Where'd that come from? I'm absolutely offended, are you trying to
polarize our community?" Green then walked out of the debate.

Though Green won the primary with 59 percent of the vote, when
Silver's assembly map was unveiled, it turned out that Jeffries's residence
had been drawn out of the district. By one block. Green later claimed
that he didn't even know where Jeffries lived. Whether intentional or
not, the fix was in. Both the assembly and the senate plans passed the
legislature by comfortable margins in April 2002, and Governor Pataki
dutifully signed them into law. Handshake deal number three was a go.

The Fourth Handshake: Sheldon Silver, Dean Skelos, and Andrew Cuomo

Joe Bruno's senate gerrymander held up for about as long as Joe Bruno's
own career as majority leader. By the time of the 2008 election, the
thirty-seven-to-twenty-five majority that the Republicans had enjoyed

in his chamber after 2002 had been whittled down to a narrow thirty-two-to-thirty edge. As GOP incumbents retired, or sought higher office, the Democrats gradually won back some of the seats where they enjoyed a voter registration advantage. In a February special election, they had flipped an upstate seat along Lake Ontario in an area that the GOP had dominated for 120 years. But the process was slow. As the general election approached, Bruno's anxiety was rising.

"If a cat has nine lives, Joe's had 30," one Democratic operative remarked. "Eventually, it's up." The historical fundraising advantage that had allowed Republican candidates to hold on in Democratic districts also appeared to be breaking. The upstate billionaire Tom Golisano, the owner of the Buffalo Sabres NHL team, had pledged $5 million to help Democrats win back control of the senate. The signs looked ominous. Bruno, perhaps seeing the writing on the wall, announced that he would not seek reelection, and resigned the position of majority leader in June. His troubles, though, were only beginning.

Sheldon Silver had no such issues in the assembly, where the Democrats never dipped below the 102 seats they had held coming out of the 2002 midterms. By 2008, they controlled more than 70 percent of the chamber. Their advantage, cemented by the 2001 gerrymander, appeared unassailable, particularly given the party's growing statewide registration advantage and the unpopularity of the Bush administration in Washington. That unpopularity deepened even further as the 2008 financial crisis played out, scuttling the campaign of the Republican presidential nominee, John McCain. Bush's approval numbers sank into the mid-20s, a low matched only by Harry Truman and Richard Nixon. It was not a good year to be running for political office as a Republican.

Barack Obama won 63 percent of the vote in New York that November, the largest margin of victory since Lyndon Johnson in 1964. Even the resignation earlier in the year of the state's Democratic governor, Eliot Spitzer, in the wake of a prostitution scandal, could not stand in the way of the party's relentless march toward victory. Obama's coattails were just long enough to finally crack the GOP's stranglehold on the senate after forty-four years of unbroken control, to the tune of a narrow thirty-two-to-thirty majority. Then things really kicked off.

On January 23, 2009, a mere two weeks after the Democrat Malcolm Smith had assumed the position of senate majority leader, Bruno was indicted by a federal grand jury on eight felony corruption charges.

The indictment alleged that for more than fifteen years Bruno had been running a consultancy business out of his Albany office, racking up $3.2 million in fees to grease the wheels for businesses that were competing for state contracts. None of the payments had been reported on his ethics disclosure forms. Such financial arrangements were apparently commonplace among state politicians, part and parcel of a system where the will of the voters was largely irrelevant to who got to control the levers of power.

Then, on June 10, two Democratic senators, Hiram Monserrate and Pedro Espada, announced that they would join with the Republicans in voting to remove Smith as majority leader. Chaos broke out on the senate floor. The remaining twenty-eight Democrats frantically attempted to adjourn the session to head off the coup, at one point walking out of the chamber en masse, turning out the lights, and ending the television broadcast. Now sitting in the dark, the thirty Republicans and two Democratic defectors purported to pass a resolution naming Dean Skelos, one of the ringleaders of the coup that had ousted Ralph Marino, the new majority leader. Democrats claimed the vote was invalid, because the session had already adjourned. In a farce befitting a Marx Brothers movie, two competing factions both claimed to be in control of the senate.

Allies of Malcolm Smith's withheld the keys to the senate chamber, locked away the copies of pending bills, and directed the stenographer, journal clerk, and sergeant at arms to ignore any directive from Skelos's office. Governor David Paterson announced that he would cancel all out-of-state travel until the crisis was resolved, amid uncertainty about who would serve as acting governor in his absence. This role was usually fulfilled by the lieutenant governor, but that office had been vacant since Spitzer's resignation. Lawsuits proliferated from both sides, but the courts refused to issue relief for either, essentially telling the senators to figure it out themselves.

Things dragged on for a month as the business of the state government effectively ground to a halt. Monserrate eventually had a change of heart, returning to the Democratic caucus on June 15, creating a thirty-one-to-thirty-one tie in the senate. This only created additional confusion, because under state law tied votes in the senate are broken by, you guessed it, the lieutenant governor. On July 8, Paterson attempted to appoint the former Metropolitan Transportation Authority chairman

Richard Ravitch to the position, a move that had never before been attempted in the history of the state. The Democratic attorney general Andrew Cuomo opined that the appointment was more than likely illegal. More lawsuits ensued.

Finally, on July 9, Espada announced that he too would be rejoining the Democrats, in return for a deal that would install him as the new majority leader, making him the fourth man to occupy that position in a little over a year. The next day, the senate passed 135 separate bills that had been held in abeyance since the crisis began. Paterson later estimated that the entire debacle had cost taxpayers almost $150 million. It was, suffice to say, not a good look for anyone involved.

The implications of the crisis for redistricting would be determined by what happened in the 2010 elections. Neither Monserrate nor Espada was around to see it. Monserrate had been expelled from the senate in February after a misdemeanor conviction for domestic assault, while Espada, now under criminal investigation by the FBI, IRS, and Attorney General Cuomo, was defeated by a landslide in his September primary election. And, amid the Republican wave that proved crucial to the subsequent implementation of REDMAP, the GOP won back the senate, returning Dean Skelos to his leadership position with a narrow thirty-two-to-thirty majority.

The state would also have a new occupant of the governor's mansion, because the embattled Paterson withdrew his candidacy amid a challenge from Andrew Cuomo, who then ran riot over his Republican opponent, Carl Paladino, in the general election. Just as it had appeared that the three-decade handshake deal streak might be broken, things were back to business as usual in Albany. And that included yet more criminal prosecutions.

In October, Monserrate had been indicted on federal corruption charges after allegedly funneling $300,000 in state funds to a nonprofit that he ran, portions of which were then used to pay his campaign expenses. He pleaded guilty and spent twenty-one months in federal prison. Then, in December, Espada was also indicted, this time on six counts of embezzlement and theft, after using public money to, among other things, purchase tickets to Broadway shows and take care of the down payment on a Bentley. He was found guilty on all counts and served five years in a federal penitentiary. Bruno was also convicted, although an appeals court later overturned the verdict. At his second trial, he was acquitted by the jury.

Across the capitol, Sheldon Silver watched the chaos as it played out. His own legal reckoning was still several years away, as was that of Dean Skelos, now once again his opposite number in the senate. But the incoming governor, Andrew Cuomo, like his father two decades before, promised to be more of an adversary to the continuation of the handshake deals than George Pataki had been.

Cuomo's 2010 campaign had come at a time when redistricting reform was front and center on the state's political agenda. Bill Samuels, described by the *New York Observer* as a "liberal activist and gadfly," had launched a campaign, in conjunction with the former New York City mayor Ed Koch, to encourage candidates to sign a pledge to pass legislation creating an independent redistricting commission. The hope was to finally break the logjam in Albany and return to the voters the power to rein in the rampant corruption in the legislature.

More than 350 candidates, including Cuomo, had signed the pledge. A hundred and thirty-eight of them were subsequently elected. Cuomo also placed redistricting reform front and center during his run, devoting as much page space to the issue in his campaign policy book as he had to that of education. And as the legislative task force convened in the wake of the 2010 census to begin drawing up new district lines, he appeared to be sticking to his guns. In public remarks in July 2011, Cuomo promised, "I will veto lines that are not drawn by an independent commission that are partisan." When asked if he believed that the task force could deliver such lines, he responded, "No, I don't. It's not non-partisan." Awkward double negatives aside, Cuomo appeared committed to following through on his pledge. But like his father, he would end up reneging on that promise, at least in the minds of his critics.

Neither Silver nor Skelos appeared to be especially deterred by the governor's public statements. Each set about drawing districts designed to once again preserve their respective majorities. But Skelos found himself in an even more unenviable position than his predecessor, Joe Bruno, had faced a decade earlier. Registered Democrats now outnumbered Republicans in the state by a two-to-one margin. And as the 2008 election had proven, such an imbalance was a significant obstacle to even the most creative of gerrymanders.

To make the map work, he was forced to resort to the same trick that Marino had employed in the 1990s, adding an additional seat to the senate, to bring the total to sixty-three. The new district, a more than hundred-mile-long monstrosity, meandered through the GOP strongholds in the suburbs and old industrial towns around Albany, before ending up in Poughkeepsie. Other than spectacular views of the Hudson River, there was very little that its disparate parts had in common. The district happened to contain the home of the Republican real estate developer and incumbent assemblyman George Amedore, who was expected to self-finance a campaign in 2012. He went on to lose to his Democratic opponent by only nineteen votes following a recount, demonstrating how thinly Skelos had been forced to slice his margins to create a map in which a Republican majority was even feasible.

The six Democratic incumbents representing Queens were redrawn into three districts, forcing them to either move or compete with one another in the primaries. District 51, west of Albany, included all or part of nine different counties and was so sprawling that the advocacy group Citizens Union estimated that it would take almost six hours to drive between its most distant corners. District 20, in Kings County, included a twenty-six-block-long corridor only a block wide that connected its main Prospect Heights neighborhood to a distant appendage in Sunset Park. District 11 in Queens crossed both the Long Island Expressway and the Grand Central Parkway before tacking on segments of Jamaica Heights that were only accessible on foot during low tide.

Almost as bizarre was District 16, also in Queens. "This absurdly drawn district," wrote Citizens Union, "while well-intended in its goal to elect an Asian American, does so through nonsensical means. The district tiptoes through Whitestone along the Cross Island Parkway, makes a sharp 90 degree turn south along the Whitestone Expressway, takes in a chunk of Flushing, and then shoots out two elongated tentacles stretching into eastern and western Queens." "District 29," they continued, "posits the false notion that Central Park and the South Bronx are a community of interest. It also includes Roosevelt Island in the East River yet not a single block on the Upper East Side."

District 31, less than a block wide in certain places, stretches almost the entire length of Manhattan. The *New York Observer* also got in on the fun, putting together a slideshow of some of the most bizarrely shaped districts, along with their alleged resemblances. These included

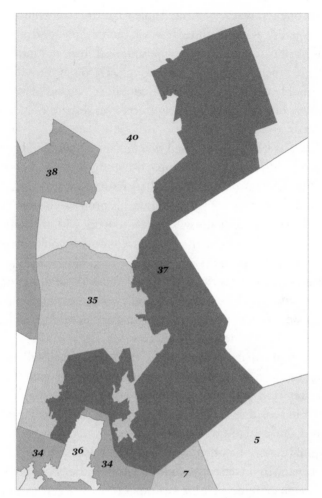

"Donald Trump urinating on a small turkey."

"the silhouetted hair of Conan O'Brien" (District 35); "an extinct Ptero-dactyl perched precariously on a tree limb" (District 27); "a man wearing an elaborate, feathered headdress while projectile vomiting" (District 51); "a male camel that's missing one leg and has a rather prominent package" (District 32); and perhaps my personal favorite, "a man with a prominent nose urinating on a small turkey." In my opinion, the uri-nating man bears more than a passing resemblance to Donald Trump.

And finally, by systematically underpopulating Democratic districts in New York City while overpopulating those held by GOP incum-bents upstate through creative prison gerrymandering, Skelos was able to allocate one less seat to the Big Apple than strict adherence to mathematical equality would require. It was a master class in extracting every ounce of juice that could possibly be squeezed from the state's electorate, and even then it was only just enough. Despite losing the popular vote by double digits in 2012, the Republicans nevertheless clung to the slimmest of majorities, winning thirty-two seats to the Democrats' thirty-one.

Sheldon Silver's assembly map was no more restrained in its creative use of oddly shaped, uncompact, community-dividing districts, although he had no particular need to resort to any of these tricks. But as Cuomo became ever squishier on his promise to veto a partisan plan, and began signaling his willingness to work with the Republicans in the senate, Silver became increasingly concerned about preserving a veto-proof majority in the assembly. This would require him to fashion more than a hundred districts that the Democrats could be reasonably assured of winning. His plan, unveiled by the task force in January 2012 alongside Skelos's senate map, contained more than its fair share of affronts to the practice of cartography.

District 13, nicknamed the donut, was drawn specifically to elect a Democrat amid the Republican Nassau County strongholds of Westbury, Oyster Bay, and Glen Cove, on Long Island's north shore. It straddles the coastline for miles, at one point jumping across Oyster Bay from Centre Island to Cove Neck, before looping back on itself and terminating on the other side of the Long Island Expressway from where it began. To traverse from one end to the other would require one to either be an extremely strong swimmer or have access to a rowboat.

But perhaps even more egregious was District 101, a 127-mile-long jagged sliver running from Oneida County east of Syracuse in the north, close to Lake Ontario, down to Orange County on the New Jersey border in the south. What do the citizens of the rural Tug Hill Plateau and the outskirts of the New York City metropolitan suburbs have in common? The answer is their tendency to vote Republican. Dubbed the "leftovers" district, the 101st was designed to vacuum up every lingering GOP community in its path, allowing the Democrats to capture surrounding seats. The district's incumbent representative, the Republican Claudia Tenney, joked to the press that she would now need a mobile home in order to visit all of her constituents.

But would her district, and the others unveiled by the task force in

January 2012, even see the light of day? A spokesperson for Governor Cuomo immediately threw cold water on the plans. "At first glance," he told the press, "these lines are simply unacceptable and would be vetoed by the governor. We need a better process and product." But when the final redistricting plan was passed by both houses of the state legislature in March, it was virtually identical to the earlier proposal. Cuomo was in a bind. While publicly insisting that he still intended to veto them ("He's not backing off his position," an administration official told the New York *Daily News*. "Nothing has changed"), in private he began angling for a deal that would allow him to save face.

The terms were simple. If Cuomo agreed to sign the heavily gerrymandered districts that had emerged from the legislature, they must commit to passing his proposed constitutional amendment to create an independent redistricting commission. Silver and Skelos agreed. On March 15, the legislature passed the amendment, and Cuomo signed the plans into law, exactly as his father had done in 1992. "It's over, once and for all," he declared. "You can't live your life in a goldfish bowl." And with that, the final handshake deal was completed. In the November 2014 election, New Yorkers endorsed the redistricting commission proposal by a 58–42 percent margin. That commission, rather than the legislative task force, would be primarily responsible for redrawing the state's assembly, senate, and congressional districts after the 2020 census.

What lessons can be drawn from this four-decade redistricting debacle? The first is that, contrary to what many may believe, gerrymandering does not require one party to be in total control of the machinery of state government to consistently subvert the will of the electorate. Politicians, above all, are motivated by self-interest. In an ideal world, they would certainly like to be in a position to rig election results in their party's favor, as the Wisconsin Republicans had done during REDMAP. But the best-laid plans of mice and men must sometimes yield to the cold hard reality of divided government. And if a deal can be struck by opposing factions to preserve the status quo to the mutual benefit of incumbents on both sides, leaving the voters to pick up the tab, such is the price of doing business.

For decades, New York's legislature was among the most corrupt and dysfunctional in the nation, and still nothing changed. *Sic semper erat, et sic semper erit.* In a two-party system, where the courts have abrogated their responsibility as the watchdogs of democracy, the voters have little recourse other than to choose their foxes. Here, the competing foxes had already agreed ahead of time to divide the chickens evenly among themselves, no matter which pack happened to make it inside the henhouse first.

The second is that gerrymandering is a potent recipe for corruption, especially when combined with lax ethics regulations and a culture of playing fast and loose with the public trust. According to research by Jeffrey Milyo and Scott Delhommer at the University of Missouri, between 2005 and 2015 no fewer than thirty New York state officials of both parties were involved in corruption cases. This was more than any other state, and twice as many as every state except Pennsylvania, which came in second with twenty-four. That same research also showed New York atop the list since at least 1986.

A report by the nonpartisan PolitiFact website similarly concluded that "the data shows New York State has led the nation in public corruption for decades." Jennifer Rodgers of the Center for the Advancement of Public Integrity opined, "While measuring corruption is a challenge, I think it's fair to say that New York remains one of the most corrupt states if not the most corrupt state." "Much of corruption is cultural, and in New York that means that you have to think about the way the New York political system has developed over more than 200 years," she continues. "So you start with these corrupt political machines like Tammany Hall, and over time the problem replicates itself as the next generation figures out how things work and how much corruption will be tolerated, and so on down the line." When gerrymandering means that nothing short of a criminal indictment will threaten your reelection odds, that tolerance is apparently pretty damn high.

Sheldon Silver and Dean Skelos both learned their lesson the hard way. After decades of lining his pockets from his lucrative side practice, Silver was arrested by federal authorities in January 2015 on seven felony counts of bribery, extortion, fraud, and conspiracy. According to the indictment, Silver had received more than $4 million in referral fees, bribes, and kickbacks from two law firms with which he was affiliated, in return for using his influence as assembly Speaker to direct business and state grants to them and their clients. After a lengthy trial, a federal jury found him guilty on all seven counts, and the judge sentenced him to twelve years in federal prison.

The conviction carried with it mandatory expulsion from the assembly, ending his career as Speaker. He remained free on bail while he pursued an appeal, and in 2017 a panel of judges on the U.S. Court of Appeals for the Second Circuit vacated his conviction on technical grounds. In 2018, he was tried again on the same charges, once again found guilty on all counts, and this time sentenced to seven years. On January 21, 2020, the appeals court again dismissed three of the charges against him but allowed the other four to stand. Finally, in June, Judge Valerie E. Caproni sentenced him to seventy-eight months in federal prison. "This was corruption pure and simple," she stated at the hearing. "The time has now come for Mr. Silver to pay the piper."

Skelos faced the music a few months later. In May 2015, he was indicted on eight felony counts of bribery, extortion, fraud, and conspiracy, along with his son, Adam, who was the main beneficiary of the scheme. The complaint alleged that he had used his position as majority leader to steer public benefits to three companies—a real estate developer, an environmental technology company, and a medical malpractice insurer—in return for some $300,000 in cash payments and benefits. Like Silver, he was alleged to have received more than $2.6 million in referral fees from a law firm to steer clients to them who had business before the state, despite performing no actual legal work on their behalf.

Less than two weeks after Silver had been convicted in the same courthouse, a jury found both men guilty on all eight counts. The Skeloses appealed, and in 2017 the Second Circuit also overturned their convictions, based on similar technical deficiencies as in the Silver case. In their second trial in 2018, both men were again found guilty on all counts, and Skelos was sentenced to four years and three months in federal prison. Having begun his sentence in January 2019, he was released in April 2020, when the Bureau of Prisons granted him permission to serve the remainder of his time in home confinement. Both Silver and Skelos maintained that they did nothing wrong.

How could corruption have run so deep throughout the government of one of the nation's largest states? How could generations of lawmakers, of both parties, be so consistently assimilated into a culture where what mattered was not what you could do to better the lives of your constituents but how best you could line your own pockets? I certainly don't mean to suggest that gerrymandering was the only reason for the Empire State's persistent dysfunction. Lax ethics rules, and a general indifference among the public toward white-collar crime, at least when it's their side that's committing it, certainly played a significant part as well. But there's scarcely a corner of New York politics or policy making that was not in some way dirtied by the stain of the handshake deals.

The state's broken budgeting process, for example, was clearly exacerbated by chronic divided government created by gerrymandering, sparking fiscal crisis after fiscal crisis for which the citizens inevitably paid the bill. The parade of lawmakers who passed through the revolving doors between Albany and the Southern District's federal courthouses were but a symptom of a broader disease. A broken system where the will of the people counts little for who wins elections and who controls the purse strings. When human beings are not held accountable in some way for their bad behavior, that behavior is allowed to fester. Stick your mitts in the cookie jar once and get away with it, and you're much more likely to go back for a second dip. Pretty soon, the grubby paws of those around you start twitching too.

The nineteenth-century British aristocrat John Emerich Edward Dalberg-Acton, better known as Lord Acton, once famously wrote, "Power tends to corrupt, and absolute power corrupts absolutely." Clearly, the leaders of the New York legislature had become accustomed to, and corrupted by, their power. But that same letter by Acton, written to Archbishop Mandell Creighton in 1887, contains another dictum that is perhaps a little more apropos. "There is no worse heresy than that the office sanctifies the holder of it," he wrote. "That is the point at which the end learns to justify the means."

Here, I think, is the harm of gerrymandering in a nutshell. Silver, Skelos, Bruno, and their ilk all came to see the offices they held, and the majorities they commanded, not as a privilege conferred on them to serve at the pleasure of the people they represented but as something they were entitled to, something that belonged to them. Their property. Or maybe it was simply greed. The great NBC television producer Don Ohlmeyer perhaps put it best of all. "The answer to all your questions," he said, "is money."

11

Hollow Hope

In 1991, the University of Chicago law and political science professor Gerald Rosenberg published a highly influential and controversial book titled *The Hollow Hope: Can Courts Bring About Social Change?* Rosenberg's thesis was a simple one. Courts, he argued, are institutionally unsuitable for driving major societal change, particularly in the areas of civil rights and social justice. They lack both the institutional capacity and, absent cooperation from the elected branches and the public, the political will to force reform on a society that is unwilling to accept it. This argument was not a new one. In Federalist 78, Alexander Hamilton had advanced a similar point of view, labeling the judiciary as the "least dangerous" branch of the federal government, wielding neither the sword of executive power nor the purse strings of legislative authority. "It may truly be said to have neither FORCE nor WILL, but merely judgment," he wrote, "and can take no active resolution whatever."

The quintessential example of the hollow hope thesis is school desegregation. When the Supreme Court decided *Brown v. Board of Education* in 1954, only one out of every thousand black students attending school in southern states had any white classmates whatsoever. Almost a decade later, after the Court directed those schools to desegregate "with all deliberate speed," that number had only risen to slightly more than one in a hundred. It was not until the executive branch stepped in to wield the sword, with JFK issuing an executive order federalizing the Alabama National Guard to enforce desegregation in the face of resistance from Governor "segregation now, segregation tomorrow, segregation forever" George Wallace, and the legislature tightened the purse strings, conditioning federal education funding on schools effectively implementing desegregation, that things began to change. By 1972, more than 90 percent of black students in the South attended integrated schools.

While *The Hollow Hope* has received its fair share of criticism—most notably from those who charge that it ignores the role of courts in setting the nation's agenda, bringing social justice issues to the forefront of the national conversation, and stimulating the evolution of public opinion (Martin Luther King, for instance, credited the *Brown* decision with igniting the civil rights movement)—it's hard not to see its relevance to the topic of gerrymandering.

When *Davis v. Bandemer* was decided in 1986, the justices were more than two decades into their excursion in the political thicket, with precious little to show for their efforts. The most egregious instances of partisan gerrymandering, like Phil Burton's adventures in modern art or the increasingly flagrant violations of representative democracy inherent in New York's handshake deals, remained unaddressed. And in the arena of racial gerrymandering, it had taken Congress's 1982 amendments to the Voting Rights Act to finally stamp out the lingering echoes of slavery embodied in the vote dilution of the 1970s, allowing African American voters a free and fair voice in the selection of their representatives in government. At least in theory. More on that later in the chapter.

"Courts ought not to enter this political thicket," Frankfurter had warned in 1946. "The fulfillment of this duty cannot be judicially enforced." The reapportionment revolution had ended the creeping gerrymanders of the first half of the twentieth century, but at what cost? Frankfurter's curse lived on.

For those who had placed their hopes in the judicial branch for salvation from the scourge of the rapidly evolving modern gerrymander, there would be still more disappointments to come. On three separate occasions, challenges to the most pervasive partisan gerrymanders of the twenty-first century found their way before the Supreme Court, only for the hopes of reformers to be repeatedly dashed. But at the same time, those petitioning the justices to undo the advances in minority representation that had been achieved through the Voting Rights Act found a surprisingly receptive audience on the bench. The lesson of the past three decades of gerrymandering jurisprudence has been a clear one: relying on the courts to fix the malaise in our democratic institutions is a fool's errand.

"Liberty may arrive or depart in a moment," wrote J. Morgan Kousser in *Colorblind Injustice,* but "equality requires not only eternal vigilance but also consensus and incremental improvement." Only a concerted effort by the people to organize, lobby their elected representatives, and rebuild our broken institutions from the ground up will get us out of this mess that we've created. Absent diligent institutional reform, history is doomed to repeat itself, and the world's most powerful democracy will be condemned to wander the purgatory of the political thicket forever. "Marx was wrong, the poor have much more to lose than their chains," Kousser concludes, referencing the straitjacket into which the privileged and politically influential have placed the levers of representative democracy. "Only the powerful can afford to be radical for long."

"All of us are children of the Voting Rights Act," declared Congresswoman Cynthia McKinney as she stood on the steps of the Capitol. McKinney was one of thirteen African American Democrats to be elected to the House of Representatives from majority-minority districts in the 1992 election. Five southern states sent their first black representatives to Washington since the aftermath of the Civil War. But despite those early signs of encouragement, America's first Reconstruction had been a failure. Following the corrupt bargain of 1877, which installed the Republican Rutherford B. Hayes in the White House in return for the withdrawal of federal troops from the states of the former Confederacy, the promise of equal rights for previously enslaved persons swiftly became an illusory one.

The Fourteenth and Fifteenth Amendments to the Constitution, rammed through Congress by the Radical Republicans amid concern that the repeal of the three-fifths compromise would give Democrats an edge in the fight for control of Congress, had nominally protected civil rights and equal access to the franchise for racial minorities. But they remained largely toothless without vigorous federal enforcement. And with their stranglehold on federal power now effectively maintained by virtue of the great statehood gerrymander discussed in chapter 4, Republicans quickly lost interest in doing so. This was all the opportunity that the racist Democrats who controlled the politics of the South needed to reassert their dominance.

Almost as soon as the federal supervision of southern elections had ended, the suppression of black participation began. At first this disenfranchisement was unofficial. White mobs blocked African American voters from accessing polling places; white supremacist paramilitary organizations like the Ku Klux Klan, which was founded in Tennessee in 1865, embarked on campaigns of violence, intimidation, assassinations, and lynchings designed to intimidate black voters into submission; and white-owned newspapers gleefully publicized their efforts, further magnifying the threat.

In 1877, Georgia became the first state to impose a poll tax, and others soon followed suit, codifying the suppression into law. State legislatures imposed numerous barriers to voting, including literacy tests, grandfather clauses, and white primaries, administered in a discriminatory fashion by complicit state elections officials so as to minimize their effect on white citizens. Eventually, these restrictions were written into the constitutions of the states themselves, superseding the constitutional protections of minority voting rights that had been imposed on them during Reconstruction. By the early twentieth century, it is estimated that less than 1 percent of African Americans in the Deep South, and only around 5 percent in the remaining southern states, were registered to vote. Actual participation in elections was rarer still, given the ongoing threat of violence and intimidation.

Curtis Graves described to me the experience of registering to vote as a black man in 1950s Louisiana. Even a century after the Civil War, the legacy of Jim Crow still loomed large. His father had sat him down at the dinner table ahead of time and walked him through the process. "Son," he said, "you're going to turn twenty-one in a few weeks, and I wanted to tell you about what you need to do to register to vote." "Well, Dad," Graves replied, "you know, I have my driver's license, I have everything that I need. It shouldn't be a problem." "No," he said, "it's going to be a problem because in Louisiana it's set up for you not to register to vote." Earlier that year, Washington Parish had conducted an audit of "illegally registered" voters, resulting in 85 percent of African American registrants being removed from the rolls. It took a protracted federal lawsuit by the NAACP to get them reinstated.

"You need to have shined shoes," his father continued, "you need to have your best suit, you need to have your best dress shirt, you need to have a tie, and you need to have all of those things on the morning that you go to register. Because if you don't look like you are a capable, competent person, they're going to give you a hard time." Even into the 1960s, this kind of "soft" disenfranchisement was still widespread. No longer able to enforce many of the overtly racist tools of Jim Crow, local officials seized on any excuse they could find, no matter how pretextual, to disqualify black voters. "Make sure you say 'yes, ma'am' and 'no, ma'am,'" he cautioned. "Because if you don't, you're going to be looked upon as an arrogant nigger, and you will never be registered to vote in the state of Louisiana."

Graves showed up at the registrar's office at five minutes to nine. "You want to get there when nobody else is there," his father had advised. "You want to be the first person in the morning because if they can make an example of you by trying to make a fool of you in some way, they will. And so you probably want no audience." After checking his license, the registrar, whom Graves describes as having "a look on her face that would break a stick," pulled out a copy of the Constitution of the United States. "Read that, and you're going to have to explain it to me," she told him, pointing to the preamble. "We the People of the United States," Graves read to himself, "in Order to form a more perfect Union, establish Justice, insure domestic Tranquility, provide for the common defense, promote the general Welfare, and secure the Blessings of Liberty to ourselves and our Posterity, do ordain and establish this Constitution for the United States of America."

"Now tell me what you just read," she barked at him, taking the book from his hand. Graves was prepared. "Well, ma'am," he replied, "what you gave me to read was the preamble to the Constitution of the United States of America. Now it sets out in that paragraph the ways in which the Constitution is going to help to govern our nation . . ." Before he could even finish, the registrar, without a word, reached beneath the counter, pulled out a large stamp, and slammed it down on the registration form. "No matter what I said," Graves reminisced, "if there were other people in the room, she might have told me that it was not the correct thing." "But I outsmarted her," he concluded, smiling to himself for a moment. At the time Curtis Graves joined the electoral rolls in 1959, less than a third of eligible African Americans in the state of Louisiana were registered to vote. In nearby Alabama, that number was 14 percent. In Mississippi, it was 4 percent.

The Voting Rights Act changed everything. America's Second Reconstruction outlawed the discriminatory tests and devices that had for so long shuttered any hope of black voter participation, let alone actual governing power. And crucially, Section 5 of the act reimposed federal supervision of the electoral practices of localities that had formerly engaged in disenfranchisement. Any state with a history of racial discrimination in voting would now have to submit all changes to their election procedures, including the redrawing of legislative districts, to either the Justice Department or a federal court for approval before they could take effect, a process known as preclearance.

It was a draconian solution, not quite analogous to the northern troops stationed at polling places during Reconstruction, but one that placed the full might and authority of federal power behind the enforcement of the Fifteenth Amendment. "The constitutional propriety of the Voting Rights Act of 1965 must be judged with reference to the historical experience which it reflects," wrote Chief Justice Earl Warren, in an 8–1 decision upholding the preclearance requirement against a constitutional challenge from the State of South Carolina. "Congress felt itself confronted by an insidious and pervasive evil which had been perpetuated in certain parts of our country through unremitting and ingenious defiance of the Constitution." The message from the justices was clear: extraordinary times justified extraordinary measures.

By the time the 1990 census rolled around, the question of how to enforce the VRA's provisions against vote dilution and racial gerrymandering had been resolved. As was noted in chapter 6, the Supreme Court had initially insisted on a combined discriminatory intent plus effects standard in *Mobile v. Bolden*. But after Congress modified the VRA in 1982, this was replaced with the totality of circumstances test established in *Thornburg v. Gingles*.

It's worth revisiting that ruling briefly, because it set the stage for what was about to occur during the subsequent decade. *Gingles* stipulated that for a claim of illegal vote dilution to be established, three criteria must be met: (1) "the minority group must be able to demonstrate that it is sufficiently large and geographically compact to constitute a majority in a single-member district"; (2) "the minority group must be able to show that it is politically cohesive"; and (3) "the minority must be able to demonstrate that the white majority votes sufficiently as a bloc to enable it usually to defeat the minority's preferred candidate."

Notice the implication. If a racial minority group is sufficiently numerous and geographically cohesive to justify the drawing of a district where they may elect a candidate of their choice, then it is illegal for a state to divide that group among two or more districts. In essence, it required states to create what are called "majority-minority districts," districts in which the members of a minority group constitute an effective voting majority. And with that command, the Republican Party sensed an opportunity. It's time for Thomas Hofeller to reenter the story.

The 1970s and 1980s had been a frustrating time for Hofeller and his colleagues at the RNC. Their redistricting successes in states like Indiana had been few and fleeting, while their failures, particularly in California, Hofeller's home state, had been dramatic. The Democrats had held a majority in the U.S. House of Representatives since 1955, in part due to their successful gerrymandering efforts. They also controlled most of the nation's state legislatures, granting them many more opportunities for redistricting shenanigans. All of that, though, was about to change.

"We must remind ourselves the GOP's success in redistricting actually had its genesis in a decade-long struggle in the federal court system beginning in the 1980's," Hofeller wrote in a 2014 memo that only became public after his death and the release of his redistricting files by his estranged daughter. "The GOP gained partisan advantage at the same time African-Americans and Latino minorities gained control of their own districts due to the application of Sections 2 & 5 of the Federal Voting Rights Act of 1965." Ground zero for this successful strategy was the South. And this time, Hofeller and his fellow GOP redistricting professionals had a powerful ally in their push for a Republican electoral edge: the U.S. Department of Justice.

Almost two full decades had passed since *Davis v. Bandemer,* the ruling that opened the door for constitutional challenges to egregious instances of partisan gerrymandering, and the legal community was growing restless. "Court Disallows Gerrymandering," proclaimed the somewhat overly optimistic headline in the *Los Angeles Times* the morning after the case was decided. That initial enthusiasm had quickly given way to frustration. The problem was that no one could make head nor tail of what the law was actually supposed to be. Partisan gerrymandering, at least in theory, was now unconstitutional. But like the proverbial tree falling in the forest, if a constitutional violation occurs with no meaningful standards by which to identify it, can it really be said to exist? The results spoke for themselves.

On no fewer than twenty separate occasions between 1986 and 2003, lower federal courts had entertained constitutional challenges to gerrymanders that were brought under the *Bandemer* precedent. The plaintiffs' record in those cases: 0-20. And it was not merely the hopelessly high bar that had been set by Byron White's plurality opinion that stymied efforts at legal redress. The increasingly conservative Supreme Court, while surprisingly active in certain other areas of gerrymandering jurisprudence, as will soon be discussed, had expressed little interest in revisiting or clarifying the mess of opinions that now represented the law of the land. Lower court judges were left with little else to do but wander around aimlessly in the now-darkened thicket, groping for a flashlight.

Anthony Kennedy was one of the justices who had watched this saga play out with interest. He joined the Court less than two years after *Bandemer,* quickly establishing himself, along with his fellow Reagan appointee Sandra Day O'Connor, as a centrist voice in an institution that was becoming ever more polarized between competing ideological camps.

He was also no big fan of gerrymandering. Kennedy later wrote, "Whether spoken with concern or pride, it is unfortunate that our legislators have reached the point of declaring that, when it comes to apportionment, 'We are in the business of rigging elections.'" But this concern was at cross pressures with his inherent judicial conservatism. And despite being presented with numerous opportunities during his first sixteen years on the bench to push his colleagues to revisit the issue, he appeared content to allow the lower courts to go about their business, however uninspiring the results. Then came Pennsylvania.

Though the excesses of REDMAP were still a decade away, the first decade of the twenty-first century saw the Republican Party achieve its most successful redistricting cycle to date. In contrast to the 1990s, where the GOP had directly controlled the line drawing in only two low-population states, forcing them to rely on the Bush Justice Department as their primary point of influence over the process, in the first decade of the new century they took control in numerous voter-rich locales, including Florida, Michigan, Ohio, Texas, and Virginia. But it was the Republican gerrymander of Pennsylvania's congressional districts that finally forced a showdown before the Supremes, calling up a full-court press from the anti-gerrymandering legal establishment to attempt to persuade the justices to bring clarity to their muddled and much-criticized jurisprudence.

In the 1994 election, the GOP had assumed full control of the elected branches of the Keystone State's government for the first time in more than a decade. And they took full advantage of that control in the wake of the 2000 census. Anemic population growth had seen the state lose two House seats, necessitating a wholesale revision of the existing district boundaries. The Republicans took full advantage, crafting a map that would virtually guarantee that their candidates would win twelve of the state's nineteen seats in Congress, no matter how the people voted.

There was nothing particularly notable about the Pennsylvania gerrymander. Yes, it contained all of the traditional redistricting tropes that are by now no doubt entirely familiar. The challengers contended that the districts were "meandering and irregular" and "ignor[ed] all traditional redistricting criteria, including the preservation of local government boundaries, solely for the sake of partisan advantage." But this was par for the course, abundantly evident in just about every modern gerrymander that this book has examined.

Nor were the results overtly discriminatory, at least at first. Republican candidates did indeed capture twelve of Pennsylvania's nineteen House seats in the 2002 election, approximately 63 percent of the available total. But they also won 58 percent of the popular vote, so Democrats had very little evidence of distortion of the will of the people on which to hang their hat. And while redistricting disputes do fall into the narrow subset of cases where Congress has provided for mandatory Supreme Court review—bypassing the regular certiorari procedures that allow the justices the option of declining to hear the appeal—this had certainly not prevented them from extricating themselves from the thicket before.

In fact, on six separate occasions between 1986 and 2004, the Court had been confronted with mandatory appeals of lower court decisions dismissing partisan gerrymandering claims. Each time they had summarily affirmed the ruling without briefing, argument, or written opinion. These included the 1988 appeal of the challenge to the Democratic gerrymander in California discussed in chapter 7; 1992 disputes

involving a Democratic gerrymander in Maryland, a Democratic gerrymander in North Carolina, and Saul Weprin's gerrymander of the New
York Assembly that was discussed in chapter 10; a 1993 case alleging
Democratic gerrymandering in West Virginia; and a 2002 challenge to
a Republican gerrymander in Michigan. And while a smattering of justices had expressed a desire to note probable jurisdiction and schedule
some of these cases for oral argument, including Byron White, John
Paul Stevens, Harry Blackmun, and Stephen Breyer, the Court did not
appear to be chomping at the bit to revisit the gerrymandering question. So why now?

The answer probably lies amid the morass of competing strategic
concerns on the minds of the nine individuals occupying the bench.
When the Court in December 2003 heard oral arguments in *Vieth v.
Jubelirer,* the case challenging the Republican gerrymander in Pennsylvania, a 4-1-4 split appeared to be emerging among the justices. On the
Court's liberal wing, Justices Stevens, Souter, Ginsburg, and Breyer were
committed to cracking down on the most egregious instances of partisan gerrymandering. While on its right flank, Chief Justice Rehnquist,
along with Justices O'Connor, Scalia, and Thomas, seemed ready to
declare these cases nonjusticiable.

Sandwiched between them was Justice Kennedy, and each side
appeared to be lobbying hard for his vote. It seems likely that the decision to take the case was motivated by a sincere belief among both factions that Kennedy was up for grabs and that the time had come to lay
their cards on the table and let the chips fall where they may. But when
the Court finally handed down its decision the next April, Kennedy,
displaying a Solomon-like commitment to compromise that dismayed
the losing side while delivering to the winners a largely Pyrrhic victory,
decided to split the baby.

The result was yet another punt. The liberal justices, while agreeing
that the most egregious instances of gerrymandering should be held
to violate the Constitution, were again divided on how that question
should be judged. Stevens, Breyer, and Souter each authored their own
separate dissenting opinions. Kennedy's opinion concurring in the
judgment, however, was a nothingburger. "The ordered working of our
Republic, and of the democratic process, depends on a sense of deco-
rum and restraint in all branches of government, and in the citizenry
itself," he pontificated. "Here, one has the sense that legislative restraint

was abandoned. That should not be thought to serve the interests of our political order."

But while conceding the evils of gerrymandering, and professing an open mind to the possibility that the courts might be able to provide redress, he then proceeded to throw up his hands. "The failings of the many proposed standards for measuring the burden a gerrymander imposes on representational rights make our intervention improper," he concluded. "If workable standards do emerge to measure these burdens, however, courts should be prepared to order relief."

Meanwhile, the conservative justices predictably signed on to Scalia's plurality opinion, in which he channeled Felix Frankfurter's plea to leave disputes about the drawing of legislative districts well enough alone. "Eighteen years of judicial effort with virtually nothing to show for it justify us in revisiting the question whether the standard promised by *Bandemer* exists," he begins, before outlining his core argument. "As the following discussion reveals, no judicially discernible and manageable standards for adjudicating political gerrymandering claims have emerged. Lacking them, we must conclude that political gerrymandering claims are nonjusticiable and that *Bandemer* was wrongly decided."

Scalia considers the standards proposed by both White and Powell in *Bandemer,* the standards proposed by the Pennsylvania plaintiffs, and the standards proposed by the dissenting justices in turn, and finds each of them wanting. But his most damning criticism is reserved for Kennedy. "Reduced to its essence, Justice Kennedy's opinion boils down to this," Scalia concludes. " 'As presently advised, I know of no discernible and manageable standard that can render this claim justiciable. I am unhappy about that, and hope that I will be able to change my opinion in the future.' What are the lower courts to make of this pronouncement?"

What, indeed? The legal establishment displayed much the same intemperance to Kennedy's display of legal cowardice, and proceeded to tear the justice a new one in the pages of law review articles. The UCLA law professor Daniel Lowenstein alleged that Kennedy's opinion had "blazed a new trail on the frontier of judicial irresponsibility." Samuel Issacharoff of Columbia and Pamela Karlan of Stanford similarly charged that "as Justice Kennedy would have it, [the Court] simply ignores the question." "Much like the protagonist in Johnny Lee's hokey country song, who had been searching singles bars for true love," mused Loyola Law School's Richard Hasen, "Justice Kennedy is embarking on a search for judicially manageable partisan gerrymandering standards 'in all the wrong places.'" The media even got in on the act, with *The Atlantic* likening the dissenting opinions in the case to "contestants in a beauty pageant parading before Kennedy to see if there was anything he liked." The headline in the *Chicago Tribune* echoed Gerald Ford's famous 1975 admonition to the city of New York: "Court to Democracy: Drop Dead."

Scalia himself probably summarized it best, in typically sardonic fashion. Now conveniently freed from the burden, courtesy of the political question doctrine, of having to choose a standard himself, he lampooned Kennedy for his failure to do so. "It is *our* job, not the plaintiffs'," Scalia charged, "to explicate the standard that makes the facts alleged by the plaintiffs adequate or inadequate to state a claim. We cannot nonsuit *them* for our failure to do so." Irony meters everywhere immediately exploded into dust. The message, both from his colleagues and from legal academia, was a clear one: you had one job, Justice Kennedy. You had one job. And with that, like the ring of power in Tolkien's epic fable, the evil of the gerrymander was allowed to endure, slumbering in the corridors of power until REDMAP would once again unleash its wrath upon the world.

North Carolina's Twelfth Congressional District is not the place where you would expect a titanic decades-long legal battle for the soul and legacy of the civil rights movement to have played out. Far removed from the well-trodden paths of the Freedom Riders, the urban unrest of the great southern metropolises, and the pitched legislative debates on the floors of Congress, here tobacco is king. The district's various iterations have included both the plantation fields of the state's southern climes and the corporate headquarters and processing plants to the north, each geared toward sustaining the nicotine habits of millions of Americans. The city of Winston-Salem, home of R. J. Reynolds, the second-largest tobacco company in the world, is named in part after the Twelfth District's very first representative, Joseph Winston, a Revolutionary War hero and first cousin of Patrick Henry. Befitting the true nature of its constituency, the district has, on occasion, included the village of Tobaccoville.

But in this sleepy corner of Appalachia, a conflict was brewing that would pit Democrats against Democrats, unite other Democrats with Republicans, and reach into the highest levels of the U.S. Department of Justice, the White House, and the Supreme Court. At stake was the preservation of America's Second Reconstruction, the meaning of the Constitution's guarantee of equal protection under the law, and the dream of a just and fair society free from the historical subjugation of the voices, votes, and interests of disfavored minorities.

The year was 1991, and line drawers across the nation were grappling with what to do in the wake of the Supreme Court's vote dilution ruling in *Thornburg v. Gingles*. Amid much uncertainty over what the decision's three-pronged test required of states when it came to redistricting, the Reagan Department of Justice stepped in to clarify. Recall that the RNC had filed a brief before the Supreme Court in *Gingles* urging the justices to rule in favor of the black plaintiffs. Their strategy, documented in the Hofeller files, was to capitalize on the federal government's efforts to require states to draw districts designed to help African American candidates win. Since these candidates would almost certainly be Democrats, those districts could be drawn in such a way as to enhance the prospects of Republicans in surrounding areas, to the detriment of white Democrats.

And under the preclearance requirements of the VRA, it would be the Justice Department that took the lead in enforcing that mandate. In the 1987 regulation issued by the Reagan DOJ, their strategy was written into law. It provided that preclearance would be denied not only when a proposed redistricting plan demonstrated "discriminatory purpose and retrogressive effect," which was the standard that had been used to police covered jurisdictions since 1965, but also when it constituted "a clear violation of the amended Section 2."

The Syracuse University professor of geography Mark Monmonier discusses the strategy in his 2001 book, *Bushmanders and Bullwinkles* (more on those shortly). The regulation, he argues, signaled that DOJ would deny preclearance to any proposed redistricting plan in a covered jurisdiction "if a different redistricting plan could further enhance the collective clout of minority voters." The implication was clear: when states got around to redrawing their districts after the 1990 census, they would have to create as many majority-minority districts as conceivably possible in order to satisfy Washington.

It must be noted here that while the Republicans' motives in pushing this approach might have been somewhat less than pure, the goal was certainly a noble one. The significant gains in African American voter registration and participation rates in the wake of the original Voting Rights Act had yet to translate into effective representation in government. Between 1900 and 1972, when Barbara Jordan blazed her trail in Texas at the expense of Curtis Graves's political career, no state of the former Confederacy had elected even a single African American candidate to the House or Senate. There was precious little progress in the next two decades either, with only Andrew Young of Georgia, Harold Ford Sr. of Tennessee, Mickey Leland and Craig Washington of Texas, John Lewis of Georgia, and Mike Espy of Mississippi following in Jordan's footsteps.

When Tim Scott won his special election for one of South Carolina's two Senate seats in 2014, he became the first African American to be elected to that chamber from a southern state since Reconstruction. It was for these reasons that the Justice Department under Bill Clinton pushed as aggressively for the creation of majority-minority districts as his Republican predecessors had done, perhaps even more so. But it's hard to ignore the cynical opportunism that appeared to be driving the Republicans' sudden embrace of the cause of minority representation.

The Democrats who controlled the North Carolina legislature were in a bind. Ideally, they would have liked to have used redistricting to create safe seats for their incumbents in the House, all of whom were white. They had emerged from the 1990 election in control of seven of the state's eleven seats, and an additional twelfth seat was now on the table by virtue of population growth, which they also coveted. But the aggressive approach being taken by the Republican DOJ made that virtually impossible. And with George H. W. Bush replacing Ronald Reagan in the White House following the 1988 election, there was now a new sheriff in town. His name will probably be a familiar one.

On November 26, 1991, Bill Barr was sworn in as the seventy-seventh attorney general of the United States. It was his first of what would prove to be two rather eventful stints as the holder of that particular office. Barr was a career Republican who had worked at the CIA during the 1970s, initially as an intern and then as an analyst and agency liaison to Congress. After graduating from George Washington University Law School in 1977, and serving as a clerk to a judge on the D.C. Circuit Court of Appeals, he worked various jobs in the Reagan and Bush Justice Departments. He eventually rose to deputy attorney general, the same position Byron White had held, before being tapped for the top job. His most controversial days, of course, still lay ahead of him, when he would return once again to head the Justice Department in the administration of Donald Trump.

Barr's initial appointment as AG occurred right in the middle of a back-and-forth dispute between the department and the North Carolina Democrats over the redrawing of the state's House districts. African Americans made up 22 percent of the Tar Heel State's population, but the state had not elected a black member of Congress in the twentieth century. The last had been George Henry White, a Republican, who had declined to seek reelection in 1900 and left his home state entirely amid the toxic atmosphere of racism, telling the *Chicago Tribune,* "I cannot live in North Carolina and be a man and be treated as a man."

Earlier in the year, the state legislature had drawn a proposed House plan that contained only a single black-majority district, located in the northeastern corner of the state, where the African American population was most heavily concentrated. Though there were sufficient black populations elsewhere to provide at least the numerical justification for a second majority-minority district, they were far more dispersed among the state's various urban centers, from Charlotte in the south to Winston-Salem, Greensboro, and Durham in the north, and Wilmington in the southeast. Connecting those disparate pockets was a challenge, but it was one that Thomas Hofeller was ready for.

Now working for the state Republicans, Hofeller produced a map that included a second minority-influence district in the state's southeastern corner, running from Charlotte to Wilmington. While only 48 percent black, he bolstered those numbers by drawing in another 7 percent consisting of members of the Lumbee Native American Tribe, demonstrating to DOJ that the creation of a second majority-minority district was possible. On December 24, less than a month after Barr assumed office, the Justice Department rejected the Democratic plan. "The price of preclearance, it was clear," Monmonier writes, "was a second district."

But how to draw one? Hofeller's map was a nonstarter for the legislature. It would have forced the displacement of a Democratic incumbent, something the Republicans saw as a feature, not a bug, of their proposal. But the alternative, the creation of a majority-black district elsewhere in the state, would require the Democrats to resort to far more creative adventures in cartography.

By shifting the city of Durham out of District 1, the existing majority-minority district, and replacing it with appendages snaking south to Wilmington and Fayetteville, the Democrats were able to create a second majority-minority district in the central part of the state (District 12) as an alternative to the more southerly district that the Republicans had proposed. This configuration had the added advantage of protecting six of the seven white Democratic incumbents, collapsing only the district of the seventh, Walter Jones, who was retiring. This virtually guaranteed the election of two new African American Democrats, and even placed one of the four white Republican incumbents, Charles Taylor, into a marginally Democratic seat.

At worst, the Democrats felt that they had locked up an eight-to-four advantage with the new map, with the outside chance of a nine-to-three romp if Taylor could be successfully unseated by a Democratic challenger. They had called the bluffs of both Barr and Hofeller, and somehow crafted a map that created two new majority-black districts without giving the Republicans an overall advantage. The legislature gratefully passed the plan into law on January 24, 1992, and Bill Barr's Justice Department approved it on February 7, only three days before the filing deadline for the state's primary elections later that year.

The result was a work of modern art of which Phil Burton would have been proud. District 12 begins its journey in the city of Gastonia in Gaston County, twenty-five miles west of Charlotte, collecting its 25 percent African American inhabitants before narrowing to the width of Interstate 85 as it begins its commute into the Queen City. After stretching feelers into the heavily black neighborhoods to the southwest and east of downtown, the district plunges north through Mecklenburg County along Interstate 77, taking an abrupt right turn as it enters Iredell County, before widening and cutting back to the northwest upon approach to the city of Statesville.

Now turning east, and after another brief detour to the northwest across Interstate 40 to collect still more black precincts, it meanders

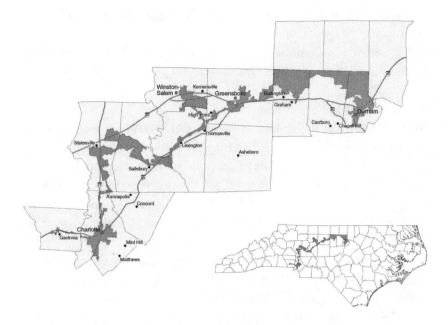

North Carolina's 12th Congressional District (1991).

southeast to pick up I-85 around Salisbury, crossing the Yadkin River between Rowan and Davidson Counties, narrowing again as it follows the highway northeast through Lexington and Thomasville. Here it divides in two, sending one tentacle northwest through Forsyth County to Winston-Salem, while the other strikes out to the east to pick up the black populations in Greensboro.

Tiring somewhat, the district narrows to a point along the border of Guilford County, before emerging refreshed and rejuvenated on the other side, widening and becoming almost compact as it sweeps across the northern reaches of Alamance County. Nearing its destination, it implodes to a fraction of its former width as it heads east through Orange County, before staggering circuitously around and through the city of Durham and collapsing, exhausted from its two-hundred-mile journey through ten different counties, east of Chapel Hill.

Ridicule swiftly ensued. Though the creation of District 12 had achieved its stated goal—delivering a second seat (56.6 percent African American as a percentage of the total population; 53.3 percent of the voting-age population) that along with District 1 (57.3 percent; 53.4 percent) was almost certain to elect an African American Democrat to

Congress—its bizarre and contorted shape provided endless fodder for politicians, the media, and the courts.

Conservative columnists gleefully compared the shape of District 12 to that of a lower intestine. *The Wall Street Journal* condemned it as "political pornography," while *USA Today* likened it to "a return to segregation." "It's not the prettiest thing in the world," pondered Mickey Michaux, the black Democratic member of the state house of representatives and a likely candidate for the new seat. "But it's what the Justice Department wanted us to do. Sometimes you have to bend over backwards to get a point across." "If you drove down the interstate with both doors open," he then joked, "you'd kill most of the people in the district. We'll just have campaign rallies at every exit along I-85 from Vance County all the way to Mecklenburg County."

Others were in a far less jovial mood. The African American Democratic house Speaker Daniel Blue described the new configuration as "an ugly plan," while Robinson Everett, the white Democratic attorney who would end up leading the legal charge against the gerrymander, branded it as "political apartheid." It was not the only majority-minority district to draw the ire of the commentariat. New York's Bullwinkle district, for example, which tacked together various Hispanic and Latino neighborhoods in the general vicinity of Brooklyn, was mocked relentlessly for its alleged resemblance to the bumbling cartoon moose. The resulting creation, according to Monmonier, "is a polygon with no fewer than 813 sides. [Its] perimeter requires 217 lines of verbal description, which read like the itinerary of a taxi driver trying desperately to run up the meter."

Aside from its bizarre and irregular shape, North Carolina's Twelfth District included several features that pushed the envelope even of the modern computer-drawn gerrymanders that have now become ubiquitous. In order to avoid bifurcating the Sixth District entirely, portions of which lie to both the north and the south of District 12, the line drawers had been forced to rely on a technique known as point contiguity, whereby the districts converge along I-85 and then diverge again, maintaining the illusion of connectedness. "Drivers in the southbound lanes would be in the Republican-controlled 6th District, while drivers in the northbound lanes would be in the new black majority 12th District," explains David Canon in his book *Race, Redistricting, and Representation.* "As they traveled down the interstate . . . , the congressional districts actually 'changed lanes.' Southbound drivers were now in the 12th District, and northbound drivers were now in the 6th District."

Elsewhere along the interstate, "drivers traveling either north or south were in the 12th, but the moment they turned onto any exit ramp (on either side of the road), they were in the 9th." It was an almost comically intricate way to ensure that the district's disparate parts remained technically connected, even though it was impossible to walk from one section to another without passing through another district. But the shenanigans did not stop there.

Monmonier also documents a section of the boundary between Districts 2 and 12 in the city of Durham that employs what I'm going to call fractal point contiguity. In the resulting conflation, which is as challenging to draw on a map as it is to describe in writing, "Districts 2 and 12 converge to a point twice, so that a part of District 2 is nested within a part of District 12, nested in turn in a part of District 2." These were crimes against the noble art of cartography egregious enough to make even the most seasoned mapmakers throw up their hands in abject frustration. Whatever tools were necessary to remove as many white voters as possible from the two majority-minority districts were employed to full effect. "Ask not for whom the line is drawn," joked one satirical law review pastiche of the famous John Donne poem. "It is drawn to exclude thee."

It should come as no surprise that the plan was immediately challenged in court. In the case of *Shaw v. Barr,* a group of white Democratic voters, including Robinson Everett, alleged that the districts represented a racial gerrymander so severe that it violated the principle of the "colorblind Constitution." This somewhat novel reading of the Fourteenth Amendment was becoming increasingly weaponized by white Americans to attack government policies that attempted to enhance the opportunities of groups that had been the victims of systemic racism. In the firing line were affirmative action in hiring and public education, programs that gave preference to minority-owned businesses when awarding government contracts, and here majority-minority districting.

They had turned the spirit of the equal protection clause on its head, taking legal principles that had been intended to protect racial minorities from government-sponsored discrimination and applying them in favor of the now-aggrieved white majority, dismayed at this new threat to their own privilege. And it was now spreading like wildfire through the conservative legal establishment. Though the panel of federal judges rejected their claims, Everett immediately appealed to the Supreme Court. And many of the same justices who a decade later in *Vieth* would find the problem of partisan gerrymandering so baffling as to foreclose even the possibility of a judicial solution had no such problem when it came to invalidating gerrymanders designed to enhance minority representation.

By the time the Court heard oral arguments in *Shaw v. Reno* in April 1993 (the election of Bill Clinton had seen Janet Reno replace Bill Barr, both as attorney general and as the named defendant in the suit), the early 1990s Bushmanders—to borrow Monmonier's term for the majority-minority districts that formed the centerpiece of the GOP's new redistricting agenda—had already proven to be a runaway success. In the 1992 election, thirteen African American candidates won election to the House from newly drawn majority-minority districts. These included Mel Watt, who had defeated Michaux in the Twelfth District's Democratic primary, and Eva Clayton, who now represented District 1.

The states of Florida and Alabama elected their first African American members of Congress since Reconstruction. Virginia and South Carolina sent their first black representatives to Washington since the nineteenth century. According to *The New York Times,* "The number of Congressional districts with black majorities [rose] to 32 from the current 17, while those with Hispanic majorities nearly double[d], to 19, from the 10 created after the 1980 census." It was the largest single expansion of elected minority federal officeholders in U.S. history.

"This is, perhaps, the negro's temporary farewell to the American Congress," George Henry White had declared in his final address to the House of Representatives in 1901, "but let me say, Phoenix-like he will rise up some day and come again. These parting words are in behalf of an outraged, heart-broken, bruised and bleeding, but God-fearing people; faithful, industrious, loyal, rising people—full of potential force." And it was African American women too, like Barbara Jordan two decades before, who were now realizing the full force of their potential. Joining Eva Clayton in the House were Barbara-Rose Collins of Michigan, Maxine Waters of California, Corrine Brown and Carrie Meek of Florida, Eddie Bernice Johnson of Texas, and Cynthia McKinney of Georgia.

None of this, however, proved persuasive to the color-blind jurists on the U.S. Supreme Court. In a 5–4 decision—the majority consisting of Chief Justice Rehnquist and Justices O'Connor, Kennedy, Scalia, and Thomas—the Court, while declining to strike down the districts directly, put the lower courts and the states on notice. "Racial classifications with respect to voting carry particular dangers," O'Connor wrote for the majority. "Racial gerrymandering, even for remedial purposes, may balkanize us into competing racial factions; it threatens to carry us further from the goal of a political system in which race no longer matters."

She then directed the lower courts to apply a constitutional test known as strict scrutiny to redistricting plans that classified voters on the basis of race. Under this standard, the challenged district must be shown to further a compelling government interest, be narrowly tailored in the pursuit of that interest, and use the least restrictive means of achieving it. On remand, the same three-judge panel who had upheld Districts 1 and 12 the first time did so again, ruling in August 1994 that while the challenged plan did classify citizens by race, it survived strict scrutiny as a legitimate good-faith attempt to comply with the Voting Rights Act, as the Justice Department had interpreted it.

By now, though, the floodgates had opened. The Supreme Court's 1993 decision signaled to litigants that constitutional challenges to bizarrely shaped majority-minority districts were fair game, and those lawsuits began proliferating. In addition to the ongoing saga in North Carolina, cases were filed in Florida, Georgia, Louisiana, New York, Texas, and Virginia. All alleged that those states' districts, drawn with the encouragement of the Bush DOJ, violated the color-blind Constitution. As lower courts continued to reach conflicting conclusions— some striking down particularly contorted majority-minority districts under strict scrutiny, others upholding them as legitimate—another showdown before the justices appeared inevitable.

In June 1995, the Court released its decision in the Georgia case, *Miller v. Johnson,* declaring that Cynthia McKinney's Eleventh Congressional District ran afoul of the equal protection clause. Then, in June 1996, the justices ruled in the second appeal of the North Carolina dispute, now known as *Shaw v. Hunt* for those keeping track at home. "This case is here for a second time," Chief Justice Rehnquist helpfully reminded the assembled onlookers, speaking for the same five-justice majority as in *Shaw I* and *Miller.* "We now hold that the North Carolina plan does violate the Equal Protection Clause because the State's reapportionment scheme is not narrowly tailored to serve a compelling state interest." On the same day, they also decided the Texas case, *Bush v. Vera,* finding similar impermissible usage of race in the drawing of three Texas districts—one designed to elect a Latino, and the other two an African American.

That all of these cases were decided 5–4 along ideological lines is a testament to the conflicting worldviews on display. For the majority, whenever race is the "overriding, predominant force" in the drawing of a legislative district—whether that force was directed at helping or hindering the political and representational interests of a racial minority group—it should be met with extreme suspicion, if not outright hostility. For the dissenters, the difference between gerrymandering as a tool of racial oppression and discrimination and gerrymandering as a form of affirmative action was one not merely of semantics but of fundamental kind.

"I have no hesitation in concluding that North Carolina's decision to adopt a plan in which white voters were in the majority in only 10 of the State's 12 districts did not violate the Equal Protection Clause," begins Justice Stevens's somewhat caustic dissent in *Shaw II.* "I am convinced that the Court's aggressive supervision of state action designed to accommodate the political concerns of historically disadvantaged minority groups is seriously misguided." He also called out the majority for the inconsistency of their approach. Though the North Carolina, Texas, and Georgia districts were struck down, similarly misshapen and distorted creations in places like California, Illinois, and Ohio were nevertheless allowed to stand.

It was as if the justices had created a Goldilocks test inside a black box that only they were able to decipher. Race must be taken into account when drawing districts in order to comply with the Voting Rights Act, but not too much, or else the Fourteenth Amendment would be violated. It could not be the "predominant" or "sole" motivating factor, as they concluded was the case in North Carolina, nor could it be ignored entirely. But somewhere along the continuum of color blindness was a level of racial motivation that was just right. Were Potter Stewart still on the bench, he probably would have known it when he saw it.

In *Colorblind Injustice,* Kousser describes the Court's heavy-handed approach to majority-minority districting in the 1990s as akin to the undoing of America's Second Reconstruction. "My conclusions are that *Shaw v. Reno* and its successors are revolutionary, contradictory, and incoherent," he charges, "that they are infected with racial and partisan bias; and that they have turned the intent of the Fourteenth and Fifteenth Amendments on their head and deliberately distorted history and language in an effort to stamp out the embers of the Second Reconstruction."

There was very little precedent to support the color-blind Constitution approach taken by the majority, either in the Court's earlier racial gerrymandering cases or in its prior rulings on the use of racial classifications. "Instead, *Shaw* was a radical departure," he concludes, "granting standing to plaintiffs who could not show specific injury; inventing largely fictitious harms to society; exalting a vague, openended, and factually unwarranted category of 'traditional districting principles,' especially aesthetically pleasing district shapes, over the original egalitarian intent of the Fourteenth Amendment; and appropriating heightened, egalitarian language from the civil rights movement in an effort to undermine some of the chief gains of that movement."

The "color-blind Constitution" had become a repackaged, repurposed version of "separate but equal," a veneer of equality grafted onto an apparatus of systemic racism and oppression to make it palatable for the white majority. That many of the same justices who less than a decade later would declare excessive partisan gerrymandering so hopelessly, bafflingly tricky to identify as to entirely foreclose any hope of a judicial solution appeared in these cases to possess such a finely tuned and precisely calibrated sense for when the creation of majority-minority districts went too far was, if you'll permit me, supremely ironic.

It's also worth noting the cynical political opportunism that the entire saga engendered from politicians on both sides of the aisle. At the federal level, the Clinton Justice Department voiced full-throated support for the creation of majority-minority districts and loudly touted their successes. But many state Democrats had major reservations, including the white voters who filed the majority of the lawsuits against them, and the white legislators whose hands were tied in the quest to protect their own seats. The GOP was no better, although somewhat more devious. Republican operatives like Thomas Hofeller could advocate for ever more contorted majority-minority districts in private, then sit back and reap what they had sown. These districts contributed in no small part to their winning back control of the House in 1994.

Republican politicians could then rail publicly against the excesses of racial gerrymandering as a further wedge issue to win support from white voters, with the Supreme Court's rulings as Exhibit A. It was a win-win. And while both Mel Watt and Eva Clayton were able to hold on to their seats even as the districts that originally elected them were systematically dismantled, others were not so lucky. Cleo Fields of Louisiana, for example, who had seen his 66 percent black district whittled down to 58 percent black and then finally 71 percent white by a series of federal court decisions, decided not to run for reelection in 1996.

Perhaps the greatest conceit in the majority's approach to these cases, Kousser notes, is the fiction they appeared to be operating under that prior to 1991 "boundary lines were regular, districts were compact, and communities of interest were carefully preserved." Nothing could have been further from the truth. The history of gerrymandering in America is replete with examples of districts that split counties, cities, and townships, that twisted themselves into ever more contorted and bizarre shapes, stretching the definition of concepts like contiguity and compactness to their very limits.

The difference, of course, is that those previous subversions of traditional districting principles, to the extent that such principles ever really existed, were employed in the service of partisan advantage, incumbent protection, and other racially neutral objectives. By framing the majority-minority districts as something new, rather than as a continuation of time-worn gerrymandering tactics older than the United States itself, the Court's conservative majority were "implying that they have deviated from them only recently, in order to grant special privileges to underrepresented ethnic minorities." It was a bait and switch unbecoming of the nation's highest Court, and Justice Stevens was prepared to call them on it.

In what Monmonier describes as a "spirited, mildly sarcastic dissent" in the Texas case, Stevens documents several white-majority districts in the same plan that were equally as misshapen as the black- and Latino-majority ones the Court struck down. "For every atrocity committed by District 30," he writes, "District 6 commits its own and more. District 30 split precincts to gerrymander Democratic voters out of Republican precincts; District 6 did the same. . . . District 30 combines various unrelated communities of interest within Dallas and its suburbs; District 6 combines rural, urban, and suburban communities. District 30 sends tentacles nearly 20 miles out from its core; District 6 is a tentacle, hundreds of miles long (as the candidate walks), and it has no core." The clear implication is that what made District 30 different from District 6 was its intent, rather than its actual character. If the Court had applied such aggressive scrutiny to the racial gerrymanders from prior decades that were designed to prevent minority candidates from getting elected, rather than assist them, the 1982 amendments to the VRA might have been unnecessary.

There was still time for one last parting shot from the Court at the Justice Department's proactive, and bipartisan, enforcement of the VRA. In the 1997 case of *Reno v. Bossier Parish School Board,* the justices heard a challenge to the 1987 Reagan DOJ regulation that had begun this entire enterprise. The goal behind the regulation had been a political one. By requiring states to create more and more majority-minority districts, Republican administrations hoped to enable GOP candidates to unseat white Democratic incumbents in surrounding areas. It paid off spectacularly. Studies have estimated that Republicans gained approximately ten to fifteen seats in the House of Representatives during the 1990s as a direct result of the strategy. In 1990, Georgia's U.S. House delegation had consisted of seven white Democrats, one black Democrat, and one white Republican. By 2000, six of the white Democrats had lost their seats to Republican challengers. Another, the future governor Nathan Deal, had defected to the GOP, leaving the state with three black Democrats and eight white Republicans.

In state legislatures across the nation, hundreds of minority candidates were elected from majority-minority districts during the 1990s. Between 1971 and 1999, the percentage of state legislative seats held by African Americans had quadrupled, from 2 percent to 8 percent. But the Court's crackdown on majority-minority districts stalled that progress. By 2015, it was only 9 percent. "Blacks are still elected from districts that are predominantly black," explained Kerry Haynie, a professor of political science and African American studies at Duke University. "Until there's a time that blacks can run and win in districts that are not majority-minority, you won't see significant increases in their representation." This is the unfortunate reality of racially polarized voting.

The justices, however, were keen to ensure that the redistricting cycle of the first decade of the twenty-first century would not be a repeat of the 1990s one, at least as far as their own caseload was concerned. By a 7–2 vote, they struck down the 1987 DOJ regulation as a misinterpretation of the VRA. States no longer had to worry about potential vote dilution, and the necessity of drawing majority-minority districts as a remedy, when submitting their redistricting plans to the federal government for preclearance. The era of Bushmanders was over.

But it would still take another two trips to the Supreme Court before the long-running legal battle over North Carolina's Twelfth District was finally settled. After the district was struck down in *Shaw v. Hunt,* the legislature, now under divided partisan control, had redrawn it in 1997, softening its most contorted edges and reducing the African American population to 47 percent of the total population and 43 percent of the voting age population. This did not satisfy the challengers, including Robinson Everett, who once again filed suit claiming that it still represented an unconstitutional racial gerrymander. The lower court agreed. But in 1999, the Supreme Court unanimously reversed its decision, ruling in *Hunt v. Cromartie* that it had erred by failing to hold a trial on whether the legislature was motivated by impermissible racial intent.

The lower court, apparently as confused as everyone else was by the majority's bafflingly opaque Goldilocks test, promptly held a three-day trial and then struck it down a second time. But not to be outdone, the Supreme Court reversed it again in 2001, ruling 5–4 in *Easley v. Cromartie* (Mike Easley had by now replaced James Hunt as the governor of North Carolina) that race was not the predominant factor in the drawing of the new district. Justice O'Connor, without explanation, had switched sides to join Justice Breyer's majority opinion, along with the other three liberals. By this point it didn't even matter. The district had already been used for the 1998 and 2000 elections and would cease to exist later that same year when the next round of redistricting ramped up in the wake of the 2000 census.

Scott Walker's tenure as governor of Wisconsin was colored by controversy from start to finish, on a scale far greater than would be expected even in a swing state in an era of intense partisan polarization. After an unsuccessful run in 2006, Walker was elected in the Republican wave election of 2010, with a 6 percent margin of victory over Milwaukee's mayor, Tom Barrett. Armed with majorities in both houses of the state legislature, he quickly set about implementing a hard-line conservative agenda. The first two years of his administration saw the passage of a strict voter ID bill; the rejection of federal grants made available under the Patient Protection and Affordable Care Act; the defunding of Planned Parenthood; and most controversially of all, the passage of the 2011 Budget Repair Act. This imposed an 8 percent pay cut on all state employees while severely curtailing their collective bargaining rights.

It was this move that thrust the Walker administration into the national spotlight. As soon as the bill was proposed, thousands of demonstrators descended on Madison to protest, and a media circus swiftly ensued. Lacking the votes to prevent the Republicans in the state legislature from moving forward with the bill, all fourteen Democrats in the thirty-three-member senate fled to Illinois, denying them a quorum to pass the legislation. With the recalcitrant Democrats announcing their intention to remain in Illinois indefinitely, Walker and his allies resorted to increasingly hardball tactics to ramp up the political pressure. As protesters occupied the state capitol, Senate Republicans voted to fine the absent members $100 per day, withheld their paychecks unless they were collected in person, and stripped staffers of their access to printing and photocopying resources.

And, in an extraordinary move, senate Republicans ordered the arrest of the absent Democrats for "contempt and disorderly behavior," instructing the sergeant at arms "to use force and enlist the help of law enforcement to bring missing members to the Capitol," according to reporting by the *Wisconsin State Journal.* Acting on a tip that at least some of the missing members were returning to Wisconsin at night in the midst of the boycott, state troopers were dispatched to the homes of the fourteen Democratic senators but were unable to apprehend them.

Walker eventually hatched a plan to bypass the quorum requirement by stripping the bill of its spending provisions entirely, thus exempting it from the rule. Months of palace intrigue eventually ended not so much with a bang as with a whimper as the senate passed the amended Budget Repair Bill by an 18–1 margin, the missing Democrats returned home, and the law went into effect on June 29, 2011.

But the damage to the state's democratic norms, and its culture of civility, was already done. Walker's aggressive tactics were met in kind by his political opponents. Under state law, a recall election may be triggered by a petition signed by a number of registered voters equal to 25 percent of the vote cast in the most recent gubernatorial election. Activists targeted Governor Walker along with his lieutenant governor, Rebecca Kleefisch, as well as numerous Republican senators. Opponents responded by attempting to recall several Democratic senators as well. Between May 2011 and March 2012, recall petitions were certified against thirteen members of the Wisconsin Senate, ten Republicans and three Democrats.

When all was said and done, ten of the thirteen survived their recall elections. Three Republicans were voted out of office, giving the Democrats a one-vote majority in the senate. Their victory proved to be short-lived, however, because the 2012 legislative session had already ended by the time the recall elections were complete. Republicans then took back their majority in the 2012 election. Front and center in the recall debate, however, was Scott Walker himself. After more than 900,000 signatures were collected to force him into a recall vote, Walker ended up defeating the same opponent he had bested in 2010, Tom Barrett, by a slightly larger margin than before, almost 7 percent of the vote. It was the highest turnout and most expensive gubernatorial election in Wisconsin history.

These high-profile and public battles, which dominated both local and national news coverage, would unfortunately obscure what was perhaps the most consequential action of Walker's tenure as governor: the redrawing of the state's assembly, senate, and congressional districts after the 2010 census. Despite all the rhetoric, controversy, and partisan rancor that surrounded the passage of the Budget Relief Act and the subsequent recall efforts, the most lasting damage to the democratic apparatus of the Wisconsin state government was perpetrated under the radar as a shadowy group of activists, political operatives, and special interests set about to remake the state's electoral map.

The resulting gerrymander, the shining jewel of Hofeller's REDMAP project, was perhaps the most pervasive and diabolically effective of all that have been encountered in this book. It would force Justice Kennedy to finally confront the effects of his vacillating in *Vieth* and decide once and for all if the Court was going to do something to crack down on the antidemocratic scourge of partisan gerrymandering. If Walker's Wisconsin gerrymander didn't violate the Constitution, then quite clearly nothing would.

Secrecy was the order of the day from the very start. "What could have—indeed should have—been accomplished publicly instead took place in private, in an all but shameful attempt to hide the redistricting process from public scrutiny," wrote the panel of federal judges overseeing the first of several legal challenges to the gerrymander. They had recently issued an order directing GOP officials to turn over eighty-four emails that had been withheld from the plaintiffs during discovery, and these emails shed considerable light on what had occurred behind the scenes during the early months of the Walker administration.

It was February 2011, and lawmakers were scrambling to pass new state legislative and congressional maps ahead of the anticipated senate recall elections later in the year. The Republicans faced the very real possibility that the party might soon lose its senate majority, and hence their control over redistricting. Attorneys from the firm of Michael Best & Friedrich, hired by Walker and the state GOP to oversee the effort, got to work implementing REDMAP's second phase. Huddled in a conference room across the street from the state capitol, the team, which included legislative staffers, attorneys, and a noted political science professor, used Hofeller's maps as a blueprint to craft one of the most pro-Republican gerrymanders in the nation.

Members of the Republican majority had gone to unprecedented lengths to keep the details of the redistricting process under wraps. Not only had the legislature contracted with private attorneys in the hopes that attorney-client privilege would shield them from being compelled to turn over documents in any subsequent litigation, but legislators themselves signed a pledge of secrecy, promising to conceal from the public the details of what was occurring behind closed doors. "Without a doubt, the Legislature made a conscious choice to involve private lawyers in what gives every appearance of an attempt—albeit poorly disguised—to cloak the private machinations of Wisconsin's Republican legislators in the shroud of attorney-client privilege," continued the court. "Quite frankly, the Legislature and the actions of its counsel give every appearance of flailing wildly in a desperate attempt to hide from both the court and the public the true nature of exactly what transpired in the redistricting process."

But setting aside the cloak-and-dagger nature of the deliberations, it was the substance of the Republican effort to manipulate Wisconsin's political boundaries that raised the greater concern. In *Gill v. Whitford*, the subsequent lawsuit challenging the gerrymander before the federal courts, the University of Chicago law professor Nicholas Stephanopoulos and the Public Policy Institute of California political scientist Eric McGhee put forward a measure of partisan gerrymandering severity known as the efficiency gap as a potential standard that could form part of a judicial test for whether a given redistricting plan violates the equal protection clause of the Fourteenth Amendment. It was a fairly nakedly transparent attempt to appeal to Justice Kennedy, part of the continuing beauty pageant of gerrymandering standards that were paraded through the courthouse doors in the hope that he might finally see something he liked. The efficiency gap metric essentially quantifies the severity of cracking and packing on exhibit in a plan, calculating the difference between the number of wasted votes for each political party and then dividing that by the total number of votes cast.

Applying the measure to Scott Walker's Wisconsin gerrymander, they found that the pro-Republican efficiency gap of 13 percent produced by the assembly plan represented the twenty-eighth worst in modern American history, out of the eight hundred plans across five decades that were included in their analysis. Relying on this and other data, the lower court concluded that "there is close to a zero percent chance that the Current Plan's efficiency gap will ever switch signs and favor the Democrats during the remainder of the decade. Furthermore, prior to the current cycle, not a *single* plan in the country had efficiency gaps as high as the Current Plan's in the first two elections after redistricting." When combined with the clear evidence of partisan intent, there can be no question that what occurred in Wisconsin was a deliberate and calculated subversion of the norms, principles, and institutions of democratic self-governance. But would the Supreme Court see it that way?

On October 3, 2017, the justices heard oral arguments in *Gill v. Whitford*. The tenor of the questioning suggested to Court watchers that Kennedy's appetite for a positive resolution to more than three decades of uncertainty might be waning. Mere seconds into the proceedings, he began quizzing the Wisconsin solicitor general about the issue of standing, a threshold procedural requirement that those bringing or appealing a legal case have a concrete and particularized stake in the outcome. "I think it is true that there is no case that directly helps Respondents very strongly on this standing issue," Kennedy mused, before dropping the hammer blow. "You have a strong argument there."

The argument he referenced was that the twelve Wisconsin voters who had filed the lawsuit, as residents of individual districts, lacked standing to challenge the plan as a whole. Not seriously debated among legal scholars prior to the arguments—it would represent an upending of decades of precedent allowing statewide challenges to redistricting plans—the standing issue gave Kennedy a way out. While Chief Justice Roberts sat back and mocked the efficiency gap as "sociological gobble-dygook," Kennedy seemed to be angling for a way to extricate himself from the pressure. Sensing defeat, the Court's liberal wing gave him an out.

On June 18, 2018, the justices issued their decision. It was yet another punt. Writing for a unanimous Court—the four liberals having apparently decided that a partial loss was better than total annihilation, and its conservatives that a partial win was preferable to another divided ruling—John Roberts declared that the Wisconsin plaintiffs lacked standing. In another case decided on the same day, *Benisek v. Lamone,* they also dodged, on even more obscure procedural grounds, another partisan gerrymandering challenge, this time to a Democratic gerry-mander of Maryland's U.S. House districts. Neither decision reached the merits of the plaintiffs' claims. They also proved to be among the final few cases that Anthony Kennedy participated in. On June 27, only hours after the Court's term had concluded, he announced his retirement after more than thirty years on the bench. The last lingering hope for a federal judicial solution to the problem of pervasive gerry-mandering was extinguished.

It was a crushing disappointment for reformers, whose hopes for the salvation of representative democracy had once again proven to be hollow. But it was not an unexpected one. The Court's rightward drift, amply illustrated by the racial gerrymandering disputes discussed earlier in this chapter, had always seemed likely to stymie this particular avenue of legal inquiry. It had become a case of when, not if, a majority would finally embrace the positions advocated by Scalia in 2004, and by O'Connor in 1986, that such claims represented nonjusticiable political questions.

And a year later, the complete withdrawal of the federal judiciary from the thicket of partisan redistricting was given the official stamp of approval. In *Rucho v. Common Cause*—the appeal of a lower court decision striking down another piece of Thomas Hofeller's REDMAP handiwork, the Republican gerrymander of North Carolina's congressional districts—the death knell finally sounded. In a 5–4 opinion by Chief Justice Roberts, joined by Justices Thomas, Alito, Gorsuch, and Kavanaugh, the doors of federal courthouses across the nation were firmly and decisively slammed shut.

"Excessive partisanship in districting leads to results that reasonably seem unjust," the majority conceded. "But the fact that such gerrymandering is 'incompatible with democratic principles' does not mean that the solution lies with the federal judiciary. We conclude that partisan gerrymandering claims present political questions beyond the reach of the federal courts."

If You Can Keep It

Remember Democracy never lasts long. It soon wastes exhausts and murders itself. There never was a Democracy Yet, that did not commit suicide.

—JOHN ADAMS

W hen the Lord closes a door," Sister Maria reminds herself in *The Sound of Music,* before departing Nonnberg Abbey to start a new life as governess for the von Trapp family, "somewhere He opens a window." The Supreme Court's decision in *Rucho* did not bring to an end the decades-long battle to cleanse our democratic system of the scourge of gerrymandering. It marks a fresh beginning, a new frontier in the never-ending holding action to preserve and defend the Republic that Benjamin Franklin had promised at the Constitutional Convention in 1787.

The French aristocrat, diplomat, political scientist, and historian Alexis de Tocqueville wrote in his famous treatise on government, *Democracy in America,* "There is hardly any political question in the United States that sooner or later does not turn into a judicial question." He might well have been right. But with almost two hundred years of hindsight, a second clause can probably now be added to his aphorism: there is scarcely a political problem in the United States for which there exists a satisfactory and effective judicial solution.

This is now our eighth decade of redistricting litigation since Felix Frankfurter's famous warning about the dangers of the political thicket. What do we have to show for it? On three separate occasions, the Supreme Court has confronted the issue of partisan gerrymandering and on three separate occasions has failed to effectively address it. The justices have found themselves hopelessly divided, unable to agree upon a definitive standard for even identifying the most severe and egregious gerrymanders, let alone remedying them.

This lack of clarity is certainly not a product of a lack of information. There is more than ample data on the harms of gerrymandering, from the efficiency gap to the multitude of other metrics and statistical techniques that researchers have developed to measure, quantify, and differentiate the manipulative effects of district line drawing. A dearth of data is not the problem here. The problem is that judges are not statisticians, lawyers are not social scientists, and courts as institutions are ill-equipped to solve complex and highly technical policy problems in a satisfactory manner.

This was true in the reapportionment revolution, where the judiciary's fixation on numerical equality as the be-all and end-all of fair representation allowed the modern gerrymander to fly in under the radar. Politicians are resourceful, strategic, and, when they need to be, devious and underhanded. When the Court closed a door on one avenue of electoral manipulation, it opened a window on another. Such is the nature of politics.

This was clear with racial gerrymandering, where the courts first failed to effectively deal with the problem of racial vote dilution in the wake of the civil rights movement, then became fixated on the highly irregular shapes of certain majority-minority districts, to the exclusion of all other relevant mitigating criteria, stymieing the dramatic expansion in minority office holding that the Justice Department had produced. Their obsession with "traditional districting principles"— applied selectively to districts that were drawn with the goal of allowing racial minority groups to elect candidates of their choice, but conveniently ignored when similarly employed to produce gross inequities between competing political parties—without first stopping to think about what those principles actually are, or if they even exist, should be troubling for any who believe in judicial salvation. If there's one thing that this book has demonstrated, it's that the only traditional districting principle that has been ubiquitous in America since before the founding is the gerrymander itself.

Where significant progress has been made in combating the harms of gerrymandering, it has almost always come from the people, rather than the courts. Either through direct action or by persuading their elected representatives to take up the cause. The pervasive use of racial vote dilution to blunt the influence of African American voters in the South was stamped out not through litigation but when Congress stepped up to pass the bipartisan 1982 amendments to the Voting Rights Act.

When the Prison Policy Initiative finally shined a light on the gross inequalities produced by counting prisoners at their place of incarceration rather than their homes, eleven state legislatures passed bills to correct those discrepancies. Hundreds of local jurisdictions have done likewise. And while the justices on the Supreme Court have repeatedly fiddled while our electoral system burned, significant progress has already been made in fighting back against the evils of gerrymandering using democratic mechanisms.

After six straight decades of partisan infighting, squabbling, and bickering, the people of California had finally seen enough. In 2008, the reform group California Common Cause collected enough signatures to place an initiative on the ballot, Proposition 11, amending the state constitution to create an independent, nonpartisan commission to take over responsibility for redrawing state legislative districts after the 2010 census. The effort was supported by such ideologically diverse groups as the ACLU, the NAACP, the League of Women Voters, the California Chamber of Commerce, the California Police Chiefs Association, and the National Federation of Independent Business.

Politicians of both parties endorsed it, including both the Democratic former governor Gray Davis and the man who replaced him in Sacramento following the 2003 recall election, the incumbent Republican, Arnold Schwarzenegger. Many of the state's largest newspapers, including the *Los Angeles Times,* the *San Francisco Chronicle,* the *San Jose Mercury-News,* the *San Diego Union-Tribune,* and *The Fresno Bee,* ran editorials in support of Proposition 11. And more than $16 million was raised by the "yes" campaign and its affiliated interest groups, compared with only $1.5 million by the "no" side. Howard Jarvis would have been proud.

But it was also not without its opponents. And when opposition did arrive, it came from the places where it would be most expected: incumbent politicians whose party held a vested interest in the preservation of the status quo. The Democratic senator Barbara Boxer, the Democratic House Speaker, Nancy Pelosi, and the California Democratic Party all came out in opposition to Proposition 11, as did numerous Democratic interest groups. With Democrats dominating the state legislature, and the term-limited Republican governor unable to run again in 2010, their control over the 2011 redistricting process if the initiative were to fail seemed likely.

While Democrats elsewhere had grown increasingly skeptical of the gerrymander since the Republican successes of the early twenty-first century, in California, as chapter 7 discussed, it was one of the party's most potent weapons. Now the state's Democratic voters faced a choice. Would they support the creation of the Citizens Redistricting Commission, even if it meant ceding some of their political power to the Republicans? Or would partisan self-interest once again rule the day?

The people of both California and Ohio had faced a similar dilemma three years earlier. In 2005, the November ballot had included both Ohio Amendment 4, a Democratic-sponsored initiative to create a commission to redraw state legislative districts, and California Proposition 77, a Republican proposal pushed by Governor Schwarzenegger that would have turned over responsibility for redistricting to a panel of retired judges. Both measures went down to heavy defeats, by a 70–30 margin in Ohio and 60–40 in California.

The takeaway was clear. In both states the majority party—Republicans in Ohio, Democrats in California—opposed giving up their own hard-earned control over redistricting. While members of the same party, now in the minority—Democrats in Ohio, Republicans in California—suddenly became proponents of good government reform. It was a neat illustration of one of this book's central arguments. Reforming partisan gerrymandering is so maddingly difficult because while everyone wants to get rid of it when they're losing, no one wants to do so when they're winning. But perhaps this too has begun to change.

In 2008, the voters of California approved Proposition 11 by the narrowest of margins, 51–49, with the "yes" campaign eking out victory by 200,000 votes in an election where nearly 14 million ballots were cast. Two years later, another ballot initiative, Proposition 20, added the drawing of congressional districts to the commission's list of responsibilities, this time by a 61–39 margin. Then, in 2018, the floodgates finally opened. The citizens of five additional states—Colorado, Michigan, Missouri, Ohio, and Utah—passed redistricting reform measures, some by even more lopsided margins. In Ohio, where Amendment 4 had been voted down by forty points in 2005, a subsequent 2015 redistricting amendment, turning over the drawing of state legislative districts to a bipartisan commission, passed with 71 percent of the vote. The 2018 reforms to the drawing of congressional boundaries passed with 75 percent support.

In blue states, red states, and swing states, the voters were being given an opportunity to have a voice in how redistricting would be conducted after the 2020 census. Their message was clear, and spoken in unison: keep politics out of it. In one election, the American people made more meaningful progress toward ending gerrymandering than the Supreme Court had managed in more than three decades. And reform is possible even where state law does not allow for policy questions to be placed on the ballot through a citizens' initiative. In New York, after four decades of redistricting dysfunction, pressure from activists, interest groups, and disgruntled voters finally persuaded the legislature to cede some of its control over the drawing of districts to a ten-member bipartisan commission. Change is happening, albeit slowly and frustratingly inconsistently.

All of which is not to suggest that lawsuits cannot sometimes be an effective tactic for combating gerrymandering. At least in certain circumstances, they can. Although I would still maintain that change at the impetus of the people is preferable to change at the direction of judges. And in the wake of the Supreme Court's decision in *Rucho,* litigants have begun to bring partisan gerrymandering challenges in state court, with several notable successes.

In Florida, a 2012 suit by the League of Women Voters alleged that the Republican-controlled legislature had violated the state's Fair Districts Amendments by impermissibly favoring GOP incumbents in the drawing of its state senate and congressional maps. After four years of litigation, during which several courts concluded that the plans violated the state constitution, the Florida Supreme Court finally approved a new map that corrected the violations in the U.S. House plan. A trial court later imposed a similarly redrawn set of districts for the state senate. Both court-drawn maps were used for the 2016 elections. Though the GOP was able to maintain their majority in both the senate and the House delegation, they had narrowed to twenty-three to seventeen and fourteen to thirteen, respectively, by the 2018 election, having been twenty-six to fourteen and seventeen to ten earlier in the decade.

In Pennsylvania, another lawsuit by the League of Women Voters targeted the gerrymandered Republican congressional map, alleging that it violated the free and equal elections clause of the state constitution. The GOP-drawn plan had produced a thirteen-to-five Republican edge in U.S. House seats in the 2012, 2014, and 2016 elections, despite the popular vote fluctuating between a two-point Democratic victory in 2012 and an eleven-point Republican landslide in 2014. This is the essence of a partisan gerrymander—a 13 percent popular vote swing from one election to the next produced precisely zero change in control of the seats in Congress.

In early 2018, the Pennsylvania Supreme Court ruled that the gerrymander was invalid, concluding that it "clearly, plainly and palpably violates the [state] Constitution." For their trouble, the four justices who made up the majority in the 4–3 decision were subjected to an impeachment attempt by twelve Republican members of the state legislature. Under the new map imposed by the court for the 2018 and 2020 elections, the eighteen districts were split nine-nine, with the Democrats picking up four seats.

Finally, in North Carolina, the congressional districts that had been drawn by Thomas Hofeller in 2011 were also subjected to legal challenge, this time by a group of fourteen voters. A parallel lawsuit was filed by Common Cause, alleging that the Republican-drawn general assembly districts violated the North Carolina Constitution's free elections clause. Under the challenged plan, Republicans had won 29 of the 50 senate seats in 2018, and 65 of the 120 house seats, despite losing the popular vote for both chambers.

In Congress, the story was remarkably similar to Pennsylvania. The popular vote had ranged from a two-point Democratic victory in 2012 to a twelve-point GOP win in 2014, but the seat totals had remained virtually unchanged. After winning nine of the thirteen seats in 2012, Republicans held a ten-to-three edge in the elections of 2014, 2016, and 2018. In 2019, the North Carolina Supreme Court ruled that all three sets of districts must be redrawn to cleanse them of their partisan taint. The result: Democrats picked up two additional seats in 2020, creating a somewhat more balanced eight-to-five split in the delegation. "After nearly a decade of voting in some of the most gerrymandered districts in the country," said Eric Holder, the chair of the National Democratic Redistricting Committee, "courts have put new maps in place that are an improvement over the status quo, but the people still deserve better."

Holder was correct about the limits of judicial remedies. These three cases, though ending in victory for the plaintiffs, illustrate some of the continuing drawbacks in relying on courts to police partisan gerrymandering. The wheels of justice, it is often said, turn slowly, sometimes agonizingly so. Each of these maps, though plainly in violation of its respective state constitution, was used for multiple elections before the judiciary was finally able to step in and ensure its replacement. The Florida gerrymander remained in place for the 2012 and 2014 elections; the Pennsylvania map was used through 2016; and Hofeller's North Carolina plan survived longer than the man himself. The districts he drew were still in place for the 2018 election, which took place several months after his death.

Courts are reactive, not proactive. And while the moral arc of the gerrymander may bend toward justice, every delay along the parabola permitting another election to be held under illegally drawn boundaries represents justice denied. Lawsuits remain a lengthy, complex, and expensive method of combating gerrymandering, one that must be undertaken every decade, in every state, with no guarantee or even likelihood of success.

So, what other options remain? So fundamentally broken is the redistricting process in the United States that any reform, no matter how imperfect, represents an improvement over the status quo. And rather than providing a singular policy prescription, I will conclude this book with a discussion of some of the strategies that have already worked, either in individual states or in other nations, along with notes on their likely effectiveness.

The redistricting reforms that have been implemented in a minority of U.S. states generally fall into one of three categories, albeit often with partial or even significant overlap. It's perhaps best to think of these solutions as existing along a continuum, with their positions dictated by the extent to which they remove the process from the hands of self-interested politicians and the degree to which they impose constraints on those who are responsible for it.

At one extreme is the status quo, the foxes-guarding-henhouses conundrum. Redistricting is the responsibility of the majority party in the state legislature or, if control of state government is divided, the product of compromise between competing factions. Constraints on the process are generally minimal. They usually amount to little more than norms favoring the types of "traditional districting principles" that have been discussed extensively in this book, such as contiguity, compactness, preservation of communities of interest, and a desire to avoid splitting counties or other municipal units. As we've seen, when a party has both the political will to subvert these norms and the political capital to effectively do so, they offer little resistance to the imposition of an egregious gerrymander. Some of these principles are also codified into individual state constitutions, although enforcing them effectively remains a challenge.

A number of states also have some variation of the free and equal elections clauses that formed the basis of some of the recent state court challenges to partisan gerrymandering. According to the National Conference of State Legislatures, "30 states have some form of constitutional requirement that elections be 'free,' 18 of these states further require that elections be either 'equal' or 'open' in addition to being free, [and] 15 state constitutions also include language that explicitly protects a citizen's right to vote from improper influence or interference." I discuss these and other types of legal restrictions on redistricting extensively in my 2017 book, *Drawing the Lines: Constraints on Partisan Gerrymandering in U.S. Politics*. Suffice it to say, while they can, and sometimes do, have marginal effects in restraining some of the worst impulses of line drawers, they are of little impediment to a party that is determined enough to implement a gerrymander.

The constitution of the State of Maryland includes a contiguity mandate, a compactness requirement, and a free elections clause, as well as requirements that those conducting redistricting follow existing political subdivisions and preserve both communities of interest and the cores of previous districts. None of these prevented the Democratic legislature from crafting a plan in 2011 that unseated one of the two Republican House incumbents, giving them a seven-to-one advantage in congressional seats from 2012 through 2020. These nominal constraints, where they exist, are enforceable only through litigation, and so suffer from the same drawbacks associated with other legal remedies that have already been discussed.

A handful of states, namely Florida, Iowa, and Ohio, have taken things further, imposing additional legal criteria designed specifically to prevent partisan gerrymandering. The Florida Fair Districts Amendments, passed with 63 percent of the vote in the 2010 election, provided that "legislative districts or districting plans may not be drawn to favor or disfavor an incumbent or political party." But, as we've already seen, these amendments are not self-enforcing. When legislators choose to ignore them, as the Florida Republicans did in 2011, the only remedy is to file a costly and time-consuming lawsuit. And though the Fair Districts Amendments did lead to the dismantling of the GOP gerrymander, it was not until two sets of elections had already been held under the unconstitutional boundaries. In essence, Florida sends the foxes a sternly worded letter warning them not to eat any chickens and lets you sue them afterward if they don't listen. Hardly a panacea.

The voters of the Buckeye State also implemented reforms to their redistricting practices, this time through a legislatively referred amendment to the state constitution. The 2018 Ohio referendum, while leaving the state legislature in control of congressional redistricting, added additional procedural requirements designed to encourage bipartisanship. Under the new rules, any proposed map must receive a three-fifths majority, along with at least 50 percent support from both Democrats and Republicans, to go into effect for the remainder of the decade. This bipartisan supermajority requirement is designed to ensure that the majority party in the legislature is unable to implement a partisan gerrymander of both chambers. And while that eventuality is foreclosed by the reform, the drawbacks of this approach are immediately obvious.

First, it is open to bipartisan incumbent protection, where the minority party agrees to the majority's proposed plan purely to safeguard their own seats, and jobs. Second, it incentivizes the kind of collusive handshake deals that became endemic in New York. If control of the legislature is divided, each side can agree to allow their respective chambers to draw their own map, institutionalizing the existing division of partisan control. In both situations, voters are precluded from any meaningful input into who wins control of the legislature and which candidates are elected to its individual seats. Basically, Ohio requires the foxes to agree beforehand how many chickens each of them gets to eat, or else the henhouse remains closed. It's a good thing foxes aren't known for their cunning.

Iowa has an entirely unique system for conducting redistricting. Since 1980, the state legislature has delegated the task to nonpartisan legislative staffers, who are required to produce district maps without any reference to political data whatsoever. This includes the addresses of incumbents, the partisan affiliations and other demographic information on registered voters, and the results of prior elections, none of which may be considered when producing a plan. The resulting maps are then submitted to the general assembly for an up-or-down vote.

Of the approaches that leave the legislature as the primary mover and shaker in the redistricting sideshow, this one is clearly superior. But it still doesn't entirely foreclose the possibility of shenanigans. If three successive proposals from the legislative staffers are voted down by the assembly, the process short-circuits, and the foxes are given free rein to craft their own alternative plan. It was also imposed by statute rather than constitutional amendment, meaning that the legislature could at any point decide to change its mind and reassume control. Nevertheless, the system appears to have worked pretty well so far. In 1991 and 2011, the first plan was adopted; in 2001, it was the second proposal; and in 1981, the third time was the charm. Iowa leaves the foxes at least technically in charge of the henhouse but takes the added precaution of locking them in cages around mealtimes.

Which brings us to the phenomenon of redistricting commissions. When reformers talk about how to fix the problem of gerrymandering, these discussions almost inevitably involve an appeal for some kind of commission. What this conceals, however, is the staggering amount of variation even among the minority of states that have already adopted one. Commissions fall into one of four broad categories, although even these often have significant overlap between them. In fact, there are almost as many different kinds of redistricting commissions as there are redistricting commissions. Basically, it's complicated.

The first are backup commissions, whose responsibilities are triggered only when the legislature is unable to pass a redistricting plan by the statutory or constitutional deadline. Backup commissions for state legislative plans have been established in Connecticut, Illinois, Mississippi, Oklahoma, and Texas and for congressional plans in Connecticut, Indiana, and Ohio. In states without backup commissions, failure to pass a plan in a timely fashion instead throws the matter to the courts, so their utility is marginal. Not much to see here.

The second are advisory commissions, an example of which is the system adopted in New York after the final handshake deal discussed in chapter 10. Here, the commission—usually appointed by some combination of the party leadership in the state legislature, the governor, or the courts—is responsible for drawing up a proposed set of district boundaries, which may then be adopted as is, amended, or rejected and replaced with an alternative map by the legislature. Five states (Maine, New York, Rhode Island, Utah, and Virginia) have so far established advisory commissions that play a role in the redrawing of their congressional and state legislative districts, while Vermont, which has had only one seat in the House since the 1930 census, uses its advisory commission only for the state legislature. While advisory commissions impose a democratic norm in favor of independently drawn district boundaries, they cannot prevent a party that is determined enough to gerrymander from successfully doing so. It's akin to handing the foxes a memo outlining the farmer's voluntary but strongly encouraged chicken protection plan before turning them loose on the henhouse.

The next step along the continuum is the bipartisan redistricting commission. Here, as the name suggests, the state has removed the logistical task of redrawing districts from the hands of the politicians who will compete in them, and vested it in a commission made up of equal numbers of Democrats and Republicans. Sometimes, these commissions also include a tie-breaking member who is independent of either side, such as a nonpartisan redistricting expert, legal scholar, or political scientist. Other times, a supermajority requirement plays the same role, ensuring at least a modicum of bipartisan consensus to successfully pass a plan. While members of the legislature themselves are not directly involved, it is generally the responsibility of the party leadership to select the commission's members, so its composition may still be subject to political influence.

Some commissions are bipartisan in name only. The very first state to adopt a redistricting commission was Arkansas in 1956, with 58 percent of the state's voters supporting the switch. The Arkansas Board of Apportionment, whose responsibilities extend only to the drawing of districts for the state legislature, is made up of the governor, the attorney general, and the secretary of state, all elected positions in the executive branch of the state government. By virtue of the 2018 elections, all three of these positions will be held by Republicans when redistricting is conducted after the 2020 census. Even on occasions when the voters have returned a bipartisan slate of executive branch officials, as was the case in 2010 when the Democratic governor, Mike Beebe, was elected alongside a Republican secretary of state, the odd number of commissioners ensures that one side will always control a majority.

New Jersey's Apportionment Commission, the next to be established in 1966, was instead created to guarantee bipartisanship. It has thirteen members, two each appointed by the senate president, the assembly Speaker, the minority leaders of each chamber, and the chairs of the state Democratic and Republican Parties. The tie-breaking thirteenth vote is selected by consensus or, if the commission deadlocks, by the chief justice of the state supreme court. In recent decades, that tie-breaking vote has been held more often than not by the late Rutgers University political science professor Alan Rosenthal, who served as the independent member of the congressional redistricting commission in 1992 and 2001 and of the state legislative commission in 2011. Some form of bipartisan commission has primary responsibility for the drawing of state legislative districts in Hawaii, Missouri, Ohio, and Pennsylvania, with Hawaii and New Jersey also using them for congressional districts. Bipartisan commissions effectively take the foxes out of the henhouse-guarding equation entirely and replace them with weasels. Sure, fewer chickens per capita are likely to find themselves getting eaten, but I doubt the residents of the coop are feeling especially secure.

Finally, there is the gold standard: the independent redistricting commission. Or at least, independent in theory; in practice, your mileage may vary. The most prominent of these in the United States is probably the California Citizens Redistricting Commission. Its fourteen members consist of five registered Democrats, five registered Republicans, and four unaffiliated voters. Politicians, legislative staffers, and lobbyists are all prohibited from serving. The process works thus. Any registered California voter may apply for a position on the commission. In 2010, there were almost thirty-six thousand applications. The state auditor's office then reviews the application materials, which include a personal essay and letters of recommendation, and narrows the list to the sixty most qualified candidates: twenty Democrats; twenty Republicans; and twenty independents. After each category is narrowed to twelve, eight commissioners are selected at random from the remaining pool, and they in turn are responsible for choosing the remaining six. The goal is to create a representative cross section of qualified citizens unbeholden to the Sacramento political establishment.

Once empaneled, the commission is subject to strict rules about how the districts must be drawn. Traditional principles like compactness, contiguity, and respect for communities of interest and political subdivisions must be followed, while the interests of incumbents, candidates, and political parties may not be considered. The commission is required to "conduct an open and transparent process enabling full public consideration of and comment on the drawing of district lines." In 2011, thirty-four public hearings were conducted during which the testimony of twenty-seven hundred citizens and organizations was heard. But the process is by no means foolproof. A widely cited article by the independent investigative journalism organization ProPublica alleged that the California Democratic Party had engaged in a systematic effort to influence the commission's deliberations, surreptitiously enlisting "local voters, elected officials, labor unions and community groups to testify in support of configurations that coincided with the party's interests." While the commission members denied that they had been unduly swayed by these tactics, the resulting maps were viewed by many observers to be somewhat more favorable to the Democrats than they were to the Republicans. An investigation by the nonpartisan Public Policy Institute of California concluded that "the CRC plans led to greater competitiveness compared to plans drawn by the state legislature in 2001," and that while "Democrats have had a slight edge under the CRC plan," this advantage nevertheless lacked "the size or durability typical of a gerrymander."

California was not the first state to experiment with independent redistricting. Montana (1972), Washington (1983), Idaho (1994), Alaska (1998), and Arizona (2000) had already established similar commissions on which elected representatives and public officials were prohibited from serving. Notably, these other states allow the legislature to have direct input into the selection of commissioners, increasing the possibility of undue political influence. But the California model seems to be one that is catching on. In 2018, the voters of both Colorado and Michigan approved constitutional amendments creating independent redistricting commissions. Both states, like California, require them to be made up of a mix of registered Democrats, Republicans, and independents, allow any interested citizen to apply for a position, and employ some form of random process to select the membership.

The takeaway from California's experiment is that attempting to constrain, incentivize, or shame the foxes into behaving themselves is futile. It is the nature of foxes to eat chickens. Nothing can change that. At the conclusion of this tour of the history of American gerrymandering, one lesson is clear. Only the chickens themselves can be trusted to guard the henhouse. And while only a handful of states have so far truly embraced the notion of independent redistricting, in the rest of the world it is very much the norm.

"During the nineteenth century, in Europe and in self-governing European colonies around the world, the drawing of constituency boundaries was the responsibility of the legislature," writes Lisa Handley, the political scientist and consultant to the United Nations on issues of democracy building and election administration. "Partisan politics and gerrymandering were more often than not a normal element of the [redistricting] process. But in most consolidated Western democracies, the idea that politicians are best excluded from the [redistricting] process has emerged, and legislators have opted out, handing the process over to independent commissions." Her essay appears in the 2008 book *Redistricting in Comparative Perspective,* perhaps the most comprehensive academic study to date of the differing practices utilized by the world's democracies to draw the districts from which the members of their legislature are elected. The results were stark.

"Today, a substantial majority of countries employ an election commission or a specifically designated boundary commission to [redraw] constituency boundaries," she continues. "Of the 60 countries in the survey that [redraw] electoral districts, 43 (73 percent) assign the responsibility for constituency [redistricting] to an election management body or to a boundary commission specially formed for the purpose." Boundary commissions, as the independent nonpartisan bodies responsible for redrawing the United Kingdom's parliamentary constituencies are known, originated in New Zealand in 1887. They have since spread throughout the British Commonwealth, including to the UK itself, Australia, Canada, India, and Fiji. Independent boundary commissions are also used in Albania, the Bahamas, Belize, Botswana, Dominica, Germany, Ireland, Japan, Namibia, Nepal, Papua New Guinea, Singapore, and Zimbabwe.

Other nations make use of an election management body, generally a government agency or commission that is responsible for election administration more generally, rather than redistricting specifically. They usually have a significant degree of independence from the executive and legislative branches. Such systems are used in Armenia, Bangladesh, Belarus, the Dominican Republic, Indonesia, Jamaica, Kenya, Lithuania, Malaysia, Mexico, Nigeria, Pakistan, Poland, Tanzania, Turkey, Ukraine, and Yemen. Of the remaining seventeen nations in the survey, the vast majority of those whose legislature has primary responsibility for redistricting also employ some form of proportional representation or mixed electoral system. These award parties a percentage of seats based on the overall popular vote, rather than the results in individual districts, making gerrymandering less of a concern. "The United States and France," Handley concludes, "are the only two surveyed countries dependent solely on single-member constituencies for the election of legislators that allow the legislature a dominant role in the [redistricting] process."

That process is now under way in the United States. Across the nation, legislatures and commissions are redrawing the boundaries that will be used for U.S. House of Representatives and state legislative elections for the remainder of the decade. The storm is already upon us. Both sides have been planning and organizing for this for almost a decade. Eric Holder and the National Democratic Redistricting Committee, along with his counterpart Scott Walker and the National Republican Redistricting Trust, are already implementing their strategies for rigging the results of American elections for the next ten years. In August 2019, the two men aired their respective grievances on Twitter. "As we said, @EricHolder doesn't want the public to know the real mission of his organization—to gerrymander Democrats into permanent control," Walker charged. "If anyone tells you that @EricHolder is 'fighting against gerrymandering' and for 'fair maps,' just look at the form his organization filed with the IRS. The truth: their mission is to 'FAVORABLY POSITION DEMOCRATS FOR THE REDISTRICTING PROCESS.'" "This is so contrary to the facts—things Scotty doesn't like—and his own efforts to gerrymander for R's that it's laughable," Holder countered. "The big lie. Challenge: Say—like me—you will support non-partisan commissions to draw the lines. Politicians not in control."

This is what we've been reduced to: the two parties' respective redistricting czars sniping at each other on social media about which side's efforts to subjugate the will of the people is more pervasive. Enough already. The blame game accomplishes nothing. I have no doubt that both Holder and Walker have exactly the same goal in mind: how best to manipulate the redistricting process to ensure that their side comes out ahead. Lather, rinse, and repeat. Always repeat. The battle for control of America's governing institutions will not be fought on the campaign trail, in the media, or by the armies of campaign volunteers, activists, and paid professionals whose job is to mobilize supporters and win over undecided voters. It will be fought and won by a handful of mapmakers, attorneys, data scientists, and redistricting professionals whose names most people will probably never even know.

"Each generation," wrote Chief Justice John Roberts in his 2019 year-end report on the federal judiciary, "has an obligation to pass on to the next, not only a fully functioning government responsive to the needs of the people, but the tools to understand and improve it." Only months earlier, he and his colleagues had dashed the hopes of millions with their decision in *Rucho,* foreclosing once and for all a federal judicial solution to the problem of gerrymandering.

Roberts, a pragmatist, an institutionalist, and a conservative in both ideology and temperament, seemed keenly aware of the backlash their decision had produced. So, he took the opportunity to remind his fellow citizens about the importance of civic education, civil discourse, and an engaged body politic for the continuing health of democracy. His colleague Justice Neil Gorsuch expressed similar sentiments in a book published the previous year. "My worry," he wrote, "is that in our country today we sometimes overlook the importance of these kinds of bonds and traditions, and of the appreciation for civility and civics they instill."

The Framers of the U.S. Constitution gave us the institutions, the philosophical traditions, and many of the tools and norms necessary to create a healthy and functioning representative democracy. But they did not supply the virtues required to maintain it. The seeds they planted were strong and hardy. The American system of government has weathered a devastating civil war, numerous attempts at demagoguery from all corners of the political spectrum, massive expansion of the franchise, civil unrest, and all manner of threats both foreign and domestic. But as we enter the third decade of the twenty-first century, the level of confidence that Americans have in the mechanisms of their democratic system is waning.

Aside from the pervasive influence of the modern gerrymander, which is today more devastatingly effective than it has ever been before, voter suppression, outdated voting technology, underfunded and often unfortunately incompetent election administration, the influence of wealthy donors and big money, and foreign interference in our campaigns have shaken the foundations of our democratic mechanisms to their very core. And if there's one thing that I hope this book has made clear, it's that the politicians who benefit from this dysfunction cannot be trusted to fix it. We have the power. Only we can act to safeguard our democracy.

It will not be easy. The mechanisms that incumbent politicians have erected to protect their cushy institutionalized jobs and insulate themselves from the public sentiment are strong and difficult to break down. Some of them may even be intractable. But that should not prevent us from affecting what we can affect, fixing what we are able to fix, and reforming what is capable of being reformed. Let's not allow the perfect to become the enemy of the good. Voting is not enough. Once rigged, elections cannot be unrigged merely through the diligent and careful exercise of the franchise. We must organize to prevent gerrymandering from creating yet another decade in which who votes in elections, and whom they vote for, matters little in a sizable percentage of American states.

Where direct democracy is available, petitions must be organized, signatures must be gathered, and initiatives must be placed on the ballot to remove redistricting from the hands of self-interested incumbent politicians and place it in the hands of independent commissions. Where it is not, state legislatures must be lobbied to sponsor popular referenda, or to pass bills achieving similar ends. Congress must be pressured to enact legislation to require independent redistricting for all federal elections. Momentum must be built and then sustained. Minor reforms beget more significant ones, and each small step in the direction of a healthy, responsive democracy makes the next giant leap not only possible but inevitable.

The good news is that the anti-gerrymandering position is the popular one. A 2019 poll by the Campaign Legal Center, a nonpartisan democratic advocacy group, found that 63 percent of Americans—including

65 percent of Democrats, 64 percent of independents, and 59 percent of Republicans—viewed partisan gerrymandering unfavorably. In that same poll, 62 percent expressed support for the creation of independent redistricting commissions, and 65 percent opined that they preferred for districts to be drawn without partisan bias, even if that bias benefited their side. We don't need to win people over, to persuade them why it's a bad idea to continue leaving the foxes in charge of guarding the henhouses. They already agree. What is needed is for them to be mobilized, for the media to shine a brighter light on the abuses of the people's charge, for rich philanthropists to fund interest groups dedicated to redistricting reform, and for politicians to be shamed, cajoled, and brought kicking and screaming into the realization that they must take action. We need to make the electoral downside to the powers that be of stymieing redistricting reform outweigh the benefits that they currently receive from gerrymandering. We have made some progress, but it's not enough.

In statehouses across the nation, the task of redrawing districts at all levels of federal, state, and local government is now playing out. The idle hands of those who have spent a decade preparing for this latest round of gerrymandering are being put to work drawing up spreadsheets, crunching census data, and tweaking boundaries. The next ten years of American elections have already happened in the mainframes of supercomputers running simulation after simulation on every conceivable combination and permutation in the game of redistricting chess. And the devil, as always, is in the details. How much do you really know about redistricting in your state? If the answer is not much, well, that's what the career politicians already huddling behind the scenes with teams of redistricting professionals, attorneys, political scientists, and strategists are hoping for. Democracy dies in darkness. It's up to us to turn on the light. "Those who cannot remember the past," George Santayana once wrote, "are condemned to repeat it."

Benjamin Franklin, at eighty-one when the Constitutional Convention concluded, was the elder statesman and among the most experienced of all the Founding Fathers. He had traveled extensively, observing how governments the world over fail to realize the dream and promise of democracy. He was acutely aware of the responsibility that later generations bore when it came to setting a watchman at the gates through which the people's elected representatives must pass. "Doctor, what have we got, a republic or a monarchy?" asked Elizabeth Willing Powel as Franklin left Independence Hall on the final day of the Constitutional Convention in Philadelphia in 1787. "A republic," he replied, "if you can keep it."

Acknowledgments

It's rare for an academic to be given the opportunity to write a book that will be read by anyone other than their fellow academics. When they are, it's usually because they've received the advice, guidance, and assistance of numerous people along the way. Oh, and luck, too. A whole lot of luck.

I was fortunate enough to begin my academic career under the mentorship of an extraordinary group of professors at the State University of New York at Buffalo. My thanks to Jim Battista, Jim Campbell, Munroe Eagles, Chuck Finocchiaro, Steve Halpern, Gregg "Bagel" Johnson, Chuck Lamb, the late Franco Mattei, Harvey Palmer, Claude Welch, and, most of all, to Josh Dyck.

Fifteen years ago, I walked into Josh's office and told him that I didn't want to be a professor. I'd enrolled in graduate school with no clear career goal in mind, but simply because I loved political science. That love had been kindled by my high school politics teacher, Patrick Walsh-Atkins, at Bromsgrove School in the United Kingdom. His classes on American government inspired me to move three thousand miles away from home and family to follow the American Dream. "Give me a year," Josh replied, "and I'll do my best to change your mind." He did.

I'd also like to express appreciation to my wonderful colleagues, current and former, at the University of North Florida. Matt Corrigan, who took the chance of hiring a twenty-six-year-old British dude to teach American politics. He saw the potential in me that I was unable to find in myself. Adrienne Lerner, who encouraged me to dream big and then helped make that dream a reality. I've never met a more supportive and dedicated colleague and friend. Mike Binder, who still laments my retirement from the game of golf. And Georgette Dumont and George Candler, to whom I'll merely say: "pip pip, socialism!" My thanks also to Mary Borg, Lauren Chartier, Natasha Christie, Sierra Ejankowski, Sean Freeder, Josh Gellers, Paul Harwood, the late Anne Hopkins, Emily Maiden, Pat Plumlee, David Schwam-Baird, Enrijeta Shino, Henry Thomas, and Pam Zeiser. You've made coming to work every day this past eleven years a pleasure.

This book became a reality thanks to the hard work of numerous people. These include my agent, Ian Bonaparte, my editor, Victoria Wilson, her assistant, Marc Jaffee, publicist Michiko Clark, art director Kelly Blair, and production editor Nora Reichard.

Finally, and most importantly, I'd like to thank my family—your boy did good! My parents, Mike and Hilary, my grandmother, Maisey, who passed away during the writing of this book at the age of 101, and my brother, Will. And most of all, my wife, Saundra. Thanks for coming on this crazy journey with me.

Notes

1. THE FIRST GERRYMANDER

16 The year was 1724: The lords proprietors were a group of eight British noble-
men who had been awarded ownership of Carolina by King Charles II in 1663.
Although the crown retained sovereignty over the land, the lords proprietors were
granted significant powers under their charter, including the ability to lay and collect taxes and to maintain law and order. In 1719, South Carolina was spun off as
its own separate royal colony, and in 1729 King George II bought off the remaining
proprietors, also bringing North Carolina under the direct control of the crown.

16 This translated into: For the original research in this chapter, I am indebted to
the Documenting the American South archive of colonial-era records, which
is maintained by the University Library of the University of North Carolina at
Chapel Hill.

17 Later that same year: In his deposition, Gale expresses that "he knows of no reason
he has ever given the said Govr for such his insupportable behavior," but specu-
lates that Burrington's enmity might have dated back to Gale's time as a customs
agent at the Port of Beaufort, where he had advised another agent at Roanoke who
was embroiled in a dispute with Burrington over the seizing of a trading vessel.

19 And Pelham's connections: In an autobiographical letter to the journal *The
Champion* many decades later, Burrington claimed that he had not made Pelham's acquaintance until the late 1720s. This assertion is doubtful, given the
contrary conclusion reached by numerous historians, and might have been an
attempt to downplay the political connections that had jump-started his career.

29 Nevertheless, he remained: The other votes against ratification were cast by
Edmund Randolph and George Mason of Virginia, who are discussed in chapter 2.

30 Adding further embarrassment: Gerry was defeated by Strong 50–44 in 1800,
56–44 in 1801, 60–39 in 1802, and 67–32 in 1803. Things were not trending in the
right direction for him.

34 In a now famous: While contemporaneous sources, not to mention early historical accounts, credit Stuart as the creator of the gerrymander cartoon, more recent
analysis argues that Tisdale was actually responsible, and I'm inclined to agree.

The identity of the newspaper editor who originally coined the term "gerry-mander" is believed to be either Benjamin Russell, his brother John Russell, or Nathan Hale.

2. JAMES MADISON'S HENRYMANDER

37 He made a name: The House of Burgesses, established in 1642, was the elected chamber of the Virginia General Assembly during the colonial era. It existed until 1776, when the Commonwealth of Virginia declared independence from Great Britain, at which time it was replaced by the house of delegates, which continues to this day.

38 In a letter to: The original correspondence referenced and quoted in this chapter is sourced from both the National Archives' Founders Online project, a joint collaboration of the National Historical Publications and Records Commission and the University of Virginia Press, and from *The Documentary History of the First Federal Elections, 1788–1790,* published by the University of Wisconsin Press.

41 Jefferson's church-state: Jefferson's bill was titled the Virginia Statute for Religious Freedom, and in addition to guaranteeing the personal right to free exercise of religion that would later be incorporated into the First Amendment to the U.S. Constitution, it disestablished the Church of England in the commonwealth.

42 Rumors of Jefferson's: Following through on a promise he had made while in Paris, whereby Hemings only agreed to return to Monticello if Jefferson pledged to release her children from bondage, he freed each of them on their twenty-first birthdays. None of his slaves other than those affiliated with the Hemings family were similarly granted freedom, either during his lifetime or in his will, although his heirs were forced to sell the 130 remaining slaves at Monticello to pay the debts incurred by his estate. In his 1873 memoir, Madison Hemings, one of Sally's children, claimed not only that Jefferson was his father but also that he had been named after his close friend James Madison at the request of Dolley Madison, James's wife.

48 According to a letter: The word "militia" here carries the same meaning as in the Second Amendment to the U.S. Constitution. It refers, in the words of the Supreme Court justice Antonin Scalia, to "those who were male, able bodied, and within a certain age range," and not, as the term is more commonly used today, to any kind of organized military or paramilitary force. Because the number of militiamen was a rough proxy for the adult male population, it could be used to draw districts that were approximately equal in terms of their respective numbers.

3. REVENGE OF THE WHIGS

62 In 1816, for example: The Constitution provides states with almost unlimited discretion to determine how their Electoral College votes will be chosen dur-

ing presidential elections. In the early republic, most states decided to allocate their electoral votes among districts, with each district sending one representative to the Electoral College. A few allowed the state legislature to pick their electors directly. Today, almost every state has transitioned to a winner-takes-all approach, where the candidate who receives the most popular votes in the state receives all of that state's Electoral College votes. Maine and Nebraska still utilize a version of the district system.

64   The former president: Adams remains the only former chief executive to be elected to the U.S. House of Representatives after leaving the office of president. He served for seventeen years before collapsing on the House floor from a massive cerebral hemorrhage during a debate on February 21, 1848, and died two days later. Andrew Johnson served for four months in the U.S. Senate before his death in 1875, while William Howard Taft enjoyed a successful nine-year career on the Supreme Court as chief justice following the end of his presidency. He's widely regarded as a far more successful justice than he was a president.

66   Fueled by voter backlash: Zachary Taylor was also elected on the Whig ticket in 1848. Though they won only two presidential elections, four Whigs would actually occupy the Oval Office, because both Harrison and Taylor contracted serious illnesses and died shortly into their administrations. Their vice presidents, John Tyler and Millard Fillmore, round out the party's fairly nondescript contributions to the presidency. Tyler, a former Democrat, was even expelled from the Whig Party while serving as president and suffered the ignominy of his own party commencing impeachment proceedings against him in the House. Both Tyler and Fillmore also managed to lose their party's nominations when running for reelection, something that only three other presidents in U.S. history have achieved. One could be forgiven for thinking that the Whig Party was not sending its best people.

67   After an Ohio jeweler: Performed to the tune of the old minstrel song "Little Pigs," the lyrics to the first verse and chorus of "Tip and Ty," as the song was originally popularized, were as follows:

> What's the cause of this commotion, motion, motion,
> Our country through?
> It is the ball a-rolling on
>
> For Tippecanoe and Tyler too.
> For Tippecanoe and Tyler too.
> And with them we'll beat little Van, Van, Van,
> Van is a used up man.
> And with them we'll beat little Van.

67   Though the Harrison-Tyler: The election in Ohio saw Harrison win 54 percent of the vote to Van Buren's 46 percent.

67   It became immediately: The term "Locofoco" originated in the machine politics of New York's Tammany Hall. Referencing a patent for a self-lighting cigar that

had been issued to John Marck in 1834, it was adopted by the Whigs as a derisive moniker for their Democratic opponents after the Jacksonian faction made use of the device to light candles at one of their meetings, the gaslights having been turned off by the Tammany men in an effort to break up the assembly. A portmanteau of the Spanish word *loco,* meaning "mad or crack-brained," and a misspelling of the Italian word *fuoco,* meaning "fire," the nickname continued to be used well into the 1850s, even after the Whig Party, which had coined it, had ceased to exist.

68 The specifics of the legislation: For the original research in this chapter, I am greatly indebted to the fantastic resources of the Ohio Memory project, a collaborative statewide digital library program created by Ohio History Connection and the State Library of Ohio. I'd also like to thank Jenni Salamon, whose article "Ohio's 1842 Election: Absquatulators vs. Gerrymanderers" inspired me to delve into the details of this largely unknown historical gerrymander.

72 "Next morning the Tin Pan": The "Tin Pan" was, according to *The Oxford Dictionary of American Political Slang,* a "secret caucus of Democratic legislators working outside normal procedures and hierarchies to develop legislation to be forced by its majority power upon the state legislature."

73 In the elections: The Apportionment Act had thrown a wrench into the 1842 midterms, with more than half of the states following suit with Ohio and delaying their elections until 1843. Maryland even waited until February 1844, almost a full year after the Twenty-Eighth Congress had begun.

74 Branded by the National: The others are Bill Clinton in 1998 and Donald Trump in 2019 and 2021. Articles of impeachment had been drawn up against Richard Nixon by the House Judiciary Committee in 1974, but he resigned his office before they could be formally voted on.

4. HONEST ABE STACKS THE STATES

84 Less than four years: Hamilton's son Philip had also been killed in a duel with George Eacker at the same location in 1801. Some historians believe that the pistols used in the Hamilton-Burr duel, which were supplied by John Barker Church, Hamilton's brother-in-law and a business partner of Burr's, were also used in that duel, and possibly another between Burr and Church himself in 1799, during which neither man was injured. While both Hamilton and Burr discharged their weapons during the duel, the question of who fired first is a matter of considerable historical debate, because, per the principles of *code duello,* all others present had turned their backs as the duel commenced. Burr's bullet struck Hamilton in the lower abdomen, above the right hip, fracturing several ribs and causing fatal damage to his internal organs. Hamilton's bullet was later found to have passed through the limb of a cedar tree, on a trajectory that would most likely have taken it above Burr's head. So, while his discharge might have been accidental—an involuntary response to the wound he had received from Burr—it nevertheless remains possible that Ham shot first.

86 Gravely wounded in the attack: A later conspiracy theory alleged that Cermak, rather than Roosevelt, had actually been the intended target of the assassination attempt. According to this account, Zangara was a hired killer working for the Chicago crime boss Frank Nitti, one of Al Capone's top henchmen, who had targeted Cermak in retaliation for his campaign promise to crack down on organized crime. Most historians dispute this conclusion, and Zangara himself stated during his confession that his goal had been to "kill kings and presidents first and next all capitalists."

89 One of those opponents: A split in the Democratic Party between pro-slavery southern Democrats and their northern counterparts, who endorsed popular sovereignty, resulted in the party nominating two different presidential tickets for the 1860 election. The northern faction backed Douglas, while the southerners rallied behind Vice President John C. Breckinridge of Kentucky, who served in the administration of James Buchanan. A group of former Whigs also established the Constitutional Union Party, which nominated the former senator John Bell of Tennessee, who sought to avoid secession by campaigning on a pro-Union platform in the South. All four of the major candidates received electoral votes, although Lincoln ran out a comfortable winner.

92 But they nevertheless moved forward: Perhaps the most fascinating, not to mention bizarre, secession story of the Civil War comes in the form of the tiny hamlet of Town Line, New York, outside Buffalo. Sometime in 1861, the men of Town Line met secretly in the local schoolhouse and voted by an 85–40 majority to leave the Union. On their minds that day was not the question of slavery but a desire on the part of the German-immigrant population, left war weary by the conflicts in their homeland, to avoid a military draft. Several residents even fled to Canada when the war broke out. Since Town Line was, and remains to this day, an unincorporated entity sandwiched between the villages of Alden and Lancaster, the vote carried no legal weight. Eighty-five years later, in a 1946 ceremony that was for some reason presided over by the Hollywood actor Cesar Romero, the residents of Town Line voted to rejoin the Union. The margin was 90–23. The insignia of the Town Line Volunteer Fire Department continued to incorporate the Confederate flag, as well as the slogan "Last of the Rebels," until 2011, when it was replaced with the state flag of New York.

92 In the aptly named case: The Court's decision entertained the somewhat narrower legal question of whether two individual counties, Berkeley and Jefferson, properly belonged in the state of Virginia or West Virginia. While the direct question of the legality of the secession itself was not before the Court, in ruling in favor of West Virginia with regard to those two counties, the justices at least tacitly endorsed its validity.

97 But like other Democratic hopefuls: There have been four presidential elections in U.S. history in which a candidate lost the popular vote and still won an Electoral College majority. On each occasion, the Democratic candidate was on the losing side. In addition to Tilden, Grover Cleveland (1888), Al Gore (2000), and Hillary Clinton (2016) all found themselves on the wrong end of a popular-electoral vote split. Andrew Jackson also won the popular vote in 1824, but no

candidate reached a majority in the Electoral College, leading to John Quincy Adams being selected as president by the House of Representatives in a contingent election.

5. FRANKFURTER'S POLITICAL THICKET

III Frankfurter's papers: In November 1972, it was discovered that more than 1,000 pages of Felix Frankfurter's papers, including his correspondence with President Lyndon Johnson and Chief Justice Charles Evans Hughes, had been stolen from the Library of Congress. An FBI investigation ensued, and a grand jury was empaneled, but no suspects were ever publicly identified or charged. Even the full scope and timing of the theft were hard to pin down. Frankfurter's papers, consisting of more than 250 boxes of documents, had been open to the public since 1967, but no comprehensive inventory had yet been compiled. The FBI suspected that the thief had been a scholar, narrowing their investigation to a list of researchers who had requested access to the other major repository of Frankfurter papers at the Harvard Law School Library, but had been denied. Decades later, Roger Newman, a journalism professor who subsequently authored a biography of Frankfurter's Supreme Court colleague Hugo Black, confirmed to journalist Jill Lepore that he was the FBI's prime suspect and had been brought before the grand jury for questioning in October 1973. He denied any knowledge of the heist. The FBI quietly ended their investigation in March 1974. None of the stolen pages have ever been recovered.

III He finished out the war: The two presidents Roosevelt, Theodore and Franklin, had remarkably similar career paths on their way to the White House. They both served as members of the New York state legislature, assistant secretary of the navy, and governor of New York.

113 The Court of the early 1930s: The *Lochner* era takes its name from the 1905 case *Lochner v. New York,* where a 5–4 majority struck down a state law regulating the working hours of bakery employees. The decision was based on a controversial theory of due process known as the liberty of contract, which posited that the Constitution prohibits government from "unreasonable, unnecessary and arbitrary interference with the right and liberty of the individual to contract." The portrayal of the Court as an activist institution during this period has been disputed by many later conservative legal scholars, who point out that from 1887 to 1910 fully 83 percent of the state economic regulations that the justices reviewed were upheld.

119 Kenneth W. Colegrove: Colegrove's second claim to fame, or more accurately infamy, in addition to lending his name to a Supreme Court decision, came when he was ousted from his position at Northwestern over his outspoken support for McCarthyism. In addition to fundraising on McCarthy's behalf, Colegrove authored a twelve-page pamphlet defending the senator, which was nationally distributed by Freedom Clubs Inc. "It is difficult to name any university where

a communist cell does not exist," Colegrove said in 1952, "nor in which there is not one or more communist professors."

6. ECHOES OF SLAVERY

128 Echoes of Slavery: The title of this chapter references a photography series by Curtis Graves, whose story as a Texas civil rights pioneer features prominently. " 'Echoes of Slavery' is from my 'Architecture of Enslavement' collection," Graves wrote in a 2013 article promoting a documentary in which he was featured, "and was taken on the Evergreen Plantation where my great grandmother, Celeste, was born, about 35 miles up river from New Orleans. The plantation still stands."

134 Meanwhile, the previous at-large system: While the legal wrangling went on even after the passage of the new apportionment plan in 1965 (House Bill 195), the court allowed the new districts to be used for the 1966 state legislative elections. In 1967, the Supreme Court in *Kilgarlin v. Hill* vacated the lower court ruling upholding the plan, and the case would continue to be mired in litigation for most of the remainder of the decade.

148 He was the first: The Wood assassination was followed by the murders of Richard J. Daronco of the Southern District of New York, who was shot and killed by the family member of a disgruntled former litigant in 1988, and Robert Smith Vance of the Fifth Circuit, who was murdered in a mail bomb attack in 1989. More recently, John Roll of the District of Arizona was shot and killed in Tucson in 2011 during the assassination attempt on Congresswoman Gabrielle Giffords by Jared Lee Loughner.

151 In 1911, the Alabama: The 1901 Alabama Constitution remains in effect to this day. At 310,296 words, most of which consist of its 977 amendments (at the time of this writing), it is both the longest and the most amended constitution in the world. One estimate places its length at more than twelve times that of the average state constitution and more than forty-four times that of the average national constitution.

154 And while he performs: For the record, those nine words were "Mr. Chief Justice, and may it please the Court."

7. A BLUE TIDE IN THE GOLDEN STATE

172 "hard-boiled San Francisco Democrat": For my research into Burton's background, I relied heavily on John Jacobs's excellent 1995 biography, *A Rage for Justice: The Passion and Politics of Phillip Burton.*

184 In an apparent attempt: Godwin's law (or Godwin's rule of Hitler analogies): "As an online discussion grows longer, the probability of a comparison involving Nazis or Hitler approaches 1."

9. WIN ONE FOR THE WHIZZER

219 In a 5–4 ruling: Though the exact wording may vary, *Miranda* requires law enforcement to advise criminal suspects of the following:

  1. They have the right to remain silent.
  2. Anything the suspect does say can and may be used against them in a court of law.
  3. They have the right to have an attorney present before and during questioning.
  4. They have the right, if they cannot afford the services of an attorney, to have one appointed, at public expense and without cost to them, to represent them before and during questioning.

226 "But if you say": Prior to 2004, the names of the individual justices who asked questions during oral arguments were not included in the publicly released Supreme Court transcripts. Interjections from the bench were instead prefaced only with the notation "Question." Though diligent court-watching sleuths may be able to identify the individual justices from the vocal cues in the recordings, I do not presume to possess either the knowledge or the experience to venture such a guess. I will only stipulate, and with some confidence, that the questions quoted in this section did not come from Justice Sandra Day O'Connor.

10. THE HANDSHAKE DEAL

259 On July 8, Paterson: The Ravitch appointment was later upheld by the New York Court of Appeals.

11. HOLLOW HOPE

284 The legislature gratefully passed the plan: Under the North Carolina Constitution, the governor has no veto authority over redistricting legislation, so the plan became law immediately upon being passed by both houses of the general assembly.
295 Lacking the votes: Wisconsin law requires at least twenty senators to be present for the passage of a fiscal bill. The Republican majority in the state assembly was sufficiently large that it constituted a quorum without a single Democrat needing to be present.

CONCLUSION: IF YOU CAN KEEP IT

307 The districts he drew: Some modifications were made to Hofeller's 2011 map after the U.S. Supreme Court's ruling in the 2017 case of *Cooper v. Harris,* which

struck down Districts 1 and 12 as unconstitutional racial gerrymanders. The overall partisan slant of the map, however, remained in place.

307 It's perhaps best: The information on state redistricting procedures in this section is sourced largely from the comprehensive resources published by the National Conference of State Legislatures (www.ncsl.org) and from the All About Redistricting website maintained by the Loyola Law School professor Justin Levitt (redistricting.lls.edu). Any errors in interpretation of their data are entirely my own.

Bibliography

Abraham, Henry. *Justices and Presidents: A Political History of Appointments to the Supreme Court.* New York: Oxford University Press, 1992.

Ammon, Harry. *James Monroe: The Quest for National Identity.* New York: McGraw-Hill, 1971.

Anderson, D. R. "Jefferson and the Virginia Constitution." *American Historical Review* 21, no. 4 (1916): 750–54.

Anderson, Eric. *Race and Politics in North Carolina, 1872–1901: The Black Second.* Baton Rouge: Louisiana State University Press, 1981.

Anderson, Jon M. "Politics and Purpose: Hide and Seek in the Gerrymandering Thicket After *Davis v. Bandemer.*" *University of Pennsylvania Law Review* 136, no. 1 (1987): 183–237.

Argersinger, Peter H. *Representation and Inequality in Late Nineteenth-Century America: The Politics of Apportionment.* New York: Cambridge University Press, 2012.

Aron, Paul. *Founding Feuds: The Rivalries, Clashes, and Conflicts That Forged a Nation.* Naperville, Ill.: Sourcebooks, 2016.

Atkins, Jonathan M. *Parties, Politics, and the Sectional Conflict in Tennessee, 1832–1861.* Knoxville: University of Tennessee Press, 1997.

Austin, James T. *The Life of Elbridge Gerry.* Boston: Wells and Lilly, 1828.

Baker, Gordon E. *The Reapportionment Revolution: Representation, Political Power, and the Supreme Court.* New York: Random House, 1966.

Banning, Lance. *The Sacred Fire of Liberty: James Madison and the Founding of the Federal Republic.* Ithaca, N.Y.: Cornell University Press, 1995.

Barbash, Fred. "Justices Limit Court Powers Under Voting Rights Act." *Washington Post,* April 21, 1980.

Barrett, Grant, ed. *Hatchet Jobs and Hardball: The Oxford Dictionary of American Political Slang.* New York: Oxford University Press, 2004.

Barron, James. "Public Lives." *New York Times,* Aug. 23, 2000.

Barron, Seth. "All-Blue Albany?" *City Journal* (Autumn 2018).

Benjamin, Gerald, and Charles Brecher, eds. *The Two New Yorks: State-City Relations in the Changing Federal System.* New York: Russell Sage Foundation, 1988.

Berkin, Carol. *A Sovereign People: The Crises of the 1790s and the Birth of American Nationalism.* New York: Basic Books, 2017.

Bernstein, Richard B., and Kym S. Rice. *Are We to Be a Nation? The Making of the Constitution.* Cambridge, Mass.: Harvard University Press, 1987.

Bethea, Charles. "A Father, a Daughter, and the Attempt to Change the Census." *New Yorker,* July 21, 2019.

Billias, George. *Elbridge Gerry: Founding Father and Republican Statesman.* New York: McGraw-Hill, 1976.

Black, Earl, and Merle Black. *The Rise of Southern Republicans.* Cambridge, Mass.: Harvard University Press, 2002.

Blacksher, James U., and Larry T. Menefee. "From *Reynolds v. Sims* to *City of Mobile v. Bolden:* Have the White Suburbs Commandeered the Fifteenth Amendment?" *Hastings Law Journal* 34, no. 1 (1982): 1–46.

Boyd, Thomas M., and Stephen J. Markman. "The 1982 Amendments to the Voting Rights Act: A Legislative History." *Washington and Lee Law Review* 40, no. 4 (1983): 1347–428.

Boyd, William K. "Some North Carolina Tracts of the Eighteenth Century." *North Carolina Historical Review* 2, no. 1 (1925): 30–82.

Boyer, Peter J. "Howard Jarvis: New Hero to the U.S. Taxpayer." Associated Press, June 7, 1978.

Brown, Ralph Adams. *The Presidency of John Adams.* Lawrence: University Press of Kansas, 1975.

Buel, Richard, Jr. *America on the Brink: How the Political Struggle over the War of 1812 Almost Destroyed the Young Republic.* London: Palgrave Macmillan, 2005.

Buhite, Russell D., and David W. Levy, eds. *FDR's Fireside Chats.* Norman: University of Oklahoma Press, 1992.

Burstein, Andrew, and Nancy Isenberg. *Madison and Jefferson.* New York: Random House, 2010.

Calabrese, Stephen. "Multimember District Congressional Elections." *Legislative Studies Quarterly* 25, no. 4 (2000): 611–43.

Campbell, Norine Dickson. *Patrick Henry: Patriot and Statesman.* Old Greenwich, Conn.: Devin-Adair, 1969.

Canon, David T. *Race, Redistricting, and Representation: The Unintended Consequences of Black Majority Districts.* Chicago: University of Chicago Press, 1999.

Carpenter, William. *The People's Book: Comprising Their Chartered Rights and Practical Wrongs.* London: W. Strange, 1831.

Castel, Albert E. *The Presidency of Andrew Johnson.* Lawrence: Regents Press of Kansas, 1979.

Chill, C. Daniel. "Political Gerrymandering: Was Elbridge Gerry Right?" *Touro Law Review* 33, no. 3 (2017): 795–825.

Clark, George. *Stealing Our Votes: How Politicians Conspire to Control Elections and How to Stop Them.* Pittsburgh: Dorrance, 2004.

Colby, Peter W., ed. *New York State Today: Politics, Government, Public Policy.* 2nd ed. Albany: State University of New York Press, 1989.

Collins, Paul M., Jr., and Lori A. Ringhand. "The Institutionalization of Supreme Court Confirmation Hearings." *Law and Social Inquiry* 41, no. 1 (2016): 126–51.

Cox, Gary W., and Jonathan N. Katz. *Elbridge Gerry's Salamander: The Electoral Conse-*

quences of the Reapportionment Revolution. Cambridge, U.K.: Cambridge University Press, 2002.

Crapol, Edward P. *John Tyler: The Accidental President.* Chapel Hill: University of North Carolina Press, 2006.

Crawford, Ann Fears. *Barbara Jordan: Breaking the Barriers.* Houston, Tex.: Halcyon Press, 2003.

Cushman, Barry. "Inside the 'Constitutional Revolution' of 1937." *Supreme Court Review* 2016 (2016): 367–409.

Daley, David. "How Democrats Gerrymandered Their Way to Victory in Maryland." *Atlantic,* June 25, 2017.

———. *Ratf**ked: Why Your Vote Doesn't Count.* New York: Liveright, 2017.

———. "The Secret Files of the Master of Modern Republican Gerrymandering." *New Yorker,* Sept. 6, 2019.

Danelski, David J., and Joseph S. Tulchin, eds. *The Autobiographical Notes of Charles Evans Hughes.* Cambridge, Mass.: Harvard University Press, 2001.

Darling, Marsha, ed. *Enforcing and Challenging the Voting Rights Act: Race, Voting, and Redistricting.* New York: Routledge, 2001.

Davidson, Chandler. *Minority Vote Dilution.* Washington, D.C.: Howard University Press, 1984.

Demos, John. *Remarkable Providences: Readings on Early American History.* Boston: Northeastern University Press, 1991.

Dionne, E. J. "Power Shift Seen in State Districting." *New York Times,* Feb. 10, 1982.

Dolan, Joseph F. "Byron White Oral History Interview—JFK #1." John F. Kennedy Presidential Library and Museum, May 6, 1964. www.jfklibrary.org.

———. "Byron White Oral History Interview—JFK #2." John F. Kennedy Presidential Library and Museum, Sept. 2, 1964. www.jfklibrary.org.

Draper, Robert. "The League of Dangerous Mapmakers." *Atlantic,* Oct. 2012.

Eason, John M. *Big House on the Prairie: Rise of the Rural Ghetto and Prison Proliferation.* Chicago: University of Chicago Press, 2017.

Ebenstein, Julie A. "The Geography of Mass Incarceration: Prison Gerrymandering and the Dilution of Prisoners' Political Representation." *Fordham Urban Law Journal* 45, no. 2 (2018): 323–72.

Eisler, Kim Isaac. *A Justice for All: William J. Brennan Jr. and the Decisions That Transformed America.* New York: Simon & Schuster, 1993.

Ekirch, A. Roger. *"Poor Carolina": Politics and Society in Colonial North Carolina, 1729–1776.* Chapel Hill: University of North Carolina Press, 1981.

Ellis, Joseph J. *American Creation: Triumphs and Tragedies in the Founding of the Republic.* New York: Vintage Books, 2008.

Elmendorf, Christopher S., Kevin M. Quinn, and Marisa A. Abrajano. "Racially Polarized Voting." *University of Chicago Law Review* 83, no. 2 (2016): 587–691.

Epstein, Reid J. "Attention, America: We've All Been Saying Gerrymander Wrong." *Wall Street Journal,* May 24, 2018.

Fallon, Michael. *Dodgerland: Decadent Los Angeles and the 1977–78 Dodgers.* Lincoln: University of Nebraska Press, 2016.

Farber, Peggy, and Rachael Fauss. *Rigged to Maintain Power: How NYS' 2012 Redistrict-*

ing Protected Incumbents and Continued Majority Party Control. New York: Citizens Union Foundation, 2014.

Feldman, Daniel L., and Gerald Benjamin. *Tales from the Sausage Factory: Making Laws in New York State.* Albany: State University of New York Press, 2010.

Feldman, Noah. *The Three Lives of James Madison: Genius, Partisan, President.* New York: Random House, 2017.

Ferling, John. *A Leap in the Dark: The Struggle to Create the American Republic.* New York: Oxford University Press, 2003.

Flores, Nicolas. "A History of One-Winner Districts for Congress." Undergraduate thesis, Stanford University, 1999. archive.fairvote.org.

Formisano, Ronald. *The Transformation of Political Culture: Massachusetts Parties, 1790s–1840s.* New York: Oxford University Press, 1983.

Foster, Eugene A., M. A. Jobling, P. G. Taylor, P. Donnelly, P. de Knijff, Rene Mieremet, T. Zerjal, and C. Tyler-Smith. "Jefferson Fathered Slave's Last Child." *Nature* 396 (1998): 27–28.

Frankfurter, Felix. "The Case of Sacco and Vanzetti." *Atlantic Monthly,* March 1927.

Galderisi, Peter F., ed. *Redistricting in the New Millennium.* Lanham, Md.: Lexington Books, 2005.

Geldzahler, Evan. "*Davis v. Bandemer:* Remedial Difficulties in Political Gerrymandering." *Emory Law Journal* 37, no. 2 (1988): 443–93.

Gorsuch, Neil. *A Republic, If You Can Keep It.* New York: Crown, 2019.

Gray, Geoffrey. "The Obstructionist." *New York,* May 20, 2008.

———. "The Un-reformed." *New York,* Feb. 28, 2008.

Griffin, John Chandler. *Abraham Lincoln's Execution.* Gretna, La.: Pelican, 2006.

Griffith, Elmer Cummings. *The Rise and Development of the Gerrymander.* Chicago: Scott, Foresman, 1907.

Grofman, Bernard. "Would Vince Lombardi Have Been Right if He Had Said: 'When It Comes to Redistricting, Race Isn't Everything, It's the Only Thing'?" *Cardozo Law Review* 96, no. 5 (1992): 1236–76.

———, ed. *Political Gerrymandering and the Courts.* New York: Agathon Press, 1990.

———. *Race and Redistricting in the 1990s.* New York: Agathon Press, 1998.

Grofman, Bernard, and Chandler Davidson, eds. *Controversies in Minority Voting: The Voting Rights Act in Perspective.* Washington, D.C.: Bookings Institution, 1992.

Handley, Lisa, and Bernard Grofman, eds. *Redistricting in Comparative Perspective.* New York: Oxford University Press, 2008.

Hanson, Royce. *The Political Thicket: Reapportionment and Constitutional Democracy.* Englewood Cliffs, N.J.: Prentice-Hall, 1966.

Harney, Sarah. "The Albany Triopoly." *Governing,* Aug. 15, 2010.

Hartman, Chester, and Sarah Carnochan. *City for Sale: The Transformation of San Francisco.* Berkeley: University of California Press, 2002.

Hasen, Richard L. "Justice Kennedy's Beauty Pageant." *Atlantic,* June 19, 2017.

———. "Looking for Standards (in All the Wrong Places): Partisan Gerrymandering Claims After *Vieth.*" *Election Law Journal* 3, no. 4 (2004): 626–42.

———. "Race or Party, Race as Party, or Party All the Time: Three Uneasy Approaches to Conjoined Polarization in Redistricting and Voting Cases." *William & Mary Law Review* 59, no. 5 (2018): 1837–86.

Haskins, Ralph W. "Internecine Strife in Tennessee: Andrew Johnson Versus Parson Brownlow." *Tennessee Historical Quarterly* 24, no. 4 (1965): 321–40.

Haywood, Marshall De Lancey. *Governor George Burrington.* Raleigh, N.C.: Edwards Broughton, 1896.

Heltzel, Emily J. "Incarcerated and Unrepresented: Prison-Based Gerrymandering and Why Evenwel's Approval of 'Total Population' as a Population Base Shouldn't Include Incarcerated Populations." *William & Mary Bill of Rights Journal* 26, no. 2 (2017): 533–56.

Henrietta, James A. *Salutary Neglect: Colonial Administration Under the Duke of Newcastle.* Princeton, N.J.: Princeton University Press, 1972.

Hess, Michael A. "Beyond Justiciability: Political Gerrymandering After *Davis v. Bandemer.*" *Campbell Law Review* 9, no. 2 (1987): 207–54.

Heyer, Rose, and Peter Wagner. *Too Big to Ignore: How Counting People in Prisons Distorted Census 2000.* Easthampton, Mass.: Prison Policy Initiative, 2002.

Hirsch, H. N. *The Enigma of Felix Frankfurter.* New York: Basic Books, 1981.

Hockett, Jeffrey. *New Deal Justice: The Constitutional Jurisprudence of Hugo L. Black, Felix Frankfurter, and Robert H. Jackson.* Lanham, Md.: Rowman & Littlefield, 1996.

Hofeller, Stephanie. The Hofeller Files. thehofellerfiles.org.

Hofeller, Thomas B. "California Congressional Reapportionment." Master's thesis, Claremont Graduate School, 1975.

———. "The GOP Redistricting Position in December of 2014." The Hofeller Files, 2014. s3.documentcloud.org/documents/6431863/Geo-GOP-Position12-2-14.pdf.

———. "The Looming Redistricting Reform: How Will the Republican Party Fare?" The Hofeller Files, 2010. www.politico.com/pdf/PPM116_rnc_hofeller _memo_051010.pdf.

———. "Redistricting 2010: Preparing for Success." The Hofeller Files, 2009. www .documentcloud.org/documents/4366661-Redistricting-2010-Preparing-for -Success.html.

———. "What I've Learned About Redistricting—the Hard Way!" The Hofeller Files, Jan. 24, 2011. www.ncsl.org/documents/legismgt/The_Hard_Way.pdf.

Holmes, Dan. " 'Whizzer' White Starred for Lions, but His 'Second' Career Was More Famous." *Vintage Detroit,* April 9, 2018.

Hunter, Thomas Rogers. "The First Gerrymander? Patrick Henry, James Madison, James Monroe, and Virginia's 1788 Congressional Districting." *Early American Studies* 9, no. 3 (2011): 781–820.

Hutchinson, Dennis J. *The Man Who Was Once Whizzer White: A Portrait of Justice Byron R. White.* New York: Free Press, 1998.

Ingalls, Gerald L., and Toby Moore. "The Present and Future of Racial Gerrymandering: Evidence from North Carolina's 12th Congressional District." *Political Geography of the South* 35, no. 1 (1995): 58–74.

Ingwerson, Marshall. "For Californians, It May Be One Gerrymander Too Many." *Christian Science Monitor,* Oct. 21, 1982.

Irish, Leon E. "Byron White: A Singular Life." *Catholic University Law Review* 52, no. 4 (2003): 883–86.

Irons, Peter H. *The New Deal Lawyers.* Princeton, N.J.: Princeton University Press, 1982.

Issacharoff, Samuel, and Pamela S. Karlan. "Where to Draw the Line: Judicial Review of Political Gerrymanders." *University of Pennsylvania Law Review* 53, no. 1 (2004): 541–78.

Jackson, John S., and Lourenke Prozesky. "Redistricting in Illinois." *Simon Review,* paper no. 2 (2005).

Jacobs, John. *A Rage for Justice: The Passion and Politics of Phillip Burton.* Berkeley: University of California Press, 1995.

Jarvis, Howard. *I'm Mad as Hell: The Exclusive Story of the Tax Revolt and Its Leader.* With Robert Pack. New York: Times Books, 1979.

Jenks, Leland Hamilton. *The Migration of British Capital to 1875.* New York: Alfred A. Knopf, 1927.

Jenson, Merrill, and Robert A. Becker, eds. *The Documentary History of the First Federal Elections, 1788–1790.* Vol. 2. Madison: University of Wisconsin Press, 1976.

Jewell, Malcolm E., ed. *The Politics of Reapportionment.* New Brunswick, N.J.: Transaction, 2011.

Justesen, Benjamin R. *Forgotten Legacy: William McKinley, George Henry White, and the Struggle for Black Equality.* Baton Rouge: Louisiana State University Press, 2020.

Katzenbach, Nicholas. *Some of It Was Fun: Working with RFK and LBJ.* New York: W. W. Norton, 2008.

Keith, Gary A., ed. *Rotten Boroughs, Political Thickets, and Legislative Donnybrooks: Redistricting in Texas.* Austin: University of Texas Press, 2013.

Kelly, Jason P. "The Strategic Use of Prisons in Partisan Gerrymandering." *Legislative Studies Quarterly* 37, no. 1 (2012): 117–34.

Ketcham, Ralph. *James Madison: A Biography.* Charlottesville: University of Virginia Press, 1990.

Kidd, Thomas S. *Patrick Henry: First Among Patriots.* New York: Basic Books, 2011.

Klein, Milton M., ed. *The Empire State: A History of New York.* Ithaca, N.Y.: Cornell University Press, 2001.

Kolbert, Elizabeth. "How Redistricting Turned America from Blue to Red." *New Yorker,* Dec. 29, 2017.

Konishi, Hideo, and Chen-Yu Pan. "Partisan and Bipartisan Gerrymandering." *Journal of Public Economic Theory* 22, no. 5 (2020): 1183–212.

Kornheiser, Tony. "A Dash for the Cash." *Washington Post,* Feb. 11, 1994.

Kousser, J. Morgan. *Colorblind Injustice: Minority Voting Rights and the Undoing of the Second Reconstruction.* Chapel Hill: University of North Carolina Press, 1999.

———. "Ignoble Intentions and Noble Dreams: On Relativism and History with a Purpose." *Public Historian* 15, no. 3 (1993): 15–28.

Kramer, Daniel C. *The Days of Wine and Roses Are Over: Governor Hugh Carey and New York State.* Lanham, Md.: University Press of America, 1997.

Kukla, Jon. *Patrick Henry: Champion of Liberty.* New York: Simon & Schuster, 2017.

Labunski, Richard. *James Madison and the Struggle for the Bill of Rights.* New York: Oxford University Press, 2006.

Lachman, Seymour P., and Robert Polner. *The Man Who Saved New York: Hugh Carey and the Great Fiscal Crisis of 1975.* Albany: State University of New York Press, 2011.

Lash, Joseph P., ed. *From the Diaries of Felix Frankfurter.* New York: W. W. Norton, 1980.

Lauck, Jon K. *Prairie Republic: The Political Culture of Dakota Territory, 1879–1889.* Norman: University of Oklahoma Press, 2010.

Lavergne, Gary M. *Before Brown: Herman Marion Sweatt, Thurgood Marshall, and the Long Road to Justice.* Austin: University of Texas Press, 2010.

Lepore, Jill. "The Great Paper Caper." *New Yorker,* Dec. 1, 2014.

Lesher, Stephan. *George Wallace: An American Populist.* Boston: Da Capo Press, 1994.

Levine, Mike, and Ed Shanahan. "Governor Who?" *Times Herald-Record,* Jan. 15, 2007.

Lindsey, Robert. "Howard Jarvis, 83, Dies; Led Drive for Tax Limit." *New York Times,* Aug. 13, 1986.

Lowenstein, Daniel H. "*Vieth*'s Gap: Has the Supreme Court Gone from Bad to Worse on Partisan Gerrymandering?" *Cornell Journal of Law and Public Policy* 14, no. 3 (2005): 367–95.

Lubasch, Arnold H. "Miller Is Found Guilty of Fraud; Speaker Loses Seat in Assembly." *New York Times,* Dec. 14, 1991.

Lynch, John Roy. *The Facts of Reconstruction.* New York: Neale, 1913.

Mader, George. "Binding Authority: Unamendability in the United States Constitution—a Textual and Historical Analysis." *Marquette Law Review* 99, no. 4 (2016): 841–91.

Malan, Rian. "BOSS: You Don't Want to Cross Phil Burton, the Man Who Carved Up California." *California,* Nov. 1981.

Mansoor, Sanya, and Madeline Carlisle. "When Your Body Counts but Your Vote Does Not: How Prison Gerrymandering Distorts Political Representation." *Time,* July 1, 2021.

Martis, Kenneth C. "The Original Gerrymander." *Political Geography* 27, no. 8 (2008): 833–39.

Mayer, Henry. *A Son of Thunder: Patrick Henry and the American Republic.* New York: Franklin Watts, 1986.

Mayer, Jane. *Dark Money: The Hidden History of the Billionaires Behind the Rise of the Radical Right.* New York: Anchor, 2017.

McCarty, Nolan, Keith T. Poole, and Howard Rosenthal. "Congress and the Territorial Expansion of the United States." In *Party, Process, and Political Change in Congress: New Perspectives on the History of Congress,* edited by David W. Brady and Matthew D. McCubbins. Palo Alto, Calif.: Stanford University Press, 2002.

McElvaine, Robert S. *Mario Cuomo: A Biography.* New York: Scribner's, 1988.

McGhee, Eric. "Assessing California's Redistricting Commission: Effects on Partisan Fairness and Competitiveness." *Public Policy Institute of California,* March 2018.

McGrane, Reginald Charles. *The Panic of 1837: Some Financial Problems of the Jacksonian Era.* Chicago: University of Chicago Press, 1924.

Meade, Robert Douthat. *Patrick Henry: Patriot in the Making.* Philadelphia: J. B. Lippincott, 1957.

Miller, Andrew P., and Mark A. Packman. "The Constitutionality of Political Gerrymandering: *Davis v. Bandemer* and Beyond." *Journal of Law and Politics* 4, no. 4 (1988): 697–735.

Miller, Peter, and Bernard Grofman. "Redistricting Commissions in the Western United States." *UC Irvine Law Review* 3 (2015): 637–68.

Monmonier, Mark. *Bushmanders and Bullwinkles: How Politicians Manipulate Electronic Maps and Census Data to Win Elections.* Chicago: University of Chicago Press, 2001.

Montgomery, Gayle B., and James W. Johnson. *One Step from the White House: The Rise and Fall of Senator William F. Knowland.* Berkeley: University of California Press, 1998.

Moore, Frank. *Speeches of Andrew Johnson, President of the United States.* Boston: Little, Brown, 1865.

Moore, Stephen. "Proposition 13 Then, Now, and Forever." Cato Institute, July 30, 1998.

Murphy, Bruce Allen. *The Brandeis/Frankfurter Connection: The Secret Political Activities of Two Supreme Court Justices.* New York: Oxford University Press, 1982.

Nussbaum, Jeff. "The Night New York Saved Itself from Bankruptcy." *New Yorker,* Oct. 16, 2015.

Parrish, Michael E. *Felix Frankfurter and His Times: The Reform Years.* New York: Free Press, 1982.

Parsons, Stanley B., William W. Beach, and Dan Hermann. *United States Congressional Districts, 1788–1841.* Westport, Conn.: Greenwood Press, 1978.

Paterson, David. *Black, Blind, and In Charge: A Story of Visionary Leadership and Overcoming Adversity.* New York: Simon & Schuster, 2020.

Pawel, Miriam. *The Browns of California: The Family Dynasty That Transformed a State and Shaped a Nation.* New York: Bloomsbury, 2018.

Pear, Robert. "Redistricting Expected to Bring Surge in Minority Lawmakers." *New York Times,* Aug. 3, 1992.

Pecorella, Robert F., and Jeffrey M. Stonecash, eds. *Governing New York State.* 6th ed. Albany: State University of New York Press, 2012.

Phillips-Fein, Kim. *Fear City: New York's Fiscal Crisis and the Rise of Austerity Politics.* New York: Metropolitan Books, 2017.

Picchi, Blaise. *The Five Weeks of Giuseppe Zangara: The Man Who Would Assassinate FDR.* Chicago: Academy Chicago, 1998.

Pierce, Olga, Justin Elliot, and Theodore Meyer. "How Dark Money Helped Republicans Hold the House and Hurt Voters." ProPublica, Dec. 21, 2012.

Pierce, Olga, and Jeff Larson. "How Democrats Fooled California's Redistricting Commission." ProPublica, Dec. 21, 2011.

Polsby, Nelson W., ed. *Reapportionment in the 1970s.* Berkeley: University of California Press, 1971.

Pooley, Eric. "The Un-Cuomo." *New York,* Sept. 19, 1994.

Price, William S., Jr. "A Strange Incident in George Burrington's Royal Governorship." *North Carolina Historical Review* 51, no. 2 (1974): 149–58.

Quinn, T. Anthony. *Carving Up California: A History of Redistricting, 1951–1984.* Claremont, Calif.: Rose Institute of State and Local Government, 1988.

Rapoport, Roger, Stephanie Harolde, and Ralph E. Warner. *California Dreaming: The Political Odyssey of Pat and Jerry Brown.* Berkeley, Calif.: Nolo Press, 1982.

Rarick, Ethan. *California Rising: The Life and Times of Pat Brown.* Berkeley: University of California Press, 2005.

Redistricting Majority Project. "Final REDMAP Report." Dec. 21, 2010. www .redistrictingmajorityproject.com.

———. "2012 REDMAP Summary Report." Jan. 4, 2013. www.redistrictingmajority project.com.

Ribble, Frederick G. "George Burrington, Sometime Governor of North Carolina: The 'Janus' of Fielding's *Champion.*" *Studies in Bibliography* 50 (1997): 272–94.

Richomme, Olivier. *Race and Partisanship in California Redistricting: From the 1965 Voting Rights Act to Present.* Lanham, Md.: Lexington Books, 2019.

Riddle, A. G. *The Life of Benjamin F. Wade.* Cleveland: Williams, 1888.

Riggenbach, Jeff. "The Revolt of the Taxpayer: An Interview with the Elder Statesman of Today's Tax Rebellion—Howard Jarvis." *Libertarian Review,* March 1, 1978, 17–24.

Rivers, Christina. "A Brief History of Felon Disenfranchisement and Prison Gerrymanders." *American Historian,* Nov. 2017.

Rives, William C. *History of the Life and Times of James Madison.* Boston: Little, Brown, 1859–68.

Roberts, Sam. "Census Bureau's Counting of Prisoners Benefits Some Rural Voting Districts." *New York Times,* Oct. 23, 2008.

Rorabaugh, W. J. "The Political Duel in the Early Republic: Burr v. Hamilton." *Journal of the Early Republic* 15, no. 1 (1995): 1–23.

Rosen, Hy, and Peter Slocum, eds. *From Rocky to Pataki: Character and Caricatures in New York Politics.* Syracuse, N.Y.: Syracuse University Press, 1998.

Rosenberg, Gerald N. *The Hollow Hope: Can Courts Bring About Social Change?* Chicago: University of Chicago Press, 1991.

Rove, Karl. "The GOP Targets State Legislatures." *Wall Street Journal,* Oct. 8, 2020.

Ryden, David K., ed. *The U.S. Supreme Court and the Electoral Process.* 2nd ed. Washington, D.C.: Georgetown University Press, 2002.

Sack, Kevin. "Incumbency Protection; Changes in the Election Laws in New York Are Less Monumental Than They Appear." *New York Times,* May 6, 1992.

Salamon, Jenni. "Ohio's 1842 Election: Absquatulators vs. Gerrymanderers." *Ohio Memory,* Sept. 6, 2013.

Saunders, William L., ed. *The Colonial Records of North Carolina.* Raleigh: State of North Carolina, 1886–90.

Schneier, Edward V., and Brian Murtaugh. *New York Politics: A Tale of Two States.* 3rd ed. New York: Routledge, 2001.

Schlesinger, Arthur M. *Robert Kennedy and His Times.* Boston: Houghton Mifflin, 1978.

Schwarz, Jordan A. *The New Dealers: Power Politics in the Age of Roosevelt.* New York: Alfred A. Knopf, 1993.

Scott, Eben Greenough. *Reconstruction During the Civil War in the United States of America.* Cambridge, Mass.: Riverside Press, 1895.

Seabrook, Nicholas R. *Drawing the Lines: Constraints on Partisan Gerrymandering in U.S. Politics.* Ithaca, N.Y.: Cornell University Press, 2017.

Seager, Robert, II. *And Tyler Too: A Biography of John and Julia Gardiner Tyler.* New York: McGraw-Hill, 1963.

Sikes, Lewright B. "Gustavus Adolphus Henry: Champion of Lost Causes." *Tennessee Historical Quarterly* 50, no. 3 (1991): 173–82.

Simon, James F. *The Antagonists: Hugo Black, Felix Frankfurter, and Civil Liberties in Modern America.* New York: Simon & Schuster, 1989.

Slayton, Robert A. *Empire Statesman: The Rise and Redemption of Al Smith.* New York: Free Press, 2001.

Smith, Adam. "East, West; Jarvis." *New York Times,* Dec. 9, 1979.

Stephanopoulos, Nicholas, and Eric McGhee. "Partisan Gerrymandering and the Efficiency Gap." *University of Chicago Law Review* 82, no. 2 (2015): 831–900.

Stevens, John Paul, Louis F. Oberdorfer, Louis Henkin, and William E. Nelson. "In Memoriam: Byron R. White." *Harvard Law Review* 116, no. 1 (2002): 1–12.

Stewart, Charles, and Barry R. Weingast. "Stacking the Senate, Changing the Nation: Republican Rotten Boroughs, Statehood Politics, and American Political Development." *Studies in American Political Development* 6, no. 2 (1992): 223–71.

Stigler, Stephen M. "Stigler's Law of Eponymy." *Transactions of the New York Academy of Sciences* 39, no. 1 (1980): 147–57.

Stith, Kate. "Byron R. White, Last of the New Deal Liberals." *Yale Law Journal* 103, no. 1 (1993): 19–35.

Summers, Anthony. *Official and Confidential: The Secret Life of J. Edgar Hoover.* New York: G. P. Putnam's Sons, 1993.

Tagliabue, Paul. "A Tribute to Byron White." *Yale Law Journal* 112, no. 5 (2003): 999–1009.

Taper, Bernard. *Gomillion Versus Lightfoot: The Right to Vote in Apartheid Alabama.* Tuscaloosa: University of Alabama Press, 2003.

Taylor, Miles. "Empire and Parliamentary Reform: The 1832 Reform Act Revisited." In *Rethinking the Age of Reform: Britain, 1750–1850,* edited by Arthur Burns and Joanna Innes. Cambridge, U.K.: Cambridge University Press, 2003.

Temin, Peter. *The Jacksonian Economy.* New York: W. W. Norton, 1969.

Thernstrom, Abigail. "Redistricting, Race, and the Voting Rights Act." *National Affairs,* April 6, 2010.

Thomason, Michael V. R., ed. *Mobile: The New History of Alabama's First City.* Tuscaloosa: University of Alabama Press, 2001.

Tocqueville, Alexis de. *Democracy in America.* Chicago: University of Chicago Press, 2000.

Trefousse, Hans L. *Andrew Johnson: A Biography.* New York: W. W. Norton, 1989.

———. *Benjamin Franklin Wade: Radical Republican from Ohio.* New York: Twayne, 1963.

Turner, Maureen. "The Prison Town Advantage." *Valley Advocate,* Oct. 8, 2009.

Turner, Wallace. "California G.O.P. Seeks to Void Redistricting." *New York Times,* Sept. 22, 1981.

Tushnet, Mark, ed. *I Dissent: Great Opposing Opinions in Landmark Supreme Court Cases.* Boston: Beacon Press, 2008.

Tyler, Gus. "What Is Representative Government?" *New Republic,* July 16, 1962.

Tyler, Gus, and David Wells. "Camel Bites Dachshund." *New Republic,* Nov. 27, 1961.

Udall, Morris K. "Reapportionment I: 'One Man, One Vote' . . . That's All She Wrote!" *Congressman's Report,* Oct. 14, 1964. speccoll.library.arizona.edu/online-exhibits/files/original/11ac559f0063813f0a80bed401b4597f.pdf.

———. "Reapportionment II: Where Do We Go from Here?" *Congressman's Report,* Dec. 11, 1964. speccoll.library.arizona.edu/online-exhibits/files/original/74147dc3693c32adb963c33cb60f0933.pdf.

Unger, Harlow Giles. *The Last Founding Father: James Monroe and a Nation's Call to Greatness.* Boston: Da Capo Press, 2009.

Valentine, Phil. *Tax Revolt: The Rebellion Against an Overbearing, Bloated, Arrogant, and Abusive Government.* Nashville: Nelson Current, 2005.

Verhovek, Sam Howe. "Saul Weprin, a Quiet Conciliator." *New York Times,* Dec. 17, 1991.

Vine, Katie. "The Agitator." *Texas Monthly,* Aug. 2015.

Wagner, Peter. "Breaking the Census: Redistricting in an Era of Mass Incarceration." *William Mitchell Law Review* 38, no. 4 (2012): 1241–60.

———. *Importing Constituents: Prisoners and Political Clout in New York.* Easthampton, Mass.: Prison Policy Initiative, 2002.

Wagner, Peter, and Avi Cummings. *Importing Constituents: Incarcerated People and Political Clout in Maryland.* Easthampton, Mass.: Prison Policy Initiative, 2010.

Wang, Sam. "The Great Gerrymander of 2012." *New York Times,* Feb. 2, 2013.

Wells, David. "The Redistricting Cartel." *City Journal* (Summer 1992).

White, Charles B. "Byron Raymond White (1917–2002): One of the Greatest." *Colorado Lawyer,* Aug./Sept. 2018, 76–81.

White, G. Edward. *The Constitution and the New Deal.* Cambridge, Mass.: Harvard University Press, 2000.

White, Ronald C. *A. Lincoln: A Biography.* New York: Random House, 2009.

Williamson, Hugh. *The History of North Carolina.* Vol. 2. Philadelphia: Thomas Dobson, 1812.

Wilson, Reid. "Pioneer of Modern Redistricting Dies at 75." *Hill,* Aug. 18, 2018.

Wiltz, Teresa. "Why State Legislatures Are Still Pretty White." *Governing,* Dec. 9, 2015.

Wines, Michael. "Thomas Hofeller, Republican Master of Political Maps, Dies at 75." *New York Times,* Aug. 21, 2018.

Woodward, Bob, and Scott Armstrong. *The Brethren: Inside the Supreme Court.* New York: Simon & Schuster, 1979.

Woodward, C. Vann. *Reunion and Reaction: The Compromise of 1877 and the End of Reconstruction.* Boston: Little, Brown, 1951.

———. *The Strange Career of Jim Crow.* 2nd ed. New York: Oxford University Press, 1966.

———. *The Strange Career of Jim Crow.* 3rd ed. New York: Oxford University Press, 1974.

Yang, John E. "Remapping the Politics of the South." *Washington Post,* April 16, 1996.

Index

Acheson, Dean, 114

Adams, John, 27, 28, 29, 84, 301

Adams, John Quincy, 64

Adams, Samuel, 27

Adequate and independent state ground
    standard, 11, 121

Adolf, Jay, 244–245

Aiken, John A., 75

Alabama, 64, 117, 142, 228, 288
    1957 gerrymander in, 140
    1985 election in, 155
    constitution of, 126, 151, 155
    African American disenfranchisement
        in, 152, 154–155, 273
    governor of, 144, 270
    racial segregation in, 215, 269–270
    racial vote dilution in, 151
    redistricting in, 105
    malapportionment in, 125–126

Alaska, 313

Alatorre, Richard, 182–184

Albany, 233–234, 239, 243–244, 249–251,
    253–254, 259–260, 268

Alito, Samuel, 300

Allen, Earl, 132

Amedore, George, 262

American Civil Liberties Union, 111, 156,
    221, 303

Anamosa, Iowa, 188–190, 200

Anderson, Warren, 239, 242, 245

Annapolis Convention, 42

Apportionment Act, 63–64, 66

Arizona, 90, 100, 104, 105, 106, 313

Arkansas, 144, 311–312

*Arlington Heights v. Metropolitan Housing
    Development Corp.*, 152–153

Articles of Confederation, 38, 41–42, 43,
    45–46

Ashe, John Baptista, 21, 22

Atlanta, 93, 124, 125, 134

Atzerodt, George, 87

Austin, 131, 133, 136–137, 139

Avery v. Midland County, 127

Badham v. Eu, 229–230

Baker v. Carr, 107, 120–126, 153, 215,
    224–225

Bailey, Thomas, 20

Baker, Bill, 182

Baltimore, 13, 194, 198

Bane, Tom, 182

Bank of England, 65

Barnes, Ben, 137–138, 144

Barr, Bill, 282–284, 288

Barrett, Tom, 295–296

Battle of Tippecanoe, 67

Beame, Abraham, 241

Beebe, Mike, 312

Bellamy, Pierre, 27

Benisek v. Lamone, 299

Benjamin, Gerald, 255–256

Berman, Howard, 170, 175, 182

Berry, William, 172–173

Beverly, Bob, 181

Bianco, Fred, 250–251

Bill of Rights, 29–30, 38, 45, 46–47, 55–56, 58

Black, Hugo, 107, 117, 119, 121, 125–126, 216

Blackmun, Harry, 149, 154, 220, 226, 228–229, 278

Blacksher, James, 154

Bladen, Martin, 21, 23, 25

Blue, Daniel, 286

Board of Trade, 24

Boatwright, Daniel, 179, 184

Boehm, Theodore, 226–227

Bolden, Wiley L., 152

Booth, John Wilkes, 74, 87, 92

Bosma, Charles, 212

Boston, 13, 27, 29, 112

Boston Tea Party, 29

Bowen, Otis, 211

Bowers v. Hardwick, 221–222

Boxer, Barbara, 303

Bracewell, Searcy, 146

Braden, Mark, 224

Bragman, Michael, 254

Brandeis, Louis, 110–111, 113

Brennan Center for Justice, 232–233

Brennan, William, 121–123, 124, 130, 157, 210, 216, 224–226, 228–229

Breyer, Stephen, 278, 294

Brooke, Edward, 135

Bromberg, Frederick G., 155

Brown, Jerry, 170, 172, 185–186

Brown, Pat, 163, 165, 169, 170

Brown v. Board of Education, 131, 151, 210, 269–270

Brown, Willie, 170, 174–175, 179, 181–184

Bruno, Joseph, 251–253, 255–256, 257–259, 260–261, 268

Bryant, Gizelle, 134

Buchanan, James, 89

Buffalo, 187–188, 246, 256

Bundy, Ted, 193

Bureau of Prisons, 267

Burgener, Clair, 175

Burger Court, 127

Burger, Warren, 149, 154, 226

Burr, Aaron, 84, 87

Burrington, George, 15–27, 31, 36, 60, 75

Burton, Harold Hitz, 120

Burton, Phillip, 172–179, 180, 182, 184, 186, 210, 212, 256, 270, 284

Bush, George W., 84, 258

Bush, George H. W., 134–135, 139, 245, 282, 289

Bush v. Gore, 10, 84

Bush v. Vera, 290

Butler, Joe Kelly, 133

Butler, Pierce, 113

Byrne, Brendan, 222–223

Cady, Michael, 191–192

Calabrese, Stephen, 63

Callender, James T., 42

California, 198, 223, 238, 275, 288
    1951 gerrymander in, 162
    1956 elections in, 172
    1958 elections in, 162–163, 173
    1966 elections in, 163
    1970 elections in, 164
    1972 elections in, 165
    1976 elections in, 166
    1978 elections in, 169–170
    1980 elections in, 170
    1981 gerrymander in, 160, 175–184, 202, 210–212, 224, 227, 277
    1982 elections in, 178–179, 184–185, 227
    1984 elections in, 179–180
    Assembly of, 7, 164, 170, 178, 179, 181–184, 224
    attorney general of, 163, 186
    Citizens Redistricting Commission in, 169, 190, 303–304, 312–313
    governor of, 163–164, 170, 172, 179, 185–186
    majority-minority districts in, 290
    malapportionment in, 106
    prison gerrymandering in, 197, 199
    Proposition 11 in, 303–304

Proposition 13 in, 168–171, 183
redistricting in, 162–164
Senate of, 179–181
Supreme Court of, 164–166, 184–185
Campaign Legal Center, 317–318
Campbell, William, 176, 177
Canon, David, 286–287
Cape Fear, 17, 20–21, 23
Capone, Al, 120
Caproni, Valerie, E., 267
Cardozo, Benjamin, 113, 117
Carey, Hugh, 240–243, 246
Carter, Jimmy, 166, 170, 186, 214, 241
Carteret, John, 19
Carrington, Edward, 52, 58
Castleton, Joseph, 16
Cato Institute, 171
census, 127, 162, 192–195, 200, 233, 318
   1800, 31
   1860, 81, 82, 93
   1870, 82, 96
   1900, 119
   1910, 104
   1930, 105, 311
   1940, 105, 119
   1950, 97, 162
   1960, 105, 163, 234
   1970, 137, 256
   1980, 165, 170, 202, 210, 288
   1990, 194, 244, 274, 282
   2000, 159, 189–192, 195–196, 254, 277, 294
   2010, 8, 193, 198, 261, 296, 303
   2020, 7, 193, 199, 265, 305, 311
   2030, 199
Census Bureau, 186, 188, 193–194, 200
Central Intelligence Agency, 139
Cermak, Anton, 86
Chaffee, Jerome, 96–97
Chagra, Jamiel, 148–149
Chapman, Mark David, 187
Cheston, E. Calvert, 208
Chicago, 82, 104, 109, 119, 152, 187
Citizens Union, 262
Civil Rights Act, 129, 144

civil rights movement, 128–129, 280, 302
Civil War, 81, 94, 95, 98, 203, 271–272
   First Battle of Bull Run in, 88
   Battle of Appomattox Courthouse in, 151
   Battle of Cold Harbor in, 93
   Battle of Gettysburg in, 91
   Battle of Paducah in, 93
   Reconstruction after, 94, 95, 98, 99, 140, 271–272, 282
   Secession and, 78
   statehood debates in, 83, 88, 91–92, 100–101
   Red River Campaign in, 93
Claremont Graduate University, 162, 164–165, 174
Claremont McKenna College, 161
Clark, George Rogers, 38
Clark, Tom, 121–123, 216
Clayton, Eva, 288, 292
Cleveland, Grover, 99
Clinton, Bill, 193, 203, 282, 291
Coelho, Tony, 175
Coffee, Linda, 219
Coffey, Bert, 169
Colavita, Tony, 253
Colegrove, Kenneth, 119
Colegrove v. Green, 107, 119–120, 122–123, 125
College of William and Mary, 53
Collins, Barbara-Rose, 288
color-blind constitution, 287–291
Colorado, 89, 192, 202–206, 208–210
   malapportionment in, 125
   prison gerrymandering in, 199
   redistricting reform in, 304, 313
   statehood and, 95–101
   territory of, 89, 94
Columbia University, 250, 279
Columbus, Christopher, 14
Common Cause, 8, 303, 306
Compromise of 1877, 98, 129, 271
Confederacy, 88, 89, 91, 93, 94, 151, 271, 282

Confederation Congress, 48, 51–53, 54
Congress, 38, 47, 51, 55, 57, 59, 66, 81,
    137, 156, 215, 280
    gerrymandering of, 6, 8, 63–64, 76,
    151, 172–179, 211, 234–237, 276–277,
    296–297
    lame-duck session of, 99–100
    malapportionment in, 105–106,
    119–120, 125, 223, 238
    minority representation in, 271, 283,
    288
    New Deal in, 114–115
    statehood debates in, 88–91, 93,
    95–96, 99–101, 310
    voting rights in, 156–157
Connecticut, 105, 106, 191, 199
Constitution of the United States, 14,
    29, 37, 45, 50–51, 54, 57, 199, 210,
    214, 217, 221, 278, 296, 316
    Article I of, 10, 63, 102, 125
    Article IV of, 10, 88, 91–92, 102
    Article V of, 46–47, 55
    Eighth Amendment to, 218–219
    Fifteenth Amendment to, 124,
    140–141, 152, 154, 157, 158, 271, 274,
    291
    Fifth Amendment to, 219
    First Amendment to, 58, 201
    Fourteenth Amendment to, 120, 147,
    152, 157, 271, 290–291, 298
    Nineteenth Amendment to, 124
    Ninth Amendment to, 220
    Preamble to, 273
    ratification of, 43–46
    Second Amendment to, 58
    Seventeenth Amendment to, 104, 124
    Twelfth Amendment to, 84
    Twentieth Amendment to, 86
    Twenty-Fifth Amendment to, 84–85
Constitutional Convention, 11, 28, 29,
    41, 42–43, 44, 46, 55, 101–102, 301,
    318–319
Continental Congress, 29, 38, 41, 42
Coolidge, Calvin, 113

Cooper, Gordon, 132
Corcoran, Thomas, 114
Cornstein, David, 252
Corwin, Thomas, 73
Cox, Archibald, 214–215
Creighton, Mandell, 268
Cruz, Lauro, 134–135
Cuomo, Andrew, 260–261, 264–265
Cuomo, Mario, 246–247, 250, 252–253
Cutrer, Lewis, 132

Dalberg-Acton, John Emerich Edward,
    268
Dailey, J. Roberts, 212
Dakota Territory, 81–82, 89, 95, 99–101
Dallas, 142, 146–147, 204, 219, 293
D'Amato, Al, 251–253
Danbury Baptist Association, 41
dark money, 6–7
Davidson, Chandler, 130
Davis, Garrett, 92
Davis, Gray, 303
Davis v. Bandemer, 222–230, 270,
    275–276, 278
Deal, Nathan, 293
Declaration of Independence, 29, 38,
    124, 154
Delaware, 105, 125
Delhommer, Scott, 266
Democratic Party, 66, 72, 75, 77, 134,
    144, 160
    gerrymandering by, 7, 11, 67–68,
    73–74, 83, 87, 164–166, 175–184,
    222–223, 256–257, 264, 284–286,
    299
    National Committee of, 139, 186
Democratic-Republican Party, 28, 31, 32,
    33, 62, 84
Demos, 198
Denis, Nelson, 254
Department of Justice, 153–154, 157,
    214–217, 274–275, 281–284, 286,
    289, 291, 293, 302
DePaul University, 193

George Deukmejian, 185

Direct Democracy, 104

  ballot initiatives in, 168–170, 303–305, 313, 317

  referenda in, 78, 91, 95, 184, 309, 313

  recall elections in, 3, 295–296, 303

Doar, John, 215

Donne, John, 287

Doolittle, John, 180

Dornan, Bob, 176–177

Dougherty, Charles, 100

Douglas, Stephen A., 83, 89

Douglas, William O., 107, 119, 121, 124, 152, 216

Easley, Mike, 294

Easley v. Cromartie, 294

Eason, John M., 187–188

Eckhardt, Bob, 135, 138–139

Edenton, North Carolina, 15, 17, 20, 21

efficiency gap, 297–298, 302

Eisenhower, Dwight D., 121, 141, 144, 154, 210, 215

elections clause, 63, 125

Electoral College, 62, 67, 84, 94, 97–98, 100, 144

Ellis, Joseph, 44–45

Enabling Acts, 89, 92, 93, 95, 97, 100

Epstein, Lee, 127

equal protection clause, 10, 120, 125–126, 201, 286, 289–291

Era of Good Feelings, 62, 114

Ericsson, John, 86

Espada, Pedro, 259–260

Espy, Mike, 282

Essex County, Massachusetts, 13, 33, 34–35

Everard, Sir Richard, 18

Evans, William, 226

Everett, Robinson, 286, 294

Evers, Tony, 3

Farley, James, 115

Farrell, Herman, 254

Featherstonehaugh, James, 251

Federal Bureau of Investigation, 111–112, 260

Federalist Papers, 43

  No. 14, 43–44

  No. 78, 269

Federalist Party, 27, 31, 33, 43, 52, 62

Felando, Gerald, 181, 183

Feldman, Daniel, 255–256

Fiedler, Bobbi, 177

Fielding, Henry, 25

Fields, Cleo, 292

Fink, Stanley, 239, 242–243

Finn, Bertha, 200

First Red Scare, 112

First World War, 111

Fletcher v. Lamone, 199–200

Florida, 84, 98, 100, 151, 160, 276, 306

  majority-minority districts in, 289

  minority representation in, 288

  prison gerrymandering in, 192–193, 196–197

  redistricting reform in, 305–306, 308–309

Ford, Gerald, 147, 152, 166, 240–241, 280

Ford, Harold Sr., 282

Ford, Johnny, 142

Foster, Lafayette S., 86, 87

Frankfurter, Felix, 107–113, 116–124, 127, 141–142, 148, 201, 210, 216, 217–218, 220, 270, 279, 301

Franklin, Benjamin, 11, 301, 318–319

free and equal elections clauses, 306, 308

Freedom Rides, 215, 280

French Revolution, 27

Fugitive Slave Act, 88

Gale, Christopher, 15–17, 20

Gallup, George, 115

Garner, John Nance, 86, 87

George I of Great Britain, 16, 23, 24–25

Georgia, 64, 144, 198, 288–290
    African American disenfranchisement
        in, 272
    malapportionment in, 124–125
    majority-minority districts in,
        289–290, 293
    minority representation in, 282,
        288
Gerry, Elbridge, 13–14, 27–35, 44, 60,
        62, 185, 235, 246
gerrymandering
    at-large elections and, 62–64, 134
    cartoon depictions of, 34, 69–71,
        234–237
    definition of, 4–6
    effectiveness of, 60–61, 79–80, 97–98,
        101, 296
    incumbent protection in, 163–164,
        179–180, 232–233, 242–243,
        246–248, 256–257, 262–264
    judicial review of, 10–11, 146–149,
        153–155, 165, 184–185, 201–202,
        223–230, 275–280, 289–294,
        301–302, 305–307
    majority-minority districts and, 262,
        281–284, 291–292
    malapportionment in, 107, 119–127,
        163–164, 223, 238
    maps of, 50, 141, 189, 236, 256, 263,
        285
    multimember districts and, 62–63,
        142, 147–148, 157, 211, 213–214
    municipal boundaries in, 140–142
    partisanship in, 158, 175–184, 202,
        211–213, 222–223, 226, 233–234,
        283–284, 296–298
    prison populations and, 188–200,
        263–264
    public opinion on, 317–318
    racial vote dilution in, 129–131,
        149–150, 153, 157, 199, 201, 213–214,
        274–275
    reform of, 11, 102, 104, 149, 159,
        302–305, 307–315, 317–318

    statehood and, 89–102
    strategies in, 50–51, 57–59, 68, 76,
        79, 101–102, 129, 175–178, 179–180,
        196–197, 243, 246–247, 256–257,
        286–287, 292
    technology and, 7–9, 51, 67, 79–80,
        107, 164, 184–185, 201, 211, 213, 286,
        316, 318
    territorial boundaries and, 82, 89–91,
        94–95, 99–100
Gill v. Whitford, 297–299
Gilmer, Thomas Walker, 86
Gingrich, Newt, 7, 160
Ginsburg, Ben, 161
Ginsburg, Ruth Bader, 278
Godard, Jean-Luc, 26
Goldberg, Arthur, 124, 217–218
Goldberg, Irving Loeb, 148, 219–220
Goldwater, Barry, 169, 171
Goldwater, Barry Jr., 177
Golisano, Tom, 257
Gomillion v. Lightfoot, 141–142
Goodhue, Mary B., 251
Gore, Al, 84
Gore, Christopher, 30–31
Gorsuch, Neil, 300, 316
Grant, Ulysses S. 97, 151
Graves, Curtis, 128, 131–140, 142, 149,
        220, 272–273, 282
Graves v. Barnes, 142–143, 145–149, 150
Grayson, William, 47
Gray v. Sanders, 124
Great Depression, 113
Green, Dwight, 120
Green, Roger, 257
Greher, Lenny, 248
Griffith, Elmer, 4, 5, 23, 58
Grofman, Bernard, 232

Halley, Edmund, 36
Hamilton, Alexander, 28, 42, 43–44, 84,
        269
Hancock, John, 29
Handley, Lisa, 214

Harding, Warren, 113
Harlan, John Marshall, 121–122
Harlan, John Marshall II, 121–123, 216
Hannah, Mack, 133
Harrelson, Charles Voyde, 148–149
Harrelson, Woody, 148
Harris, Isham G., 76
Harrison, Benjamin, 99, 100
Harrison, William Henry, 66–67, 85
Harvard University, 28, 109–112, 114,
    214
Hasen, Richard, 279–280
Hauteval, Lucien, 27
Hawaii, 64, 312
Hayes, Rutherford B., 97–98, 271
Haynes, Landon Carter, 76
Haynie, Kerry, 293
Haywood, Marshall De Lancey, 16, 20,
    21, 26
Hemmings, Sally, 42–43
Henry, Gustavus Adolphus, 76–77
Henry, Patrick, 37–60, 67, 73, 123, 280
Heslop, Alan, 164, 174
Hevesi, Alan, 237
Hill, Alger, 114
Hillenbrand, John, 210–211
Hofeller, Stephanie, 8, 165, 171
Hofeller, Thomas B., 3, 7–8, 161–166,
    170, 174, 176, 181, 186, 223–224, 235,
    275, 281, 283–284, 291–292, 296,
    306–307
Holder, Eric, 306, 315–316
Holmes, Dan, 208
Homestead Act, 75, 81–82
Hoover, Herbert, 113, 167, 223
Hoover, J. Edgar, 111–112
Hottinguer, Jean-Conrad, 27
House of Representatives, 10, 62–64, 74,
    83, 88, 96–97, 144, 157
    1789 elections to, 47, 48, 51, 53–57
    1840 elections to, 67
    1842–43 elections to, 67, 72–73, 75
    1962 elections to, 237
    1964 elections to, 237

    1982 elections to, 178, 186, 227
    1984 elections to, 186
    1990 elections to, 282
    1992 elections to, 271, 288
    1994 elections to, 7, 253, 292
    1998 elections to, 294
    2000 elections to, 294
    2012 elections to, 8, 306
    2014 elections to, 306
    2016 elections to, 8, 306
    2018 elections to, 8–9, 306
    2020 elections to, 306
    Judiciary Committee of, 139
    reapportionment of, 210, 222, 234
Houston, 131–133, 134, 137–138, 140, 143,
    145
Hubble, Edwin, 35–36
Hughes, Charles Evans, 113
Hukari, Harvey, 174
Humphrey, Hubert, 144
Hunter, Thomas Rogers, 50–51, 58
Hunt, James, 294
Hunt v. Cromartie, 294
Hutchinson, Dennis, 203–204

Idaho, 90, 100, 106, 313
Illinois, 295, 310
    1850 gerrymander in, 83
    General Assembly of, 83, 119
    governor of, 120
    majority-minority districts in, 290
    malapportionment in, 105, 119–120
    prison gerrymandering in, 187, 195,
    198
    redistricting reform in, 199
Indiana, 222, 310
    1980 elections in, 210–211
    1981 gerrymander in, 202, 210–213,
    275
    1982 elections, 211–212
    constitution of, 35
    General Assembly of, 149–150, 158,
    211
    racial vote dilution in, 149

Industrial Revolution, 14, 104
Internal Revenue Service, 260
Iowa, 308–310
Irish, Leon, 203
Issacharoff, Samuel, 279

Jackson, Andrew, 62, 65, 66
Jackson, Robert, 120
Jankowski, Chris, 6
Jarvis, Howard, 166–172, 183, 303
Jay, John, 43–44
Jay Treaty, 27
Jefferson, Thomas, 28, 37–43, 45, 47–48,
    58, 60, 81, 84, 122, 123
Jeffries, Hakeem, 257
Jim Crow, 98, 129–130, 132, 134, 140,
    151–152, 210, 215, 269–274
John, Susan, 256–257
Johnson, Andrew, 74–79, 87, 94,
    95–96
Johnson, Eddie Bernice, 288
Johnson, Gabriel, 24
Johnson, Lyndon B., 129, 133, 135, 139,
    143, 144, 169, 210, 214, 237, 258
Johnson, Ross, 181
Jones, Sam, 155
Jones, Walter, 284
Jordan, Barbara, 134–139, 143, 282, 288
judicial activism, 118–119, 218
Judicial Procedures and Reform Bill,
    115–116
judicial restraint, 109–110, 218, 220–221
Justice, William Wayne, 143, 145–146,
    148

Kansas, 89, 94, 98
Kansas-Nebraska Act, 88
Karcher v. Daggett, 202, 222–223
Karlan, Pamela, 279
Katzenbach, Nicholas, 214–215, 217
Kavanaugh, Brett, 300
Kean, Thomas, 222–223
Keeney, Bernie, 189–190
Keever, Charles M., 142

Kelly, Jason P., 196–197
Kennedy, Anthony, 276, 278–280,
    296–299
Kennedy, Edward, 176–177
Kennedy, John F., 124, 207–208,
    209–210, 214–217, 222, 269–270
Kennedy, Robert F., 214–215
Kentucky, 78
Kilgarlin v. Martin, 133
King, Martin Luther, 270
King, Rufus, 62
Kleefisch, Rebecca, 296
Koch, Ed, 261
Kopechne, Mary Jo, 177
Korean War, 172
Knight, Goodwin, 162–163
Knowland, William, 162–163
Kousser, J. Morgan, 155–156, 271,
    290–292
Ku Klux Klan, 272

Landis, James M., 111
Landon, Alf, 114–115
Lawson, William, 133
Lash, Joseph, 119
League of Women Voters, 305
Lee, Henry III, 49
Lee, Richard Henry, 47
Lee, Robert E., 91, 151
Lefcourt, Gerald, 245
Leland, Mickey, 282
Lemaître, Georges, 36
Letterman, David, 250
Levi, Edward, 147
Lewis, John, 282
Lincoln, Abraham, 74, 78, 81–83, 86–95,
    96, 256
Lincoln, Benjamin, 29
Lochner v. New York, 113, 118
Locofocos, 67
London, 24, 25, 64–65
Lords Proprietors, 16
Los Angeles, 11, 167–168, 176–177,
    181–182

Louisiana, 93, 98, 132, 144, 192
   African American disenfranchisement
     in, 272–273
   majority-minority districts in, 289
   minority representation in, 293
Louisiana Purchase, 81
Lowenstein, Daniel, 279
Lumbee tribe, 283
Lynch, John Roy, 96

Madison, Dolley, 85
Madison, James, 11, 28, 35, 37–60, 73, 74,
   85, 103, 122, 151
Magna Carta, 14
Maine, 32, 33, 115, 190, 311
malapportionment, 15, 32, 49–50,
   101–102, 104–107, 119–127, 163–164,
   223
Maloney, Andrew, 244
Maloney, Tommy, 173
Manatt, Charles, 186
Mangum, Willie Person, 85, 87
Marbury v. Madison, 11, 122
Marguth, Gilbert, 182
Marino, Ralph, 245–247, 250–253, 259,
   262
Marks, Milton, 186
Maryland, 91, 125, 194, 278
   1812 gerrymander in, 13–14
   1816 gerrymander in, 62
   2011 gerrymander in, 299, 308
   Prison gerrymandering in, 198–199
Marshall, John, 27, 28, 45, 122
Marshall, Thurgood, 131, 132, 154, 226,
   228–229
Mason, George, 39, 43, 44, 48, 49
Massachusetts, 27, 29, 42, 112
   1780 elections in, 29
   1788 elections in, 29
   1810 elections in, 30
   1812 gerrymander in, 13–14, 31–35, 49
   1812 elections in, 13, 35
   General Court of, 31–33
   governor of, 29–31

   House of Representatives of, 33
   Senate of, 32, 33
   Supreme Judicial Court of, 113
Mayo Clinic, 220
McCain, John, 155, 258
McCarthy, Leo, 169–170
McCarty, Nolan, 94
McCorvey, Norma, 219–220
McDonald, Laughlin, 156
McEwen, Robert C., 234–235
McGhee, Eric, 298
McKinney, Cynthia, 271, 288
McReynolds, James Clark, 113
Meek, Carrie, 288
Michaux, Mickey, 286, 288
Michigan, 160, 172, 304
   2001 gerrymander in, 276, 278
   2011 gerrymander in, 8–9
   minority representation in, 288
   prison gerrymandering in, 197
   redistricting reform in, 304, 313
Miller, Mel, 242–245, 254
Miller, Peter, 232
Miller v. Johnson, 289
Milyo, Jeffrey, 266
Miranda v. Arizona, 219
Mississippi, 64, 96, 105, 144, 273, 310
Missouri, 160, 304, 312
Mobile, 150–152, 155
Mobile v. Bolden, 153–157, 214, 228,
   274
Monmonier, Mark, 281–283, 286–288,
   292
Monroe, James, 50, 53–57, 59, 60, 62,
   103
Monserrate, Hiram, 259–260
Montana, 81, 90–91, 99–100, 313
Montgomery, 128, 151
Montgomery, John, 20, 22, 25
Mooney, Thomas, 111
Moore, Frank, 77
Moore, Stephen, 171
Moscone, George, 169
Murtaugh, Brian, 231

Nabrit, Sam, 132
Nashville, 75, 77, 78, 121
National Aeronautics and Space
    Administration, 139
National Association for the
    Advancement of Colored People,
    131, 140, 152, 153, 156–157, 212, 272,
    303
National Conference of State
    Legislatures, 308
National Constitution Center, 74
National Democratic Redistricting
    Committee, 306, 315
National Federation of Independent
    Business, 303
National Football League, 202, 205–208,
    217
National Industrial Recovery Act, 114
National Labor Relations Act, 116
National Park Service, 174
National Republican Redistricting Trust,
    7, 315
National Voting Rights Institute, 198
Naylor, Robert, 178, 184
Nebraska, 89, 95, 98
Nessen, Ron, 240–241
Nevada, 89, 91, 93–94, 97, 98, 100, 106,
    199
New Deal, 107, 113–116, 117, 144, 218
New Frontier, 214
New Hampshire, 45, 64, 106
New Jersey, 84, 224
    1980 elections in, 222–223
    1981 gerrymander in, 202, 223–224
    malapportionment in, 228
    prison gerrymandering in, 199
    redistricting reform in, 312
New Mexico, 64, 89, 97, 99–101, 104
New York, 31, 125, 162, 266–267, 286,
    309
    1894 constitution of, 233–234, 239, 242
    1962 elections in, 237
    1964 elections in, 237
    1974 elections in, 238
    1978 elections in, 254

1982 gerrymander in, 242–243
1982 elections in, 243
1991 gerrymander in, 246–247, 278
1994 elections in, 247–248, 253
2001 gerrymander in, 256–257
2002 elections in, 257–258
2002 elections in, 257–258
2010 elections in, 260
2011 gerrymander in,
2012 elections in, 264
2014 elections in, 265
    assembly of, 188, 191, 234, 239,
        243–244, 256–248, 249–250,
        253–257, 258, 264, 278
    governor of, 112–113, 233–235, 239,
        240, 243, 252–253, 264–265
    Independent Redistricting
        Commission of, 265, 305, 310–311
    Legislative Task Force on
        Demographic Research and
        Reapportionment, 191, 239,
        242–243, 261, 264–265
    majority-minority districts in, 289
    prison gerrymandering in, 198–199
    Senate of, 188, 191, 198, 234, 239,
        245–248, 251–253, 259–260,
        262–264
New York City, 48, 51, 53, 65–66, 67,
    104, 108–110, 112, 190, 192, 198,
    233–237, 240–242, 248–249, 253,
    256, 262–265, 280
New York University, 232, 242
Nixon, Richard M., 139, 144, 149, 152,
    154, 156, 162–163, 166, 214, 223, 258
No Representation Without Population
    Act, 198–199
North Carolina, 280–281
    1732 gerrymander in, 22–24, 60
    1990 elections in, 282
    1992 elections in, 288
    1998 elections in, 294
    2000 elections in, 294
    2011 gerrymander in, 8, 299–300
    attorney general of, 20
    chief justice of, 15–17

General Assembly of, 157, 306
governor of, 15–27
majority-minority districts in,
    283–286
minority representation in, 288
Province of, 16–17, 25, 27
provincial assembly of, 21–22
provincial council of, 17, 21, 22–23
racial vote dilution in, 157
North Dakota, 100
Nozzolio, Michael, 191
Nuremburg Trials, 120

Oakes, Bunny, 204
Obama, Barack, 193, 231, 258
Ohio, 64–67, 82, 87, 160, 172
    1842 gerrymander in, 67–74, 87
    1837 elections in, 87
    1843 elections in, 72–73
    2011 gerrymander in, 8–9, 172
    Amendment 4 in, 304
    General Assembly of, 67–68
    governor of, 97
    majority-minority districts in, 290
    redistricting reform in, 304–305,
        308–309, 310, 312
    Senate of, 87
Oklahoma, 141, 310
O'Connor, Sandra Day, 226, 276, 278,
    289, 294, 299
Ohlmeyer, Don, 268
O'Malley, Martin, 198
one person, one vote, 32, 64, 108,
    124–127, 137, 140, 142, 154, 158,
    163, 197, 212–213, 223, 228, 234,
    237–239, 256
Orange County, Virginia, 48, 50–51, 53,
    55–56, 103
Oregon, 104, 105, 175
Organic Acts, 89–91
Orr, Robert, 211
Ortloff, Chris, 191

Panic of 1837, 64–66
Paris, 27, 41, 42

Parks, Rosa, 128
Parliament of Great Britain, 14–15, 29
Pataki, George, 250–253, 255, 261
Paterson, David, 199, 259–260
Patient Protection and Affordable Care
    Act, 295
Patterson, John Malcolm, 215
Patterson, Thomas, 97
Payne, William, 63–64
Pelham-Holles, Thomas, 19, 21, 24, 25
Pelosi, Nancy, 303
Pendleton, Edward, 51
Pennsylvania, 91, 160, 266
    1994 elections in, 277
    2001 gerrymander in, 8–9, 276–277
    2002 elections in, 277
    redistricting reform in, 305–306, 312
    Supreme Court of, 306
Pettit, John, 35
Philadelphia, 29, 30, 42–43, 44, 46, 53,
    55, 101, 104, 319
Pinckney, Charles Cotesworth, 27
Pittman, Thomas Virgil, 154–155
Planned Parenthood, 295
political question doctrine, 11, 120, 201,
    225–227, 278–279, 300
Polk, James K., 75
Poole, Keith, 94
Porter, Edmund, 21
Povich, Shirley, 217
Powel, Elizabeth Willing, 319
Powell, Lewis, 149, 154, 226, 228–229,
    279
president of the United States, 60, 88
    1836 election of, 85
    1840 election of, 67
    1844 election of, 75
    1852 election of, 78
    1860 election of, 83, 88, 91, 94
    1864 election of, 74, 169, 171, 258
    1876 election of, 97–98
    1980 election of, 170, 186
    1888 election of, 98–99
    1932 election of, 112–113
    1936 election of, 114–115

president of the United States
  (continued)
  1960 election of, 163
  1964 election of, 144, 237
  1968 election of, 144–145, 149, 151
  1980 election of, 186
  1984 election of, 160, 186
  1988 election of, 282
  1992 election of, 252
  2000 election of, 84
  2008 election of, 231, 258
  assassination attempts against, 74,
    86–87, 96
  contingent election of, 84
  impeachment of, 74, 85, 96, 139
  signing statements of, 63
  vetoes by, 65, 95
Presidential Succession Act, 85
Prewitt, Kenneth, 193
Princeton University, 196, 198
Prison Policy Initiative, 190–191, 194,
  198, 199, 303
Progressive Era, 104–105
Public Policy Institute of California,
  298, 313
Pythagoras, 36

Quasi-War, 27
Quinn, T. Anthony, 166, 169, 170, 179,
  180, 182, 183, 186

racially polarized voting, 130–131, 293
Radical Republicans, 74, 88, 95–96, 271
Raleigh, Sir Walter, 18
Randolph, Edmund, 42, 43, 44–45,
  51, 60
Rappleyea, Clarence, 252–253
Ravitch, Richard, 260
Reagan, Ronald, 157, 160, 163–164, 170,
  171, 184, 186, 276, 281–282, 293
reapportionment revolution, 15, 62, 102,
  119–127, 163, 234, 270
Reed, William, 19–20
Reed, Stanley Forman, 117, 120

redistricting
  1970s cycle in, 137–138, 143, 145–147,
    159–160, 164–165
  1980s cycle in, 7, 159, 175–184,
    185–186, 201–202, 210–212, 222–223
  1990s cycle in, 7, 246–248, 276,
    283–286
  2000s cycle in, 159–160, 256–257,
    276–277
  2010s cycle in, 6–9, 198–199, 296–300
  2020s cycle in, 199, 315–316, 318
  backup commissions in, 310–311
  bipartisan commissions in, 311–312
  international approaches to, 314–315
  independent commissions in, 312–314
REDMAP, 6–9, 32, 51, 61, 73, 159–160,
  178, 260, 265, 276, 280, 297, 299
Rehnquist, William, 149, 154, 226, 278,
  289–290
Reno, Janet, 288
Reno v. Bossier Parish School Board,
  293–294
Representation of the People Act, 15
Republican Party, 83, 93, 96, 134,
  159–160, 163, 199, 275
  gerrymandering by, 3, 6–9, 11, 83,
    89–102, 159–160, 164–165, 211–213,
    233–234, 238, 256, 262–264, 288,
    296–298, 300
  National Committee of, 161, 165, 167,
    174, 223–224, 275, 281
Republican State Leadership
  Committee, 6
residential segregation, 129–130
Revere, Paul, 29
Revolutionary War, 29, 30–31, 41, 42, 48,
  52, 53–54
Reynolds v. Sims, 126–127, 133, 218
Rhode Island, 311
Rhyne, Charles, 153
Rice, Grantland, 204
Rice, Nathaniel, 21, 22, 25
Rice University, 204
Richardson, Bill, 180

Richmond, 44, 46, 49, 51, 55
Rivers, Christina, 193, 195
Rives, William Cabell, 56
Roberti, David, 179, 184
Roberts Court, 225
Roberts, John, 10, 299–300, 316
Roberts, Owen, 113–114, 116–117
Robinson v. California, 218–219
Rockefeller, Nelson, 234–235, 238
Rodda, Albert, 180
Rodgers, Jennifer, 266
Roe v. Wade, 219–221
Rooney, Art, 206, 217
Roosevelt, Franklin D., 86, 110–118, 120, 121, 141, 167, 222
Roosevelt, Theodore, 110
Roosevelt, Theodore Jr., 234
Root, Elihu, 233–234
Rose Institute for State and Local Government, 164, 174–175, 181–182
Rosenberg, Gerald, 269
Rosenthal, Alan, 312
Rosenthal, Howard, 94
Rothgerber, Ira C., 217
Rotten borough, 15, 32, 91
Rousselot, John, 177
Rucho v. Common Cause, 225, 299–300, 301, 305, 316
Rutledge, Wiley Blount, 120
Ryan, William, 250–250
Ryder, John, 164

Sacco, Nicola, 112
Sacramento, 7, 162, 163, 171, 174, 179, 180, 185, 312
Salem Witch Trials, 13
Samuels, Bill, 261
San Antonio, 142, 146–147, 148
San Diego, 161, 175
San Francisco, 172–174, 175–176, 186
Santayana, George, 318
Scalia, Antonin, 278–280, 289, 299
Schiff, Jacob, 111
Schlesinger, Arthur, 217

Schneier, Edward, 231
Schumer, Chuck, 253
Schwarzenegger, Arnold, 304
Scott, Tim, 282
Scott, Winfield, 78
Second Bank of the United States, 65
Second World War, 129, 167, 207–208, 242
Secretary of State, 48, 60, 85, 86
Secretary of the Navy, 86, 111
Secretary of War, 95, 110–111
Second Party System, 62
Securities and Exchange Commission, 111
Seminerio, Anthony, 252
Senate, 78, 83, 87, 89, 94, 96–97, 98, 115, 144, 157, 179
    1788 elections to, 47, 51
    1851 elections to, 88
    1958 elections to, 163
    1982 elections to, 185
    2014 elections to, 282
    Judiciary Committee of, 10, 117, 157
    malapportionment of, 101–102
    president pro tempore of, 85, 86, 96
Shanker, Al. 241
Shapiro, Kenneth, 254
Shawcross, Arthur, 252
Shaw v. Hunt, 289–290, 294
Shaw v. Reno, 288–289, 291
Shays's Rebellion, 42
Sharpstown scandal, 139
Shelley, John F., 173
Sherman, William Tecumseh, 93
Siena College, 74
Silver, Nate, 3
Silver, Sheldon, 248–250, 253–257, 258, 261–262, 264–265, 266–268
Sioux tribe, 81–82
Skelos, Dean, 253, 259, 260–265, 266–268
Smith, Al, 233–234, 240
Smith, Malcolm, 258–259
Smith, Preston, 139

Smith, Robert, 43
Smith v. Allwright, 132
Soifer, Ari, 156
Solicitor General of the United States, 113
Solid South, 7, 144–145
Souter, David, 278
South Carolina, 24, 44, 98, 282
South Dakota, 100
Southern Strategy, 149
Soviet Union, 112, 114
Spano, Nick, 253
Special Circular, 65
Spitzer, Eliot, 258–259
Stanford University, 280
Stanton, Edwin, 95
Stearns, Eldrewey, 132–133
Steingut, Stanley, 254
Stephanopoulos, Nicholas, 298
Stevens, John Paul, 152, 154, 226, 228, 278, 290, 292–293
Stevens, Thaddeus, 88, 92
Stewart, Charles, 91, 93
Stewart, Chris, 251
Stewart, Potter, 10, 121–122, 154, 155–156, 216, 290
Stigler, Stephen, 35–36
Stimson, Henry, 110
Stith, Kate, 218
Stockton, Robert, 85–86
Stone, Harlan Fiske, 113, 120
Strict scrutiny, 289–290
Strong, Caleb, 30, 35
Stuart, Gilbert, 34
Sumner, Charles, 88
Supreme Court of the United States, 84, 92–93, 107–108, 111, 147, 163, 197, 269
    appointments to, 10, 45, 116–117, 119–122, 127, 149, 152, 210, 216–217, 276
    court-packing of, 115
    ideological balance of, 113–114, 116–119, 124, 149, 216, 220, 228–229, 276, 278

malapportionment decisions of, 120–127, 202, 222–223
oral argument before, 116, 120, 122, 153–154, 226 278, 288, 298–299
partisan gerrymandering decisions of, 223–227, 278–280, 298–300
prison gerrymandering decisions of, 199
racial gerrymandering decisions of, 140–142, 153–154, 157–158, 288–294
Sutherland, George, 113
Sweatt, Heman Marion, 131
Sweatt v. Painter, 131
Syracuse University, 281

Taft, William Howard, 110
Talleyrand-Périgord, Charles Maurice de, 27–28
Taylor, Charles, 284
Taylor, Nathaniel, 77
Tennessee, 74, 75, 78, 81, 153, 272
    1841–42 elections in, 75
    1850–51 elections in, 76
    1852–53 elections in, 76–77
    1852 gerrymander in, 76–77
    General Assembly of, 121
    malapportionment in, 105, 121
    minority representation in, 282
    Secretary of State of, 121
    Supreme Court of, 121
Tenney, Claudia, 264
Tenure of Office Act, 95
Texas, 84, 139, 145, 192–193, 198, 219–220, 276, 288–290, 292, 310
    1966 elections in, 133–136
    governor of, 84, 139, 145
    House of Representatives of, 133–134, 136–137, 139
    Legislative Redistricting Board of, 137–138, 143, 145–147
    lieutenant governor of, 145
    majority-minority districts in, 289–290, 292
    minority representation in, 282, 288

prison gerrymandering in, 196–197
racial vote dilution in, 142–143,
    145–149, 150
Senate of, 133–134, 138–139, 145–146
Texas Southern University, 131, 133
Thomas, Bill. 177
Thomas, Clarence, 278, 289, 300
Thornburg v. Gingles, 157–158, 223,
    274–275, 281
Three-Fifths Compromise, 271
Tilden, Samuel, 97–98
Tisdale, Elkanah, 34
Tocqueville, Alexis de, 301
totality of circumstances test, 157–158,
    274–275
Truman, Harry S., 120, 141, 144, 258
Trumbull, Lyman, 83
Trump, Donald, 193, 252, 263
Turberville, George Lee, 51–52
Turner, William, 153–154
Tuskegee, AL, 140–142
Tuskegee Institute, 140–141
Tyler, Gus, 237
Tyler, John, 63, 67, 73, 85–86

Udall, Morris K., 105–106, 126
Uniform Congressional District Act, 64
University of Chicago, 4, 35, 130, 269,
    298
University of Colorado, 202, 204–206,
    217
University of Florida, 63
University of Missouri, 266
University of North Dakota, 82
University of Saint Andrews, 24
University of Texas at Austin, 131
Upshur, Abel P., 86
USS *Princeton* disaster, 85–86
U.S. Term Limits v. Thornton, 52
Utah, 89, 93, 98, 100–101, 106, 166–167,
    304, 311
Utah State University, 167

Van Buren, Martin, 66
Van Devanter, Willis, 113, 117

Vanzetti, Bartolomeo, 112
Vermont, 105, 106, 115, 190, 311
vice president of the United States, 31,
    35, 84–85, 86, 87
Vieth v. Jubelirer, 278–280, 288, 296
Vietnam War, 161, 174, 191
Vinson, Fred M., 209
Virginia, 20, 22, 31, 38, 39, 41, 46, 51, 53,
    54, 67, 91–92, 125, 199, 276
1788–89 elections in, 47, 48, 51–57
1788 gerrymander in, 37–38, 43, 48–53,
    57–60
constitution of, 39–40, 43
Council of State of, 39
Declaration of Rights of, 39
Fifth Convention of, 39, 53
General Assembly of, 38, 41, 48–49,
    51, 52
governor of, 39, 42, 44
House of Burgesses of, 37, 53
House of Delegates of, 38, 48–50, 54
majority-minority districts in, 289
minority representation in, 288
Ratifying Convention in, 44–46, 48,
    50, 55
redistricting reform in, 311
Senate of, 49
Virginia v. West Virginia, 92–93
Volker, Dale, 191
Voting Rights Act, 135, 156, 158, 197,
    198, 270–271, 273–275, 282, 288,
    293–294
1982 amendments to, 157, 214, 270,
    303
Section 2 of, 275, 281, 281
Section 5 of, 147–148, 156, 274

Wade, Benjamin, 83, 87–88, 89–91, 93,
    95–96
Walker, Scott, 3, 7, 294–298, 315–316
Wallace, George, 144–145, 150–151, 270
Walpole, Sir Robert, 25
War on Drugs, 190, 197
Warren Court, 62, 118, 124–127, 149,
    218–219

Warren, Earl, 107, 124, 126, 127, 133, 167, 210, 216, 274
Washington, 99–100, 199, 313
Washington, Booker T., 140
Washington, Craig, 138, 282
Washington, DC, 85, 87, 88, 91, 97, 98, 100, 139, 149, 152, 165, 177, 258, 271, 282, 288
Washington, George, 42, 43, 47, 48, 49, 52, 53, 54, 57, 60, 86
Washington v. Davis, 152
Watergate Scandal, 166, 238
Waters, Maxine, 288
Watt, Mel, 288, 292
Weddington, Sarah, 219
Weingast, Barry, 91, 93
Weinstein, Harvey, 187
Weinstein, Murray, 254
Welch, Louie, 137
Wells, David, 235
Wells v. Rockefeller, 238
Weprin, David, 250
Weprin, Saul, 245–248, 249–250, 278
Wesberry v. Sanders, 125–126, 154, 218
West Coast Hotel v. Parrish, 116
West Virginia, 91–93, 94, 278
Whig Party, 66–67, 68, 72–73, 75, 78, 85, 87
    Gerrymandering by, 76–77
Whitcomb v. Chavis, 149–150
White, Byron, 147, 150, 202–210, 214–222, 223–229, 276, 278–279
White, George Henry, 283, 288

White, Hattie Mae, 133
Whittaker, Charles Evans, 121–122, 215–216
William III of England, 19
Wilson, Pete, 185
Wilson, Woodrow, 110–111
Wisconsin, 172
    2010 elections in, 6, 294–295
    2011 gerrymander in, 3, 6–7, 8, 265, 296–298
    2012 elections in, 3, 7
    2014 elections in, 3
    2016 elections in, 3, 7
    Assembly of, 3, 7
    Senate of, 3, 7, 295–296
Wolf v. Colorado, 210
Wood, John H. Jr, 148–149
Woodward, C. Vann, 129
Wright, Cathie, 188–190
Wright, Jim, 172
Wright v. Rockefeller, 150
Wyoming, 81, 100

Xavier University, 131
XYZ Affair, 27–28

Yale University, 204, 207–209, 218, 250
Young, Andrew, 282
Young, Danny, 188–190, 200

Zangara, Giuseppe, 86
Zarb, Frank, 252
Zimmerman, Donald, 242

ILLUSTRATION CREDITS

ABOUT THE AUTHOR

Nick Seabrook is a professor in the Department of Political Science and Public Administration at the University of North Florida. The author of *Drawing the Lines: Constraints on Partisan Gerrymandering in U.S. Politics,* he lives in Jacksonville, Florida.

A NOTE ON THE TYPE

This book was set in Adobe Garamond. Designed for the Adobe Corporation by Robert Slimbach, the fonts are based on types first cut by Claude Garamond (c. 1480–1561). It is to him that we owe the letter we now know as "old style."

Composed by North Market Street Graphics, Lancaster, Pennsylvania
Printed and bound by Berryville Graphics, Berryville, Virginia
Designed by Maggie Hinders